Leadership Development in the Middle East

In memory of Yousif Abdullah, for an introduction to Bahrain and, through Bahrain to the rich and endlessly fascinating region of the Middle East.

Beverly Dawn Metcalfe

To my parents who have taught me: to be a leader is to be humble.
To my wife and children for their warmth and support.

Fouad Mimouni

Leadership Development in the Middle East

Edited by

Beverly Dawn Metcalfe

Institute for Development Policy and Management, University of Manchester, UK

Fouad Mimouni

Researcher on leadership development and practitioner in talent management and executive coaching in the Middle East

Edward Elgar

Cheltenham, UK • Northampton, MA, USA

Published by
Edward Elgar Publishing Limited
The Lypiatts
15 Lansdown Road
Cheltenham
Glos GL50 2JA
UK

Edward Elgar Publishing, Inc.
William Pratt House
9 Dewey Court
Northampton
Massachusetts 01060
USA

A catalogue record for this book
is available from the British Library

Library of Congress Control Number: 2011929455

ISBN 978 1 84720 615 2 (cased)

Typeset by Servis Filmsetting Ltd, Stockport, Cheshire
Printed and bound by MPG Books Group, UK

Contents

Figures

Tables

Contributors

Samir Abuznaid, Ph.D. is President of Hebron University, Palestine Associate Professor of Management and Marketing and former Acting Governor of Hebron.

Abbas J. Ali, Ph.D. is Professor of Management and Director, School of International Business, Indiana University of Pennsylvania, US.

Rashid Althakhri, Ph.D. is Strategic Officer, Abu Dhabi Police, UAE.

Richard Common, Ph.D. is Senior Lecturer in Public Management at Manchester Business School, University of Manchester, UK.

Rehana Hayat, Ph.D. is Associate Professor in the Faculty of Business, Canadian University of Dubai, UAE and teaches at the American University of Ras al Khaimah, UAE.

Kate Hutchings, Ph.D. is Professor of Human Resource Management and Deputy Head of Department, Griffith Business School, Griffith University, Australia.

Aminu Mamman, Ph.D. is Reader in International and Comparative Management, Institute for Development Policy and Management (School of Environment and Development), University of Manchester, UK.

Beverly Dawn Metcalfe, Ph.D. is Senior Lecturer in Human Resource Development, Institute for Development Policy and Management (School of Environment and Development), University of Manchester, UK.

Fouad Mimouni, Ph.D. is a researcher in leadership development and practitioner in talent management and executive coaching in the Middle East.

Kavoos Mohannak, Ph.D. is Lecturer in Business and Management in QUT Business School, Queensland University of Technology, Brisbane, Australia.

Tony Murfin, MA, MSc is a freelance researcher and author.

Lulwa Mutlaq, Ph.D. is a Senior Vice President at the Arab Banking Corporation, Kingdom of Bahrain, President of Golden Trust Business

Consultancy, Vice Chairwoman Women Empowerment Committee at the Supreme Council for Women (Bahrain) and President of Bahrain Women's Society.

Mustafa F. Özbilgin, Ph.D. is Professor of Organizational Behaviour, Brunel Business School, London, UK.

Christopher J. Rees, Ph.D. is Senior Lecturer in Organization Development and HRM, Institute for Development Policy and Management (School of Environment and Development), University of Manchester, UK.

Gillian Rice, Ph.D. is Professor Emerita at Thunderbird School of Global Management, Arizona, US

Sen Sendjaya, Ph.D. is Senior Lecturer in the Department of Management, Faculty of Business and Economics, Monash University, Australia.

Abubakr M. Suliman, Ph.D. is Head of the MSc HRM Programme at the Faculty of Business, British University in Dubai, UAE

Nabil Sultan, Ph.D. is Award Director of International MBA at Liverpool Hope University's Faculty of Science and Social Sciences, UK.

David Weir, Ph.D. is Head of the School of Business, Leadership and Enterprise University Campus, Suffolk and Professor of Business and Enterprise at Essex University, UK, and Affiliate Professor, ESC Rennes, France.

Rodney Wilson, Ph.D. is Professor in the School of Government and International Affairs and Director of the Islamic Finance Programme at Durham University, UK.

Abbreviations

ABA	Alexandria Business Association.
ADP	Abu Dhabi Police.
AFED	Arab Forum for Environment and Development.
AGFUND	Arab Gulf Fund for UN Development Organizations.
AHDR	Arab Human Development Report.
BBS	Bahrain Businesswoman's Society.
BRIC	Brazil, Russia, India and China (considered comparable in newly advanced economic development).
CAWTAR	Center for Arab Women Training and Research.
CDS	Center for Development Service.
CLT	Culturally Endorsed Implicit Leadership Theory.
CPI	Corruption Perceptions Index.
CSR	Corporate Social Responsibility.
DFID	Department for International Development (UK).
DIFC	Dubai International Financial Centre.
DWE	Dubai Women Establishment.
FDI	Foreign Direct Investment.
GCC	Gulf Cooperation Council.
GDP	Gross Domestic Product.
GLOBE	Global Leadership and Organisational Behaviour Effectiveness (study).
GNI	Gross National Income.
GPC	General People's Congress (Yemen).
GPYW	General Presidency of Youth Welfare, (Saudi Arabia).
GWU	General Women's Union (UAE).
HPI	Human Poverty Index.
HRD	Human Resource Development.
HRM	Human Resource Management.
ICT	Information and Communications Technology.
IDRO	Industrial Development and Renovation Organization (Iran).
IEA	International Energy Agency.
ILO	International Labour Organization.

ILT	Implicit Leadership Theory.
IMC	Industrial Modernization Center (Egypt).
INGO	International Non-Governmental Organizations.
ITF	International Transport Forum.
JAFZA	Jebel Ali Free Zone.
JCCI	Jeddah Chamber of Commerce and Industry.
KAUST	King Abdullah University of Science and Technology.
KSA	Kingdom of Saudi Arabia.
MDGs	Millennium Development Goals.
MENA	Middle East and North Africa.
MMC	Muslim majority country.
MIT	Massachusetts Institute of Technology.
MNC	Multi-National Corporation.
MTD	Management Training and Development.
NAP	National Action Plan.
NATO	North Atlantic Treaty Organization.
NDP	National Democratic Party (Egypt).
NGO	Non-Governmental Organization.
NHRD	National Human Resource Development.
OCD	Organizational Change and Development.
OECD	Organization for Economic Co-operation and Development.
OPEC	Organization of the Petroleum Exporting Countries.
PANDE	Public Authority for National Development and Employment (UAE).
PDRY	People's Democratic Republic of Yemen.
QFD	Quality Function Deployment.
SABIC	Saudi Basic Industries Corporation.
SME	Small to Medium-sized Enterprise.
SWP	Springboard Women's Programme.
TNC	Trans-National Corporation.
TUBITAK	Scientific and Technological Research Council of Turkey.
WHO	World Health Organization.
UAE	United Arab Emirates.
UN	United Nations.
UNDP	United Nations Development Programme.
UNESCO	United Nations Educational, Scientific and Cultural Organization.
UNICEF	United Nations International Children's Emergency Fund (now United Nations Children's Fund).
UNIFEM	United Nations Development Fund for Women.

WEF	World Economic Forum.
WTO	World Trade Organization.
YAR	Yemen Arab Republic.
YSP	Yemeni Socialist Party.

Acknowledgements

There are many inspirational and supportive people who assisted with the development of this work.

Yousif Abdullah, to whom this book is dedicated, provided constant support and guidance. His faith and personal generosity enabled the initial contacts with leaders in government, diplomatic services, public agencies, industry and women's development organizations from which this volume developed. He is sadly missed.

Thanks to Dr Lulwa Mutlaq for her support and commitment to women's leadership development, both personally and as part of the Bahrain Management Society. Thanks also to Susan Kanani at the Institute of Productivity and Human Resource Development, IDRO, Tehran.

We would like to acknowledge the support of the current leaders at the Institute of Public Administration in Saudi Arabia and, in particular, we thank Dr Saeed al-Garni, Head of Research; Dr Hanan al-Mahdi, Director General of the Women's Branch; and Khalid Baltal for their encouragement, critical insight and reflection on the process of writing about leadership. We are honoured to be involved with their scholarly deliberations on organization and human development issues in the region.

Also key in the development of this book are those colleagues who have supported this academic endeavour including Jawad Syed (University of Kent), Mustafa Özbilgin (Brunel University), Kate Hutchings (Griffith University) and Maged Botros (American University in Cairo).

To all those we have taught in Bahrain, Iran, Saudi Arabia, United Arab Emirates and Oman: we hope this book provides inspiration to examine Middle East leadership from a global perspective, and global leadership from a Middle Eastern perspective.

Finally, a note of appreciation to Tony Murfin for his work on the manuscript, his guidance, his support and encouragement: and as her husband, from Beverly, a personal note of love and thanks.

Dr Beverly Dawn Metcalfe and **Dr Fouad Mimouni**,
January 2011

Editors' preface

December 17 2010: Mohammed Bouazizi, a 26-year-old man trying to support his family by selling fruits and vegetables in the central town of Sidi Bouzid, doused himself in paint thinner and set himself on fire in front of a local municipal office.

Police had confiscated his produce cart because he lacked a permit and beat him up when he resisted. Local officials then refused to hear his complaint.

Rifai, 2011

It will be for future scholars to unpick the web of events that led from the immolation of a fruit seller to the downfall of the heads of state in Tunisia and Egypt; to civil unrest in Algeria, Bahrain, Iran, Syria and Yemen and to open revolt in Libya. As we write, the final outcome of these events, for the region and for the world, are unknown and unknowable.

Some of these states are considered in this volume. And, although the events themselves are surprising, even shocking, they are to some extent anticipated by the contributors. Leaders, especially long-serving ones, have become distanced from the populations of their states. More fundamentally than this, they have failed to understand a new generation of politically-aware, technologically-savvy citizens. But most importantly, they have ruled states with governance that is to some extent imported or imposed, and certainly without the *ijma*, the consensus of the community. Whether this is the gradual erosion of rights under Mubarak or military dictatorship of Gaddafi, these leaders have lost their mandate. The position of the Al Khalifa family in Bahrain, Sunni rulers of a Shi'i majority, remains unresolved.

Yet we would contend that our thesis remains unchanged. We argue for a culturally appropriate leadership model which is derived from the fundamental faith and circumstance of the region. This is, more than ever, a necessity.

SCOPE OF THE WORK

The text which we present provides a critical overview of leadership development in the Middle East. As we hope to demonstrate, a focus on the organizational and social practices in the region of our study requires immersion in a broad range of disciplines in social sciences, the humanities, geography, development and religion in order to present a more complete and balanced view of leadership development in the Middle East. If this causes offence to pure 'discipline' scholars, we apologize: but our intention is to engender critical engagement as a way of opening out and radicalizing resistance to dominant Western conceptualizations of leadership and management.

In our introduction we touch on the issues surrounding resource, especially oil, wealth in the region and the national, regional and global consequences of the exploitation of that wealth. We take the opinion that to fail to mention resource issues and human-caused global warning would be a far stronger and more contentious political stance than it is to critically assess their impact on the region.

DEFINITIONS, USAGE AND NOMENCLATURE

This book deals to some extent with 'contested territories,' not only intellectually but in terms of national boundaries, nomenclature and Arabic usage. As editors, it is not our intention to take a political stance on leadership as manifested in the nations covered and expressed by the individual authors. Similarly, this volume contains some maps. We would like to stress that these are included for illustration only: they do not aspire to strict cartographic correctness and they do not imply any opinion on boundaries which may be contested.

The title of this book assumes that a recognizable 'Middle East' exists. We discuss this further in Chapter 1, but would like to acknowledge here that this is an extrinsic construct, necessarily coined outside the region and likely to be not only contestable but contested in some of the territories concerned. As for Arabic usage, while acknowledging that inconsistencies in spelling and construction in terms transliterated from Arabic are almost certainly unavoidable, we have chosen to follow, as far as possible, the transliteration guide of the *International Journal of Middle East Studies*. We have attempted to be consistent with these guidelines where such matters as general spelling, use of the articles *al* and *El*, use of the Arabic u as in Qur'an, Muhammad, Umar, Muslim, etc., and usages such as Shi'ism, Shi'i and Shi'a are concerned.

A number of Arabic terms are used in the body of the book. In general, the definitions given in and the context of individual chapters are to be used to determine the approximate English meaning. However, as a summary and for ease of reference, a glossary is given below.

THE SECTS OF ISLAM, ISLAMIC JURISPRUDENCE AND INTERPRETATION

It is far beyond the scope of this volume to attempt a thorough explanation of the sects of Islam or the schools of Islamic jurisprudence. We are, however, conscious that a reader new to this area of study may encounter unfamiliar terms and concepts related to such matters. All we can hope to do for those readers is to provide an overview and to give some indication of the patterns of belief that will be encountered in the countries of the Middle East included in this study. Our aim is to assist the reader of this volume, not to give a comprehensive overview. We can only apologize if this seems partial or – as it inevitably must be – incomplete, and if in order to explain, we necessarily concentrate more on historical developments than on current knowledge, interpretation and understanding. For a further introduction, we recommend the *Oxford Dictionary of Islam*, edited by John L. Esposito (2004).

Most people outside the region and outside the faith of Islam are aware of the terms *Sunni* and *Shi'i* (often rendered as Shiite), and to the existence of some historical schism between the two. We believe this is fundamental to scholars attempting to understand leadership in the modern Middle East as this schism goes to the very heart of leadership in Islam, as we will expand on in Chapter 1.

An estimated 85 per cent of Muslims belong to the Sunni branch of the faith. To explain this further we must first introduce some concepts, starting with Shari'a: ideal Islamic law or, 'God's eternal and immutable will for humanity' (Esposito 2004, p. 287): law making or establishing rules is only part of the concept of Shari'a.

The more fundamental meaning of Shari'a has been translated as, 'the road to the watering hole, the straight path to be followed' (Esposito 2005, p. 78) or as Ramadan eloquently puts it: 'the path that leads to the spring' (2005, p. 31). This is expressed in the Qur'an and in the example, in sayings and action, of Muhammad. These do not, however, provide an exhaustive body of laws, and the requirement to delineate Islamic law in a comprehensive fashion led to the development of Islamic judisprudence (*fiqh*). Fiqh is the science or discipline that has sought to ascertain, interpret and apply God's guidance. In all, there are four sources or roots of law: the Qur'an; *sunna*; consensus (*ijma*) of the community; and analytical reasoning or deduction (*qiyas*).

Sunnis stress the *sunna* and *ijma*. In full they are the *Ahl al-Sunnah wa'l-Ijma*, the people of the sunna and consensus. To Sunnis, the other Islamic sects have introduced *bidah* or innovations, departing from the sunna. In contrast, Shi'i Muslims are guided also by the wisdom of the descendents of Muhammad through his son-in-law Ali and daughter Fatima.

This precedence to the Shi'a of the descendents of Muhammad is at the root of the schism. The Sunni accept the legitimacy of the first four successors to the Prophet, chosen from among his Meccan companions and known as the Rightly Guided Caliphs. Ali was the fourth caliph, but is to the Shi'a the first legitimate successor to Muhammad, the first Imam, and the succession continued through Ali and Fatima's sons, Hasan and Huseyn. The term Shi'i is a contraction of *Shiat Ali* or partisans of Ali. It is this belief that Muhammad's divine guidance was passed on through his descendents that differentiates Shi'i from Sunni Muslims.

There are three main branches of Shi'i Muslims, distinguished in general by those of the later Imams whom they recognize. The Zaydis are discussed in the chapter on Yemen: the other branches are the Isma'ilis and the Ithna Isharis (also known as Twelvers). Shi'a form a majority of the population only in Iran and Bahrain, with a significant minority in Iraq.

The Sunni sect of Islam comprises four schools of legal thought: Hanafi, Maliki, Shafii and Hanbali. Today they are dominant in different parts of the Islamic world – the Hanafi in the Arab Middle East and South Asia, Maliki in North, Central and West Africa, Shafii in East Africa, Southern Arabia and Southeast Asia and the Hanbali in Saudi Arabia. Hanbali traditions were reinvigorated in the seventeenth century by ibn Abd al-Wahhab and have since maintained a close connection with the al Sa'ud dynasty, as discussed in Chapter 7.

Two other groups are referred to in this volume. Sufism is an Islamic mysticism whose followers strive to be constantly aware of God's presence. Ibadis, dominant in Oman, are a sect derived from the Kharijis or 'seceders' and are neither Sunni nor Shi'i, having initially supported Ali and later turned against him. An approximate breakdown of the religious affiliation of populations in the countries considered in this volume is given in Chapter 1, Table 1.2 and Figure 1.5.

One final point that we would like to stress is that, in an era of global scholarship, we have made a concerted effort to be inclusive and to draw on a wide range of sources including, as well as those from the Anglo-American and European traditions, others from Arab and Persian sources including some still unpublished in English translation. We have consciously aspired to avoid exclusively citing a narrow range of US-dominated organization and management journals.

REFERENCES

Esposito, John L. (2003), *The Oxford Dictionary of Islam*, paperback edn (2004), New York: Oxford University Press.

Esposito, John L. (2005), *Islam: The Straight Path*, 3rd edn, New York: Oxford University Press.

IJMES Transliteration Guide, accessed 16 January 2011 www8.georgetown.edu/departments/history/ijmes/Transliteration_Guide.pdf.

Rifai, Ryan(2011), *Timeline: Tunisia's civil unrest*, Al Jazeera English television: accessed 24 February http://english.aljazeera.net/indepth/spotlight/tunisia/2011/01/201114142223827361.html.

Glossary

'Adl	justice, equilibrium, equity.
'Ahd	integrity and keeping one's word.
Amanah	trust, honesty; something given to someone for safekeeping.
Abkari	genius.
Asabiyya	tribal solidarity; putting the needs of the tribe or clan ahead of the community as a whole.
Aql	human intellect or reason.
Azim	great.
Bidah	innovation; any act departing from the Sunnah.
Birr	righteousness; good conduct; fair dealing.
Bukra	tomorrow.
Caliph	to Sunni Muslims, successor to Muhammad as leader of the Islamic community.
Din	religion; the way of life for which humans will be held accountable.
Diwan	here, consultative decision making; administration or branch of government.
Falah	wellbeing: to thrive, prosper, become happy, as a result of *Taqwa*.
Fatwa	judgement; specific legal ruling.
Feth	distinctively competent and uniquely capable.
Fiqh	understanding; Islamic jurisprudence.
Fuqaha	religious scholars.
Ghabi	idiot.
Ghasi	merciless.
Hadith	an account; narrations and reports of the deeds and sayings of the prophet Muhammad.

al-Hakimiyyah	sovereignty of God.
Halal	permitted; lawful activities.
Haram	forbidden; unlawful activities.
Hijab:	veil or headcovering.
Ihsan	doing good or excelling; one of the highest degrees of *Iman* (faith).
Ijma	consensus; agreement of the community, a source of Islamic law.
Ijz	humility.
Imam	leader; prayer leader. To Shi'i Muslims, successor of Muhammad.
Iman	belief in the articles of faith enunciated in the Qur'an and the sunna.
Insha'allah	God willing.
Islam	The term Islam comes from the Arabic root *slm* meaning peace and submission. Islam means peace with Allah, with oneself and willing submission to Him.
Itihad	unity.
al-Jahiliyyah	decadence of society.
Jihad	struggle; the struggle to follow Islam; can include defence of the faith, armed struggle, holy war.
Khaleeji	of the Gulf; the distinctive culture of the Gulf region.
Khalifah	the representative of God on Earth: trusteeship; see also caliph.
Khutbah	sermon at Friday prayer.
Ma'alesh	(Egypt) that's all right; it doesn't matter.
Mal	wealth.
Majlis	place of sitting; a gathering; legislature.
Maslahah	concern for the public good and welfare.
Mu'azarah	caring; mutual respect and understanding.
Mujahadah	personal control, critical self-reflection.
Musahabah	self-reflection.
Musawat	equality.
Musleh	reformer, conciliator.
Mutasaled	suppressor.
Muwahiddun	Monotheists or Unitarians: term used for themselves by *Wahhabis*.

Nafs   self.
Nasab   family heritage, kinship.
Nasl   posterity; progeny/generation/lineage.

Qadhf   slander.
Qiwama   protection.

Rahima   mercy; rahim merciful.

Sabr   patience.
Safah   murderers.
Shari'a   the path of faithfulness, the way to the source: ideal
                    Islamic law.
Sheikh   literally 'old'; a ruler, religious leader or tribal leader.
Shukr   thankfulness.
Shura   consultation; consultative process of decision making.
Sukuk   Islamic financial instrument.
Sunna   the example of Muhammad, his 'sayings and doings'.

Taqwa   the consciousness of God.
Tawhid   unity of God: absolute monotheism.

Ubudiyyah   servitude.
Umma   community: the worldwide Muslim community.

Wasta   connections; see discussion in Chapter 8.

Zakat   alms giving.
Zulm   inequity, injustice, exploitation; (*zalim* (noun): the
                    oppressor).

This glossary has been compiled from various sources including:

Beekun, Rafik I. and Jamal Badawi (1999), *Leadership, an Islamic Perspective,*
    Beltsville, MA: Amana Publications.
Esposito, John L. (2003), *The Oxford Dictionary of Islam*, New York: Oxford
    University Press.
Esposito, John L. (2005), *Islam: The Straight Path*, 3rd edn, New York: Oxford
    University Press.
Ramadan, Tariq (2004), *Western Muslims and the Future of Islam*, New York:
    Oxford University Press.

1. Leadership, social development and political economy in the Middle East: an introduction

Beverly Dawn Metcalfe and Tony Murfin

Hold fast to God's rope all together; do not split into factions. Remember God's favour to you: you were enemies and then He brought your hearts together and you became brothers by His grace; you were about to fall into a pit of Fire and He saved you from it – in this way God makes his revelations clear to you that you may be rightly guided.

Qur'an, sura, The Family of 'Imran, 3:128

Among the Arabs there were no distinctions, traditional or natural, except the unconscious power given a famous sheikh by virtue of his accomplishment; and they taught me that no man could be their leader except he ate the ranks' food, wore their clothes, lived level with them, and yet appeared better in himself.

T.E. Lawrence, *The Seven Pillars of Wisdom*, 1926

This volume advances scholarship of leadership theorizing by exploring the socio-cultural, political and economic context of leadership identity formation in the Middle East. Central to this analysis is the role of Islam in shaping leadership behaviour and social practices. Our contention is that Islamic philosophy and science are at the very heart of conceptualizing leadership roles and relations in the Middle East, but are often silenced in contemporary global discourse.

We begin this chapter by investigating the historicization of Islamic cultural and intellectual heritage and the legacy of the period immediately following the death of the Prophet Muhammad in which Islamic leadership traditions were formed (Campbell 2008). Current theological scholarship attempts to reinterpret and reimagine the dynamic processes of leadership and we position these arguments within contemporary discourses of leadership in the Islamic world. As the contributors maintain throughout the book, the retrieval and renewal of such insights are vital if scholars, whether in theology, development, management, economics, women's studies or sociology, are to achieve new insights into the 21st century world of leadership, and for new, marginalized voices to emerge from that world.

We go on to discuss how re-Islamization, or Islamic resurgence, has recently grown all over the world. We show how this relates to processes of Westernization and globalization, their cultural interaction and the complex activity of mapping leadership practices. In exposing how Western and Islamic civilizations are historically entwined, we also identify opportunities for mutual exchange, growth and development.

We then summarize the historical development of Western leadership theory and practice, showing how a focus on leadership traits and competences has moved on to consider situational factors, the leader's relationship with followers and critical accounts including social constructionist approaches. Finally, we briefly review contemporary thinking on leadership and ethics as it relates to our considerations of Middle East leadership ideology and practice. Building on this debate, we review leadership thinking through an Islamic lens. Here, we emphasize the significance of moral codes and ethical conduct and stress a radical departure from Western models, with their focus on leadership in organizations, to one that engenders the holistic development of an individual's intellectual and spiritual identity, as well as the social transformation of communities and societies.

To position our debate, we feel it appropriate and necessary to define the geographic territories of the Middle East and their role and historical significance in the global political economy. We will outline the religious, dynastic and colonial forces that have shaped national boundaries in the region, putting into perspective the areas in which specific Islamic traditions are prevalent and making postcolonial legacies evident. We will examine human development in a region which contains states in widely differing stages of economic, social and political development. We position the Middle East centre-stage in the global political economy by stressing the significance and power of the region in terms of natural resources in the form of oil and gas, while acknowledging that these resources have a complex relationship in the fabric of the international political economy, impacted by the complexity of power relations between international development agencies, nation states and regional networks such as OPEC (Bebbington 2008; Utting 2006). Unequal power dynamics and relations in shaping economic and social agendas are further highlighted in a region which can be considered as divided between resource-rich and resource-poor economies. Finally, we discuss the vulnerabilities and opportunities in the region in its response to current and future development and environment issues including 'peak oil', water resources, population growth, global trade routes and global warming, including opportunities in alternative energy resources.

We do not intend this text to merely restate myriad leadership theories, but rather to go some way in opening up communication and dialogue and thereby to reinterpret and reintegrate the knowledge territories of East and West (Escobar 1998; Ramadan 2009), and help *re-imagine* development discourses (Crush 1998). In doing so, we hope to unveil and open out the possibility of envisioning alternative development leadership paradigms inspired by knowledge from the Global South, as well as those, largely untranslated, Arabic texts that have shaped and influenced Middle Eastern thinking, reflection and comprehension: texts that build on a tradition of thought and intellectual investigation that was once the common link between both East and West civilizations and the scholarship of antiquity (see, inter alia, Morgan 2007; Ramadan 2009), a connection that the West and the Global North are belatedly rediscovering (Asutay and Zaman 2009; Morgan 2007).

The dynamic of political leadership and its intimate connection with leadership strategies in organizations is unfolded in this introduction (Platteau 2010). Weaving together the knowledge territories of development studies, organization and management, human resource development and environmental agendas with Islamic scholarship, we provide a rich account of the complexities of leader behaviours in the Middle East and the challenges that development stakeholders face to build leadership knowledges and human capabilities as the twenty-first century progresses.

CULTURE, POLITICAL ECONOMY, RELIGIOPOLITICS AND INTERNATIONAL RELATIONS

The Legacy of History

Our perception of the past depends on how we choose to collect and assemble the mosaic pieces of history – in the words of Arthur Miller (1947), 'the past is always present, and cannot be ignored, forgotten or denied' – yet it is absolutely essential to assemble those pieces correctly if we are to construct an understanding of the Middle East in which prosperity, stability and inter-state collaboration can be achieved (Ramadan 2004, 2009; Woolgar 1978). As Lewis and Churchill (2009) argue, the rehistoricization of social and political processes reveals insights that may otherwise fade away and be lost.

Islam has been pained for centuries by events that took place in the 50-year period following the death of the Prophet Muhammad in 632 CE. The Sunni majority of Muslims believe that Muhammad died having left no instruction as to who, if anyone, should succeed him in the Islamic community; but some believed that he had designated his son-in-law Ali as his successor. This group, the partisans of Ali (*Shiat Ali*), were later to be called Shi'a (Campbell 2008; Cleveland and Bunton 2009; Esposito 2005; Wilson 1985; see also discussion in the Editors' preface). These events gave rise to enduring ruling dynasties but also produced a schism between the Sunni and Shi'a. From this historic turmoil, distinctive leadership styles would develop and schools of thought on leadership would grow up which can only be understood in the context of the region, its history and culture, and the processes that formed the historical and modern states. Although there is an enduring legacy of colonial involvement in the region, to assume that this is the only, or even the dominant cultural influence is inaccurate and hubristic (Halliday 2010), and Western models are incomplete or inadequate to understand the reality of leadership in this complex region. While we acknowledge that cultural ideologies are shaped by a society's location in the hierarchically organized global economy, it is important to appreciate that they also vary according to the organization and development discourses that have evolved (Escobar 1998), and the historical and social context in which they have been embedded in each country (Crush 1998; Fairclough and Chiapello 2005; Woolcock 1998).

Leadership succession, long a central concern of the region, became an issue of global urgency beginning in December 2010 and continuing into 2011. The issue of political leadership succession to long-serving and relatively aged rulers in Egypt, Oman and Saudi Arabia was well known, but no one could have predicted the decisive mass action that caused, first, Zine El Abidine Ben Ali to be forced out of power in Tunisia and then Hosni Mubarak to be deposed in Egypt. Other protests have occurred in Bahrain – where they have been violently suppressed – Algeria, Jordan, Iran, Syria and Yemen. Libya has descended into civil war. Table 1.1 gives a summary of current governance regimes and the current leaders of selected states in the region. This is correct at July 2011.

As can be seen in Table 1.1, of the 11 nations considered, five have heads of state born in or before the year 1940. It should be noted that there is no single method to determine succession common to these states and no simple rule of succession such as primogeniture. In all cases, however, there is a degree of consensus (*ijma*) involved in appointing a legitimate successor.

The questions that remain of who will take control, and who should be involved in choosing a successor, are central to contemporary international relations and development, just as they were to the Muslim world in the early decades of Islam, and some commentators have suggested that the Muslim world faces the same problems it has faced since

Table 1.1 Culture and leadership in selected Middle East countries

Country	Population (millions)	Political System	Head of State	Year of birth	Year of accession	Notes
Bahrain	0.81	Constitutional monarchy Elected Chamber of Deputies since 2002.	King Hamad bin Isa al Khalifah	1950	1999	Ruling family of Al Khalifah are Sunni
Egypt	84.5	Presidential republic	Supreme Council of Egyptian Armed Forces	n/a	2011	Mohamed Hosni Mubarak (b. 1928) stood down 11 Feb 2011.
Iran	75.1	Presidential theocracy	Supreme Leader Ali Khameini	1939	1989	
Jordan	6.5	Constitutional monarchy	King Abdullah II	1962	1999	
Kuwait	3.1	Constitutional monarchy	Amir Sabah al-Ahmed al-Jabir al Sabah	1929	2006	
Oman	2.9	Traditional monarchy Appointed Consultative Assembly Elected legislature (Council of Oman)	Sultan Qaboos bin Said al Said	1940	1970	
Qatar	1.5	Constitutional monarchy	Amir Hamad bin Khalifa Al Thani	1932	1972	
Saudi Arabia	26.2	Islamic monarchy	King Abdallah bin Abd al-Aziz al Saud	1924	2005	

Table 1.1 (continued)

Country	Population (millions)	Political System	Head of State	Year of birth	Year of accession	Notes
Turkey	75.7	Parliamentary republic	President Abdullah Gül	1950	2007	
UAE	4.7	Presidential Federation of Traditional Monarchies Appointed consultative assembly (FNC)	Sheikh Khalifa bin Zayed al Nahyan	1948	2004	
Yemen	24.3	Presidential Republic Elected Council of Deputies Appointed Shura Council (advisory)	President Ali Abdullah Saleh	1946	1978 (Yemen Arab Republic)	

Sources: Long, Reich and Gasiorowski (2011), UNDP 2010

its inception: that same issue of succession to the Prophet Muhammad (Cleveland and Bunton 2009; Rodenbeck 2010; Platteau 2008). As Berkey (2003) argues:

> . . .probably no set of issues proved so contentious to Muslim posterity, or so critical in subsequent definitions of what it meant to be a Muslim, than that surrounding the question of leadership after the Prophet's death. (2003, p. 70)

It should be noted that the majority of the states analysed are governed by Islamic Shar'ia. This means that governance regimes and legal frameworks are premised on Islamic jurisprudence (see Editors' preface), although there is a great deal of variety in how this is interpreted and organized with respect to state – society relations. Platteau (2010) argues that there remains an instrumentalism of Islam in political organization and development. When we take a retrospective look at the deep political history of Muslim countries, it becomes apparent that authoritarian political regimes were dominant throughout, and that in these regimes politics and religion co-existed as separate entities linked through an asymmetric relationship of mutual recognition.

Countries of the Middle East differ in their historical evolution, social composition, economic structures and state forms. All the countries are Arab except Afghanistan, Israel, Iran and Turkey. All are predominantly Muslim except Israel. All Muslim countries are predominantly Sunni except Iran and Bahrain, with Sunni and Shi'a roughly equal in Iraq. State structures, some of which are set out in Table 1.1, vary from theocratic monarchy (Saudi Arabia) to secular republic (Turkey) and Gulf states all have constitutions premised on Islamic Shar'ia. Political scientists have used various terms to describe state organization including 'radical Islamist' (Iran); 'patriarchal conservative' (Jordan and Saudi Arabia) and 'authoritarian privatizing' (Egypt and Turkey) (Moghadam 1993).

The complexities of religious affiliation and organization are shown in Table 1.2, which includes the key schools of Islamic jurisprudence in Sunni governed states and Shi'i groups in Shi'i states. The process of Islamic interpretation of the Qur'an and Hadith is called *fiqh* and is undertaken by clerical scholars or *muttawa*. *Fiqh* is an ongoing process and revivalist scholars have argued for interpretations to be reassessed in light of contemporary Western knowledge and sciences (Ramadan 2009). However, as the chapters will reveal, the complexity of *fiqh* illustrates ways in which language is socially constituted, as Muslim leaders can often gain affirmation of political action by recourse to widely acknowledged and respected religious scholars.

Table 1.2 Religious affiliations in global regions and selected Middle East countries (2009 estimate)[1]

	Total Popu-lation	Muslim Population Total, millions		Breakdown and Sect if available Sunni	Shi'i	Other
Bahrain	0.79	0.64	81.2	25%	57%	Christian 9% Other 9%
Egypt	83	78.5	90[2]	89%	<1	Coptic Christian 9% Other Christian 1%
Iran[2]	75.1	73.8	98	9%	89%	Other 2%
Jordan	6.5	6.2	95	94%	<1	Christian 6% Other up to 2% (reported)
Kuwait	3.1	2.8	90	70	20%	10
Oman	2.9	2.5	86	≈4.5%	6.5%	Ibadi Muslim 75%
Qatar	1.5	1.2	77.5	69.5	8	Christian 8.5% Other 14%
Saudi	26.2	25	97	85%	12%	Other 3%
Turkey[2]	75.7	74	98	86%	12%	Other 2%
UAE	4.7	3.6	76	68%	8%	Other 14%
Yemen	24.3	23	99	64%	25% Zaydi 10% Other Shi'i	Other 1%
MENA Total	345	315	91.2			
Asia-Pacific	4037	973	24.1			
Other Africa	801	241	30.1			
Europe	731	38	5.2			
Americas	920	4.6	0.5			
World Total	6,860	1571	22.9			

Notes:
1. Compiled from multiple sources including Pew Forum on Religious and Public Life 2009; Long, Reich and Gasiorowski (2011); UNDP 2010; population figures are constantly changing due to natural growth and migration and census data is often out of date. These figures are in the end a judgement on the consensus between multiple, often contradictory sources and should be used with caution. This is an area for further research.
2. Both Turkey and Iran are included in total for Asia-Pacific.

Globalization, Culture and the Resurgence of Islam

Deetz et al. (2000) have argued that globalization and changes in social relations and in the nature of products and work processes have created a crisis of control in contemporary global organizations. They cite issues such as increasingly professionalized workplaces, geographically dispersed facilities and turbulent world markets that have contributed to the difficulty of coordination and control. These changes signal a shift to more ambiguous leadership roles and leader-follower relations which identify that relationships are not fixed but must be negotiated (Fairclough 2007; Fairclough and Chiapello 2005; Grint 2005, 2009; Meindl 1995; Swan et al. 2009; Yukl 2008). They further challenge individualistic orientations in leadership theorizing: the self preservation, self interest and self-promotion implicit in neo-liberal conceptions of political economy and industrial growth. It is, however, important that the revision and reinterpretation of the concept and dynamic of leadership is viewed as multi-layered.

Castells' (2009) observations inject into our deliberation the connectedness of international political economy, social movements, international organizational interventions, regional state alliances, conflicts and post-conflicts. The constitution of leadership as the property of a collective rather than as an individual characteristic mitigates against conventional representation of individual heroic leadership behaviours (Grint 2009, p. 2), and suggests that this quest to depart from what we term heroic social justice and ethical positions in Islamic states will be a difficult endeavour, as the following chapters will elaborate. Our discussion of Islamic leadership will show that the *collective* and *relational* orientation of a social ethic is embedded in Islamic leader-follower behaviours.

As Grint argues, the West's search for post-heroic versions of leadership closes off the 'romance' of heroic leadership (Meindl 1995). Adopting a multi-layered, multi-contextual and multi-cultural position, Grint argues that leadership scholarship: 'closed off from radical alternatives not because of its relationship to capitalism, or patriarchy, or ethnicity, or any other variable, but because it is so closely related to the realm of the sacred' (2009, p. 15). Repositioning the sacred and reconfiguring its dynamic interaction with leadership political processes will ultimately assist in attaining new perspectives not generally admitted by Western epistemologies. Within Islamic states, of course, no reimagining is necessary: faith, devotion and the sacred are integral to the practice of leadership and to revealing the qualities of that leadership (Beekun and Badawi 1999).

It is important to note, however, the potential confusion between Islam as a religion and Muslim, or Arab, or other relevant cultures. A religion is usually embedded in one or more cultures, but it cannot be reduced to a single culture (Roy 2002). Although our focus is on the Middle East (as defined later in this chapter), Said (1978) argued that we should avoid equating Islamic ideology only with the territories of the Middle East, a concept that underpins approaches he termed 'Orientalism'. This suggests that the role of Islam in shaping contemporary societies has been overemphasized. Westernization (globalization) is a social and cultural force whatever the official ideology of certain countries has to say to the contrary.

Re-Islamization and Westernization

Islam is an all-encompassing ideology which provides the organizing structure of meaning for political, social and cultural life. Thus Islam represents religion and state, and a system of belief and law that governs both spiritual and material conditions of everyday life and, as such, is central to state formation and governance.

Islam, or re-Islamization, can be observed in personal behaviour, growth in religious practices and a return to patriarchal family structures. Esposito (2005) uses the phrase, 'Islamic resurgence'. This is described by the author as an increased emphasis on religious identity in individual and corporate life. This involves a noticeable increase in religious observance (mosque attendance, fasting during Ramadan, abstention from alcohol); a new vitality in religious literature and media broadcasting (for example, Al Jazeera); the growth of Islamic associations concerned with reform, especially women's organizations; and the reassertion of Islam in regional politics. Re-Islamization requires organizations of dedicated and trained Muslims who, by their example, call on others to challenge social injustices. Esposito (2005, p. 165) summarizes the ideological framework of Islamic revivalism as follows:

1. Islam is a total and comprehensive way of life. Religion is integral to politics, law and society.
2. The failure of Muslim societies is due to their departure from the 'straight path' of Islam, and their following a Western secular path.
3. The renewal of society requires a return to Islam, an Islamic religiopolitical and social reformation role or revolution.
4. To restore God's rule and inaugurate a true Islamic social order, Western-inspired laws must be replaced by Islamic law.
5. Although the Westernization of society is condemned, modernization as such is not.

Islamization provides an alternative development model and questions dominant neoliberal understandings of modernity (Platteau 2010). The significance of this resurgence requires an understanding of how social, political and economic relations are constructed (Islam 2009). First, the condition of modernity which in the West separates religion and politics is not the only way to view development. Second, for many Muslims, Islam is a 'program of life' (Ahmed 1992; Esposito 2005). However, this modern resurgence in nations as widespread as Algeria and Iran was a result not of state legislation, but, on the contrary, accompanied the process of Westernization. As Roy (2002) argued: 'We tend to overemphasize the Islamic factor in the very process of Islamization, and miss all the others. Relationships between Islamization and globalization must be scrutinized more closely therefore' (p. 14).

The process of Westernization does not only include changes in economic and social relations. It also includes religiosity and a focus on increasing forms of transnational communication and knowledge exchange: global networking logic, interconnectedness, harbouring social movements and ideas concerned with ethics, moral values, professional development and personal success (Castells 2009; El Ghazili 1994). These are 'symbolising mobilisers' that bring into play new network organizations and configurations of power. The perception of a clash of civilizations between West and Middle East, and on values inherent in social and political organization, blurs the complexity of international relations. Norris and Ingleheart's 2002 treatise on the 'cultural clash' assumes a Western superiority and dominance in world order and is being challenged by social movements (Castells 2009; Bebbington 2008).

Thus, one cannot discuss religion and politics, but rather *religiopolitics* (Esposito 2005, p. 159). Islam is believed to be relevant and integral to politics, law, education, social life and economics. The question is not whether religion should inform life, but when and how. It is impossible to understand the salience of religion and the strength of Islamic resurgence without bringing into context decisive historical events. These include the Al Saʻud's successful conquest of much of the Arabian peninsula and espousal of *Wahhabism* as state ideology, and the challenges associated with the abundance of Saudi Arabia's oil resources, a theme we explore later. This has led to an accumulation of frustration at the inadequacy of state leaders in meeting the challenge of modernization, engendered by a series of military defeats by the West (Platteau 2010, p. 256-7). To appreciate, critique, analyse and debate the nature and practice of leadership one must look at the world through an Islamic lens. There is no 'secular', and no sharply defined dichotomy between the sacred and the profane. Islamic symbols, slogans and ideology have become prominent fixtures in Muslim politics. This historical logic is affirmed by Lewis: 'The idea that any group of persons, any kind of activities, any part of human life, is in any sense outside the scope of religious law and jurisdiction is alien to Muslim thought' (2002, p. 111).

The observations of critical social theorist Grint (2009) reflect this when he states that a critique is necessary of romance leadership, both heroic and collaborative notions (Meindl 1995), and that we need to reconfigure the dynamic relations of the sacred *in* and *through* leadership concepts and processes, *in* and *of* the sacred as it is constituted in diverse cultures, rather than attempting to eliminate this relationship (Grint 2009, pp. 14-15).

The cross fertilization of ideas and the deterritorialization of Islam and the Middle East in an age of globalization is nicely phrased by Princess Adelah bint Abdullah of Saudi Arabia:

> We should have an open mind and borrow the good from other cultures, including the West. There should be a process of a cultural give and take. Western civilization is indebted to Islam on several counts. The only thing is that we should be careful to take the good and leave the bad. Without doing that, we cannot progress. In the age of globalization, it is impossible to erect barriers. Let us take what is best in Asia, Europe, and America and use it for the healthy growth of society. (Arab News 2006)

Islamic revivalism, then, is a response to some aspects of Western values and development interventions that have challenged Arab knowledges and identities (Ahmed 1992; Roy 2002). Several scholars have argued that twenty-first century leadership requires a way for organizational actors and development stakeholders to re-envision their position in an era of post-industrialization and globalization (Ahmed and Donnan 1994; Grint 2005; Sinclair 2007; Western 2008). This requires a shift from the values and cultural norms of the industrial (Western) paradigm which fosters rational, control oriented, performance focused, self-interested, hierarchical structures and the expression of individualism to one that engenders collaboration, inclusiveness, commitment to human development and an ethics of care (Deetz et al. 2000; Greenleaf 1977; Grint 2007, 2009). A critical interpretative view of Islamic leadership challenges neoliberal models since behaviour orientation focuses on social change, emancipation and humanistic development (Ahmed 1992; Chapra 1993; Choudhury 1993; Platteau 2008).

LEADERSHIP: CONTEMPORARY DEVELOPMENTS IN WESTERN LEADERSHIP THEORIZING

A vital issue to be addressed in a critical review of leadership development in the Middle East is that current scholarship is still largely premised on Western constructions of leadership identities, relationships and behaviours (Metcalfe 2010; Syed 2010; Syed and Ali 2011), and this is reflected in much social science scholarship (Storey 2004). As the authors in this volume will elaborate, few scholars have paid attention to the importance of history, national identity, extensive governance reforms across the region and – especially relevant to our studies here – the terrain of international relations over the last three decades. The Iran-Iraq war, Iraq's invasion of Kuwait, the events of 11 September 2001 and the bombings of Madrid and London, the US-led invasions of Iraq and Afghanistan, the attack on the USS Cole in Aden harbour, coupled with economic turbulence and ongoing uncertainties in state leadership succession and the varying degrees to which religion influences social and organizational relations: all are components of cultural inquiry that have been underemphasized by recent scholarship which has therefore presented only a partial picture of Middle East leadership (Halliday 2010; UNDP 2010).

The Western conception of leadership incorporates myriad culturally specific assumptions, from democratic state leadership to a free market, capitalist structure for business. As Dunning (2007) has argued, modern capitalism has failed on at least three basic dimensions: failure of markets, failure of institutions, and failure of moral virtues. In response to this, Western writers have attempted to build an understanding of leadership that includes as a subset ethical principles such as trust, trustworthiness and cooperativeness. This values-based leadership promotes ethical and moral behaviour so as to advance human wellbeing for all organization actors. Attention has been placed on the inner qualities of ethical values as well as the representation of organization leaders themselves as embodying the ethical codes that they have internalized. This helps to build and sustain trust behaviours in organization relations, as well as associated networks (Ciulla 1995, 2005). This is, however, premised on the development of organizational competitiveness through ethical practices, not on wholesale ethical and economic rejuvenation of societies (Chapra 1992; El Ghazali 1994; Platteau 2008; Wilson 1985).

As we will go on to show, the organization leader is only one part of a social system. A clear difference between Western and Middle Eastern states is the latter's belief in integration via *umma* (El Ghazali 1994). The Islamic community is inextricably connected. Conceptualizations of leadership are thus wholly different when examining society through an Islamic lens, since there is no secular alternative (Metcalfe 2010; Metcalfe and Rees 2010). Leaders in Islamic states regard responsibilities as encompassing social, organizational and community-oriented responsibilities.

Leadership Theorizing: A Brief History

Figure 1.1 provides a diagrammatic overview of the historical development of leadership theorizing. Traditional leadership studies reflected assumptions about leadership in the post World War II period in the US.

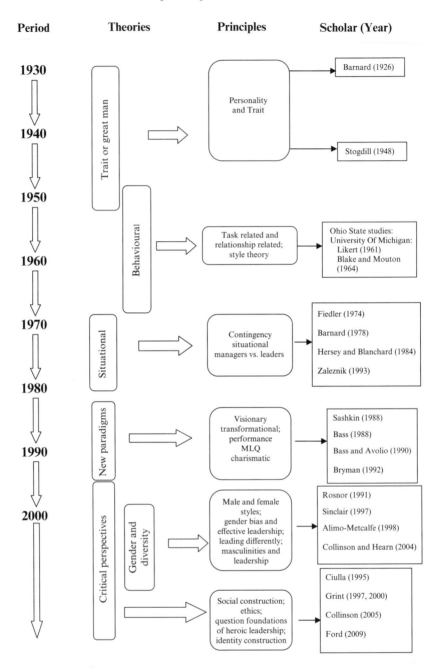

Figure 1.1   Historical development of leadership theory

Barnard (1938) argued initially that there is no single form of leadership. Behavioural psychologists, principally Stogdill (1950) and his team of researchers at Ohio State University, focused on 'trait' approaches that characterized leadership competencies such as intelligence, dominance, control orientation, task focus, objectivity and so on. Later in the 1950s, psychologists investigating leadership shifted their attention to 'behaviours'. Scholars, again at Ohio State University, measured behaviours via questionnaires and tended to focus on two dimensions: a 'concern for task' and a 'concern for people undertaking the task'. They identified behaviours termed 'consideration' and 'initiating structure' which correlated positively with employee satisfaction (Fleishman 1953, Stogdill 1974 in Alimo-Metcalfe 1998). Subsequent scholars paid more attention to context. Fiedler's contingency approach reflected developments in other social sciences where organization leadership was determined by strategy (Chandler 1962) and technology (Woodward 1970; see also Grint 1997, pp. 83-85).

The later 1970s and early 1980s marked a watershed in the history of leadership studies since the situation and contingency models, whilst including the complex context situations of leadership practice, provided little advice as to how to approach leadership in an era of economic volatility and significant social and economic change. It was in this environment that new leadership paradigms emerged. This new paradigm (Bryman 1992) encompassed visionary (Sashkin 1988), transformational and transactional approaches (see Bass and Avolio 1990, 1994). This reignited concerns for work productivity and human relationships. These were not necessarily at opposing poles. Zaleznik (1992) argued that there was a clear distinction between leaders and managers and that transactional approaches were about coordination, control and organization: in essence a management function. While these activities are not significantly associated with leaders, transformational techniques encourage trusting behaviours (idealized influence), motivate and enthuse (inspirational motivation), challenge employees (intellectual stimulation), and build meaningful relationships (individual consideration) (Bass and Avolio 1994).

Critical perspectives, which emerged in the early 1980s, include a broad range of approaches that challenged epistemological frames and questioned grand narratives of leadership, whom they benefited and for whom they were written (Utting 2006). Importantly, however, they were underwritten by Western-based knowledges. Gender and feminist critiques helped to stress how leadership theorizing was premised on masculinized constructions of knowledge (Calas and Smirchich 1991; Collinson and Hearn, 2004; Sinclair 2005, 2007). Critical perspectives highlighted the importance of the social construction of knowledge, power relations in leader-follower interactions and, importantly, the way in which language meaning is socially and culturally variable (Sinclair 2007).

Although not the first to broaden critical investigations, J.M. Burns was typical: 'Leadership over human beings is exercised when certain motives and purposes mobilise, in competition or conflict with others, institutional, political, and other resources so as to arouse, engage and satisfy the motives of the followers' (Burns 1978, p. 18).

To Burns, leaders are a particular kind of power holder. While acknowledging the importance of power, some scholars stressed effectiveness. De Vries, for example (1994, in Grint 1997), noted that 'effective leadership' depends on the complex patterns of interactions and relationships among leaders and followers, and importantly the situational and cultural context. For de Vries (1994), effective leaders are very good at 'building alliances' and creating commitment so that others will share (and accept – our insertion) their 'vision' (see also Yukl 2008).

Grint's review of the historical formation of leadership theorizing is interesting, as he suggested that contingency approaches and relationships between leaders and followers had been part of the original thinking of Barnard. Grint highlights how leaders need to be aware of, have empathy with, and understand the goals and orientations of the workers. Barnard concluded that informal relations and informal authority were important skills which the leader needed to nurture to ensure the cooperation and trust of followers:

> The followers make the leader, though the latter also may effect and guide the followers. Barnard, in Grint (1997, p. 85)

The dynamics of leader-follower relations, and the psychological make-up of all involved, have become central to understanding effective leadership behaviours, superseding earlier schools of belief in a universal theory of leadership (Storey 2004). Critical leadership studies have also shown the necessity of exploring language, cultural context and social interaction amongst leaders and followers and how they help constitute and reconstitute fluid and dynamic identities.

This brief overview of the historical foundation of leadership knowledge is relevant to understanding the socio-cultural dynamic of leadership behaviours in the Middle East since, as we will show, even early accounts of the interactions of the Prophet Muhammad and early *caliphs* with their followers presented leadership as a relational and group activity, enacted through a mutual commitment to a social ethics of humanistic development, and required trust behaviours (Al-Attas 1995; Noor 1999).

The GLOBE Leadership Study

As already highlighted, the dominant leadership writings are premised on Western values and norms and have largely examined states that are developed rather than developing. This is also the case in the growth of cross-cultural writings on leadership. Indeed, Western scholars have seemingly given precedence to some geographic regions over others. While scholarship on Asia and transition states is now expansive, there is a dearth of organization and management literature on the Middle East, Africa and Latin America (Metcalfe 2010; Metcalfe and Rees 2010). An exception is the GLOBE Leadership Study, which focused on values and practices as well as leadership attributes in 61 nations. National cultures were examined in terms of nine dimensions: performance orientation, future orientation, assertiveness, power distance, humane orientation, institutional collectivism, in-group collectivism, uncertainty avoidance and gender egalitarianism (House et al. 2004). The first six dimensions had their origins in the landmark study of Hofstede (1980, 1983). The overall goal of GLOBE was to examine the effect of specific cultural variables on leadership and organizational processes in order to discern any underlying patterns prevalent in specific socio-cultural contexts. However, there is also critique that attests to the differentiation in norms and values, both ideologically and structurally, and especially over time. Fifty-four researchers from 38 countries agreed a universal definition of leadership: 'the ability of an individual to influence, motivate and enable others to contribute towards the effectiveness and success of organizations of which they are members' (House et al. 2004, p. 5). The research team could not agree a definition of culture, however.

The GLOBE project specifically determined its parameters as the *organization* and not leadership in general. Four countries from the Middle East were included in the study: Iran, Kuwait, Turkey and Qatar, two of which are discussed in detail in this volume. Hofstede, in an attempt to assign regional countries to a cluster in what he termed the *Near East*, grouped together Egypt, Lebanon, Libya, Kuwait, Iraq, Saudi Arabia and the United Arab Emirates, based on his own research. He analysed them in terms of: (1) power distance and individualism; (2) power distance and uncertainty; and (3) uncertainty avoidance and masculine scales.

In the power distance and individualism matrix, Iran and Turkey represented high power distance and low individualism cultures. This displays an orientation to accept one's place in a hierarchy and be committed to broader community and group goals. In addition to a strong collectivist character, all displayed strong uncertainty avoidance and masculine characteristics (Hofstede 2003; Kabaskal and Dastmalchian 2001).

Recent political conflicts in Tunisia, Egypt and Libya attest to the ways in which cultural values and ideologies evolve and change in relation to social and economic relations. These observations are significant in providing an overview of shared cultural meanings and norms, but do little to expand the specificities and nuances of the myriad stages of development, governance and political institutions and gender relations, as well as the different state formations and social practices associated with Islam in daily life, and its association – or not – with individual Islamic national regimes. This is all the more significant when House et al. (2004) argue that their focus is on institutional leadership. In our view this represents an Anglocentric view of leadership roles and relations, as the varied discussions on leadership in this volume clearly demonstrate.

Ethics in Leadership

A key aspect of critical scholarship relevant to an examination of Middle East leadership is the nature of ethics in shaping leadership behaviours. The ethos of leadership varies fundamentally across nation states. How a particular society perceives and constructs leadership needs to be understood and debated in context. For example, Fairclough (2007), drawing on a Weberian analysis of formal rationality and substantive rationality, details the impact of what he terms 'ideational systems' (cultural, religious and political) on social institutions. A key observation was that the educational institutional framework laid the greatest impact on conceptualizations of leadership.

The focus on knowledge is significant. 'Leaders' and the 'led' participate in social and organizational interaction informed by their ideological and cultural knowledge, transmitted from generation to generation and learned through families and communities, a phenomenon explained by Bourdieu and Passerson (1977) as 'habitus' (Bebbington 2008). As different cultures, societies and communities construct leadership in diverse ways, the need to explore these social constructions becomes highly relevant in multi-cultural and international contexts (Javidan et al. 2006).

Doh and Strumph (2005, p. 15) devised a model of responsible leadership and governance as shown in Figure 1.2. They argue: 'Many companies are pursuing a mission of responsible leadership and governance . . . responsible leadership and governance are morally preferable to alternative approaches to management and oversight and economically beneficial to the companies and organizations that adopt it' (p. 15).

While advocating a humanistic commitment to leadership, underpinning their logic is still a neoliberal performative notion, illustrated by

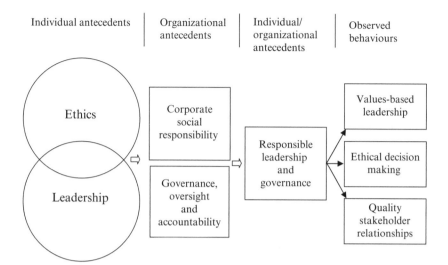

Source: Doh and Stumpf (2005), *Handbook on Responsible Leadership And Governance in Global Business*, p. 15.

Figure 1.2   *A framework of responsible leadership and governance: antecedents, construct and behaviours*

their focus on economic benefits. The observed behaviours – values-based-leadership, ethical-based decision making and quality stakeholder relationships – represent, it could be argued, the commoditization and objectification of a global business ethic to preserve and promote organization competitiveness. What is lacking in this model is a linkage to the social system that the organizations are part of, and a determination of who evaluates outcomes, and what the measures are for evaluating the ethical behaviours observed.

Maak extends the ideas of responsible and ethical leadership by bringing 'such vision to life by mobilizing stakeholders inside and outside the organization to contribute to business sustainability and legitimacy' (2007, p. 34). This vision is formed through social interaction and relies on commitment to build social capital through trust behaviours and relations (Bourdieu and Passeron 2007). Citing Balkundi and Kilduff, he states: 'To a considerable extent, organizations and environments exist as *cognitions* in the minds of leaders and followers' (our italics) (2005, p. 946, in Maak 2007, p. 334).

Maak further posits that the building of social capital by leaders, through organization networks and social ties, can benefit all stakeholders

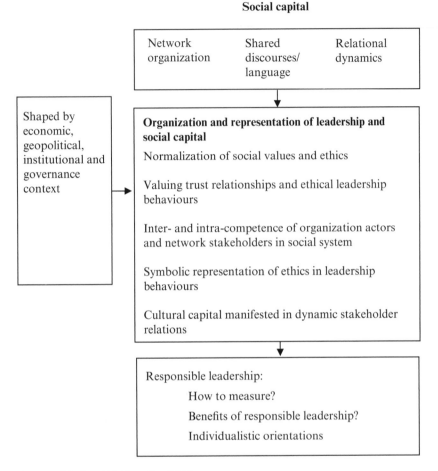

Social capital

Network organization	Shared discourses/ language	Relational dynamics

Shaped by economic, geopolitical, institutional and governance context

Organization and representation of leadership and social capital

Normalization of social values and ethics

Valuing trust relationships and ethical leadership behaviours

Inter- and intra-competence of organization actors and network stakeholders in social system

Symbolic representation of ethics in leadership behaviours

Cultural capital manifested in dynamic stakeholder relations

Responsible leadership:

How to measure?

Benefits of responsible leadership?

Individualistic orientations

Source: Maak (2007); Bourdieu (2001).

Figure 1.3   Social capital and responsible leadership

and bring about responsible, or transformational, leadership (see also Burns 1978). The 'humble networker' (Maak 2007, p. 340) is still, however, the weaver of 'value networks' (Maak 2007, p. 339) aiming to contribute to both sustainable business and a common good. A model of responsible leadership and social capital is shown in Figure 1.3. Our concern is that this leadership ethic is often constituted in neo-liberal market environments where social and ethical intelligence is about value creation for organization systems, not societies themselves. Specifically, if responsible leadership is embedded in organization behaviours, how can one check which ethics embrace the social good as opposed to individual orientations? Also, as already touched on, how are stakeholder orientations inside and outside the organization, in diverse geopolitical and governance regimes, measured and evaluated – and by whom? (Ciulla 2005; Chapra 1993).

In the next section, we address how stakeholder social capital can be constructed as a means of enhancing all human livelihoods and wellbeing. We explore what is meant by leadership in an Islamic context and draw on contemporary scholarship to elucidate the similarities and differences in leadership behaviour.

LEADERSHIP: AN ISLAMIC LENS

Islamic Resurgence and State Formation

We discussed previously the processes of globalization, Islamization and Islamic resurgence. The vision of Islam as a revealed religion is to achieve the wellbeing (*falah*) of men and women and to establish an environment and civilization in which all can live in peace and harmony. This is achieved through a process of continued development governed by shar'ia, ethics and morality. If the objectives of shar'ia, are realized, then *falah* is also realized. These objectives are aptly summarized by Muslim scholar Imam Hamid al-Ghazali:

> The objectives of the Shariah is the well-being of the people, which lies in safeguarding their faith (*din*), their self (*nafs*), their intellect (*aql*), their posterity (*nasl*) and their wealth (*mal*). Whatever ensures the safeguard of these five principles serves public interest and is desirable, and whatever hurts them is against public interest and its removal is desirable. (Al-Ghazali, in Ahmad 1995)

As Chapra observed (1993), revivalism has led to the ideologization of Islam. Instrumentalism in political Islam need not be an impediment to development, but the interwoven nature of Islam and governance adds complexities not configured in Western accounts. All the countries of the Middle East and North Africa, for example, score comparatively low in measures of public accountability, quality of public administration and the efficiency of state bureaucracy (Platteau 2010). This means that Islam has impacted the organization of the political arena more than the economic, but current Islamic constitutions have economic ambitions premised on Islamic shar'ia and jurisprudence.

Islam is an all-encompassing ideology which provides the organizing structure of meaning for political, social and cultural life. Thus, Islam represents religion and state, and a system of belief and law that governs both the spiritual and material conditions of everyday life. Islam is thus central to state formation and governance. As Table 1.1 indicates, Islamic states are not homogeneous and include regimes that operate with a theocratic establishment and state supported clerical leaders as well as monarchs and elected presidents.

Defining Leadership within an Islamic Framework

Leadership in Islam is a trust (*amanah*). It represents a psychological contract in which the leader commits to try his best to guide his followers, to protect them and to treat them justly. Hence the leadership process in Islamic communities is concerned with social welfare and moral justice as well as with attaining economic development goals. Sahih Bukhari, an eminent Islamic scholar, cites a hadith that all Muslims are the: 'shepherd of a flock and hold leadership positions' (Bukhari, in Beekun and Badawi 1999). Beekun and Badawi argued as early as 1999 that ethics will be a defining feature of the way leaders are judged and evaluated. This has been precipitated by the rise of religiosity worldwide (Norris and Ingleheart 2002), the growth of ethical codes and global conventions such as the UN social compact and a response to specific organization malpractices (for example Enron) as well as the multitude of humanitarian injustices committed by transnational corporations in developing nations, including exploitation of workers, denial of basic human needs and rights, sexual exploitation and contribution to environmental degradation (Pearson 2007; UNDP 2009a).

According to Islam, leaders have two primary functions: as *servant leaders* and as *guardian leaders*. Leaders are servants of their followers and leadership through service is embraced in a hadith: 'A ruler who has been entrusted with the affairs of Muslims, but makes no endeavour for their material and moral uplift and is not merely concerned for their welfare will not enter paradise with them' (reported by Abu Malih in Sahih Muslim 1:82, Chapter 44, Hadith no. 264).

The idea of leader as servant is embedded in Islamic philosophy and was more recently adopted by Greenleaf (1977). The guardian leader has a role in protecting his community against tyranny and oppression, in encouraging *taqwa* (duty and responsibility) and in promoting justice. A leader embraces natural feelings of wanting to lead, and then from the leader's conscience arises the aspiration to lead justly (Sarayrah 2004).

The characteristics of the servant leader as codified by Larry Spears include the following:

Listening: leader seeks to identify different points of view and listens receptively to what is 'said and 'unsaid'.

Empathy: strives to promote empathy in order to help legitimize his or her role/special gift of serving.

Healing: healing of relationships is a powerful force for social transformation.

Awareness: self-awareness and critical reflection strengthens understandings of ethics power and values.

Persuasion: a process of convincing rather than coercion is seen as appropriate for negotiations and building trust behaviours.

Conceptualization: servant leaders need critical judgement and analytical reasoning to seek a balance between concepts and practical action.

Foresight: have insights into the realities of the present, reflections on the past, and potentialities of the future.

Stewardship: a strong commitment to the service of others.

Commitment: to the growth of every individual and organization.

Building Community: building alliances between individuals, organizations and public and international institutions to engender community of care and ethics to prosper.

Spears 2000, quoted in Sarayrah 2004, pp. 63-64

A Model of Islamic Leadership

According to Beekun and Badawi (1999) leadership is rooted in belief and willing submission to the creator, Allah. The key task of leaders is to do good deeds and work towards the establishment of Allah's *din*. This involves attempting to sustain social cohesiveness while also exemplifying openness, willingness to learn and reflect and showing compassion to subordinates. Beekun and Badawi's model of the moral bases of Islamic leadership is shown in Figure 1.4.

The definitions of the terms used in Figure 1.4 are as follows:

Iman: the core of the moral character is Iman or faith in Allah. A belief in oneness of Allah (tawhid).

Islam: the term Islam comes from the Arabic root *slm* meaning peace and submission. Islam means peace with Allah, with oneself and willing submission to Him.

Taqwa: an inner consciousness of one's duty toward Allah and an awareness of one's accountability.

Ihsan: love of Allah. *Ihsan* embraces the attainment of personal qualities associated with self-actualization and completeness. This includes characteristics such as *sabr* (patience), *ubudiyqah* (servitude), *shukr*

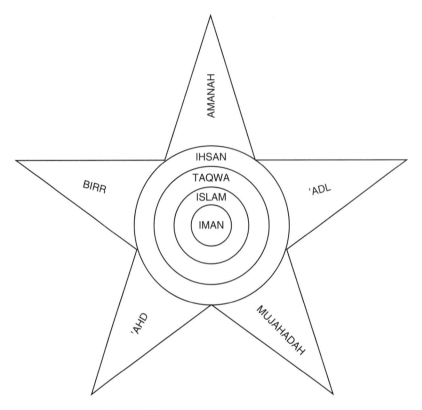

Source: Beekun and Badawi 1999, p. 15.

Figure 1.4   Moral bases of Islamic leadership

(thankfulness), *jihad* (struggle) and *ijz* (humility) (Zaman and Asutay 2009).

Adl: balance and harmony. Organization and social relations should be configured to maintain stability and complement the unique qualities of men and women. It is a dynamic characteristic that each Muslim must strive to develop, whether he is a leader or a follower (see Umar-ud-Din 1991).

Mujahadah: concerned with struggle within oneself for self improvement. Embraces self-reflection about one's leadership practice.

'Ahd: integrity and keeping one's word.

Amanah: trust and responsibility towards stakeholders. Individuals should speak the truth, keep one's promise, fulfil one's trust. Practice modesty and behave justly (Qur'an, sura Joseph (Yusuf), 12:54–55).

Birr: righteousness (goodness), or keeping one's word: 'Goodness does not consist in turning your face towards East or West. The truly good are those who believe in God and the Last Day, in the angels, the Scripture, and the prophets. . .' (Qur'an, sura Al Baqara (2:177)

It is worth expanding upon *birr* and its application to leadership. The following significant attributes of leaders derive from *birr*:

- They act justly and do not allow their personal feelings to hinder justice.
- They have *Iman* since they believe in Allah, the Last Day, the angels, the Books and the messengers.
- They take care of those in need, and do so for the love of Allah.
- They are steadfast in prayer and practice charity.
- They observe all contracts, and.
- They are patient no matter what type of adversity or personal suffering they may be experiencing.

Beekun and Badawi 1999, pp. 30–31

Similar to Beekun and Badawi, Noor (1999) is among the first modern Muslim management writers who proposed an integrated model for organizational effectiveness based on the Prophet Muhammad's leadership style and interaction with his followers. The major dimensions of this theory are: (1) alignment, which takes its roots from *tawhid* (oneness of God), and thus inspires a sense of social mission; (2) attunement to the systemic purpose and mission, which incorporates the shared communal values such as commitment, trust, mutual respect and working for the overall advancement of society and individuals; (3) empowerment, or enablement, which induces the leader with more responsibility and accountability for the community, thus embodying the role of the vicegerent (*khalifah*) of God on earth. When all these three elements have been addressed, then we have *al-falah*, which gives synergy – the total convergence of the elements into a symbiotic whole. Synergy entails the attainment of success and prosperity for all who share the common vision of greatness (Noor 1999, p. 3).

Building on these insights, we argue that the social ethics and relational dynamic is imperative to effective leader-follower interactions. Islamic scholarship on leadership is labelled 'purposeful' (Al Attas 1995; Al-Omar 1999; Al-Faruqi 1982). 'Purposeful' is used in the sense that it has genuine intent in terms of *tawhid*, understanding the oneness of creator and human beings, and understanding the responsibility of humanity as Allah's vicegerents on earth. Leadership in Islam, therefore, is a relational social practice, a process of interaction between leaders and followers which should be based on mutual engagement and trust. In this way, business leaders can be seen as corporate *khalifah*, who are not only responsible for the growth of their businesses, but are also accountable to God for their actions as leaders. The principle of *maslahah* (concern for the public good and welfare) governs actions and behaviours of leaders and followers. Therefore, instead of typical aggressive, ego-centric, personal-interest oriented leaders, more humane and ethical conduct is expected from leaders in Islam who are tasked with serving the public good. This is a holistic view of leadership which is concerned with the moral growth and development of individuals, organizations and societies

Purposeful Leadership, Knowledge and Becoming

From an Islamic perspective, 'leading' has a strong connotation of leading toward knowledge and righteousness through words and acts, entailing a knowledge figurehead for the leader, as well as perceiving him or her as a role model in a holistic sense. The role of leadership as engaged in knowledge building, and in guiding individuals to rise to higher levels (Qur'an, sura Ripped Apart, 84:19), reflects concern with a 'process of becoming' (Choudhury 1993, p. 6; Beekun and Badawi 1999), a learning journey achieved through *jihad* (struggle) and an acknowledgement of the sacred (Grint 2009). In developing purposeful knowledge, a purposeful leader also requires 'systemic environment insight' (Al-Faruqi 2000). This involves self-awareness and self-assessment – the process of *mujahadah* (critical self-reflection: Metcalfe 2008). However, in building trust relations and working towards balance and harmony (*adl*), a leader needs to build the capacities of his/her followers. Islamic scholars argue that a fundamental work ethic consists in feedback being 'a gift' to be reflected and acted upon (Al-Omar 1999). Purposeful feedback helps employees learn from their mistakes and improve their productivity: lack of feedback can build tension and conflict. Destructive behaviour such as that represented by cultural masculinism when giving feedback, or succumbing to one's ego, are primary causes of leadership derailment. If trust behaviours are developed through *shura* (consultation), there is respect and honour for those with authority: '. . .pardon them and ask forgiveness for them. Consult with them about matters, then, when you have decided on a course of action, put your trust in God' (Qur'an, sura The Family of 'Imran, 3:159).

Consultation is extremely important in Islamic communities, as seeking knowledge has a collective dimension: each individual is responsible for sharing and dissemination. This process incorporates building the *umma* (community) and local or national Muslim societies and communities. Thus, institutional leadership (whether religious or organizational) continues to involve more than organizational management, it also includes a moral obligation for the holistic development of the leaders and followers of the community. Purposeful leadership is thus holistic, and about 'becoming', as it is concerned with the moral growth and development of individuals, organizations, communities and states. Leadership without a holistic purpose is at best a demonstration of the deployment of interpersonal and intrapersonal qualities to manage social and organizational change (Al Faru 1982). However, an effective leader in the Islamic sense is firmly grounded in a strong ethical foundation that guides all his or her activities and thinking. Human beings are managing life in its totality, fully aware that while there are ongoing challenges which require reflection, there are also constants such as a humanity's value system. As previously stated, Islam is a programme of life (Ahmed 1992) requiring commitment to lifelong learning and *umma*, with a responsibility to improve both material and moral wealth. The worldview represented by Islam is: 'A vision of reality and truth that appears before our mind's eye revealing what existence is all about; for it is the world of existence in its totality that Islam is projecting' (Al-Attas 1995, p. 7). Thus, every member of the community is a leader and a guardian in his or her local context. The sense of responsibility and accountability is a shared one. In the Prophet's words: 'Each one of you is a guardian, and each one of you will be asked about his subjects; a man is a guardian over the members of his household and he will be asked about his family members; a woman is a guardian over the members of her family. . ... Each one of you is a guardian and each one of you will be asked about his subjects' (Al-Omari 2005).

Comparison with Western Leadership Ethics

Similarities with Maak's responsible leadership model (2007) are striking. The development of organization social networks, a concern for social justice and broader social development agendas, community building and stakeholder involvement – are all involved in achieving advances in human and social development. Woolcock (1998) and Bebbington (2008) are more critical of international political relations and question the power dynamics of social capital in the global world order (also central to Bourdieu's thesis) and how institutions, whether TNCs or international organizations, yield control and exercise power.

Monitoring and evaluation of ethical leadership behaviour seems to have little influence if not accompanied by legislative measures. 'Big ego' type leaders abound in the global leadership literature (whether in the US,

UK, Russia or China; Maak 2007, p. 340), as represented by corporate scandals contained within the ongoing global financial crisis. To make the point of trans-cultural miscommunication, when Maak states (quoting Plato) 'leaders are not shepherds' (a fundamental metaphor in understanding the role and responsibility of a leader in Islam) but weavers who weave together different stakeholders in a coalition and brokers of social capital. This could be read just as well as a 'good deal maker' in the UK or US. The politics and power of social capital is not deliberated in Maak's concept, but is central to understanding international power relations and diplomacy. Unequal power relations are also a general concern amongst intelligentsia and statesmen in MENA territories (Metcalfe and Rees 2010; Utting 2006), but unlike Western states, *umma* and religious codes act as regulators of individual and, ultimately, organizational behaviour.

However, as Ahmed (1992) and Roy (2002) note, globalization, the internationalization of technology and economic universalism are drawing the world closer (Castells 2009) and smoothing out many differences in diverse fields of human activity. As previously highlighted, Muslim identity and the impact of ideational systems are especially important in spite of modernization and 'meta narratives' of democracy, equality and social justice (Metcalfe 2010). Cultural fluidity and exchanges in value systems have re-ignited the politicization of Islamic identity. As previously discussed, Ahmed (1992) attributes this escalation to the revival of the religious in the modern world (see also Esposito 2005). A consequence is for Muslims to highlight their commitment to religious identity. The growth in Islamic revivalism is being expressed in national systems of education and curriculum planning. For example, the first aim of Pakistan's National Education Policy (1998–2010) is 'Within the context of Islamic perception, education is an instrument for developing the attitudes of individuals in accordance with the values of righteousness to help build a sound Islamic society' (Shah 2006, p. 372). Similarly, as highlighted when discussing state formation, the constitutions in Islamic states are explicit in upholding principles of Islamic shar'ia and in maintaining a commitment to Arabic and Persian heritage and legacy (Metcalfe 2010). Arabic scholars of leadership are concerned that waves of globalization and the intersecting flows of norms, values and practices across cultures are acting as 'disengagement' practices (Ramadan 2009) and potentially distorting the value of leadership behaviours and traditions, which are principally about the passion to motivate and nurture human wellbeing, sustainability and profitability in their communities. While ethical dilemmas concerning Western leadership practices have been broadcast widely in the media, little has been said of instances of labour trafficking and the poor treatment of migrants in GCC states and how this is influenced by globalization and this is an area for future inquiry (but see for exceptions Metcalfe 2010; Platteau 2010). As we have argued previously, a model of leadership that is culturally sensitive and appropriate is necessary in order to resist Westernization values that undermine Islamic governance regimes.

Our critique suggests that models of Islamic leadership are necessary a parts of a corrective and resistance strategy to Westernization processes, and Western leadership discourses that undermine Islamic governance regimes and thus cultural diversity (for example in Pakistan, Iran, Iraq, Saudi Arabia and Egypt; Grint 2009). Islamic leadership models also offer alternatives to the styles of economic governance and public administration favoured in Western states (see Chapra 1993, Choudhrey 1990).

Our aim in this section was not to merely restate myriad leadership theories, but rather open up communication and dialogue and thereby reinterpret and reintegrate the knowledge territories of East and West, the Global North and Global South (Ramadan 2009; Morgan 2007). Leadership theorizing needs to acknowledge the fluidity of ethical principles beyond those applied to neo-liberal governance regimes and to recognize that a flow of knowledge from the Global South to the Global North can offer new tools of thinking about the ethics of leadership behaviours (see Campbell 2008; Maak and Pless 2009). Ramadan argues for a liberation of ethics that can assist transnational reform toward enlightened leadership. He argues that Islamic ethics requires reflection about meaning and coherence and calls for 'dialogues':

> with one's own and with other civilizations, and be apt to tackle the respective inconsistencies of practice rather than ethereal ideals or theories. Goals and ethics train the heart to the intensity of questioning and the mind to build bridges – between self and self, oneself and others, values and behaviours, and means and ends. (Ramadan 2009, pp. 312–13)

THE MIDDLE EAST AND INTERNATIONAL RELATIONS: DEFINING THE TERRITORY

The large body of criticism by international leadership scholars (for example House et al. 2004; Western 2008; Yukl 2008) has tended to ignore the social and historical formations of state society relations, identity and political ideology. To step back and glimpse the complexities of Middle East social relations and national and international relations in the political economy is an approach that requires what Halliday termed 'a subtle mind, freed of modernist hubris' (Halliday 2010, p. 2). He proposed the prevalence of a religious discourse in all human activity. As previously highlighted, unlike modernist accounts of social change and transformation in the West, in the Middle East there is no secular lens.

A central tenet of this book is the influence of Islam in shaping political and governance systems and, consequently, leadership behaviour and relations. It is important to highlight the changing contours of territories allied to Islamic regimes and identities (Ali 2005). In the discussion above, we provided an overview of contemporary Islamic leadership theory. In support of this analysis, we present interpretations of leadership behaviours, relations and practices by mapping schools of Islamic jurisprudence (see Preface) and how they are bound to the geography of the region. Such ties are inexact, since migration and conflict have continuously altered allegiances, yet there are generalizations that can be observed between geographic territories. This identification with space and place, Islamic governance and ideology provides a backdrop to how historical connections between time, place, identity and Islamic affiliation are interwoven and continually interactive.

In Figure 1.5 we give a representation of the Sunni and Shi'i schools and their associated branches, as discussed in the Editors' preface, and identify the nations in which the various sects and schools are dominant. In Table 1.2 we provide a breakdown of the religious affiliations of the populations in selected countries of the Middle East. The data presented is in part estimated, as religious affiliations are often ignored or assumed in censuses: in particular, accurate statistics are often unavailable for minorities, which may be misreported by individuals or merely assumed into the majority figure (Pew Research Center 2009) and members of migrant populations are often reluctant to participate in the census. This geographic mapping illustrates the complexities of regional and Islamic populations and illustrates diversity rather than homogeneity.

Defining Middle East Territories

The contemporary Middle East is portrayed as a mysterious 'other', separate and distinct from the dominant cultural associations of space, place, values and identities attached to the West in the global political economy (Halliday 2000, 2010; Said 1978) and currently associated with intrigue and conflict, with the origination and propagation of terrorism, with religious extremism and non-democratic government (Norris and Ingleheart 2002).

In this section, in order to elucidate some of the complexities of these relationships, we discuss the Western construct of the region of the Middle East and its constituent nations, including those discussed in more detail in the remainder of this volume. The discussion that we develop provides

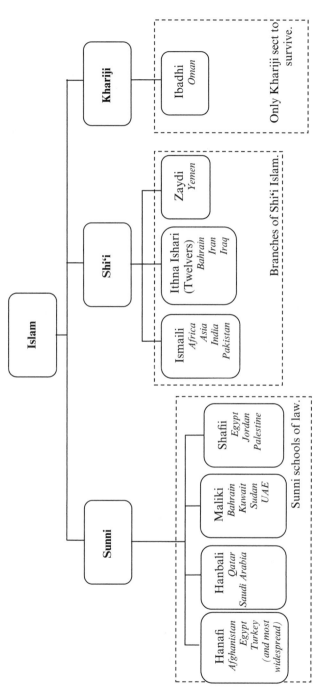

Source: Compiled from Esposito (2003) and other sources given in Editors' preface. Countries shown are those particularly associated with the sects or schools, but most are widespread.
Not shown: Sufi Islam and its orders.

Figure 1.5   Schools and branches of Islam

insights into how the Middle East as a concept and its constituent nation states came into being, how boundaries were set and reformed, and the colonial influence on that reconfiguration (Davidson 2008, 2009; Halliday 2000; Owen 1991). It is suggested that the colonial legacy still has ramifications for Middle East identity, but as subsequent chapters will demonstrate, the colonial past and colonial principles are being consigned to history in a renewal of cultural identity, bound to the nation or to Arab, Maghreb, Iranian and other identities (Ali 2005).

In order to contextualize the subject of leadership it is helpful to look at recent global developments pertinent to understanding sociocultural and geopolitical changes and to include themes such as democratization, gender, ethnicity and political economy. The justification for these themes is that, in their interrelation, they will reveal the complex multilayered factors that shape nationalisms, nation state building, organization systems and managerial policies, as well as gender and ethnic relations. Before these are examined, however, it is necessary to define the concepts and territories of the Middle East.

What we mean by 'Middle East' and its constituent nations is a controversial subject. The region provides rich contrasts in political, cultural, social and economic spheres. The three great monotheistic religions, Judaism, Christianity and Islam, were established through prophets and followers in these lands. The golden age of Islam (Ramadan 2009) witnessed the spread of Islam to Europe to the West and Asia to the East. The rich heritage of literature, thought, poetry and story telling – for example, as known in the West as the 'Arabian Nights', or the works of Omar Khayyam or Ibn Khaldun – composed in Arabia and communicated to Europe, informs us of great empires and a great respect for scientific reason, philosophy and the acquisition of knowledge (Ramadan 2009).

More recently, in the nineteenth and twentieth centuries, the Middle East was subject to colonial competition, resulting in moves towards modernization and economic development (Ali 2005). The modernization process has however been uneven and sporadic (Halliday 2010; Long et al. 2011; Milton-Edwards 2006).

The region is vast, with a number of borders and boundaries disputed and interpreted differently across cultures. Depending on which definition of the Middle East is used, the area stretches from Mauritania in the West to Iran in the East, and can include the East coast of sub-Saharan Africa and Turkey, Afghanistan and the Persian Gulf. Within this geographic territory there are vast deserts, ultra-modern cities such as Dubai, snow-capped mountains and vital natural resources, as will be discussed later in this chapter. The countries of this region differ in their historical evolution, social composition and governance regime. Many of the countries can be considered Arab – on a definition based on language rather than geography – but not Afghanistan, Iran, Israel or Turkey, and several including Afghanistan, Iran and Iraq are ethnically diverse. All except Israel are predominantly Muslim, and of those all except Iran and Bahrain (Shi'i) and Oman (Ibadhi) are predominantly Sunni: 'however, the "Arab world" is not congruent as a concept with the 'Muslim world' as consideration of the status of, for example, Israel, Iran, Turkey, Pakistan and Afghanistan, or indeed Europe, will show' (Hurd 2006). However, the Arab League of 22 Middle East and North African nations remains a significant political and cultural organization.

That the region is inhabited by many religious groupings, despite the dominance of Islam, is linked to migration as well as to a resurgence in religiosity in general. Migration has created a diverse cultural mix of ethnic identities and religious affiliations, and many non-Muslims, for example Christian and Hindu expatriates, have played a large part in the development of the region. This is summarized in Table 1.2.

What, then, does define the Middle East? There are common historical reference points such as the death of the Prophet in 632 CE, or the fall of the Ummayad empire in 750 CE: events common to the Islamic world as a whole, rather than to distinct regions. It is argued, however, that the Arabic language is in some sense an essence of Arab identity even beyond such shared historical legacy.

For the purposes of this book, we will define the Middle East as comprising the 16 states identified in Figure 1.6. Also shown but not identified are the nations of the 'Broader Middle East and North Africa' (BMENA) defined by the G8 and consisting of Afghanistan, Algeria, Bahrain, Egypt, Iran, Iraq, Jordan, Kuwait, Lebanon, Libya, Mauritania, Morocco, Oman, Pakistan, Qatar, Saudi Arabia, Sudan, Syria, Tunisia, Turkey, UAE, West Bank/Gaza and Yemen (G8-BMENA 2007).

The US has gone further in proposing policy based on a definition of a 'Greater Middle East', 'a large swath of Arab and non-Arab Muslim countries, stretching from Morocco in the west to as far east as Pakistan in southeast Asia' (Sharp 2005).

As Özbilgin states (Chapter 11), positioning Turkey with the Middle East is contentious. Although part of Turkey is geographically in Europe and the country is a candidate for EU accession, its relationship to Europe is debatable, although the concept of Europe is as amorphous and political (Hurd 2006; Yukleyen 2009) as is that of the Middle East. Further, Egypt is an African state with a strong Islamic heritage; however, so are others such as Sudan. Ultimately, we have chosen to adopt a 'traditional' definition of the Middle East consistent with that given in Esposito (2005,

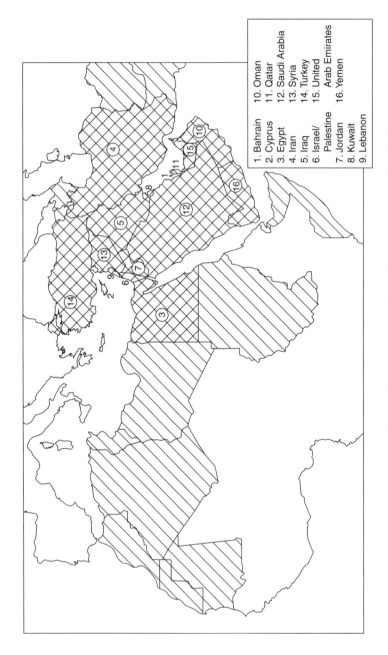

Note: Map is for illustrative purposes only, and does not imply acceptance of or opinion on any disputed boundaries.

Figure 1.6   Map of the Middle East

p. 200), while accepting that this is an arbitrary delineation. Within this definition, this book does not cover all countries but aims to provide a representative sample, including resource rich and resource poor, democratic and authoritarian states, along with generic chapters providing a detailed critique of specific issues across a broader range of countries.

COLONIAL DISENGAGEMENT AND THE MIDDLE EAST

The discussion in the section above brings to the fore the significance of how the Middle East as a geographic label has been constructed. The term is relatively new: this is important since the name creator was outside the geographical space which has become identified as Middle East: 'the Orient was almost a European invention' stated Palestinian academic Edward Said in *Orientalism*, his classic critique of the dominant Western concepts of the Middle East (Said 1978, p. 1). He went on to elucidate in poetic prose a dualism of night and day in which the Orient stood as the moon, the black, the negative, the backward, while the Occident represented the sun, the white, the positive, the enlightened and the progressive. Despite a homage to cultural knowledges, the West's construction of a Middle East positioned it as 'less than': less educated, less democratic and less developed – the 'other' against which are positioned dominant, developed Western nations:

> The Orient is not only adjacent to Europe; it is also the place of Europe's greatest and richest and oldest colonies, the source of its civilizations and languages, its cultural contestant, and one of its deepest and most recurring images of the Other. (Said 1978, p. 1)

Western societies began to constitute themselves in a series of oppositions, for example: centre/periphery; developed/underdeveloped; scientific/superstitious, and so on. This social construction led to a Western self-image as a superior civilization. Once a link between superior West and inferior non-West was formed, colonialism became a culture and identity project that was acceptable to assist the process of 'improving, helping and civilizing' those states and peoples that were 'lagging behind' (Escobar 1998). Scholarship on the Middle East has progressed since Said's text brought to the fore debates between East and West about what constitutes development and reaffirmed both postcolonial and poststructuralist understandings of knowledge, world order and power relations across and within developed, developing and transitional states (Utting 2006). These themes re-emerge throughout this book for, as we shall see, Arab Gulf states in particular are re-imagining development advances through an Islamic lens and thus have fundamentally different perspectives on transformation and change compared to Western states (Asutay 2007; Sharabi 1990).

Halliday (2007) takes a more pragmatic view, arguing that what happens in these societies is not as distinct or apart as imagined, but evolves from the cultural transference of ideas, concepts and interactions, aided by information and communication technology growth in the last twenty years and the advent of globalization (see also Castells 2009).

This discussion has indicated the complexity of the way in which the Middle East is defined. Orientalists and post colonialists have presented convincing debates about ongoing influence and control. In fact, for many states, colonial rule in the twentieth century was short lived, as will be discussed in the chapters that follow. It is beyond the scope of this text to examine this history in detail, but we feel it is necessary to touch on the most pertinent period, that between the First and Second World Wars.

It was at the end of World War I, associated with the break up of the Ottoman Empire, that governance regimes were comprehensively restructured. By 1922 the 'new' Middle East was emerging. New states were mandated to Britain and France under League of Nations auspices, states such as Jordan, Syria, Lebanon and Iraq, the boundaries of which paid little or no regard to the rich and diverse cultural and ethnic identities within them. During the inter-war period, colonial powers attempted to extend their control over the region, notably to Egypt and the Gulf: Milton Edwards (2005) coined the phrase 'merchants and missionaries', who impacted trade routes and development agendas across the region, communicating and infusing European ideals, values and practices.

After World War II the colonial powers faced greater resistance. There is no uniform picture that reflects and explains disengagement from British and French rule. However, the involvement of the newly established powers, the US and USSR, following the discovery of oil, altered international relations irrevocably. Perhaps only by 1956 and the Suez Crisis was the situation finally clear to the former powers. The new, developing links between the Middle East and the rest of the world forged new patterns of conflict and cooperation. This is summarized in Table 1.3.

Within these regions the issue of naming and labelling is one of identity, setting boundaries and social and political space between the peoples of the region and the world where the state seeks to create and establish identities which compete with other group identities focused on tribe, family, gender, ethnicity and religious affiliation. Platteau (2010) asks what exactly is Islamic influence, and is it Arab or Muslim identity that matters? Given

Table 1.3   Twentieth century state formation in the Middle East

Year	Event	Notes
1916	Sykes-Picot Agreement	Britain and France secretly plan to divide up Arab Middle East.
1917	Balfour Declaration	British pledge to support Jewish settlement in Palestine.
1918	Ottomans leave N. Yemen	Imamate established.
1920	Treaty of Sèvres	Division of the Ottoman Empire. Establishment of British and French mandates.
1921	Transjordan created	
1921	Military coup in Iran	Reza Shah Pavlavi supplants Qajar regime.
1941	British seize Lebanon	
1943	Lebanon independence	Granted by 'Free French' authorities.
1943-6	Syria independence	Formal independence from Free French in 1943, withdrawal complete in 1946.
1946	Transjordan independence	Hashemite Kingdom of Jordan established.
1947	Partition of Palestine	UN partition into Jewish state, Arab state and International area of Jerusalem.
1948	Israel independence	First Arab-Israeli war.
1951	Libya independence	British and French petitions of 'trusteeship' rejected by UN.
1952	Military coup in Egypt	Nasser deposes King Farouk.
1953	Egypt independence	
1953	Coup in Iran	Backed by Britain and US and organized by CIA.
1956	Suez Canal nationalized	Suez War results, ended by intervention of US and USSR.
1956	Tunisia independence	
1957	British leave Jordan	British-Jordanian treaty terminated by Jordan.
1958	Military coup in Iraq	Monarchy overthrown and independence established.
1961	Kuwait independence	
1962	Military coup in N. Yemen.	Formation of Yemen Arab Republic.
1962	Algeria independence	
1967	S. Yemen independence	Formation of People's Democratic Republic of Yemen.
1968	British declaration of intent	Britain declares intention to withdraw from all bases East of Suez within three years.
1971	Bahrain, Qatar & UAE independence	
1979	Iranian revolution	Shah deposed and Islamic Republic of Iran created.
1990	Unification of Yemen	

Sources: Cleveland and Bunton 2009; Long et al. 2011; Milton-Edwards 2007.

the legacy of geopolitical, religious and historical dimensions, we argue that ethnicity and religion combine to form subjective positions at their intersection, and so are both pertinent (Escobar 1998; Ovendale 1998).

HUMAN AND SOCIAL DEVELOPMENT

As discussed above, Western powers have sustained authoritarian regimes and permitted theocracy governance to remain unchallenged despite ongoing scrutiny by Amnesty International and Human Rights Watch (Halliday 2000; UNDP 2003; UNDP 2009a; Utting 2006). The social development of Middle East countries is varied and characterized by uneven development (Pearson 2007; Utting 2006), with very diverse economies: Table 1.4 indicates that the Gross Domestic Product (GDP) per capita varies enormously across the region, with the richest country, Qatar, having an average income 43 times that of the poorest, Yemen. Even discounting these outliers, income levels in the region vary substantially. The most important factor driving these disparities is the huge variation in natural resource wealth, oil in particular, as the region includes oil-rich economies poor in other resources, oil-poor economies and mixed economies (Moghadam 1993) and what Moghadam (1993) terms 'city', 'desert' and 'normal' states. Natural resources are discussed later in this chapter. Another vital factor explaining uneven development is that the Arab region has suffered almost three times as much as any other region in the world in terms of years of conflict, over an 18-year period from 1990 to 2008 (UNDP 2010).

Demographic and social conditions also vary considerably across the Middle East. As Table 1.2 indicates, these countries differ widely in population, with three having populations greater than 60 million, six above 20 million and seven lower than 5 million.

Millennium Development Goals

Instability in governance regimes and the progress of democratization in most of the Middle East's resource-rich states has, to some extent, undermined development (Platteau 2010) as expressed in the Millennium Development Goals (MDGs) – what has been described as 'the world's biggest promise' (Hulme 2009). It is worth quoting from Ban Ki-Moon, UN secretary general, on the nature of the MDGs:

> The Millennium Development Goals set timebound targets, by which progress in reducing income poverty, hunger, disease, lack of adequate shelter and

Table 1.4 Selected development indicators

Country	HDI[a]		GDP	Labour Force Participation		Adult literacy		Enrolment in 3y education		Immigration	Adult Unemployment		
	Value[1]	Rank[1]	per capita US$ 2008[1]	Male[2] %	Female[2] %	Overall[1]	Female[2]	Male %[2]	Female %[2]	Share of popn 2005[3]	Total[1] %	Women 15-24[2]	Men 15-24[2]
Bahrain	0.80	39	27838	86	34	90	89	18	44	38.2	nd	11	4
Egypt	0.62	101	5840	79	24	66.4	58	31	24	0.3	8.7	19	6
Iran	0.70	70	11891	76	33	82.3	77	34	39	2.9	10.5	16	9
Jordan	0.68	82	5700	78	25	91.1	89	39	43	42.1	12.7	24	10
Kuwait	0.77	47	50284	84	47	94.5	93	12	27	69.2	0.8	nd	–
Oman	nd	nd	26258	79	27	86.3	81	27	32	25.5	nd	nd	–
Qatar	0.80	38	77178	93	51	93.1	90	5	31	80.5	nd	13	2
Saudi Arabia	0.75	55	24208	82	22	86.7	80	23	37	26.8	5.6	13	4
Turkey	0.68	83	13359	74	26	88.7	81	43	34	1.9	9.4	9	9
UAE	0.82	32	56485	93	43	90.0	91	36	17	70.0	3.1	7	3
Yemen	0.44	133	2595	74	21	63.2	43	14	6	2.2	nd	nd	13

Notes:
a. 'The premise of the HDI . . . was elegantly simple: national development should be measured not simply by national income, as had long been the practice, but also by life expectancy and literacy.' (UNDP 2010, p. 4).

Sources: (1) UNDP 2010; (2) WEF 2010; (3) UNDP 2009.
nd – No Data.

exclusion — while promoting gender equality, health, education and environmental sustainability — can be measured. They also embody basic human
rights — the rights of each person on the planet to health, education, shelter
and security. The Goals are ambitious but feasible and, together with the comprehensive United Nations development agenda, set the course for the world's
efforts to alleviate extreme poverty by 2015. (UN n.d.)

The Arab Human Development Report 2009 (UNDP 2009b) presents
a useful critical overview of progress against MDGs. While progress
against some measures has flourished beyond expectations, no progress
has been made against other indicators. We will briefly discuss some of the
indicators most relevant to this volume here.

The first of the goals is to eradicate extreme poverty and hunger. These
issues are related, and hunger is also related to water availability for
agriculture, which further impacts the target of improved access to safe
drinking water, part of Goal 7 (ensure environmental sustainability). The
challenges of economic stability and water availability are discussed later
in this introduction, but it is significant that although the total numbers
of undernourished in the Arab world are low, they rose between the study
periods of 1990–1992 and 2002–2004 – one of the only two world regions
where this was the case (UNDP 2009b).

Another example of the interconnectedness of MDGs is the relation
of education (Goal 2) to a number of factors including maternal health
(Goal 5). According to the Arab Human Development Report (AHDR):
'WHO statistics indicate that the most important factors accounting for
disparity in health levels within Arab countries are income level, place
of residence (urban or rural), and mother's educational level' (p. 151).
Significant progress has been made in the area of education and particularly in women's education. As can be seen from Table 1.3, women's
enrolment in tertiary education outstrips that of men in the majority of
the nations considered. However, the gender inequality index shows that
only 32 per cent of women in the region over 25 have completed secondary education, compared to 45 per cent for men (UNDP 2010). University
enrolment shows the reverse, with 132 women enrolled for every 100 men
(UNDP 2010).

More significant in terms of the MDGs is the illiteracy rate, a component
of the UNDP's Human Poverty Index (HPI), referring to exclusion from
reading and communication. Human poverty affects children's attendance and continuation in schooling: for example, in Egypt the attendance
of poor children is 7 per cent lower than that of more affluent children in
elementary school, 12 per cent lower at intermediate level and 24 per cent
lower at secondary level (UNDP 2009b). The only nation covered in this
volume with an HPI considered high is Yemen (36.6 per cent where the

threshold is 30 per cent). Significantly, this is a nation where insecurity from lack of access to safe water and child nutrition is also significant.

Comparison with poverty reduction in other developing counties shows that Arab nations 'could do better': for example, the United Arab Emirates with a Human Development Index (HDI) rank of 31 has performed three times worse than Hungary with an HDI rank of 38. This is true generally for Arab countries but not for Lebanon, Syria and Jordan – the education sector of which is discussed in Chapter 8. The significance of education indicators for women in particular will be discussed further in Chapter 13, but in general efforts to tackle poverty with respect to income, access to health services, and empowerment indicators such as access to resources and political decision making have been poor compared to other regions. There has also been criticism of revisions in reporting criteria in the 2010 Human Development Report. The UNDP changed the basis of inequality and poverty measures in this report, and commentators argue that this has blurred reporting of actual progress against development indicators, especially concerning gender indicators, and limits the ability to compare data series over time. Further, statistics on unemployment are questioned – many Arab states have high unemployment: Egypt and Turkey do not hide it, whereas other states, including the Gulf states, may do so, hiding the development challenges of high unemployment among women and young (15 to 24-year-old) males.

The biggest obstacle to consistent development without overlooking poverty may be bureaucratic and monolithic state institutions (Platteau 2010), lack of democracy, and issues as discussed in the section below on strategic resources regarding rentier economies, migrant labour and the so called 'resource curse' (Bebbington 2008; Utting 2006; Wiefen 2008).

Migration

Migration and the international mobility of labour have made the states of the Persian Gulf unique in the world (Fragues 2006; World Bank 2008). The GCC states have by far the largest number of world migrants among them – 18 per cent of the world total, comprising 38.6 per cent of their combined populations (UNDP 2009a). Nowhere other than in the GCC countries are local indigenous populations a minority of inhabitants: nowhere else does the majority of the population consist of migrants, with temporary residency, no access to citizenship and limited membership in society: nor are labour markets anywhere else so highly dependent upon the international recruitment of the workforce. This has highlighted a number of leadership and organization development challenges and is elaborated on in the chapters on Oman, Saudi Arabia and the UAE.

The differential employment of nationals and expatriates shapes employment relations and strategy management, including HRD planning and career management, as well as efforts to integrate women (Metcalfe and Rees 2010). The dynamic of different employment status and the associated difference in – or absence of – rights, benefits and opportunities creates tension and conflict and will provide leaders with HR challenges for years to come. Moreover, it is HR skills that are particularly in demand to rectify this situation.

The characteristics of the migrant population are diverse. Many are the 'working poor' who tend to have limited education qualifications, who often do not appear in official statistics, and who are employed in construction, service and domestic work. Originally, migration strategies were adopted by states as a strategy to build the Arab nation. Gulf States adopted nationalization – so-called 'Gulfization' (Saudization, Emiratization, Omanization, etc.) – policies along two lines: on one side, reducing the supply of migrant workers by reinforcing barriers at entry and providing disincentives to stay, and on the other, limiting the demand for migrant workers by expanding the list of jobs reserved for nationals and placing a tax on employers who hire non-nationals. Gulfization policies have had mixed results and labour markets' dependency on migrant workers is still at a peak.

Economic and social developments are currently impacting Gulfization planning and it is difficult to assess how these influences will impact in the long term. There is still a rising demand that local supply may not be able to match for high-skill workers, either for lack of an adequate skills base or because an insufficient population of highly skilled nationals will increasingly expose the Gulf to what has become a global competition for talent. This is attributed to the inadequacy of local vocational and university programmes in matching requirements in skills and numbers. In contrast to low-skilled workers, who will still be needed (although in smaller numbers) in the construction sector or in domestic services and whose potential supply can be considered unlimited, high-level professionals needed for ambitious programmes such as the development and leadership of world-class universities like KAUST in Saudi Arabia remain a scarce resource worldwide. Their recruitment may test the competitiveness of Gulf labour markets in attracting the best and the brightest. In addition, the rise of global advocacy for migrants' rights, and the adoption of Corporate Social Responsibility ethics by organizations, may influence migrants' choice of destination (Pearson 2007). A further concern is local resistance to increased migration, and social movements may play a role to curb decades-old patterns of migration to the Gulf. Increasing competition between nationals and migrants, or mounting protests by migrant workers claiming their rights, may foster anti-immigration reactions and eventually affect stability.

'ARABIA FELIX': THE MIDDLE EAST AND NATURAL RESOURCES

A current knowledge gap in cross-cultural management and leadership studies is the uneven distribution of natural resources and the current and future effect of this on power relations in the global political economy (Hulme 2009; Utting 2006). In this section we look at the implications for leadership in the Middle East of the existence and distribution of natural resources, at the continuing importance of the region as a transit route for resources from within and outside its borders, and as a physical and symbolic link between East and West (Said 1978).

In the modern era, any discussion of the resources of the region must inevitably concentrate on fossil fuels, and especially oil. It must be recognized however that the region has been important as the source or shipment route for valuable resources since antiquity; and from this time observers have recognized that these resources were not homogeneously distributed. The Romans, translating the term *Eudaimon Arabia* recorded by Ptolemy, recognized *Arabia Felix* or fortunate Arabia; the Arabia of the relatively fertile South roughly congruent with modern Yemen. This is the land of which Herodotus wrote, 'The whole country is scented with [the spices of Arabia], and exhales an odour marvellously sweet'. By contrast, they also identified *Arabia Deserta* and *Arabia Petraea*, the desert and rocky lands of the interior and North (Halliday 2000; Ovendale 1998).

It is tempting to look at modern Arabia and define an *Arabia Felix* in terms of the presence or absence of oil. However, as Maass has observed of nations with reserves of oil: 'Petrodollars can make them richer but not more honest, efficient or intelligent' (Maass 2009, p. 6) – part of the so-called 'resource curse' discourse (Ross 1999). As discussed in the chapters that follow, the leaderships of the countries under discussion are facing up to the challenges of the presence or absence of oil, to inevitable 'peak oil', and to the environmental consequences of oil extraction and consumption, in their individual ways. This is commented on further in the conclusion to this volume.

Complicating the resource issue is the fact that the resource rich nations in the region, primarily the GCC states, tend to be short of the labour required for the proper functioning of their economies. Conversely, the labour-rich, resource-poor nations from which they source their workforce are highly reliant on the remittances sent back by workers in the resource-rich countries; but these have proved vulnerable to both global economic instability and the geopolitical shifts of the region, as will be seen in the chapter on Yemen (Bjorvatn and Selvik 2008; Losman 2010; Marcel 2006; UNDP 2009b). The current balance of resources and remittances can be understood with reference to Table 1.4, with the resource-poor nations relevant to this volume Egypt, Jordan, Turkey and Yemen. Additionally, ongoing nationalization programmes in the countries studied are already placing emphasis on the employment of local, national citizens (Hutchings, Metcalfe and Cooper 2010; Metcalfe and Rees 2010). As the preceding discussion on migration revealed, it is doubtful whether labour market policy and education reform will suffice to reverse nationalization programmes in line with millennium development goals and the development plans of individual states.

The result of the situation described in this section is that, as the Arab Human Development Report 2009 points out, the flow of oil wealth within the region is less significant than it once was. The AHDR summarizes this according to three reasons:

> First, population increases in non-oil countries offset much of these flows. Second, worker remittances from the oil states have been hit by the practice of 'job nationalization'; and third, non-oil countries are incurring higher energy costs through rising oil import bills and expensive fuel subsidies. (UNDP 2009b)

Between East and West: The Middle East and World Trade

The Middle East also remains, as mentioned above and as its name suggests, a vital link between East and West. Several authors in this volume refer to the influence of ancient trade routes, known collectively as the Incense Route, which date back at least to the first millennium BCE and possibly back to the late Bronze Age (Artzy 1994). The most obvious symbol of ongoing trade through the region is the Suez Canal, which has been a key indicator of changing control and leadership in the region, from its construction as a colonial project (completed in 1869) to nationalization and the Suez Crisis – or tripartite aggression – of 1956, emblematic of the end of the colonial era, and the blockade and closure of the canal between 1967 and 1975 as a result of the Arab-Israeli wars. The canal and associated trade routes continue to develop into the twenty-first century: the Sumed pipeline allows the trans-shipment of oil from the Red Sea to the Mediterranean, and The Suez Canal Container Terminal now allows the same process with dry goods (Rodenbeck 2010, p. 8).

Elsewhere in the region, the routeing of the Baku–Tbilisi–Ceyhan pipeline, as discussed in the chapter on Iran and designed as a matter of policy to decrease the influence of Iran and increase that of Turkey, can be seen as indicative of growing neocolonial influence.

Another aspect of the Middle East as a trade conduit is the development of Islamic finance. There are opportunities for, and competition between, countries, in the development of the expanding Islamic banking sector (Wilson 1995). Islamic finance in the form of Shar'ia-compliant *sukuks* is discussed in Chapter 2, but Dubai faces competition from Bahrain and the Kingdom of Saudi Arabia in the development of a model of finance which may connect to Western financial institutions, but is Shar'ia compliant.

As they affect leadership across many of the states discussed in this volume, this introduction will look in more detail at some of the issues mentioned above. We will discuss water resources, oil and gas, labour resources and remittances, and response to climate change below.

Water, Development and Economic Growth

Water has always been a critical resource for the region. Sheikh Yamani, former Saudi oil minister and head of OPEC, is famously quoted as saying: 'All in all, I wish we had discovered water' (quoted in Ross 1999). This reflects the fact that in the region considered by the Arab Human Development Report (UNDP 2009b), congruent with the Wider Middle East discussed above, 5 per cent of the world's population live in a region that contains only 1 per cent of the world's water supply. There are also food supply and security issues discussed at length in the same report. The region's ratio of agriculturally usable land to total land surface is only 35 per cent, 'the lowest in the world' (UNDP 2009b, p. 138). Exacerbating this, it is predicted that global warming will cause the climate to become hotter and drier, and desertification is an observable issue, threatening a fifth of the total land area of Arab nations (UNDP 2009b). The population is still growing rapidly in the region and the economic instability of 2008 caused a rise in world food prices which forced a re-evaluation of food strategy. Saudi Arabia and the UAE are prominent in investing in land, particularly in Sudan. Fahad Balghunaim, Saudi Arabia's agriculture minister, told an industry event: 'In Saudi we have given a priority to water security and therefore are phasing out the production of water-intensive crops and as part [of] our security strategy we are encouraging the private sector to invest in agriculture abroad' (Sudan Commerce News 2010). However, there is an element of irony that the country in which Arab states are investing to secure their food supply is the one with the largest population of people living in hunger (more than eight million) in the Wider Middle East (UNDP 2009b).

There is, however, the potential to develop other resources. Again, as attributed to Sheikh Yamani: 'The Stone Age came to an end not for a lack of stones' (quoted in Greider 2000) and there are significant alternatives to 'doomsday scenarios' of the end of the oil economy, including the exploitation of relatively abundant solar energy and, to a lesser extent, wind power. This will be discussed briefly in the section below on climate change.

Strategic Resources: Gas and Oil

One factor of enormous significance to the countries of the Middle East and the world is the future of oil reserves. The distribution of these across the region is highly non-homogeneous, but the social and economic effects have influence across national boundaries. This has both global geo-political effects and short-distance effects, as on migrant labour, discussed above.

The oil-rich states of the Middle East are repeatedly referred to in the chapters that follow as 'rentier states'. This term originates in the concept of the landowner who lives entirely off the income from property that is rented out. In the context of this volume, it refers to the 'renting out' of natural resources, principally oil, to external bodies (Losman 2010). National income is then overwhelmingly derived from these revenues, which brings issues of its own. Losman (ibid.) argues that rentier states can be unstable. Rather than raising taxation income, the state is responsible for the distribution of rental incomes, leading to discontent among those unhappy with their share; and the legitimacy of rentier governments is based on culture, ideology and religion, which can become areas of conflict. However, elections 'are not the only source of legitimacy' (ibid. p. 430) and Common, discussing Oman in this volume, argues that an authoritarian regime can be more stable (Chapter 6).

Such economies contribute to the concept of a 'resource curse' as introduced above. This proposes that the citizens of oil-rich states do not benefit from the oil revenues that remain in the hands of relatively small elites. This concept is much discussed and it is reasonable to say that there is no strong correlation between resource wealth and development: 'There was prosperity and a measure of freedom in just a few cases, usually in tiny countries with disproportionately large reserves' (Maass 2009, p. 6) and, as will be seen in the rest of this volume, the culture, wealth and development of each state should be critically analysed on a case-by-case basis.

Migrant workers are critical not only to the economies of such rentier

Table 1.5 Remittances

Country	HDI Rank	Remittances: Inflows US$ millions	Outflows US$ millions	Inflows per capita US$	As % of GDP	Ratio to FDI
Bahrain	39		1483			
Egypt	123	7656	180	101	6.0	0.7
Iran	88	1115	nd	16	0.5	1.5
Jordan	96	3434	479	580	22.7	1.9
Kuwait	31		3824			
Oman	56	39	3670	15	0.1	0.0
Qatar	33	nd	nd	nd	nd	nd
Saudi Arabia	59		16068	16	0.2	0.1
Turkey	79	1209	106			
UAE	35	nd	nd	nd	nd	nd
Yemen	140	1283	120	57	6.1	1.4

Sources: (1) UNDP 2009 pp. 159–62.
nd – No Data.

states but also to those of their nations of origin. As highlighted previously, the nations of the GCC together attract 18 per cent of all world migrants, forming 38.6 per cent of their combined populations (UNDP 2009a). The importance of remittances to the economies of Egypt, Yemen and Jordan, in particular, is apparent from Table 1.5 and is discussed further in the relevant chapters of this volume.

The countries of origin and destination of the workers providing the remittances are not shown in Table 1.5. However, as pointed out in the 2009 Human Development Report, 'Most movement occurs within regions' (UNDP 2009a, Map 2.1, p. 24). In essence, migration and remittances are mechanisms for the transfer of wealth, in this case primarily oil wealth, across national borders in the region. This makes the recipient nations especially vulnerable to future economic challenges associated with 'peak oil', climate change and new technology introductions. These challenges, discussed below, can only be met by developments in leadership capability, nationally, in business and in education, which will enable each society to foster private sector growth and respond to profound, rapid change.

The situation is complicated by political instability and conflict in the region (Maass 2009). Figure 1.7 indicates the effect of regional events on global oil prices. It is apparent that events in the Middle East are critical to global economics. In fact, not shown on the diagram are the effects of

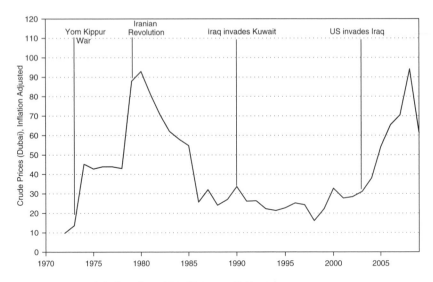

Source: BP Statistical Review of World Energy 2010.

Figure 1.7   Oil price history

interventions by OPEC to smooth out the effects of external events by regulating production. Without such efforts the fluctuations would certainly be even more dramatic.

However, the influence that can be exerted by such supply-side control will soon be diminished, as the ability of the oil fields to increase supply to meet growing global demand diminishes and then disappears. This phenomenon, known as 'peak oil', is inevitable, but the complex and interacting effects on demand both for oil and for alternative energy sources are unpredictable. Many authorities believe that global 'peak oil' is imminent, with Owen, Inderwildi and King (2010) suggesting that demand will outstrip supply at some point between 2010 and 2015.

It is reasonable to assume that the importance of the Middle East in a world in which oil supply and demand are mismatched will only become more significant. As Aleklett observes:

> Only in the Middle East and possibly the countries of the former Soviet Union is there a potential to significantly increase production rates to compensate for decreasing production rates in other countries. Saudi Arabia is a key country in this context, providing 95 million barrels per day (11% of the current global production rate). Their proven reserves are 130 billion barrels and their reserve base is said to include an additional 130 billion barrels. Iraq also has considerable untapped oil reserves. (2007, p. 61)

It is then reasonable to ask, what is the effect of such developments on leadership in the region? Iraq's justification for the 1990 invasion of Kuwait was alleged Kuwaiti 'theft' of Iraqi oil by lateral drilling, and it is generally believed that at least part of the US motivation for 'regime change' in Iraq has been control of oil supply: 'The question is not *whether* the war is about oil but *how* it is about oil' (Maass 1999 p. 159).

The effects of such struggles for the resources of the region can be less direct but just as devastating. Yemen paid a high price in the Gulf War of 1990, when the government supported Iraq and consequently found expatriate labour displaced from Iraq and Kuwait and forced out of Saudi Arabia by the tens of thousands (Colton 2010). The effects of these events have persisted to the present day, as discussed in the chapter on Yemen.

The distribution of oil in the region under consideration is shown in Table 1.6.

It should be noted that the reserves to production (R/P) ratio provides only a crude indication of future oil (and gas) supply. It does not take into account growth or other variation in demand, especially from developing economies, nor their interaction with price or the economics of recovery of the reserves. External factors such as economic sanctions or conflict may artificially depress production and exaggerate the apparent longevity of reserves (Bjorvatin Selvik 2008).

Reserves of gas, in particular, may be under-exploited, despite the West's 'dash for gas' of the 1990s. This arises from the relative difficulty of transporting gas from remote production areas to markets. Multinational corporations are investing hugely in liquefaction plant and refrigerated shipping for liquefied natural gas (LNG) and in gas to liquids (GTL) technologies. For example, Shell is involved in the Qatargas IV LNG facility, the final stages of which are commissioning at the time of writing, with a total investment from all sources of $8 billion (Reuters): also in Qatar, Shell is investing in the Pearl GTL plant, the total project cost of which is $19 billion (LNG World News). These investments will inevitably have implications for leadership development in the region, beyond that associated with traditional oil exploitation, and this is an area worthy of further study.

As the IEA states: 'oil production is projected to concentrate in an ever-shrinking group of countries with large reserves – notably Middle East OPEC member countries and Russia' (IEA 2007). Such a concentration will inevitably have an impact on political leadership in the region. The nature of such impacts will be unpredictable (Halliday 2010) .

The foregoing discussion suggests that strategic approaches at national level, particularly in the Arabian Gulf, have been slow to consider broader environmental and development impact. Christopher Davidson's work on

Table 1.6　Proven fossil fuel reserves

OIL			
Country	Proven Reserves	Production	Reserves to Production (R/P) Ratio
	gigabarrels	*1000 barrels/day*	*Years*
Bahrain	–	–	–
Egypt	4.4	742	16.2
Iran	137.6	4216	89.4
Iraq	115.0	2482	126.9
Kuwait	101.5	2481	112.1
Oman	5.6	810	18.9
Qatar	26.8	1345	54.6
Saudi Arabia	264.6	9713	74.6
Syria	2.5	376	18.2
UAE	97.8	2599	103.1
Yemen	2.7	298	24.8
Other ME	0.1	37	7.4

GAS			
Country	Proven Reserves	Production	R/P Ratio
	trillion cubic metres	*billion cubic metres/yr*	*Years*
Bahrain	0.09	12.8	7.0
Egypt	2.19	62.70	34.9
Iran	29.61	131.20	225.7
Iraq	3.17	–	–
Kuwait	1.78	12.50	142.4
Oman	0.98	24.80	39.5
Qatar	25.37	89.30	284.1
Saudi Arabia	7.92	77.50	102.2
Syria	0.28	5.80	48.3
UAE	6.43	48.80	131.8
Yemen	0.49	–	–
Other ME	0.06	4.50	13.3

Source:　Compiled from BP Statistical Review of World Energy 2010.

the growth of the UAE, Abu Dhabi and Dubai in particular, illustrated 'disconnected' logistics in Ministry regimes, and the pursuit of 'flamboyant development' to attract foreign direct investment (FDI), tourism and other income without consideration of an integrated infrastructure to manage transport, water, housing and public services. The global financial crisis has exaggerated such deficiencies in 'joined up' environmental planning, but it has been carefully monitored in global media representations (see also Asutay 2007).

Climate Change

In 2004, the authors of this introduction were given a tour of Bahrain by a senior, Western-educated manager with the national gas producer, Banagas. On being shown the highest point of the low-lying island, he was asked whether there was much concern about the effects of global warming. His reply was, 'What is global warming?'

This response may have been characteristic of Middle East attitudes only a few years ago, but the nations have been making a rapid effort to catch up with a more rational and widely-accepted approach to the environmental consequences of uncontrolled burning of fossil fuels. The formation of the Arab Forum for Environment and Development (AFED) in 2006 was a significant forward step. Still, in the Climate Change Performance Index 2009 comparing the climate change performance of the 57 countries responsible for 90 per cent of energy related CO_2 emissions, Saudi Arabia was ranked last.

Yet the nations of the Middle East are vulnerable to climate change. Sea level rise may impact the most densely populated regions of Egypt severely, but it will also have an effect on low-lying states such as UAE, Qatar, Bahrain and Kuwait (Tolba and Saab 2009). It is also predicted that the distribution of rainfall will be altered, projected to make the Middle East hotter and dryer than at present. As the 2009 AFED report found:

> virtually no work is being carried out to make the Arab countries prepared for climate change challenges. Specifically, no concerted data gathering and research efforts could be traced regarding the impacts of climate change on health, infrastructure, biodiversity, tourism, water and food production. The economic impact seems to be totally ignored. Reliable records on climate patterns in the region barely exist. (Tolba and Saab 2009)

As Reiche (2010) has pointed out for the GCC states, there is potential for renewable energy development in the region, especially in terms of solar energy (see Table 1.7) (ibid. p. 2401). It has also been pointed out that the situation of Egypt is equally propitious for solar energy generation, but also has high potential for wind power generation which it has now begun to exploit with windfarms on the Gulf of Suez and World Bank support to connect these to the Nile valley (Rodenbeck 2010).

Table 1.7 Driving forces for climate protection policies in GCC countries

Country	Ratification of the Kyoto protocol	Administrative capacities dealing with climate change issues	Government targets	Implemented policies	Large scale pioneer projects for renewable energies	Registered CDM projects	Political freedom for environmental NGOs	Vulnerability to climate change	Solar energy potential	Potential for wind electricity generation
Bahrain	2006	Public Commission for the Protection of Marine Resources, Environment and Wildlife	No	No	Bahrain World Trade Center	No	Not allowed	High	Very good opportunities	Moderate opportunities
Kuwait	2005	Environment Public Authority	No	No	No	No	Allowed, but restricted	High	Very good opportunities	Moderate opportunities
Oman	2005	Ministry of Environment and Climate Change	No	No	No	No	Not allowed	High	Very good opportunities	Moderate opportunities
Qatar	2005	Supreme Council for the Environment and Natural Reserves	No	No	Energy City	Al-Shaheen Oil Field Gas Recovery and Utilization project	Not allowed	High	Very good opportunities	Moderate opportunities

Saudi Arabia	2005	Presidency of Meteorology and Environment	No	No	Solar villages: Sustainable campus (KAUST)	No	Not allowed	High	Very good opportunities	Limited potential
UAE	2005	Ministry of Environment and Water Resources	No	No	No	No	Not allowed	High	Very good opportunities	Limited potential
Dubai		Dubai Electricity and Water Authority	No	Green building code	No	No	Not allowed	High	Very good opportunities	Limited potential
Abu Dhabi		Environment Agency	7% reduction in CO_2 emissions and 7% of renewables in power generation capacity by 2020.	No	Masdar City	No	Not allowed	High	Very good opportunities	Limited potential

Source: Reiche (2010).

SUMMARY

This volume offers views of leadership from studies of individual Middle East states. As such, many of the dominant Western constructions are challenged, reconfigured or resisted. The collection reflects a critical interpretative account of leadership by drawing on knowledge territories as diverse as Middle East studies, feminism, geography, international relations and postcolonial development, as well as Western organization and leadership writings that examine diverse geographical regions.

This multidisciplinary approach arises inevitably from a field of study in which the intersection of a range of factors is critical: factors that include the resurgence of Islam, the intricacies of governance regimes, social development and the complex influence of climate change, all provide challenges for leaders in political and organizational spheres. We position leadership in the broader political economy, as not to do so would present only a partial, inadequate portrayal of leadership behaviour and identities as defined by the economic, religiopolitical and environmental dynamics.

Our aim is to advance new knowledge about leadership behaviour and practice, and arising from our review of the leadership scholarship of the West, we reaffirm that this is partial: restating or reconfiguring Western leadership theories cannot provide an adequate model for Middle East leadership. By integrating myriad subject domains and opening up communication and dialogue between East and West, Global South and Global North, a richer view of leaders is developed that allows us to rethink, freshly reimagine and represent the concept of leadership.

REFERENCES

Ahmed, A.S. (1992), *Postmodernism and Islam*, London and New York: Routledge.
Ahmed, A.S. and H. Donnan (eds) (1994), *Islam, Globalization and Postmodernity*, London and New York: Routledge.
Aleklett, K. (2007), *Peak Oil and the Evolving Strategies of Oil Importing and Exporting Countries: Facing the hard truth about an import decline for the OECD countries*, Organisation for Economic Cooperation and Development/ITF discussion paper no. 2007-17, Uppsala, Sweden.
Ali, A.J. (2005), *Islamic Perspectives on Management and Organizations*, Cheltenham, UK and Northampton, MA, USA: Edward Elgar.
Alimo-Metcalfe, B. (1998), *Effective Leadership*, London: Improvement and Development Agency.
Arab News (2006), 'Princess Adelah bint Abdullah talks of women's issues', accessed 22 December 2010 at http://archive.arabnews.com/?page=21&section=0&article=90234&d=22&m=12&y=2006.
Artzy, M. (1994), 'Incense, camels and collared rim jars: desert trade routes and

maritime outlets in the second millennium', *Oxford Journal of Archaeology*, **13**, 121–47.

Asutay, M. (2007), 'A political economy approach to Islamic economics: systematic understanding for an alternative economic system', *Kyoto Bulletin of Islamic Area Studies*, **1** (2), 3–18.

Asutay, M. and N. Zaman (2009), 'Divergence between aspirations and realities of Islamic economics: a political economy approach to bridging the divide', *IIUM Journal of Economics and Management*, **17** (1), 73–96.

Al-Attas, S.M.N. (1995), *Prologomena to the Metaphysics of Islam: An Exposition of the Fundamental Elements of the Worldview of Islam*, Kuala Lumpur: International Institute of Islamic Thought and Civilization.

Barnard, C. (1938), *The Functions of the Executive*, Cambridge, MA: HUP.

Bass, B.M. and B.J. Avolio (1990), *Multifactor Leadership Questionnaire*, Palo Alto, CA: Consulting Psychologists Press.

Bass, B.M. and B.J. Avolio (1994), *Improving Organization Effectiveness Through Transformational Leadership*, London: Sage.

Bebbington, A.J. (2008), 'Social capital and development studies II: can Bourdieu travel to policy', *Progress in Development Studies*, **7** (2), 155–62.

Beekun, J. and R.I. Badawi (1999), *Leadership: An Islamic Perspective*, Beltsville, MD: Amana Press.

Berkey, J.P. (2003), *The formation of Islam: religion and society in the Near East, 600-1800*, Cambridge: Cambridge University Press.

Bjorvatin, K. and K. Selvik (2008), 'Deconstructing competition: factionalism and rent seeking in Iran', *World Development*, **20**, 1.

Bourdieu, P. and J.C. Passeron (1977), *Reproduction in Education, Society and Culture*, London and Beverly Hills, CA: Sage.

Bryman, A. (1992), *Charisma and Leadership in Organizations*, London: Sage.

Burns, J.M. (1978), *Leadership*, New York: Harper and Row.

Calas, M.B. and L.L. Smirchich (1991), 'Voicing seduction to silence leadership', in K. Grint (ed.) (1997), *Leadership: Classical, Contemporary and Critical Approaches*, Oxford: Oxford University Press.

Campbell, R.A. (2008), 'Leadership succession in early Islam: exploring the nature and role of historical precedents', *The Leadership Quarterly*, **19**, 426–38.

Castells, M. (2009), *The Rise of the Network Society: The Information Age: Economy, Society, and Culture*, vol I, 2nd edn, Chichester: John Wiley.

Chapra, U. (1993), *Islam and Economic Development*, Pakistan and Malaysia: Institute of Islamic Thought and Islam Research Institute.

Choudhury, M.A. (1993), 'A critical examination of the concept of Islamisation of knowledge in contemporary times', *Muslim Education Quarterly*, **10** (4), 3–34.

Ciulla, J.B. (1995), 'Leadership ethics: mapping the territory', *Business Ethics Quarterly*, **5** (11), 5–28.

Ciulla, J. B. (2005), 'Integrating leadership with ethics: is good leadership contrary to human nature?', in J.P. Doh and S.A. Stumpf (eds), *Handbook on Responsible Leadership and Governance in Global Business*, Cheltenham, UK and Northampton, MA, USA: Edward Elgar.

Cleveland, W.L. and M. Bunton (2009), *A History of the Middle East*, 4th edn., Boulder, CO: Westview.

Colton, N.A. (2010), 'Yemen: a collapsed economy', *The Middle East Journal*, **64** (3), 410–26

Collinson, D. and J. Hearn (2004), 'Men and masculinities', in M. Kimmel,

J. Hearn and R.W. Connell, *Handbook of Studies on Men and Masculinities*, Thousand Oaks, CA: Sage.

Crush, J. (1998), 'Imagining development,' in J. Crush (ed), *The Power of Development*, London: Routledge, pp. 1–24.

Davidson, C. M. (2008), *Dubai: The Vulnerability of Success,* New York: Columbia University Press.

Davidson, C.M. (2009), *Abu Dhabi: Oil and Beyond*, New York: Columbia University Press.

Deetz, S., S. Tracy and S. Simpson (2000), *Leading Organizations through Transitions: Communication and Cultural Change*, Thousand Oaks, CA: Sage.

Doh, J.P. and S.A. Strumph (2005), 'Toward a framework of responsible leadership', in J. Doh and S. Strumpf (eds), *Handbook on Responsible Leadership and Governance in Global Business*, Cheltenham, UK and Northampton, MA, USA: Edward Elgar, pp. 114–34.

Dunning, J.H. (2007), 'A new zeitgeist for international business activity and scholarship', *European J. International Management*, **1** (4), 278–301.

Escobar, A. (1998), 'Imagining a post development era', in Crush, J. (ed.), *The Power of Development*, London: Routledge.

Esposito, J.L. (2003), *The Oxford Dictionary of Islam*, paperback edn. (2004), New York: Oxford University Press.

Esposito, J.L. (2005), *Islam: The Straight Path*, 3rd edn, New York: Oxford University Press.

Fairclough, N. and E. Chiapello (2005), 'Understanding the new management ideology. A transdisciplinary contribution from critical discourse analysis and new sociology of capitalism', *Discourse & Society*, **13** (2), 185–208.

Fairclough, N. (2007), 'The contribution of discourse analysis to research on social change', in N. Fairclough, P. Cortese and P. Ardizzone (eds), *Discourse in Contemporary Social Change*, New York: Peter Lang.

Fargues, P. (2006), 'International migration in the Arab region: trends and policies', United Nations Expert Group Meeting on International Migration and Development in the Arab Region, May 2006, Beirut accessed 17 January 2011 at www.un.org/esa/population/migration/turin/Symposium_Turin_files/P09_Fargues.pdf.

Al-Faruqi, I.R. (1982), *Tawhid: Its Implications for Thought And Life*, Kuala Lumpur: IIIT.

Al-Faruqi, I.R. (2000), *Meta-Religion: A Framework for Moral Theology*, Washington, DC: Institute for Strategic Studies.

G8-BMENA (2007), accessed 9 December 2010 at www.g8-bmena-education.de/en/101.php.

El Ghazali, A.H. (1994), *Man is the Basis of the Islamic Strategy for Economic Development*, Jeddah, Saudi Arabia: Islamic Research and Training Institute (IDB).

El Ghazili, Abdel H. (2002), 'Ihyaa Uloum Addin' 'The revival of religious sciences', in H.H. Ahmad (ed.), (1995), *Al-Idarah al-Ammah Fi al-Islam: al-Osoul wa al-Tatbiq [Public Administration in Islam: Foundations and Practices]*, Riyadh: Al-Nawabi Publishing.

Greenleaf, R.K. (1977), *Servant Leadership,* Mahwah, NJ: Paulist Press.

Greider, W. (2000), 'Oil on political waters', *The Nation*, **271** (12), 5–6.

Grint, K. (ed) (1997), *Leadership: Classical, Contemporary and Critical Approaches*, Oxford: Oxford University Press.

Grint, K. (2005), 'Problems, problems, problems: the social construction of leadership', *Human Relations*, **58** (11), 1467–94.

Grint, K. (2009), 'The sacred in leadership: separation, sacrifice and silence', *Organization Studies*, **31** (1), 89–107.

Halliday, F. (2010), *The Middle East in International Relations: Power, Politics and Ideology*, 2nd edn, Cambridge: Cambridge University Press.

Halliday, F. (2000), *Nation and Religion in the Middle East*, London: Saqi.

Hausmann, R., L.D. Tyson and S. Zahidi (2010), *The Global Gender Gap Report 2010*, Geneva, Switzerland: World Economic Forum.

Hearn, J.B.D. Metcalfe and R. Piekarri (2011), 'Gender, intersectionality and IHRM', in G.K. Stahl and I. Björkman (eds), *Handbook of Research in International Human Resource Management*, Cheltenham, UK and Northampton, MA, USA: Edward Elgar.

Hersey, P. and K.H. Blanchard (1988), *Management of Organisation Behaviour*, 5th edn, Englewood Cliffs, NJ: Prentice Hall.

Hofstede, G. (1980), *Culture's Consequences:International Differences in Work Related Values*, London: Sage Publishers.

Hofstede, G. (1983), 'The cultural relativity of organization practices and theories', *Journal of International Business Studies*, **14** (2), 75–89.

Hofstede, G. (2003), *Culture's Consequences, Comparing Values, Behaviors, Institutions, and Organizations Across Nations*, 2nd ed, London and Thousand Oaks, CA: Sage Publications.

House, R.J., M. Javidan, P.J. Hanges, P.W. Dorfman and V. Gupta, (eds) (2004), *Culture, Leadership, and Organizations: The GLOBE Study of 62 Societies*, London and Thousand Oaks, CA: Sage.

Hulme, D. (2009), 'Global poverty reduction and the millennium development goals: a short history of the world's biggest promise', Brooks World Poverty Institute working paper.

Hurd, E.S. (2006), 'Negotiating Europe: the politics of religion and the prospects for Turkish accession', *Review of International Studies*, **32**, 401–18.

Hutchings, K., B. D. Metcalfe and B. Cooper (2010), 'Exploring middle eastern women's perceptions of barriers to, and facilitators of, international management opportunities', *International Journal of Human Resource Management*, **21**(1), 61–83.

IEA (2007), *Oil Supply Security*, Paris: OECD/IEA.

Islam, G. (2009), 'Animating leadership: crisis and renewal of governance in 4 mythic narratives', *Leadership Quarterly*, **16** (5), 777–806.

Javidan, M., P.W. Dorffman and M. Sully de Luque and R.J. House (2006), 'In the eye of the beholder: cross cultural lessons in leadership from project GLOBE', *Academy of Management Perspectives*, **20** (1), 67–90.

Kabasakal, H. and A. Dastmalchian (2001), 'Introduction to the special issue on leadership and culture in the Middle East', *Applied Psychology: An International Review*, **50** (4) 479–88.

Lawrence, T.E. (1926), *Seven Pillars of Wisdom*, London: Private.

Lewis, B. (2002), *What Went Wrong? Western Impact and Middle Eastern Response*, London: Weidenfeld and Nicholson.

Lewis, B. and B.E. Churchill (2009), *Islam: The Religion and the People*, Upper Saddle River, NJ: Wharton School Publishing.

Long, D.E., B. Reich and M. Gasiorowski (eds) (2011), *The Government and Politics of the Middle East and North Africa*, Boulder, CO: Westview Press.

Losman, D.L. (2010), 'The rentier state and national oil companies: an economic and political perspective', *Middle East Journal*, **64** (3), 426–45.

Maak, T. (2007), 'Responsible leadership, stakeholder engagement, and the emergence of social capital', *Journal of Business Ethics*, **74**, 329–43.

Maass, P. (2009), *Crude World: The Violent Twilight of Oil*, London: Allen Lane.

Marcel, V. (2006), *Oil Titans: National Oil Companies in the Middle East*, London: Chatham House.

Meindl, J.R. (1995), 'The romance of leadership as follower-centric theory: a social construction approach', *Leadership Quarterly*, **6** (4), 329–41.

Metcalfe, B.D. (2008), 'Women, management and globalization in the Middle East', *Journal of Business Ethics*, **81** (1), 85–100.

Metcalfe, B.D. (2010), 'Reflections on difference: women, Islamic feminism and development in the Middle East', in J. Sayed and M. F. Özbilgin (eds), *Managing Gender Diversity in Asia*, Cheltenham, UK and Northampton, MA, USA: Edward Elgar.

Metcalfe, B. D. and C. Rees (2010), 'Gender, globalization and organization: exploring power, relations and intersections' *Equality, Diversity and Inclusion: An International Journal*, **29** (1), 5–22.

Miller A. (1947) *All My Sons*, London: Penguin.

Milton-Edwards, B. (2006), *Contemporary Politics in the Middle East*, 2nd edn, Cambridge: Polity Press.

Moghadam, V.M. (2003), 'Towards gender equality in the Arab/Middle East region: Islam, culture, and feminist activism', Human Development Report Office occasional paper, background paper for HDR 2004, United Nations Development Programme.

Morgan, M.H. (2007), *Lost History: The Enduring Legacy of Muslim Scientists, Thinkers and Artists*, Washington, DC: National Geographic Association.

Noor, I. (1999), *Prophet Muhammad's Leadership: The Paragon of Excellence and Altruistic Management*, Kuala Lumpar, Utusan Publications.

Norris, P. and R. Ingleheart (2002), 'Islamic culture and democracy: testing the "clash of civilizations" thesis', *Comparative Sociology,* **1** (3-4), 235–63.

Al-Omar, F.A. (1999), *Akhlaqu-al-Amal [Work Ethics]*, Jeddah, Saudi Arabia: Islamic Research and Training Institute.

Al-Omari, J. (2005), *The Arab Way: How to Work More Effectively with Arab Cultures*, Oxford: Howtobooks.

Onley, J. and S. Khalaf (2006), 'Shaikhly authority in the pre-oil Gulf: an historical–anthropological study', *History and Anthropology*, **17** (3) (September), 189–208.

Ovendale, R. (1998), *The Longman Companion to the Middle East Since 1914*, London: Longman.

Owen, R. (1991), *State, Power and Politics in the Making of the Modern Middle East*, Oxford: Polity Press.

Owen, N.A., O.R. Inderwildi and D.A. King (2010), 'The status of conventional world oil reserves – hype or cause for concern?', *Energy Policy*, **38**, 4743–9.

Pearson, R. (2007), 'Beyond women workers: gendering corporate social responsibility', *Third World Quarterly*, **28** (4), 731–49.

Pew Research Center (2009), *Mapping the Global Muslim Population*, Washington, D.C.: Pew Research Center.

Platteau, J.P. (2008), 'Religion, politics, and development: lessons from the lands of Islam', *Journal of Economic Behaviour*, **68** (2), 329–51.

Platteau, J.-P. (2010) 'Political instrumentalization of Islam and the risk of obscurantist deadlock' *World Development*, **39** (2), 243–60.

Qur'an (2004), translated by M.A.S. Abdel, Haleem, New York: Oxford University Press.

Ramadan, T. (2004), *Western Muslims and the Future of Islam*, New York: Oxford University Press.

Ramadan, T. (2009), *Radical Reform: Islamic Ethics and Liberation*, New York: Oxford University Press.

Reiche, D. (forthcoming), 'Driving forces for climate protection policies in GCC countries', *Energy Policy*.

Rodenbeck, M. (2010), 'A special report on Egypt', *The Economist*, 15 July.

Rosnor, J. (1990), 'Ways women lead', *Harvard Business Review*, Nov/Dec, 119–25.

Ross, M. (1999), 'The political economy of the resource curse', *World Politics*, **51** (2), 297–322.

Roy, O. (2002), *Globalised Islam: The Search for a new Ummah,* London: C. Hurst & Co.

Said, E. (1978), *Orientalism: Western Conceptions of the Orient*, revised edn (1995), London: Penguin.

Sarayrah, Y.K. (2004), 'Servant leadership in the Bedouin-Arab culture', *Global Vitue Ethics Review*, **5** (3), 58–79.

Sashkin, M. (1988) 'The Visionary Leader', in J.A. Conger and R.N. Kanungo (eds), *Charismatic Leadership: The Elusive Factor in Organizational Effectiveness,* San Francisco, CA: Jossey-Bass, pp. 122–60.

Shah, S.J.A. (2006), 'Educational leadership: an Islamic perspective', *British Educational Research Journal*, **32** (3), 363–85.

Sharabi, H. (ed) (1990), 'Introduction', in *Theory, Politics, and the Arab World: Critical Responses*, New York: Routledge.

Sharp, J.M. (2005), *The Broader Middle East and North Africa Initiative: An Overview*, Washington, DC: Congressional Research Service, The Library of Congress, accessed 9 December 2010 at www.fas.org/sgp/crs/mideast/RS22053.pdf.

Sinclair, A. (2005), *Doing Leadership Differently: Gender, Power and Sexuality in a Changing Business Culture*, revised edn, Carlton, VIC.: Melbourne University Press.

Sinclair, A. (2007), *Leadership for the Disillusioned: Moving Beyond Myths and Heroes to Leading that Liberates*, Sydney, NSW: Allen and Unwin.

Stogdill, R.M. (1950), 'Leadership membership organization', *Psychological Bulletin*, **47**, 1–14.

Storey, J. (2004), 'Changing theories of leadership and leadership development', in J. Storey (ed.), *Leadership in Organisations: Current Issues and Key Trends*, London: Routledge.

Sudan Commerce News (2010), UAE, Saudi to lease more farmlands, 25 November, accessed 15 December 2010 at http://sdeconews.com/story-z3426498.

Swan S.E., V. Stead and C.J. Elliott (2009), 'Research futures: women, diversity and management learning', *Management Learning*, **40** (4), 431–7.

Syed, J. and F. Ali (2011), 'The white woman's burden: from colonial civilisation to third world development', *Third World Quarterly*, **32** (2), 349–68.

Syed, J. (2010), 'Reconstructing gender empowerment', *Women's Studies International Forum*, **33**, 283–94.

Tolba, M.K. and N.W. Saab (eds) (2009), *Arab Environment: Climate Change*, Beirut: Arab Forum for Environment and Development.

Umar-ud-al-Muhammad (1991), *The Ethical Philosophy of al Ghazzali*, Lahore, Pakistan: Sh. Muhammad Ashraf.

United Nations (n.d.), 'Millennium goals: background', accessed 18 December 2010 at www.un.org/millenniumgoals/bkgd.shtml.

United Nations Development Programme (UNDP) 2003, *Arab Knowledge Report.*

UNDP (2009a), *Human Development Report 2009: Overcoming Barriers: Human Mobility and Development*, New York: UNDP.

UNDP (2009b), *Arab Human Development Report: Challenges to Human Security in the Arab States*, New York: UNDP.

UNDP (2010), *Human Development Report 2010: The Real Wealth of Nations*, New York: UNDP.

Utting, P. (ed.) (2006), *Reclaiming Development Agendas: Knowledge, Power and International Policy Making*, Basingstoke: Palgrave Macmillan.

De Vries, K. (1994), 'The leadership mystique', in K. Grint (ed.) (1997), *Leadership: Classical, Contemporary and Critical Approaches*, Oxford: Oxford University Press.

Western, S. (2008), *Leadership: A Critical Text*, Thousand Oaks, CA: Sage Publications.

Wiefen, B. (2008), 'Liberalising autocracies in the Gulf region: reform strategies in the face of a cultural-economic syndrome', *World Development*, **36**, (12), 2586–604.

Wilson, R. (1985), 'Islamic business: theory and practice', *Economist Intelligence Unit Special Report*, no. 221, London.

Wilson, R. (1995), *Economic Development in the Middle East*, London: Routledge.

Woodward, J. (1970), *Industrial Organization: Behaviour and Control*, New York: Oxford University Press.

Woolcock, M. (1998), 'Social capital and economic development: toward a theoretical synthesis and policy framework', *Theory Culture and Society,* **27** (2), 151–208.

Woolgar, S. (1978), *Knowledge and Reflexivity: New Frontiers in the Sociology of Knowledge*, London: Sage Publishers.

World Bank (2008), 'Education and migration', in *The Road not Travelled. Education and Reform in the Middle East and Africa*, MENA Development Report, The World Bank, Washington DC, pp. 245–77.

Yukl, G. (2008), 'How leaders influence organizational effectiveness', *The Leadership Quarterly*, **19**, 708–22.

Yukleyen, A. (2009), 'Redefining "Islam" and "Europe" in Turkey's European Union membership process', paper presented at the annual meeting of the ISA's 50th annual convention, 'Exploring the Past, Anticipating the Future', New York Marriott Marquis, 15 February, New York.

Zaleznik, A. (1992), 'Managers and leaders: are they different?', *Harvard Business Review*, March – April.

Zaman, N. and M. Asutay (2009), 'Divergence between aspirations and realities of Islamic economics: a political economy approach to bridging the divide', *IIUM Journal of Economics and Management*, **17** (1), 73–96.

2. Globalization, governance and leadership development in the Middle East

Rodney Wilson

INTRODUCTION

The question of whether management culture is universal or society specific has long been debated in the Middle East, with those who accept the latter suggesting that there may be some characteristics of Arab and Islamic culture that are inimical to business development. Business leaders in the Middle East appear to accept cultural relativist arguments, believing that their values are rooted in their culture and religion. For much of the twentieth century business leaders in the Middle East were rather defensive of these values, fearing that they were being marginalized in a global business culture dominated by Western thinking. In the twenty-first century, however, a new confidence is emerging, as global business becomes more culturally diverse and Middle Eastern entrepreneurial role models become increasingly prominent.

The revival of political Islam has legitimized governance regimes administered by shari'a doctrine and jurisprudence and distinctive models of Islamic leadership are increasingly advocated as stimulating economic advancement. However, as Chapra (1993) observes, with Middle East Islamic states there is a need to reinforce moral values in leadership roles by socio-economic means in such a manner that individuals in society serve their own self interest within the constraints of social well-being and economic stability.

Although values are crucial for business, an organization's success also depends on its systems of control and governance. Hence increasing international attention has been paid to issues of corporate governance, but it is only very recently that this has received any attention in the Middle East. Corporate governance debates do not arise in family businesses, but as companies expand with external capital, as is happening throughout the Middle East, each stakeholder group becomes more concerned with their formal rights and obligations. Formal systems of corporate governance can constrain but at the same time provide opportunities for business leaders in the Middle East. Entrepreneurs have to rethink their relationships with other stakeholder groups, which has implications for management culture.

In this chapter the aim is to examine both management culture and corporate governance in a Middle East context and the links between the two. It is not just a matter of management having to adapt to socio-economic change, but of the organizations in which they aspire to play a leadership role developing in a way that could not have been envisaged even a decade ago. Rather than hosting foreign multinational companies with a predominantly Western business culture, the Middle East now has its own home-grown multinationals which are spreading their own culture across Asia and Europe, a complete reversal of the situation for most of the nineteenth and twentieth centuries (Wilson 2005). Middle Eastern management culture is subject to new types of international engagement both within and outside the region. It remains to be seen how far this will result in the emergence of distinctive corporate governance structures, or whether corporate governance will simply emulate practices from elsewhere, both good and bad (Halliday 2010).

Specific examples of the expansion of Arab multinational companies globally should help clarify matters. The case studies analysed include Orascom of Egypt; Dubai Ports World (DP World); Emaar, the UAE-based real estate company; the Saudi Basic Industries Corporation (SABIC); and Prince al-Waleed's investment company, Riyadh-based Kingdom Holdings. These companies were chosen because they are involved in different fields of activity and are domiciled in different Middle Eastern countries, but are all regarded as success stories and are all managed by the region's leading business personalities, all of whom proudly identify themselves with Arab culture.

Business is of course dependent on economic conditions, which ultimately determine leadership opportunities and the scope for management action. It therefore seems appropriate to provide a brief overview of the changing economic conditions that have resulted in many economies in the Middle East becoming net exporters rather than net importers of capital, including foreign direct investment flows, as Arab multinational companies expand their global operations.

THE ECONOMIC AND BUSINESS ENVIRONMENT

For almost two centuries the Middle East was marginal to the global economy as, although it was an important source of energy, agriculture

Table 2.1   Real GDP growth of leading Middle East economies

	1996-99	2000-03	2004-06
Algeria	3.1	4.1	3.9
Egypt	5.2	3.8	5.2
Iran	4.0	5.8	5.1
Jordan	2.9	4.9	7.2
Kuwait	1.9	5.9	7.0
Morocco	4.2	4.0	4.4
Qatar	11.8	7.1	11.5
Saudi Arabia	2.7	3.3	5.9
Syria	4.1	3.4	4.5
UAE	5.2	7.1	9.6

Source: World Bank (2007), *Economic Developments and Prospects: MENA Region,* Washington, Table 1.3, p. 8.

in much of the region stagnated and new industries struggled to achieve viability. Regional conflicts distracted from development priorities, and the postcolonial attempt to achieve a measure of economic self-reliance to match political independence largely failed (Halliday 2010). State-run industries expanded with protectionism, but their mediocre performance was blamed on ineffective management, with companies in the public sector run like government bureaucracies (Richards and Waterbury 1990, pp. 223–37). The first oil price boom of the 1970s resulted in some improvements in basic infrastructure, but with little domestic business confidence there was substantial capital flight and the oil revenues deployed locally were too often used to expand government bureaucracy, creating rentier economies (Wilson 1995, p. 9).

Much of this legacy remains, but there has been a reversal of fortunes in the region, enhanced by the second oil price boom which has been continuing since 2000, with prices trebling from 2003 to 2008 (see Chapter 1, Figure 1.5). As a consequence, the oil-rich economies comprising the Gulf Cooperation Council (GCC) have enjoyed unprecedented growth, not just in the oil sector, but also in non-oil activities including construction, retail and financial services, tourism, transportation and distribution (International Monetary Fund 2007, pp. 5–18 and 21–26).

The United Arab Emirates, with an economy larger than that of Egypt, is perhaps the outstanding success story, but Saudi Arabia's economy is now the largest in the Islamic world, while Qatar is the world's richest country in terms of per capita income. The growth performance has been especially impressive during the most recent period, as Table 2.1 shows,

Table 2.2   Business climate percentile ranks: 0 = worst, 100 = best

	Business reform	Administration quality	Accountability index
Algeria	36	43	28
Egypt	2	34	23
Iran	26	17	21
Jordan	59	71	34
Kuwait	77	65	30
Morocco	38	72	32
Qatar	N/A	54	15
Saudi Arabia	76	59	6
Syria	33	14	6
UAE	54	61	20

Source: World Bank (2007), *Economic Developments and Prospects: MENA Region,* Washington, Table 3.5, p. 111; Table 3.6, p. 130 and Table 3.7, p. 131.

especially in Qatar, UAE, Jordan, Kuwait and Saudi Arabia, with good prospects for this continuing. All these economies have flourishing private enterprise sectors and state-owned corporations, with real management autonomy from political interference, unlike economies such as Egypt, Iran, Morocco and Syria, where governments still, all too often, continue to crowd out private initiatives.

The business climate is related to economic performance, although the direction of causation can be debated. The attractiveness of the business climate is evaluated by the World Bank on the basis of the ease of start ups, closing a business, hiring and firing, contract enforcement, registering property, paying taxes, investor protection and dealing with licences. Using these criteria, the Middle East lags behind all other regions of the world apart from South Asia. However, within the region, as Table 2.2 shows, there is significant variation, with Kuwait and Saudi Arabia performing best and Egypt worst. The GCC states and Jordan also ranked higher in terms of public administration, although their position with respect to public sector accountability and transparency was much less satisfactory.

ARAB MANAGEMENT CULTURE

There are two separate bodies of literature on management culture in the Middle East, the first being specifically Arab and the second stressing

Islamic influences. The literature on the latter is much more extensive, but only the former will be dealt with here, as Abbas Ali is focusing on leadership in Islam in Chapter 3.

Farid Muna's study of the Arab Executive is a good starting point, published in 1980 and based on a doctoral thesis submitted to the London Business School (Muna 1980, pp. 1–25). The study involved semi-structured interviews with 52 leading Arab executives from six countries: Egypt, Jordan, Kuwait, Lebanon, Saudi Arabia and the UAE. Socio-cultural pressures identified by respondents included the low value placed on time, lack of industrial mentality and dislike of manual work, restrictions on women, and an individualistic rather than a team approach to work. Perhaps surprisingly, it was the respondents from Saudi Arabia who were the strongest supporters of women in management.

Pressures from the business and social community included insistency by clients in dealing only with the top man and the difficulty in keeping business and family matters separate, resulting, in extreme cases, in nepotism. However, apart from in Lebanon, there was little support for downgrading the role of family and traditions. While the executives surveyed usually consulted others in reaching decisions, especially on human resource issues regarding promotion or dismissals, they mostly made decisions themselves regarding business expansion and product development.

Although attitudes may have changed since Muna's research was undertaken, some of the themes identified still appear significant in the autobiography of a leading Arab entrepreneur, Kamal A. Shair. Although not perhaps the author's prime intention, the work reveals much about his attitudes and factors determining his motivation. Shair provides useful insights into the business culture of the Middle East, and the factors that resulted in his Beirut-based company, Dar al-Handasah, being successful. Although a much smaller engineering consultancy firm than its Western competitors, its advantage was the cultural empathy of the staff with clients from the region, who preferred to work with a company that spoke their language rather than a foreign multinational. The Christian background of its founder did not seem to be a disadvantage when dealing with clients; the important factor was that Shair was Arab, and throughout the book he stresses his nationalist credentials (Shair 2006, pp. 35–44).

The book provides an interesting perspective on political developments in the region, as Shair had business dealings with many of the politicians and rulers in the region, including the Emir of Kuwait, Skeikh Jaber al-Ali. It was the management of a contract for a power station in Kuwait that was the first big breakthrough for Shair's engineering consultancy firm. The work of the consultancy was disrupted by the civil disorder and political conflicts in Beirut in 1958, as Shair's company was based there, but the additional funding that Skeikh Jaber al-Ali generously provided saved the company, illustrating how important close personal relations with political clients were, and remain, in the Middle East. Although in Beirut the troubles of 1958 were to be the first of many that adversely affected the company because of Lebanon's factional strife and its centrality for Middle Eastern conflicts, Shair had no regrets about basing his business there, as the city had a better pool of highly educated engineers than anywhere else in the region.

COUNTRY RISK FACTORS

The Middle East is perceived to be a region where there are significant political and economic risks that are potential, or even actual, threats to business (Coface 2006). These risk perceptions help explain the relatively low amounts of foreign direct investment that have flowed into the region in comparison to other parts of Asia and even Latin America (White and Fan 2006, pp. 1–19). Regime change was traditionally not considered to be a significant political risk factor in the Middle East, as rulers lasted much longer than in the West (see Chapter 1, Table 1.1). Until the events of late 2010 and 2011, the absence of meaningful elections in much of the region was seen as contributing to political stability rather than being destabilizing, and this remained the case until the demand for democracy spread from elite, Western educated groups to the popular, widespread reform movements of the Arab Spring. The ability of political leaders to make decisions concerning business without real accountability can in theory facilitate a fast track approach, but in practice, although there may be an absence of democratic checks and balances, there are other forces, not least vested interest groups, that result in government ministers seldom having a free hand (Brink 2004, p. 30).

Cabinet government does not function well in much of the Middle East, with individual ministries enjoying much autonomy, which can result in confusion in business decision making. Many countries have established agencies to deal with inward foreign direct investments, the Saudi Arabia General Investment Authority being a prime example (Sagia n.d.), but although they can provide useful advice, they often lack authority to override government ministries. One way forward has been to establish free zones, subject to their own independent laws and regulations, the Jebel Ali Free Zone in Dubai being the most successful example of such an initiative (introduction to JAFZA n.d.).

In much of the Middle East there are restrictions on which sectors are open to foreign investment, and many countries, including Saudi Arabia, maintain negative lists (Askari 2006, pp. 216–17). The oil sector is often closed to foreign investors, yet this is the most attractive area for investment given the region's reserve base, and although investment is permitted in gas exploitation, usually local partners have to be involved through joint venture arrangements and there are often many restrictions on what are permissible operations for foreign companies. Restrictions also apply to investment in water resources, telecommunications and the media, all potentially attractive sectors for foreign investors. In Saudi Arabia foreigners cannot invest directly in any company listed on the local stock market, the only way of getting exposure being to invest through a locally registered mutual fund.

Legal risks are the greatest deterrent to foreign investment in the Middle East, the concern being what happens when local counterparties do not meet their contractual obligations, especially with respect to payments. There are often concerns over how disputes will be dealt with and the delays before cases are heard. In Saudi Arabia the Board of Grievances, which hears most cases involving commercial litigation, has a two-year backlog of work before cases reach the Court of First Instance, and there are inevitably further delays when one of the parties to the dispute seeks redress through the Appellate Panel. The Board of Grievances often spends much time in trying to reconcile the parties, but this is regarded as a waste of time by companies facing payment defaulters who have an interest in delaying matters for as long as possible (Malik 2004, pp. 131–3). The shari'a Courts can reach decisions in a much shorter time, and have less of a backlog, but they largely deal with family cases, and lack the expertise to handle commercial disputes. Cross-border contracts written under English law are not recognized by the Saudi Arabian courts where the arbitration could have been settled under Saudi Arabian law.

CORPORATE GOVERNANCE

The relationship between corporate governance and economic development appears to be complex, as it is not merely a matter of promoting competition and avoiding monopoly abuse through insider systems (Mayer 1996, pp. 8–31). In the Middle East there is often only limited competition due to barriers to market entry and the protection of established companies. Business leaders often expect and obtain political patronage, as a result of government procurement policies or exclusive agency contracts where they enjoy distribution and servicing privileges not granted to potential rivals. This inevitably increases the opportunity for corruption through illicit payments to public servants to ensure privileges are maintained. Such practices have a price, lowering returns on investment and distorting the distribution of any gains from economic growth. On the other hand, the long-term relations between governments and selected businesses in the Middle East can increase confidence in the latter, raise ratings and lower the cost of external capital. This can increase competitiveness, even if such government support is regarded by foreign critics as unfair (Halliday 2010).

Deficiencies in national governance can potentially be compensated for by sound corporate governance, and indeed it may be easier to introduce corporate reforms than political reforms given the suspicion and sensitivity in the Middle East to the latter and to any externally imposed democratization agenda (Halliday 2010). Hence, it is not surprising to see international bodies such as the Organization for Economic Co-oporation and Development (OECD) promoting better corporate governance in the region and institutions such as the World Bank and World Economic Forum increasingly interested in these issues. Hawkamah, the Institute for Corporate Governance in the Middle East and North Africa (MENA) region, organized the region's first ever corporate governance conference in Dubai in November 2006 (Hawkamah n.d.).

As the Dubai declaration resulting from the conference is likely to set the agenda for corporate governance in the Middle East in the coming years, it is worth elaborating on its key components (Hawkamah 2006). These include regulation, the role of the courts in handling disputes, procedures concerning insolvencies, corporate governance in state owned enterprises, and the importance of sound banking supervision. Regulatory bodies independent of government are rare in the Middle East, but it is seen as important that institutions such as central banks have a clear mandate and have the resources to carry out their responsibilities in an effective manner. Too often the approach is that of enforcing rules and checking procedures in a rather bureaucratic manner rather than focusing on where the problems lie and regulating sound institutions with a light touch.

The Dubai declaration stresses the importance of an efficiently functioning court system in handling disputes over payments and other matters, and the need for competent judges who have the specialist knowledge to understand the often complex issues involved in financial fraud. Creditors should have their rights upheld in a fair and equitable manner, and debtors should not be allowed to evade their responsibilities regardless of who they are and the positions they occupy. The OECD asserts that the judicial system in many Middle Eastern countries is subject to political pressures, with long delays in cases being heard and poor enforcement (Miteva 2007, p. 10). Deficiencies in the rule of law are seen as undermining the credibility of the corporate governance framework and the prospects of diversifying access to capital.

Progress with privatization has been slower in the Middle East than in most other areas of the world and, as a consequence, wholly or largely state-owned enterprises continue to play a major role in the economies of the region (Saidi 2004, p. 17). This has major implications for corporate governance as, given defective and malfunctioning systems of public administration and limited political accountability, there is often little effective control over the managers of state-run enterprises. Political interference, the lack of commercial incentives, deficient financial discipline and the availability of low-cost credit are all seen as contributing to the inefficiencies of the public sector in the Middle East (Miteva 2007, p. 19). Often, state-owned enterprises are over manned, with top-heavy management layers. Governments have sought to expand the payrolls of state enterprises as 'employers of last resort' for local citizens. The blurring of the separation between the public and private sectors also makes corporate governance more problematic, and results in conflicts between public and private interests.

Within the private sector in the Middle East there are also factors that impede effective corporate governance, not least that ownership is highly concentrated. Large family-dominated companies predominate alongside the state sector and even banks are often family owned. In the past family-run enterprises often served the economies well due to strong leadership and their entrepreneurial spirit, but widespread rent-seeking behaviour has increasingly undermined this, and relationship-based systems often fail to function effectively as competition increases (Miteva 2007, p. 8). There are often uncertainties and disputes over the leadership succession in such businesses and, where boards are simply packed with family members, there is little independence from family interests.

Most small and medium-sized enterprises are not listed, but have even less transparency and accountability than private equity companies (Bohn 2005, p. 3). Listed companies are also characterized by a high degree of ownership concentration, usually from individuals of high net worth, including members of the ruling elites, rather than institutional shareholders such as insurance companies and private pension funds. State pension funds often have ownership stakes in listed companies, but they usually put government political priorities above the interests of their members.

Detailed corporate governance guidelines have been produced for Egypt and Lebanon, but there have been no specific documents for the GCC states, despite most large Middle Eastern firms being based in these economies. There have been some improvements in financial sector governance in Saudi Arabia, with the banks adopting the Basel II standards on risk-based capital adequacy from January 2008 (Arab News 2007), but wider corporate governance rules due to be introduced by the end of 2006 by the Capital Markets Authority have yet to appear (Khaleej Times 2006).

A detailed corporate governance assessment for Egypt was undertaken by a joint World Bank and IMF team in 2004 with the OECD standards used as the benchmark (Berg and Capaul 2004, pp. 1–21). Subsequently, revised guidelines were drawn up, which are admirable for their clarity. These outline the procedures for company annual general meetings and the responsibilities of boards of directors, the external and internal auditors and the audit committee (El-Din 2005, pp. 7–14). The Board of Directors is seen as being primarily responsible to the shareholders, and it should include a majority of non-executive members to ensure the management does not dominate. As a further safeguard for shareholder interests the guidelines recommend that the managing director should not be chair of the board. Remuneration of directors should be disclosed and executive directors should not serve for more than three years unless they get the approval of the annual general meeting. Board members can receive stock options, but caution is urged if such options might bias directors towards pursuing short-term financial objectives rather than being concerned with the medium and long-term future of the business.

A corporate governance code for Lebanese small and medium-sized enterprises (SMEs) has also been drafted based on the OECD good governance principles (Abu Samra and Bishara 2006, pp. 1–19). Lebanon has been at the forefront of work on corporate governance in the Middle East, partly due to the work of the Lebanese Transparency Association, the most active non-governmental organization (NGO) in its field in the region, which has been operating since 1999. Its report on corruption in postwar reconstruction, contrasting the position of Lebanon with that of other countries, including Iraq and Kuwait, is especially informative (Large 2003, pp. 9–52). In the code for Lebanese SMEs emphasis is placed on shareholder rights including their right to freely trade their shares, call shareholder meetings and place items of concern on the agendas (Abu Samra and Bishara 2006, pp. 6–8). The responsibilities of Boards of Directors are also spelt out, including their duties of care, loyalty and obedience: issues not raised in the Egyptian code. However, as in the case of Egypt, a separation of the functions of Chairman of the Board and the General Manager is recommended, and contract terms of three years are specified for board members, but in the Lebanese code a minimum of only one-fifth of board members should be non-executive members, which raises doubts about how much control they can exercise on behalf of the shareholders (Abu Samra and Bishara, p. 12).

INCREASING GLOBAL IMPACT OF ARAB-OWNED CAPITAL

Corporate governance issues are not only of interest to Western business leaders directing multinational companies, but also to Middle Eastern entrepreneurs running their own multinational companies. These companies increasingly have the resources and capacity to invest anywhere in the world where there are potentially profitable opportunities, or where strategic involvement in overseas markets may enhance the profitability of the home companies, as in the case of downstream petrochemicals where guaranteed access to host country markets through wholly or partially-owned subsidiaries can keep out competitors and bring substantial gains in the long run. The case of the petrochemical giant SABIC will be considered later. It is perhaps appropriate first to review Orascom, and in particular its subsidiary Orascom Construction Industry, as it is based in Egypt, where, as already mentioned, corporate governance guidelines already exist. To what extent has Orascom followed the guidelines and how far has the management culture evolved during the transition of the firm from family partnership to multinational giant?

Orascom Construction Industries

Orascom is a conglomerate of which Orascom Construction Industries represents only one division, the others being in telecommunications, hotels and technology solutions (Orascom n.d.). The construction company is involved in major engineering projects including power, pharmaceuticals, fertilizers and cement plants. Its major operations are in Egypt and Algeria and the company is also involved in industrial construction in northern Iraq, Pakistan and Nigeria. At the end of 2006 it was engaged in 59 projects in nine countries (Orascom 2006, p. 31). The hotel and resort developments are in Sinai and on the Red Sea coast of Egypt, with other major projects at Aqaba in Jordan and Ras El Khaimah in the UAE. The telecommunications division provides mobile services in Algeria, Pakistan, Egypt, Tunisia, Bangladesh and Zimbabwe and in 2007 became involved in the Italian market.

Construction and cement had always been the core business of the group, as Onsi Sawiris, the founder and president of Orascom, was originally involved in contracting for real estate and infrastructure development (Hassan 1999). Sawiris was from a family of landlords, part of the historical Egyptian elite, and his father pursued a career in law. After graduating in Engineering from Cairo University, Onsi Sawiris founded a contracting company specializing in irrigation work and soon won valuable contracts from the Ministry of Irrigation. The business was however nationalized during the Arab socialist period during the 1960s and Sawiris left for Libya to exploit his business talents, building a substantial fortune. After the 1977 Camp David Accords, when Egyptians were expelled from Libya, Sawiris returned to Cairo, where the business climate was now more favourable. He used his fortune to establish a new contracting business, which by 1998 had grown sufficiently to seek a listing on the Cairo and Alexandria stock markets.

As is the case of Kamal A. Shair in Jordan and Lebanon, and similar to the case of Hayel Saeed Anaam in Yemen, as discussed in Chapter 12, Sawiris, as founder, was very much in control of the business and had a top down approach to management. Sawiris' management style could be described as patriarchal. He has passed everyday control to his three sons, who themselves appear to be formidable business leaders. All are Western educated, thanks to the money their father made in Libya, with Naguib, the eldest, attending the Polytechnic in Zurich, Sameeh studying Engineering in Berlin and Nassef studying Economics at the University of Chicago. Orascom is structured as a conglomerate as this enables each son to head a different division, although Onsi himself continues to chair Orascom Construction, with Naseef, the youngest son, serving as CEO.

Despite remaining family dominated, Orascom Construction has a small board of seven directors, including the Chairman and CEO, three of whom are non-executive directors representing shareholder interests. As Onsi Sawiris himself is a significant shareholder, it could be said that a majority of the board represent the shareholders. Orascom Construction has a code of corporate governance which is in line with international best practice and OECD guidelines. Corporate governance is important for the company, as apart from its Cairo and Alexandria Stock Exchange listing it has also issued Global Depository Receipts which are listed on the London Stock Exchange. Naguib and Sameeh Sawiris resigned as non-executive directors in 2003, reducing family control, and were replaced by outside non-executive directors including Alaa Sabaa, founder of EGF-Hermes, and a former Vice President of Kidder Peabody in New York (Orascom 2006, p. 37). The code of corporate governance covers the responsibilities of the board of directors, the internal control and risk management procedures, business conduct and ethics and relations with shareholders.

DP World

The government of Dubai, not content with operating the largest transit port in the Middle East at Jebel Ali, established DP World in 1999. Its major initial success was in securing a 20-year management contract to operate Jeddah Islamic Port, the largest on the Red Sea, making it the main port operator on both sides of the Arabian Peninsula. By 2000 it had won the management contract to operate the port at Djibouti on the African side of the Red Sea and the gateway to East Africa.

DP World next looked east, winning a 30-year concession to develop a new container terminal in India in September 2002. Its major breakthrough in India was in March 2004 when it won the contract to operate the Rajiv Ghandi Container Terminal, which it has made the most efficient shipping facility on the subcontinent. Its first European venture was in Romania near the mouth of the Danube, where it won an 18-year concession in 2003 to manage the largest port on the Black Sea.

DP World has become a leading international logistics company, as it replicated the success of its pioneering free port ventures in Dubai in other neighbouring countries and, more recently, has established a global presence through its audacious takeover of the United Kingdom port and ferry group P&O (Financial Times 2006). Despite subsequent controversy concerning the ownership of six US ports that were part of the P&O group, such a takeover deal, worth $5.7 billion, would have been unthinkable a decade ago, but although the announcement on 29 November 2005 surprised many shipping analysts, the bid has to be seen in the context of the oil price boom in the Gulf, the relatively low cost funding available, and the confidence of the financial institutions backing the company in Dubai's diversification strategy.

DP World is not a listed company, its sole shareholder being the government of Dubai. Like other companies in the Emirate however, its objectives are purely commercial and there is no political interference (Hvidt 2007, pp. 557–77). The aim is profit maximization and the board of directors has the autonomy to achieve this objective. The company adheres to a code of corporate responsibility, the focus being on providing a safe environment for its workforce (DP world website n.d.). It also seeks to limit the environmental impact of its activities by monitoring consumption of diesel oil and electricity and reusing and recycling where possible. It is important to note that the stress is on corporate responsibility not corporate governance as, like other government-owned entities in Dubai, DP World does not want to be constrained by international norms that might limit management choices.

Ultimately the management is accountable to Sheikh Mohammed bin Rashid al-Maktoum, the entrepreneurial ruler of Dubai and Vice President of the UAE. The company considered seeking a listing in London but, in November 2006, postponed the decision for six to twelve months, and then in July 2007 abandoned the planned listing (Lindsay 2007). It gave as its reason the lower cost of issuing bonds, but the real explanation may have been the reluctance to introduce the corporate governance standards required for companies listed in London. P&O included a comprehensive and transparent statement of corporate governance in its annual reports, but this was abandoned when the company was taken over (P&O 2005). It is perhaps ironic, given the prominence of the Dubai declaration on corporate governance for the Middle East, that the Emirate where it was issued is reluctant to apply the standards itself.

The management of DP World is nevertheless highly professional, with Mohammed Sharaf, the CEO, having a degree in Business Administration from the University of Arizona. The management structure is relatively flat, with just three top layers: the CEO, a second layer including the vice presidents for business development, planning, human resources, law and the CFO, and a junior layer of vice presidents responsible for operations, communications and procurement. Mohammed Sharaf is directly accountable to Sultan Ahmed Bin Sulayem, the Chairman of Dubai Ports, which owns DP World. If DP World was floated independently this line of control would be lost. Sulayem is also Chairman of Nakheel, the second largest real estate company in Dubai, and Istithmaar, the Dubai Investment Company, and he is regarded as one of the three closest confidants of the Ruler (FT Business 2003; Martinson 2006).

The DP World expansion in the United Kingdom and elsewhere was interesting, not least because it was partly financed through the issuance of the largest ever Islamic *sukuk* security offering valued at $2.8 billion. This interest-free financing, which complies with Islamic Shari'a law, was handled by the Dubai Islamic Bank, the oldest Islamic commercial bank in the world and the third largest. As already indicated, DP World is not a listed company, and hence cannot raise equity finance, and as the Government of Dubai only provided initial seed finance and not continuing subsidies it has to raise debt finance. Obtaining this through Shari'a-compliant facilities makes such funding more acceptable in the region, although it is not necessarily cheaper than conventional equivalents despite being interest free. In July 2007 DP World listed a $1.75 billion conventional bond and a $1.5 billion *sukuk* on the Dubai International Financial Exchange (DIFX), augmenting its resources for further expansion (Khaleej Times 2007).

Emaar Properties

The largest real estate development company in the Middle East is Dubai-based Emaar, the growth of which was initially propelled by the construction boom at its home base, but which has subsequently diversified its interests to the wider Arab world, Turkey and South Asia (Emaar n.d.). In contrast to the unlisted DP World, Emaar is the largest listed company on the Dubai Financial Market, but the Government of Dubai and the ruling family own significant stakes, although it is unclear what proportion of the shareholding this represents. Despite being only founded in 1997, the company's revenues exceeded $3.8 billion in 2006 and net profit rose to almost $1.3 billion (Emaar 2006). Emaar is rated A- by Standard and Poors and A3 by Moodys, reflecting market confidence in its risk management strategy and its financial strength (Emaar 2007).

Emaar's major projects in Dubai include the Burj Khalifa, the world's tallest building, completed in 2010 (BBC 2010) and the Dubai Mall, the world's largest entertainment and shopping mall. Emaar was awarded the contract to build King Abdullah Economic City, the largest ever private sector investment in Saudi Arabia valued at $26.6 billion. This new logistics hub near Jeddah will have a population exceeding 500 000. Emaar's international acquisitions include John Laing Holmes, the second largest privately-owned house builder in the United States, and Hamptons International, the London-based estate agency (Al Asaad and Nivine 2007). The company is diversifying into private health and education provision, as this is viewed as an essential complement to its residential developments.

Emaar's executive director is Mohamed Bin Ali Alabbar, who is one of the three closest confidants of Dubai's ruler, Director General of Dubai's Department of Economic Development and a member of Dubai Executive Council and Chairman of Dubai Bank, Amlak Finance and the Dubai Aluminum Company (FT Business 2006). Alabbar, like other Middle Eastern business leaders, is Western educated, having graduated from Seattle University where he specialized in finance and economics in 1981. He is passionate about golf, being Chairman of the UAE Golf Association, and in 2007 was named one of the top ten golfing personalities in the world by Golf World magazine. Emaar generously sponsors the annual, PGA-recognized Dubai Desert Classic golf tournament.

Emaar being a listed company, in contrast to DP World, adheres to OECD standards of corporate governance. The company's board consists of eight directors in addition to the Chairman and Vice Chairman, with a majority of non-executive directors, and a separate Group Chief Executive Officer who runs the businesses in consultation with Alabbar who, as Chairman, represents the shareholders' interests (Emaar, 'Corporate Governance' n.d.). The board meets quarterly, but there is a separate Executive Committee which meets when required. It is responsible for strategy, policy matters and the establishment and operation of risk management systems. The Executive Committee is chaired by Alabbar, who plays a hands on role, together with two non-executive directors, but not the Group Chief Executive Officer, who has a more limited remit for policy implementation.

As Emaar is only a decade old, its management structure reflects its establishment as a listed company, with no prior history as a family business or partnership. It was the Ruler of Dubai himself, together with the Dubai Executive Council, who approved the original structure. As Emaar has diversified internationally and into new sectors, its management structure has evolved, with Emaar acting increasingly as a holding company, while day-to-day executive operations are handled by its ten subsidiaries: Emaar Dubai, Emaar International, Emaar Investment Holdings, Emaar Malls, Emaar Hotels and Resorts, Emaar Education, Emaar Healthcare, Dubai Bank and Emaar Industries. This diversified holding structure was approved by the shareholders in 2007. Further restructuring is likely, as the costs of overseas expansion have been high, and the company does not want to burden itself with excessive debt. One plan is for Emaar to issue convertible bonds to Dubai Holdings in exchange for land, giving the government a 51 per cent majority stake in the company (Das Augustine 2007). This would undoubtedly have implications for management and corporate governance.

SABIC

The largest Middle Eastern multinational company is SABIC, a major force in global petrochemical production and the largest company in the Arab world, with net assets worth almost $20 billion, sales of $23 billion annually and a net income of almost $5.4 billion (SABIC 2006). Although most of its plants are at Jubail on the Gulf coast of Saudi Arabia and at Yanbu on the Red Sea, it has established a subsidiary, SABIC Europe, based in Sittard in the Netherlands. The company plans to expand further in Europe and purchase more petrochemical plants where it can add value based on the supply of basic inputs from the Saudi plants. SABIC has 17 major industrial complexes in Saudi Arabia and three in Europe, including petrochemical plants at Geleen in the Netherlands, Gelsenkirchen in Germany and Wilton and North Teesside in the United Kingdom, the latter being acquired from Huntsman Petrochemicals in October 2006 in a deal worth $700 million.

The company is the seventh largest petrochemical producer in the world and the leading global ethylene glycol producer. By 2006 its workforce exceeded 17000 employees, of whom around 2300 are in Europe. This is set to expand further to 30000 as in May 2007 SABIC acquired General Electrics (GE) plastics unit in the United States in a deal worth $11.6 billion (MEED 2007a).

SABIC was established by Royal Decree in 1976, the original objective being to invest some of the revenues from the first oil boom of the 1970s into creating world class petrochemical facilities, which would add value in the oil sector and contribute to the Kingdom's economic diversification plans. The expansion involved the creation of joint ventures with foreign petrochemical and basic industry companies and the Saudi partners that comprised SABIC. The competitive advantage was based on cheap and abundant energy, but many sceptics doubted that the ventures would succeed in Saudi Arabia's harsh climate and high-cost environment. However, SABIC's performance has proved the sceptics wrong, and vindicated the ambitious plans of its executives, notably Mohamed al-Mady, who has served as Chief Executive Officer since 1998.

Although the original business strategy was for each SABIC plant to have a foreign joint venture which could provide technical expertise and market the output, as the company matured it started to undertake research and development itself. SABIC's own marketing offices in Asia were established in the 1990s, the first being in Singapore in 1992, followed by New Delhi in 1993. A marketing office in France was established in 1994 to complement the London office, which had been opened seven years earlier. This meant the company could market its own products directly, without the need for foreign partners, who were subsequently bought out.

SABIC remains 70 per cent government owned, with 30 per cent of the share capital subscribed by Saudi Arabian and other Gulf Cooperation Council (GCC) investors (MEED 2001). Gulf investors are free to invest in each other's markets, but the Saudi Arabian stock market remains closed to foreign investors. In practice there are few UAE or Kuwaiti investors with significant holdings of SABIC shares. The Saudi government does much to promote SABIC's commercial interests through its diplomatic efforts, and when the King travels abroad, he is often accompanied by SABIC officials and other Saudi business leaders. One of the major benefits of Saudi Arabia's World Trade Organization accession in December 2005 was to create a level playing field for SABIC, whose exports to the European Union had been subject to a discriminatory tariff. The Saudi Foreign Ministry is also keen to ensure that SABIC will not experience the hostility that DP World encountered with regard to its brief ownership of six ports in the US after its purchase of P&O.

Rather than raising additional equity, SABIC has relied largely on debt finance to fund its expansion at home and acquisitions abroad, and its debt financing requirement for the 2007–2012 period is estimated at $28 billion (MEED 2007b). In June 2006 SABIC secured a $4.8 billion syndicated loan on behalf of its subsidiary, the Saudi Kayan Company, which is building a new petrochemical complex at Jubail with an annual capacity of four million metric tons of chemical products. The lead managers were BNP Paribas, Arab Banking Corporation and SAMBA, formerly the Saudi American Bank. However, in this deal the Saudi Kayan Petrochemical Company is to be floated separately on the Saudi stock market, with 35 per cent of the capital owned by SABIC, 20 per cent by Kayan, and 45 per cent of the capital offered to Saudi and GCC investors.

The most innovative financing arrangement, announced in July 2006, was the launch by SABIC of a *sukuk* security issue, a type of Islamic bond which yields a non-interest-based return. To comply with shari'a principles the *sukuk* must also be asset backed, so that Muslim investors who buy and sell the *sukuk* are trading rights to real assets and not merely paper. The *sukuk* was worth $700 million with HSBC, which has an Islamic financing subsidiary, acting as lead manager. The Capital Markets Authority of Saudi Arabia has issued new rules that permit the trading of *sukuk* on the Saudi stock market. Until the SABIC issuance there had only been two corporate *sukuk* by Saudi companies, but the market is now anticipating rapid expansion, with Saudi Arabia overtaking Malaysia by 2009. A second *sukuk* issuance was announced in July 2007 with HSBC again acting as lead manager (Arab News 2007b). SABIC, although a listed company, seems, like DP World, to prefer to finance expansion through debt issuance rather than equity, which would dilute the government's shareholding.

The SABIC Board of Directors is chaired by Prince Saud bin Abdullah bin Thenayan al-Saud, a member of the Saudi royal family, who could be regarded as primarily representing the government rather than private shareholders, although there is not necessarily a conflict of interest as both constituencies want to see SABIC operate on commercial lines as a profitable company. It does not have a state-company ethos, and although the company has played an important role in recruiting and training local nationals to a high level of technical expertise, it has never been pressurized by government to take on employees to solve unemployment or social problems.

Mohamed al-Mady, the low profile Vice Chairman and Chief Executive Officer, is responsible for the day-to-day management of SABIC (Harrison 2007). There are five other board members, a small number for such a large company. No distinction is drawn between executive and non-executive members, indeed SABIC has no policy for corporate governance, preferring to emphasize its mission and social responsibility (SABIC 2007). It stresses the value of its products to the community, its care over the health and safety of its employees and its concern for the environment. A more formal code of corporate governance defining the roles and responsibilities of SABIC's different stakeholder groups may become more likely as its overseas expansion continues.

Kingdom Holdings

Arab investment companies and banks are also expanding internationally, the best known investment company being Kingdom Holdings, the vehicle owned by Prince Al Waleed bin Talal of Saudi Arabia and his associates. This company is not interested in controlling what it invests in, the prime objective being to spread risk by having a diversified portfolio. At the end of 2006 its assets were worth over $25 billion (Kingdom Holding Company n.d.). Major holdings include a 5 per cent stake in Apple Computers, 4 per cent of Citigroup, 5 per cent of Fairmont Hotels and Resorts, 22 per cent of Four Seasons Hotels and 33 per cent of Mövenpick Hotels. There are almost 50 companies in the portfolio, most in the West, but also with significant exposure in the Middle East and Africa, although the portfolio is surprisingly light in Asian stock.

As Kingdom Holdings is dominated by its larger than life chairman Prince Waleed, it is relevant to provide considerable detail on his background. He is the most successful investor in the Middle East and currently the nineteenth richest person in the world (Forbes.com 2010). Although a member of the Saudi royal family, his main interest is business, not politics. Prince Waleed's investments are global, but he has a strong commitment to the development of the private sector in Saudi Arabia, demonstrated through his financial decisions and not merely words.

Prince Waleed was born in 1955, his father being Prince Talal, one of the many sons of the founder of Saudi Arabia, Abdul-Aziz al-Saud. His mother was Princess Mona El-Solh, daughter of Riad El-Sohl, leader of the Lebanese independence movement and the country's first Prime Minister. His family links in the Arab world extend to Morocco, where Prince Moulay Hicham is his cousin. Prince Waleed is married to Princess Ameera, and has a son and a daughter, Khalid and Reem (Khan 2005, pp. 15–40).

Prince Waleed completed his undergraduate degree at Menlo College in California in 1979. This is a highly reputable liberal arts university where the Prince obtained a BSc in Management, specializing in international management and marketing communication, subjects that were to serve him well in his subsequent business career. Later, after a break to pursue his early business interests, Prince Waleed enrolled at Syracuse University in New York State, adding East Coast experience to his previous West Coast exposure. At Syracuse he joined the prestigious Maxwell School for postgraduate studies where he completed an MA in Social Sciences in 1985.

Although a member of the Saudi royal family, like other Princes, and contrary to some false perceptions, Prince Waleed was not provided with a fortune because of his birth. Rather, after his first graduation, his father provided him with a modest loan of $30 000, which Prince Waleed augmented by mortgaging his own house for $300 000, a property whose value had increased substantially after being purchased by the Prince. With this limited start-up capital, all of which was through borrowings, Prince Waleed founded Kingdom Holdings in 1980. Prince Waleed's investment strategy is long term, to buy and hold, and not to speculate or to go short in falling markets. In other words the strategy is that of an investment company, or a mutual fund, but not a hedge fund that seeks to take positions in markets, and engage extensively in derivatives trading. Prince Waleed, like Warren Buffet (the world's richest investor, whom he knows well), is concerned with corporate fundamentals. He picks stock based on research into companies, rather than simply being obsessed with trends in financial markets (Arab News 2005).

Prince Waleed indicated in 2005 that he planned to float Kingdom Holdings on the Saudi stock market when conditions are optimal, enabling other Saudi and Gulf investors to share in his good fortune while at the same time releasing equity for other ventures. Had the market not fallen so much in 2006, there is little doubt that the flotation would have occurred sooner (MEED 2007c). The flotation, when it was finally announced in June 2007, was fairly modest with only 5 per cent of the company being offered, valuing the company at $17.2 billion (Gulf News 2007). The shares were made available to Saudi and other GCC investors only, with half reserved for institutional investors and the other half available for private investors. Mohammed al-Qassimi, a well known Saudi Islamic cleric, issued a *fatwa* against investing in the company, as he regarded some of its investments as not complying with shari'a principles. Indeed he branded Prince Alwaleed as '*al-amir al-majin*', meaning the depraved prince, but the *fatwa* did not deter Saudi investors from buying into the IPO.

In fact, Kingdom Holdings has a generous social responsibility policy, and sponsors the Kingdom Foundation. Like other successful businessmen, Prince Waleed feels that he should give something back through his charitable activities. As with his investments, these are also focused, one of his aims being to promote a greater understanding of Islamic culture in the West, hence his $20 million donations to Harvard and Georgetown Universities to help fund their Islamic studies programmes and a similar donation to the Louvre in Paris for a new wing displaying Islamic art. Prince Waleed has always sought to help the Palestinians in concrete ways, one of his investments being a 5 per cent stake in the Palestine Real Estate Investment

Company. He also donated $27 million to a Saudi government fund to help Palestinian refugees. Business success has not resulted in Prince Waleed neglecting to address the problems of his own troubled region; indeed, money has been put to good use to aid the victims of political conflict.

Kingdom Holdings stresses that its corporate governance standards are in line with best international practice, but, as with SABIC, these are not spelt out by the company. Prince Waleed as the Executive Chairman is supported by three with responsibility executive directors for domestic, international and private equity investment. The Chief Financial Officer also sits on the board as the fifth member, resulting in a very compact governance structure. There are no non-executive directors, which may become an issue if more shares are sold. The audit committee and nomination and compensation committee are accountable to the board, and there are separate audit and legal and compliance departments.

CONCLUSION

The emergence of Arab multinationals is a symbol of the increasing business dynamism of the Middle East, despite the region's enduring political problems. The revenues from the current oil boom are being invested wisely, and lessons have been learnt from the mistakes of the 1970s. The climate for business is increasingly favourable, and even Islamists see no problem in shari'a–compliant capitalism. Despite the low per capita incomes of some Arab states, wealth creation is occurring, and the region's most outward-looking companies can increasingly compete with the best in the world.

Business leaders in the Middle East identify strongly with Arab and Islamic culture, but this does not necessarily manifest itself in a distinctive approach to management, as Farid Muna suggested. Strong leadership is respected, as with the cases of Kamal Shair, Onsi Sawiris, Mohammed Sharaf, Mohamed bin Ali Alabbar, Mohamed al-Mady and Prince Waleed, but this is the case globally and it is far from being unique to the Middle East. Family businesses were the dominant structure, but as businesses expand and seek market listings, family influences and links become less significant, especially when confronted with the need to adhere to international best practice in corporate governance. In Orascom Construction, Onsi Sawiris had to remove two of his sons from the board to have the necessary majority of independent non-executive directors and reduce family influence. Prince Waleed continues to play the major role in Kingdom Holdings, but his family is not involved in the company and his position will inevitably evolve as more shares are offered to investors.

State ownership of large-scale companies in the Middle East became the norm from the 1960s onwards, often with disastrous consequences for efficiency as management decisions were constrained by political considerations and the companies became overmanned bureaucracies rather than business enterprises. In the GCC states, however, new models of state-sponsored enterprises emerged, as typified by SABIC, DP World and Emaar, where the emphasis was on profitability and competitiveness, with management given a relatively free hand to exercise leadership and think globally rather than simply operating within a national framework. That said, there is a world of difference with respect to political and business leadership. It is true to say that, in the Gulf states, political and corporate governance are inextricably entwined. It is significant that the leadership qualities espoused in Western-oriented writings are at odds with the leadership qualities embodied by the individuals discussed above. A commitment to humility, listening, consensus building and nurturing underpins leadership decision making. Leadership development capabilities are associated with building individuals' skills, dynamic organizational capabilities and the overall societal development of the nation (Ahmed 1999; Ali 2005; Osland et al. 2006).

Mohamed al-Mady, CEO of SABIC, has focused on expanding the company's international operations, initially as a means of guaranteeing outlets for Saudi petrochemical feedstock, but now on acquiring plants that can make the company the global leader in an increasing number of downstream activities.

Corporate governance is usually deficient in traditional state-owned industries in the Middle East, where there is minimal public accountability, little transparency and unclear delineation of stakeholder interests. Within the new GCC models, although corporate governance remains informal accountability and transparency are improving and stakeholder interests are becoming clearer. In SABIC, government interests are protected by Prince Saud bin Abdullah bin Thenayan, but Mohamed al-Mady and the other executive directors are focused on business development. In Dubai where the ruler can himself be regarded as a business leader and government policy making is entrepreneurial, there is no real conflict between state and business. Hence Mohammed Sharaf of DP World and Mohamed bin Ali Alabbar of DP World have the freedom to exercise real business leadership knowing that they have the long-term backing of the ruler and that their success will be measured on commercial, rather than political, criteria. This is what business leadership is about and how it should be judged. The executive and the political are operating within the same corporate and societal framework.

REFERENCES

Abu Samra, Nada Abdel Sater and Norman D. Bishara (2006), *Corporate Governance Code for Lebanese Joint Stock SMEs,* Beirut: Lebanese Transparency Association.

Ahmed, Akbar S. (1999), *Islam Today: A Short Introduction to the Muslim World,* London and New York: I.B. Tauris.

Al Asaad, N. and W. Nivine (2007), 'Emaar properties records record net profits for first half 2007', *AME Info,* 16 July, Dubai, UAE.

Ali, Abbas J. (2005), *Islamic Perspectives on Management Organization,* Cheltenham, UK and Northampton, MA, USA: Edward Elgar.

Arab News (2005), 'Alwaleed: The man with the Madras touch', 8 December, Jeddah.

Arab News (2007a), 'Saudi banks to adopt Basel II in January 2008', 23 May, Jeddah.

Arab News (2007b), 'HSBC to joint lead manage SABICs *sukuk* issuance', 17 July, Jeddah.

Askari, Hossein (2006), *Middle East Oil Exporters: What Happened to Economic Development?* Cheltenham, UK and Northampton, MA, USA: Edward Elgar.

BBC News (2010), '*World's tallest building opens in Dubai*', accessed 21 June 2010 at http://news.bbc.co.uk/1/hi/business/8439618.stm.

Beblawi, Hazem and Giacomo Luciani (1987), *The Rentier State,* London: Croom Helm, pp. 1–25.

Berg, Alexander and Mierta Capaul (2004), *Report on the Observance of Standards and Codes (ROSC): Corporate Governance Country Assessment – Egypt,* Cairo: World Bank – International Monetary Fund.

Bohn, John (2005), *Regional Corporate Governance Forum,* Amman: Centre for International Private Enterprise.

Brink, Charlotte H. (2004), *Measuring Political Risk: Risks to Foreign Investment,* London: Ashgate.

Chapra, M. U. (1993), *Islam and Economic Development,* Islamabad: International Institute of Islamic Thought and Islamic Research Institute.

Coface (2006), *The Handbook of Country Risk 2006-2007: A Guide to International Business and Trade,* London: GMB Publishing.

Das Augustine, Babu (2007), 'High costs hit Emaar profit', *Gulf News,* 17 July, Dubai, accessed 16 June 2010 at: www.zawya.com/story.cfm/sidGN_17072007_10139771/%20High%20costs%20hit%20Emaar%20profit.

DP World (n.d.) website accessed 16 March 2009 at www.dpworld.ae.

El Din, Ziad Bahaa (2005), *Egyptian Code of Corporate Governance: Guidelines and Standards,* Cairo: CIPE.

Emaar (n.d.), 'About Emaar', accessed 16 March 2010 at www.emaar.com/index.aspx?page=about

Emaar (2006), *Annual Report,* Dubai: Emzer, pp. 4–5.

Emaar (n.d.) 'Corporate governance', accessed 16 March 2010 at www.emaar.com/index.aspx?page=investorrelations-corporategovernance.

Emaar (2007), Press release, 10 July, Dubai.

Financial Times (2006), 'Interview with Mohammed Sharaf, CEO, DP World', 16 March, London.

FT Business (2003), *FDI Magazine*, 20 June.

FT Business (2006), 'Mohammed Alabbar – property developer', *FDI Magazine*, 1 August.

Forbes.com (2010), 'The World's Billionaires', accessed 16 March 2010 at www.forbes.com/lists/2010/10/billionaires-2010_The-Worlds-Billionaires_Rank.html.

Gulf News (2007), 'Alwaleed's Kingdom Holdings opens IPO', 11 July.

Halliday, Fred (2010), *The Middle East in International Relations: Power, Politics and Ideology*, 6th edn, Cambridge: Cambridge University Press.

Harrison, Roger (2007), 'London Business School honours CEO of SABIC', *Arab News*, 7 July, Jeddah.

Hassan, F. (1999), 'Onsi Sawiris: a capital idea', *Al Ahram Weekly*, **439**, 22–28 July.

Hawkamah (2006), 'Hawkamah's first MENA Conference issues Dubai Declaration on Corporate Governance', accessed 16 March 2010 at www.hawkamah.org/news_and_publications/news/2006/18.html

Hawkamah (n.d.), 'Hawkamah, the Institute for Corporate Governance', accessed 16 March 2010 at www.hawkamah.org.

Hvidt, Martin (2007), 'Public-private ties and their contribution to development: the case of Dubai', *Middle Eastern Studies*, **43** (4), 557–77.

International Monetary Fund (IMF) (2007), *Regional Economic Outlook: Middle East and Central Asia*, Washington, D.C.: IMF.

JAFZA (n.d.) 'Introduction to JAFZA', accessed 16 March 2010 at www.jafza.ae.

Khaleej Times (2006), 'Saudi Arabia's new corporate governance rules by end 06', 16 July, Dubai.

Khaleej Times (2007), 4 July, Dubai.

Khan, Riz (2005), *Alwaleed: Businessman, Billionaire, Prince*, New York: Collins.

Kingdom Holding Company (n.d.), 'Fast facts', accessed 16 March 2010 at www.kingdom.com.sa/en/MC_FastFacts.asp.

Large, Daniel (2003), 'Corruption in post-war reconstruction', presentation to 11th International Anti-Corruption Conference, Seoul, Republic of Korea, May 2003.

Lindsay, Robert (2007), 'Dubai ports scraps London listing plans', *The Times*, 13 July, p. 53, London.

Malik, Monica (2004), 'The role of the private sector', in Rodney Wilson (ed.), *Economic Development in Saudi Arabia*, London: RoutledgeCurzon, pp. 131–33.

Martinson, Jane (2006), 'Dubai Ports boss with a P&O boarding pass', *Guardian Unlimited*, 17 February, accessed 18 June 2010 at www.guardian.co.uk/business/2006/feb/17/2.

Mayer, Colin (1996), 'Corporate governance, competition and performance', *OECD Economic Studies*, **27**, 8–31.

MEED (2001), 'Company profiles: Saudi Basic Industries Corporation', *The Middle East Business Weekly*, 9 November, London.

MEED (2007a), 'SABIC buys GE unit in $11.6 billion deal', *The Middle East Business Weekly*, 22 and 25 May, London.

MEED (2007b), 'SABIC to keep credit rating after $28 billion debt raining', *The Middle East Business Weekly*, 8 June, London.

MEED (2007c), 'Floating kingdom', *The Middle East Business Weekly*, 28 May, London.

Miteva, Elena (2007), *Advancing the Corporate Governance Agenda in the Middle East and North Africa: A Survey of Recent Developments,* Paris: MENA – OECD Investment Programme.

Muna, Farid A. (1980), *The Arab Executive,* New York: St Martin's Press.

Orascom (n.d.), 'Orascom companies', accessed 16 March 2010 at www.orascom.com/.

Orascom Construction Industries (2006), *Annual Report,* Cairo: Orascom.

Osland, Joyce S. (2006), 'Developing global leadership capabilities and global mindset: a review', in Günter K. Stahl and Ingmar Björkman (eds), *Handbook of Research in International Human Resource Management,* Cheltenham, UK and Northampton, MA, USA: Edward Elgar.

P&O (2005), *Annual Report,* London: P&O, pp. 24–25.

Richards, Alan and John Waterbury (1990), *A Political Economy of the Middle East: State, Class and Economic Development,* Boulder, CO: Westview Press.

SABIC (2006), *Annual Report and Accounts,* Riyadh: SABIC, p. 3.

SABIC (2007), Corporate brochure, Riyadh: SABIC, p. 1 and pp. 16–18.

Saudi Arabia (n.d.), 'Advancing your business', accessed 16 March 2010 at www.sagia.gov.sa.

Saidi, Nasser (2004), *Corporate Governance in MENA Countries: Improving Transparency and Disclosure,* Beirut: Lebanese Transparency Association, p. 17.

Shair, Kamal A. (2006), *Out of the Middle East: The Emergence of an Arab Global Business,* London: I.B. Tauris.

White, Colin and Miao Fan (2006), *Risk and Foreign Direct Investment,* London: Palgrave Macmillan, pp. 1–19.

Wilson, Rodney (1995), *Economic Development in the Middle East,* London: Routledge, p. 9.

3. Leadership and Islam

Abbas J. Ali

Whether in business or politics success is, to a large extent, attributed to effective leadership. Over centuries, a consensus has evolved that leadership is the most important factor in the continuity and growth of any organization and, for that matter, any nation. While the subject of leadership has always captured the attention of the masses and intellectuals its significance has, in recent years, reached an unprecedented turn. This is the inevitable result of the growing belief that the effective performance of groups or organizations is characteristically linked to the existence of sound leadership and, conversely, lack of performance is often attributed to an absence of leadership.

Because leadership encompasses both practical and idealistic aspects, it plays a pivotal role in defining reality and designing and shaping events. Indeed, the importance of leadership stems not only from organizational competencies, but also from the ability to foster curiosity among followers; the courage to confront abuses and assume responsibility; and the foresight to articulate a purposeful vision to make change desirable and to regard new possibilities in a positive light. The importance attached to these functions and roles, however, differs over time and across cultures and civilizations. Nevertheless, leaders have to creatively maintain a balance of priorities, clarify possibilities, inspire followers and maintain focus on achieving goals.

This chapter is designed to tackle the issue of leadership from an Islamic perspective. It examines leadership in light of the foundations of Islamic thought. Furthermore, it discusses forms of leadership in the contemporary Middle East. In addition, the chapter contrasts the authoritarian style of leadership with the Islamic ideal.

CULTURE AND LEADERSHIP

Initially, most leadership studies were conducted in the United States and this has shaped the research methodologies and perspectives of researchers in other cultures. Faced with a dynamic business environment in the US and growing demand for a better understanding for the existence and differences among leaders, these researchers have placed considerable emphasis on specific attributes (Blau 1963; Dow 1969; Stogdill 1974). Certainly the American culture and its emphasis on assertiveness and self-interest has shaped researchers' orientations and priorities in terms of leadership research. At the same time, it has been important to identify what differentiates effective leaders from others.

The popularity and intensity of research on leadership has motivated researchers from other cultures to examine leadership in different contexts. These researchers have concluded that cultural norms and values play a significant role not only in moulding leaders' outlooks, but also in defining leaders and their roles and functions. That is, societies differ in their perception of leadership and what makes an effective leader. Hofstede (1999; 1980), for example, notes that such differences are primarily determined by cultural values. He argues that values are specific to national cultures and are never universal. Values represent what is desirable and generally there is a preference for one state of affairs over others. Shaw (1990) suggests that each culture, based on its values and beliefs, appears to categorize leaders differently. I assert that perceptions of leaders are culturally bound. As such, the perception of whether a person is a leader involves simple categorization. My proposition is that in each culture there are pre-existing leadership prototypes and expectations which are a potential source for variation across cultures. Recently, in their cross-cultural study of leadership, House, Javidan and Dorfman (2001) argued that cultural attributes and practices not only differentiate cultures from each other but also serve as predictors for leader attributes and behaviour. Recent empirical studies provide support for such a proposition. Brodbeck (2000) led a group of researchers to study cultural variations of leadership prototypes across 22 European countries. The researchers indicated that the results reaffirm the concept that leadership is culturally bound. For example, they found that Nordic countries ranked high on the attributes for outstanding leadership of integrity, inspiration, vision, team integration, and performance. In contrast, managers in Latin countries ranked the attributes of team integration, performance, inspiration, integrity, and vision, in order, as the most desired. That is, cultures differ in their prioritization of the desired attributes for effective leaders.

In their recent study of leadership Howell and Shamir (2005) provided support to culture-based theories. These authors argued that in the context of charismatic leadership there are two types of relationship: personalized and socialized. The first relationship is based primarily on followers' personal identification with the leader. The socialized relationship revolves primarily on followers' social identification with the group or organization. Both relationships are culturally bound and the meaning attached to them is culture specific. The point is, each culture has a set of values and beliefs and these values, despite some similarity in economic system or development, exhibit a degree of endurance. Furthermore, in traditional societies where the pace of social change is much slower than that found in less traditional countries, norms and expectations tend to be deep rooted. The interplay of social norms and religion appears to strengthen cultural influence and the relative stability of societal values.

ISLAMIC PERSPECTIVES ON LEADERSHIP

Religion constitutes a major component of any culture and is, in some cases, the dominant one. The latter situation is mostly found in traditional cultures and particularly in Muslim societies. In these societies, though there is a gap between beliefs and practices, people in general identify with Islamic tenets and aspire toward achieving the ideals prescribed in the Qur'an and the sayings of the Prophet Muhammad. Whether or not people internalize these directives is not the subject of this chapter. However, since these sayings and directives are often forcefully stated by people, it is possible to propose that they have an impact on the vast majority of the population. For these people, the ideal is treated as reality and contemporary conditions are considered temporary and subject to change or disappearance. It is this widely observed attitude, which often impedes or obstructs practical transformation in the arena of politics and economy, that confuses Western observers.

The Islamic view on leadership is influenced by Qur'anic instructions, the practice and sayings of Prophet Muhammad, and the practice of his immediate followers. As in any other religion, however, the view is subject to manipulation and obstruction. Nevertheless, in recent years the subject of leadership has been given serious and close attention in Muslim countries for three primary reasons. First, there is a deeply held belief among Muslim scholars and the population that leaders are instrumental in safeguarding the community and building prosperous societies. Second, the existence of effective leaders and quality leadership is considered important for sustaining the faith and spiritual conduct. Third, the downfall of Muslim states and the tragic events that have occurred to Muslims since the eleventh century are attributed largely to the absence of leadership, as discussed in Chapter 1.

Three philosophical assumptions about leadership situate the Islamic view apart from those of Christianity and Judaism. These assumptions are discussed below.

Leaders are not Divinely Ordained

The Qur'an states clearly that Muhammad is just a human (18:110): 'I am but a man like yourself,' and (7:188): 'I have no power over any good or harm of myself except as God willeth. If I had knowledge of the unseen I should have multiplied all good and no evil should have touched me, I am but a warner' and (88:21–22): 'So thou reminding; Thou are only a reminder. Thou art not, over them a compeller.' The four successors of the Prophet Muhammad, the Rightly Guided Caliphs (632–661 CE), considered their involvement and functions to be civic duties. These Caliphs were humble, shied away from extravagant spending and avoided imposing their will on the community. For example, the first caliph Abu Bakr requested that the senior members of the community determine his salary, stating: 'Increase my base pay as I have to support my family and the Caliphate position prevents me from performing my private business, trade.' Furthermore, upon his appointment by the community as a caliph, he stated: 'I have been given authority over you, but I am not the best of you. If I do well help me, and if I do ill, then put me right.' This stands in contrast to Christianity where leaders are treated as ordained by God. This was articulated in Romans 13:1: 'Let everyone submit himself to the ruling authorities, for there exists no authority not ordained by God.'

Leadership is a Trust

The community entrusts a leader with the authority to conduct affairs on behalf of and for the benefit of the people. The Prophet Muhammad stated: 'A ruler who has been entrusted with the affairs of the Muslims, but makes no endeavour [for their material and moral uplift] and is not sincerely concerned [for their welfare] will not enter paradise along with them' and 'authority is a trust; one must be qualified for it and execute it duly otherwise, in the day of judgment, it is a shame and regret.' It was reported (see Abu Dawod 1996, p. 64) that in his usual investigation of the affairs of his subjects, the second Caliph Omer saw a poor lady whose children were crying because of hunger and asked her, if she had any complaints. She responded, 'my only complaint is against Omer.' Then Omer asked her, 'what did he do wrong?' She replied: '[Became] a leader but ignores the state of his followers.' Omer, to rectify the situation, compensated her for his shortcomings, and apologized for overlooking the condition of his people.

Followers' Acceptance is the Foundation of Leadership

Theologically, the community in Islam is the source of legitimacy and that leadership position is contingent upon the approval of the community. Leaders are therefore assumed to act according to people's expectations; otherwise followers would desert the leader. The Qur'an (3:159) commands leaders to be responsible and always maintain *ihsan* (goodness, kindness): 'Wert thou severe or harsh-hearted, they would break away.' In his mandate for the ruler of Yemen, the Prophet Muhammad declared: 'Be gentle [to the people] and be not hard [on them], and make [them] rejoice and do not incite [them] to aversion' (quoted in Muhammad Ali 1977, p. 404). That is, in Islamic teaching, the approval of followers is a prerequisite for effective leadership. Once leadership is established both followers and leaders have reciprocal obligations and entitlements. The fourth Caliph, Ali, stated (p. 244): 'When both the constituencies and leaders observe each other's due, right is strengthened, religion tenets are respected, justice prevails, and the society will benefit.'

TRAITS AND NATURE OF LEADERSHIP

The above assumptions constitute the foundations for leader selection and the nature of leadership. In terms of leader selection, the qualities of leaders are given considerable attention in Islamic teaching and early tradition. The Qur'an repeatedly prohibits oppression and calls for justice and kindness (16:90): 'God commands justice and goodness' (28:27); 'The oppressors will not prosper' (42:40); 'Loveth not those who are oppressors.' An additional quality (28:26) is the mandate to be, 'competent and trustworthy.' Prophet Muhammad placed considerable emphasis on three qualities: *rahima* (mercy), *ihsan* (goodness, kindness) and *adl* (justice). These are considered prerequisites for leadership without any consideration to age or ethnicity. For example, when the Prophet Muhammad appointed Zaid bin Thabit to lead Muslims, Thabit placed under his command senior members of the Muslim community. In terms of ethnicity, Muhammad asserted: 'Listen to and obey whoever is in charge, even though he is an Ethiopian [black].'

Almost all Islamic thinkers agree on the above qualities. There are variations, however, in details and additional qualities that are specific to certain tasks, or events. For example, *Ikhwan-us-Safa* (a tenth century intellectual society) asserts that leaders must be intellectually sound, display an unwavering commitment to justice, and should have the following qualities in order to sustain power and governance: the ability to follow up on, and be concerned with, the affairs of the people; to treat people according to their deeds; to apply justice with no exception; to avoid brutality; to reward the knowledgeable and uneducated people accordingly in terms of position and compensation; to select and appoint subordinates who have the best reputations and are independent; to supervise and conduct people's affairs; to select advisers from those who share his/her faith and outlook; to select a chief of staff in terms of faith and worldly affairs; to protect the rights of the weak and the oppressed people and to make certain that people who have been wrongly treated are given justice. Previously, Tahir Ben al-Hussein, an extraordinary chief administrator during the Caliph al-Mamun's era (813–33 CE), wrote that a leader has three major roles: custodian, preserver and protector. He asserted that members of constituencies are called followers if a leader is consciously directing them and making sure that their interests are served well. According to him, leadership is sustainable if the leader shoulders responsibility, accepts praise for doing well, and expresses accountability for wrongdoings.

The collapse of Baghdad and the end of the Abbasid era after the Mongol invasion in 1258 left most Muslim societies in total disarray. This event was a turning point in Islamic history as it represented the end of rationalistic thinking and the beginning of the domination of a doctrine of predestination in all its gloom and pessimism. One of the few Muslim thinkers who emerged after the demise of the Islamic golden era, Ibn Khaldun (1332–1406 CE), claimed that the Arabs contributed significantly to civilization because there was a sound leadership and the people followed their leaders. He noted:

> Consider the moment when religion dominated their policy and led them to observe a religious law designed to promote the moral and material interest of civilization. Under a series of successors to the Prophet, how vast their empire became and how strongly it was established. (quoted in Mansfield 1985, p. 37)

Ibn Khaldun (ibid, p. 112) attributed the decline of Islamic culture and state to the absence of group solidarity and thoughtful leadership. He argued that goodness (*ihsan*) and an inclination for collective or group feeling are prerequisites for any leader. These are necessary qualities and the absence of these qualities, he asserted, 'would be like the existence of a person with his limbs cut off.' Ibn Khaldun made a powerful argument that the decline of a nation is linked to absence of leadership. And when a nation persists in its rejection of its leaders, its virtues subside and eventually leadership ceases to exist. He prescribed several qualities needed by leaders to ensure acceptance by followers. These are: generosity, forgiveness of errors, tolerance toward the weak, hospitality toward guests, support of subordinates, maintenance of the indigent, patience in adverse circumstances, faithful fulfilment of obligations, generosity with money for the preservation of honour, respect for the religious law and for the scholars who are learned in it, high regard for religious scholarship, belief in and veneration for men of religion and a desire to receive their prayers, respect for the elderly and teachers, justice for those who call for it, fairness to and care for those who are too weak to take care of themselves, humility toward the poor, attentiveness to the complaints of supplicants, fulfilment of the duties of the religious law and divine worship in all details, and avoidance of fraud, cunning, deceit and shirking of obligations.

Recently, in terms of business, Asaf (1987) provided two categories of traits and qualities that a leader must have: moral discipline and personal character. The first includes eight identified attributes: goodness, patience, forgiveness, an ability to make peace among conflicting parties, selflessness, cooperation, a sense of responsibility, and tenderness and compassion in conversation. The second category encompasses avoidance of lies, arrogance, envy, anger, suspicion and spying. Those leaders who exhibit these qualities are assumed to show kindness, moderation, consultation and delegation in dealing with their subordinates, do not inflict intentional damage on others and are committed to the development and growth of the organization.

NATURE OF LEADERSHIP

In the early years of Islamic civilization, leadership was viewed as a process of influence, shared in nature, whereby a leader and followers engaged in certain activities to achieve mutual goals. There is a wide consensus among Muslim scholars and experts that the era of the Prophet Muhammad and his immediate four successors represents genuine Islamic thinking and approximates what might be considered an ideal state in terms of observing Islamic principles and ethics. Therefore, a better understanding of the nature of leadership from an Islamic perspective is possible by critically referencing the sayings and practices of the Islamic leaders during that era.

As was suggested above, the Prophet Muhammad looked at leadership as a process of shared influence. In his general conduct of affairs, whether religious or otherwise, Muhammad maintained two-way communication with his followers. He utilized both open public debate and sermons to introduce desired changes and reiterated that every person, regardless of his or her position, is a leader, stating:

Every one of you is a leader and every one of you shall be questioned about those under his supervision; the Imam is a leader and shall be questioned about his subjects; and the man is a leader in his family and he shall be questioned about those under his care; and the woman is a leader in the house of her husband, and shall be questioned about those under her care; and the servant is a leader in taking care of the property of his master, and shall be questioned about those under his care. (Muhammad Ali 1977)

It appears that Muhammad recognized that leadership is a shared influence process and that such influence must be goal oriented to serve the community. He declared: 'God blesses those who benefit others.' That is, leadership is valid only when it results in a benefit to the society, regardless of the setting. When linking leadership to societal contribution, Muhammad appeared to underscore the significance of shouldering responsibility to achieve cohesiveness and the prosperity of the community. Furthermore, Muhammad highlighted two necessary qualities for leadership: persuasion and moderation. In terms of persuasion, the Qur'an (16:125) instructs, 'Argue with them in manners that are best [kind] and most gracious.' In terms of moderation, seeking the middle way is considered a virtue as the Prophet asserts: 'The best way is the middle-way.' The Qur'an (2:143) declares, 'Thus we have made you a middle-way nation.'

The immediate successors to the Prophet seemed, in general, not to deviate from the Islamic view of leadership set out in the Qur'an and the teachings and examples of Muhammad. During their era, the newly emerged Islamic State expanded, acquired more resources, and in the process faced more complex challenges. In fact the leaders, who for a long time were under the supervision of the Prophet, had to answer questions related to managing the State and coping with existing military threats while being responsive to a much larger, more vocal, and diverse constituency. In meeting these emerging difficulties, these successors articulated a vision of leadership that captured the essence of Islamic thinking and energized followers to participate actively in building new institutions and vibrant communities in Arabia and surrounding regions. Their vision of leadership is based on four interrelated assumptions.

Leadership Responsibility is a Civic Duty

In the early years of Islam, Muslims viewed the role of Caliph as a secular position that represented a successor to the Prophet, but that was neither an heir to his right nor a replacement for him (Arkoun 1986; Ashmawy 1992). In Islam, the government is considered a civic system that is entirely built on the will of the community. Community approval of how things should be done and who should assume the leadership position is needed to ensure legitimacy and continuation. The first and second Caliphs, Abu Baker and Omer respectively, affirmed this. The first declared:

> I am not the best of you. If I do well help me, and if I do ill, then put me right . . . The weak among you shall be strong in my eyes until I secure his right if God wills, and the strong among you shall be weak in my eyes until I wrest the right from him . . . Obey me as long as I obey God and his apostle, and if I disobey them you owe me no obedience. (quoted in Armstrong 1992, p. 258)

He further said: 'I prefer that someone else was chosen, rather than me, for this task.' The second Caliph, Omer stated, 'If you see me doing wrongs, then straighten me.' In both cases, followers have the right to change or remove the leader and the leader is responsible and has to answer directly to the community.

Leadership is a Shared Influence

While the above point highlights the civic dimension of authority, it implies, too, that leaders are influenced by their followers' expectations and demands. The Fourth Caliph, Ali, stated (p. 256): 'If the elected person rejects or contests their [people's] decision, they will bring to his attention the issues that need to be addressed. If he persists in his deviation, they will fight him for not following the consensus of the Muslims.' Thus, consensus in the decision-making process is the foundation for governance. During that time, public debate and transparency in decision making were a policy choice. This was exemplified by an incident that took place between the Second Caliph and a community member in a public meeting. The individual criticized the second Caliph, and some in the audience thought the criticism was harsh. Omer's answer was that it was the duty of the leader and followers to listen to each other and to voice concerns. He was quoted saying, 'When followers do not participate and provide input, they are not contributing something useful. And we are not useful if we do not consent to their contributions.'

Leadership is a Reciprocal Relationship

In line with the above two points, Islamic teaching asserts that leadership is reciprocal. The philosophical assumption is that there will be neither leaders nor leadership without followers. The followers give meaning and legitimacy to leadership. The First Caliph, Abu Baker, argued that, 'When a leader is good in conduct, followers will be sincere for him.' The fourth Caliph, Ali, articulated the nature of reciprocity between a leader and followers and argued that it was essential for legitimacy (p. 245):

'God has made it an obligation for his creatures to observe their obligations toward each other. He made them equitable and interdependent. The greatest of those obligations are the mutual rights of the ruler and the ruled. God has made them reciprocal so that they constitute a basis for their cohesion.'

Leadership is an Attribution Phenomenon

Followers attribute certain qualities to leaders. These attributes are mostly behaviour based; followers observe leaders and make corresponding relations between observed behaviour and character. Accordingly, followers make attributions whether the person is a leader or not. The fourth Caliph states (p. 303): 'Good rulers are known by what their subjects say about them. So, the best stock you can build is your good deeds.'

In recent years researchers, in their quest to theoretically explain the emergence of leadership, have moved beyond the trait approach and attempted to provide sound justifications for its presence. These justifications appear to be similar to the general outlook and understanding of leadership which prevailed in the early years of the Islamic State. Of course, at that time, the senior members of the Islamic community were not interested in providing conceptualization of leadership or constructing a model for explaining or predicting organizational phenomena. Rather, they were motivated by outlining what they thought to be a practical faith-based approach for conduct and governance and for being responsible and responsive leaders. Nevertheless, their views seem contemporary and in line with present thinking on leadership in the West. For example, Hughes, Ginnett, and Curphy (2006) suggest that leadership is a result of the interaction between a leader and followers. Willner (1984) argues that leadership is neither personality-based nor contextually-determined but is largely a relational and perceptual phenomenon. Conger and Kanungo (1987) agree with Willner and view leadership as an attribution phenomenon. The authors suggest that leadership, and specifically a charismatic one, is an attribution made by followers who observe certain behaviours on the part of the leader within organizational contexts. They propose that attribution of charisma to leaders depends on four interrelated components: the degree of discrepancy between the status quo and the future goal or vision championed by the leader; the use of innovation and unconventional means for achieving the desired change; a realistic assessment of environmental resources and constraints for bringing about such change; and the nature of articulation and impression management employed to inspire followers in the pursuit of the identified vision.

CURRENT RESEARCH ON LEADERSHIP IN THE MIDDLE EAST

In various ways, today's Middle East does not resemble either the era of the birth of Islam or the golden age where the Muslim states stretched from Morocco deep into India. It does however resemble, in terms of fragmentation and powerlessness, the era that followed the collapse of Baghdad at the hands of the invading Mongol forces in 1258 CE. In recent decades the region has undergone profound changes and, despite serious setbacks, holds the potential to be economically competitive, culturally vibrant, and politically inclusive. This makes research on leadership and organization professionally rewarding and intellectually interesting and challenging.

Most of the research on managerial leadership reveals that Arab managers are mostly consultative (Ali 1989; Ali and Swiercz 1986; Ali and Schaupp 1992; Muna 1980, 2003). Furthermore, Ali (2005) and Kozan (1993) find that there is a strong preference for the participative style among managers in the Middle East. Similarly, al-Jafary and Hollingsworth (1983) and Ali and al-Shakhis (1985) provide some evidence that Arab executives display a high preference for participative styles. Yousef (1998) found a preference for autocratic and consultative styles in the UAE. In Turkey, Kozan (1993) found that there is a discrepancy between managers' belief in participative practices and in employees' capacity for leadership and initiative. The author indicates that managers in Turkey usually resort to a dominating style in handling differences with subordinates. He postulates that traditional culture in Turkey reinforces a benevolent, autocratic style of leadership. Mellahi (2000) found that Arab managers adopt Western leadership values and simultaneously hang on to traditional leadership values. Similarly, Abdalla and al-Homoud (2001) found that, in the Arabian Gulf region, leaders endorse implicit leadership theory (the most desirable leadership dimensions are charismatic-value based, self-protective, and considerate). These leaders believe that integrity, competence, diplomacy, inspiration skills, and future and performance orientations contribute more positively to their success. These desirable leadership profiles are consistent with ideal Islamic values. Nevertheless, the authors argue that these desirable tendencies are different from what is practiced and what fits the local culture (such as autocratic values). It should be noted that these findings are consistent with the proposition of Khadra (1990) and Jasim (1987) that Arabs, in general, long for a prophetic leader and desire qualities that encompass participation, openness and transparency.

Most of the empirical findings, conceptual studies and commentaries, in the context of leadership in Islam, assert two things: that leaders are assumed to be consultative and participative, and that these leaders promote competency and performance. A consultative process is advocated in the Quran (42:38): 'This reward will be for those . . . who conduct their affairs with consultation among themselves,' and (3:158): 'Consult them in affairs [of moment].' This is viewed as participation in decision making (Arkoun 1986; Ashmawy 1992; Baali and Wardi 1981; Delo 1985; Hitti 1964; Jasim 1987). In fact, Jasim (1987) argues that consultation, during the early years of Islam, meant the full participation of the members of the community in the selection process. According to Jasim, during that time democratic debate and active collective involvement were the appropriate instruments for deciding who would be the ruler and shape the political system. Likewise, Armstrong (1992) indicates that elements of democratic practices are part of the Islamic faith and that the Prophet Muhammad set the stage for democratic practices unmatched during that era. She also argues that during the rule of the fourth Caliph, the leader was primarily responsible to the people and that in practice he was a democratic leader and on a par with his followers. For him, justice was the foundation of authority and prosperity: 'Justice is the mainstay of a nation.'

Whether in business or politics, the unity of contradiction is exemplified in leaders' behaviour and especially in decision-making. While people are generally infatuated with the ideal (that is, consultation and participation) and the prevailing social norms condone consultations, decisions are often made at the top. Muna (2003) observed that managers in the Gulf essentially retain the decision-making power. Previously, Al-Rasheed (2002) found that there is a clear centralization of decision at the top in most Jordanian organizations. Similarly, Sabri (1997, p. 205) found that it is a common practice in Jordan-based organizations, as in the rest of Arab organizations, for there to be a high concentration of authority at the top. Leaders in government and business organizations have developed their own mechanism for sustaining unity of contradictions: an ideal (Islamic principles) is held officially, but violated in practice. The leaders focus on projecting the image of consultation, caring and inclusiveness. They hope that neither their immediate subordinates nor the community at large will notice these contradictions. In the process, the leaders treat illusion as reality and begin to believe that they are literally representing the ideal form of leadership. This alternative view of reality is similar to what Child (1976) calls mental cheating. Leaders' behaviour, which remains strictly within the framework of the authoritarian system, seeks to disguise their authoritarian propensities by projecting a false image of idealism onto their subordinates and followers.

The above discussion and the survey of empirical studies demonstrates that, in terms of leadership, inconsistencies between the ideal and reality, and between what is practised and desirable, are common in the Middle East. Perhaps these contradictions may be responsible, in large part, for current economic and political stagnation and, consequently, for impairing organizational and national performance. Indeed, these contradictions may shed light on the nature of current business and political affairs and future trends in the Middle East. In fact, the apparent contradictions between the desire for inclusion and consultation and participative approaches and the authoritarian practices hold a key to understanding the current tension between followers and leaders and between governments and their own citizens, and to a large extent to understanding the nature of instability in the region and its accompanying semi-chronic crisis of identity that people in the region experience.

TYPOLOGY OF LEADERSHIP

In the Middle East people have traditionally attributed certain characteristics to leaders. Whether they agree or disagree with those in power, people develop their own expectations of what is right or wrong and who should be responsible and accountable. The absence of openness and tolerance, at organizational and national levels, neither conveys approval of authoritarian practices nor indicates that subordinates are indifferent and passive. In their collective experiences over centuries, individuals and groups in the region have constructed images of leaders in the context of their actions and relation to followers. These images are cognitively grouped into categories: *ahal alaqel* or *ahal alkher* (camp of reason – those who are inherently responsible and good) and *ahal al-sher* (camp of evil – those who are driven by selfish motives and hunger for power). The first include those who are called *musleh* (reformer, conciliator), *rahim* (merciful) *abkari* (genius), *azim* (great), and *feth* (distinctively competent and uniquely capable). These positive attributes are contrasted with their opposites, the second camp: *zhalim* (oppressor), *ghasi* (merciless), *ghabi* (idiot), *safah* (murderer), and *mutasaled* (suppressor).

In the last two centuries, due to interactions with, and openness to, Western countries and education, terms like democratic and autocratic have become popular in the media and general discourse. Nevertheless, native researchers have attempted to categorize leadership in terms that are relevant to history and culture. Khadra (1990) groups leaders into two categories: 'ordinary man' (caliphate model) and 'great man' (prophetic leader). Using these categories, Khadra attempts to capture both the reality of leadership in the Arab world and the aspiration and longing of the masses for exceptionally visionary leaders. These two categories are in line with what Jasim (1987) and others call dominating and inspiring leaders.

In a survey of groups and organizations in the Arab and Muslim worlds, Ali (2005, 2007) identifies four forms of leadership: autocratic, sheikocratic, tradition-guided (group-oriented), and spiritually enlightened. These leaders are found in most of the Middle East, but the degree and intensity of their presence varies from one country to another. Below is a brief definition of each.

Autocratic: Decisions are made at the top. There are strict rules and regulations regarding procedures and coordination. Subordinates are expected to do things according to specific guidelines. There are two commonly-found types of autocratic leaders: the first are those who are driven by the belief that efficiency is possible only through strict observation of procedures. These leaders believe in institutional set procedures, that subordinates must follow specified rules to perform tasks and that subordinates respond well to a leader who does not change his mind and has clear instructions. The second type of autocratic leader believes blindly in rules and regulations. They use elaborate rules to cover their incompetence and lack of confidence in their followers' ability to perform without fear. Under both situations, employees and workers exist to serve the organization's economic interests and the leader always plays a dominant role in designing organization mission and policies. Such leaders are common in public sectors and private organizations established by new graduates.

Sheikocratic: Leaders are driven by personal relations and place emphasis on open-door policy and caring for the welfare of subordinates inside and outside the organization. These leaders, too, set specified rules and policies. This type of leadership is a product of the interaction of a colonial bureaucratic, Ottoman autocratic system and paternalistic orientation and behaviour inherent in tribalism. Leaders attempt to maintain a fine balance between traditional values and norms and the demand of business for performance and efficient operations. The primary characteristics of Sheikocratic leadership are: hierarchical authority, rules and regulations contingent on the personality and power of the individuals who make them, an open-door policy, subordination of efficiency to personal relations and personal connections, indecisiveness in decision making, informality among lower-level managers and a generally patriarchal approach. Nepotism is often evident in selecting upper-level managers, but qualifications are emphasized in the selection of middle-and lower-level personnel. Furthermore, there is an apparent emphasis on unity of command, scalar principles, and division of labour. Like an autocratic organization, the executives consider the organization to be their fiefdom: an extension of their personal property and in the service of their interest and that of their extended family. This type of leadership was common in old bazaars and in businesses in the Gulf region which thrived from the 1960s to the 1980s.

Tradition-driven (group-oriented): Concerns for group harmony and the viability of the organization are not divorced. This type of leadership is common among small enterprises across Muslim countries. It is more likely that *ihsan* is present in design and conduct, but not as a result of conscious thinking and deep internalization of Islamic principles. Rather, it is because these leaders have learned, through upbringing, experience and observations of their forefathers and role models, what is sanctioned and not sanctioned by societal norms and that taking care of their fellow men ensures harmony and advances the welfare of the group. That is, these leaders know that their behaviour and actions are essentially good but might not be familiar with the theoretical reasoning or assumptions upon which these good actions are based. These leaders might make decisions at the top and centralize control and information but often maintain informality in operational aspects and conduct. They are found mostly in small and medium-sized business organizations in many parts of the Middle East.

Spiritually enlightened: Aligns organization interests with the welfare and viability of the community furthering the interests of the community; society at large is given high priority. There are a few leaders scattered throughout Muslim countries but mostly in business organizations. These leaders are guided by *ihsan* and general Islamic assumptions. Whether in politics or business, these leaders seek to take advantage of opportunities in business and the political arena, but are directly influenced by intrinsic motivation to pursue goodness and are guided by deeply held beliefs. Two-way communications, mutual trust and respect foster organizational arrangements and procedures that are flexible and informal.

The presence of these leaders varies according to the sector of enterprise and country. It is possible to suggest, however, that the first two are more common than the last two. Muna (2003) argues that there is a trend in the Gulf region, and to a degree in the Middle East in general, toward power sharing. This proposition is contingent on the interplay of various factors, chief among them the economic and business environment and politics. At the business level, economic openness, competition, interactions with foreign counterparts, and the rising influence of an educated professional class ease the transformation toward more democratic approaches. At the macro-political and social levels, the change is slow. The UN's *Arab Human Development Report 2004* underscored the essence of leadership and the importance of participative leadership in the region when it asserted (p. 4): 'Of all the impediments to an Arab renaissance, political restrictions on human development are the most stubborn. For that reason, this Report focuses on the acute deficit of freedom and good governance in the Arab world.' In fact, for the last five decades, there has been a consensus among Middle East experts that the absence of foresighted and visionary political leaders has made any positive change in the region an impossible task. This, however, is subject to change as younger generations long for change and economic opportunities corresponding with their educational achievements. Their aspiration for change arises from an increasing awareness of the extent of economic stagnation and freedom deficit and their consequences in the context of cultural renewal and the ability to be a vital contributor to civilization.

CONCLUSION

Islamic perspectives on leadership offer researchers and policy makers a powerful and practical framework for leadership and motivation. Indeed, these perspectives are in line with enlightened and humanistic views of leadership and, if applied wisely, could lead to a positive change in the Middle East. Of course, these views are subject to manipulation by those who are in power. Nevertheless, the fact that religious instructions and guidelines constitute a foundation for building a relevant and practical model for leadership reinforces the hope that people in the Middle East may have a promising opportunity to join the rest of the world community in contributing energetically and enthusiastically to world economic development and civilization.

In this chapter, we briefly outlined the nature of leadership in Islamic thought, the evolution of thinking regarding leadership, and the forms of leadership that appear to exist in the Middle East. Despite the fact that leadership practices in the region are not yet compatible with major developments in the world, there are significant trends in the region toward openness and power sharing. These trends and their underlying assumptions, along with forces in the global arena, make change not only desirable but also feasible. In today's politics and economic globalization, the region is situated at the crossroads and is torn by contradictory forces. Its natural and human resources enable it to be a powerful economic region. This, however, depends on the nature and quality of leadership in the years to come.

REFERENCES

Abdalla, I. and M. al-Homoud (2001), 'Exploring the implicit leadership theory in the Arabian Gulf states', *Applied Psychology*, **50** (4), 506–31.

Abu Dawod, E. (1996), *The Directory of Inquirers*, Jeddah, Saudi Arabia.

Ali, A. (1989), 'Decision style and work satisfaction of Arab executives', *International Studies of Management and Organization*, **19** (2), 22–37.

Ali, A. (2005), *Islamic perspectives on Management*, Cheltenham, UK and Northampton, MA, USA: Edward Elgar.

Ali, A. (2007), 'Organizing: structuring and methodology', keynote address at the International Conference on Management from Islamic Perspectives, Kuala Lumpur, 15–16 May.

Ali, A. and D. Schaupp (1992), 'Value systems as predictors of managerial decision styles of Arab executives', *International Journal of Manpower*, **13** (3), 19–26.

Ali, A. and M. al-Shakhis (1985), 'Administrators' attitudes and practices in Saudi Arabia', paper presented at the Annual meeting of the Midwest Academy of International Business, Chicago.

Ali, A. and M. Amirshahi (2002), 'The Iranian manager: work values and orientations', *Journal of Business Ethics*, **40**, 133–43.

Ali, A. and P. Swiercz (1986), 'The relationship between managerial decision styles and work satisfaction in Saudi Arabia', in E. Kaynak (ed.), *International Business in the Middle East*, New York: Walter de Gruyter.

Ali, I. (1989), *Nahjul Balagah*, translated by F. Ebeid (ed.), Beirut, Lebanon: Dar Alkitab al-Lubnani.

Arkoun, M. (1986), *The Historical Base of Arabic-Islamic Thought*, Beirut: Center for National Growth.

Armstrong, K. (1992), *Muhammad: A Biography of the Prophet*, New York: HarperCollins.

Asaf, M. (1987), *The Islamic Way in Business Administration*, Cairo: Ayen Shamis Library.

Ashmawy, M. (1992), *Islamic Caliphate*, Cairo: Siena Publisher.

Baali, F. and A. Wardi (1981), *Ibn Khaldun and Islamic Thought Style*, Boston, MA: Haland.

Blau, P. (1963), 'Critical remarks on Weber's theory of authority', *American Political Science Review*, **57**, 305–15.

Brodbeck, Felix et al. (2000), 'Cultural variation of leadership prototypes across 22 European countries', *Journal of Occupational & Organizational Psychology*, **73** (1), 1–29.

Child, J. (1976), 'Participation, organization, and social cohesion', *Human Relations*, **29** (5), 429–451.

Conger, J.A. and R.N. Kanungo (1987), 'Toward a behavioral theory of charismatic leadership in organizational settings', *Academy of Management Review*, **12**, 637–47.

Delo, B. (1985), *Mushama Fe Eadit Katabit al-Taryk al-Arabi [A Contribution in Rewriting Arab-Islamic History]*, Beirut: Dar al-Farabi.

Dow, T. (1969), 'The theory of charisma', *Sociological Quarterly*, **10**, 306–18.

Hitti, P. (1964), *History of the Arabs*, London: Macmillan.

Hofstede, G. (1976), 'Nationality and espoused values of managers', *Journal of Applied Psychology*, **61** (2), 148–55.

Hofstede, G. (1980), *Culture's Consequences: International Differences in Work-Related Values*, Beverly Hills, CA: SAGE Publications.

Hofstede, G. (1999), 'Problems remain, but theories will change: the universal and the specific in 21st century global management', *Organizational Dynamics*, **28** (1), 34–43.

Holy Qur'an (1989), *English Translation of the Meanings and Commentary*, al-Madinah al-Munawarah, Saudi Arabia: King Fahd Holy Qur'an Printing Complex.

House, R., M. Javidan and P. Dorfman (2001), 'Project GLOBE: an introduction', *Applied Psychology: An International Review*, **50** (4), 489–505.

Howell, J. M. and B. Shamir (2005), 'The role of followers in the charismatic leadership process: relationships and their consequences', *Academy of Management Review*, **30**, 96–112.

Hughes, R., R. Ginnett, and G. Curphy (2006), *Leadership*, Boston, MA: McGraw Hill.

Ibn Khaldun, Abd al-Rahman (1989), *The Magaddimah*, translated by F. Rosenthal and edited by N.J. Dawood, Princeton, NJ: Princeton University Press.

Ikhwan-us-Safa (1999), *Letters of Ikhwan-us-Safa*, vol 3, Beirut: Dar Sader.

Al-Jafary, A. and A.T. Hollingsworth (1983), 'An exploratory study of managerial practices in the Arabian Gulf region', *Journal of International Business Studies*, **14**, 143–52.

Jasim, A. (1987), *Muhammad: al-Hagigaha al-Kubra [Mohammed: the Greatest Truth]*, Beirut: Dar al-Andalus.

Khadra, B. (1990), 'The prophetic-caliphal model of leadership: an empirical study'. *International Studies of Management and Organization*, **20** (3), 37–51.

Kozan, K. (1993), 'Cultural and industrialization level influences on leadership attitudes for Turkish managers', *International Studies of Management and Organization*, **23** (3), 7–18.

Mansfield, Peter (1985), *The Arabs*, 3rd edn, London: Penguin.

Mellahi, K. (2000), 'Western MBA education and effective leadership values in developing countries: a study of Asian, Arab and African MBA graduates', *Journal of Transnational Management Development*, **5** (2), 59–73.

Muhammad Ali, M. (1977), *A Manual of Hadith*, New York: Olive Branch Press.

Muna, F. (1980), *The Arab Executives*, London: Macmillan Press.

Muna, F. (2003), *7 Metaphors*, Aldershot: Gower Publishing.

Al-Rasheed, A. (2002), 'Structure of Jordanian business organizations: managers' attitudes towards formalization and centralization and factors affecting them', *Dirast, Administrative Sciences*, **30** (1), 217–35.

Sabri, H. (1997), 'The impact of the national culture on organizational structure and culture', PhD dissertation, University of Leeds.

Shaw, J. B. (1990), 'A cognitive categorization model for the study of intercultural management', *Academy of Management Review*, **15**, 626–45.

Stogdill, R. (1974), *Handbook of Leadership: A Survey of the Literature*, New York: Free Press.

UN (2005), *The Arab Development Report 2004*, New York: United Nations Development Programme.

Willner, A. (1984), *The Spellbinders: Charismatic Political Leadership*, New Haven, CT: Yale University Press.

Yousef, D.A. (1998), 'Predictors of decision-making styles in a non-Western country', *Leadership & Organizational Development Journal*, **19** (7), 366–73.

4. Leadership in the UAE

Abubakr M. Suliman and Rehana Hayat

INTRODUCTION

The United Arab Emirates (UAE) as a modern nation came into being following Britain's 1968 announcement of its decision to withdraw from its colonial holdings East of Suez within three years. Up to this date, Britain had been the dominant foreign power in the region for over 200 years (Crystal 2011), concluding a series of treaties with local rulers including the Treaty of Maritime Peace in Perpetuity (1853) and exclusive agreements for the defence and foreign affairs of what had become known as the Trucial States.

With Britain's withdrawal, the seven Emirates of the Trucial States (Abu Dhabi, Dubai, Ajman, Fujairah, Sharjah, Ras al-Khaimah and Umm al-Qaiwain) became the federal nation that is the UAE. In the context of the region, the politics of the UAE has been relatively stable: Sheikh Zayed came to power in Abu Dhabi in a widely supported palace coup in 1966, and Sharjah has seen power disputed in 1972 and 1987, but recent successions have been smoother (Crystal 2011; see also Milton-Edwards 2006) despite the recent resurrection of the succession dispute in Ras al-Khaimah (Kerr 2010). The UAE has also been fortunate in its natural resources, with around 9 per cent of world oil resources (see Chapter 1, Table 1.6). However, this has led to particular challenges in other ways, especially in dealing with large numbers of migrant workers – up to 80 per cent of the population (Davidson 2008; UNDP 2009) – a challenge that will be discussed in more detail later in this chapter. Also, the very federal nature of the UAE leads to further strains, with a disparity in oil reserves, political power and development.

This chapter will critically examine the manner in which strong political leadership in the UAE has enabled the young nation to rise to these challenges. It provides an in-depth review of leadership practices in the country, focusing on the thoughts and practices of the nation's leaders and assessing how they themselves have led organizations and economic transformation, developed leadership potential and fostered community improvements and advances in society. The chapter also explores leadership in the UAE business education sectors and looks at leadership development challenges for the future as set out in the World Economic Forum scenario report (WEF 2007). Finally, the chapter provides an overview of the particular challenges facing women and of women's leadership in the community. The importance of women as inspirational leaders is illustrated in studies of two women leaders. Sheikha Lubna in particular has acted as a champion of business and political leadership worldwide. In contrast, Sheikha Fatima has promoted women's leadership role in building family communities, underpinned by Islamic cultural values.

It should be noted that, in general, role models in the domestic and workplace contexts include both genders while those in the national or international context are exclusively male. This aspect is worthy of further analysis in relation to cultural and religious perspectives (Metcalfe 2010).

POLITICAL AND ECONOMIC ENVIRONMENT

The United Arab Emirates is a member of the Gulf Cooperation Council (GCC) along with Saudi Arabia, Kuwait, Bahrain, Qatar and Oman. A young nation, it is characterized by rapid ongoing development across all sectors of its society. The population of the country has increased continuously since federation, from 500 000 in 1975 to 4.1 million in 2005, and is expected to reach 5.3 million by 2015 (UNDP 2007). At the same time the seven small, impoverished desert principalities have been transformed into a modern state with a high standard of living, an advanced educational system and a cutting-edge infrastructure. This could not have been achieved without the inspirational leadership of the late President His Highness Shaykh Zayed bin Sultan al-Nahyan, who led the country from its formation in 1971 until his death in November 2004 (Davidson 2009).

UAE comprises the Emirates of Abu Dhabi, Dubai, Sharjah, Ajman, Fujairah, Umm al-Qaiwain and Ras al-Khaimah (Ras al-Khaimah, after initially holding out, joined the union in 1972). The new federal system included an independent judiciary with the Federal Supreme Court at its apex, a Council of Ministers, the Federal National Council (FNC), and a Federal Supreme Council (FSC), the paramount policy-making body (Milton-Edwards 2006).

The FSC consists of the rulers of each of the seven Emirates and a President and Vice President are elected from among them for a five year term: however, by informal agreement, the presidency remains with the ruler of Abu Dhabi and the vice presidency and position of Prime Minister with the ruler of Dubai. One issue of contention is that Abu Dhabi and

Dubai each have the power of veto on substantive issues (Crystal 2011, p. 189). The Council of Ministers, or Cabinet, includes the usual complement of ministerial portfolios and is headed by a Prime Minister, chosen by the President in consultation with his colleagues on the Supreme Council. The Prime Minister, currently the Vice President, selects the ministers, who may be drawn from any of the Federation's component Emirates, although the more populous Emirates have generally provided more cabinet members (Metcalfe 2010).

According to Articles 120 and 121 of the Constitution, the federal authorities are responsible for foreign affairs; security and defence; nationality and immigration issues; education; public health; currency; postal, telephone and other communications services; air traffic control and licensing of aircraft; and a number of other topics specifically prescribed, including labour relations, banking, delimitation of territorial waters and extradition of criminals.

The success of the UAE is always assumed to be attributable to the political stability of the country and visionary view of its leaders (Bin Khirbash 2005). The vision is that of breaking down barriers to the operation of markets, openness and competition and the strategy is one of economic diversification and regional and international economic and financial integration.

Under Sheikh Zayed's leadership the UAE was able to develop a diversified economy with one of the world's highest mean standards of living. Many of its petrodollars have been used to build infrastructure and to broaden the country's economy. The market-oriented economic policies that the UAE has implemented for the last four decades have promoted a liberal business and economic environment and expanded the role of the private sector in the economy. They have helped to diversify the range of economic activity, reducing vulnerability to energy price shocks and volatility, and strengthening the position of the UAE as a regional trade and financial hub (Davidson 2008a, 2008b, 2009; Milton-Edwards 2009; UNDP 2009).

Table 4.1 presents a summary of the country's labour force by economic sector. The majority of the UAE's labour force is employed by the private sector which is heavily dominated by the trades and services. The Dubai International Financial Centre (DIFC) was recently established as part of the UAE's strategy to position itself as a globally recognized hub for institutional finance and as the regional gateway for capital and investment to and from the Middle East.

For example, re-export of goods is the mainstay of the trading system, although the provision of top-quality services abroad and the sale of domestically produced non-oil goods is of growing importance. The value

Table 4.1   Employment and unemployment rates in the UAE

			Items			
Unemployment rate			Employment by economic activity			
Unemployed people (thousand) 1996-2005	Total (% of labour force) 1996–2005	Female (% of male rate) 1996–2005	Total (thousand) 1996–2005	Agri-culture (%) 1996–2005	Industry (%) 1996–2005	Services (%) 1996–2005
41	2.3	118	1779	8	33	59

Source: The United Nations Development Programme (UNDP), Report of Human Development of 2007/2008.

of the UAE's recorded re-exports in 2006 was around US$46 billion, compared with US$56.4 billion in crude oil sales.

The UAE has enjoyed buoyant growth in general, but has, along with the rest of the world, been significantly affected by the global recession. Initial projections indicated a contraction in the economy of up to 4 per cent in 2009 (Kawach 2009) with a slowdown in construction affecting Dubai in particular and an OPEC mandated reduction in oil output. In the event, the economy slowed but maintained a growth rate of 1.3 per cent in 2009 with forecasts of growth for 2010 in the range of 2 to 3.2 per cent (Hall and Fattah 2010). This contrasts with an increase in GDP from 2007 to 2008 of 7.4 per cent to a high of Dh535.3bn (approximately US$145.8 bn) (Kawach 2009). This economic strength and resilience is often attributed to Sheikh Zayed and his successor Sheikh Khalifa. Sheikh Zayed in particular, as father of the nation, embraced the challenge of not only building a nation from disparate states, but also of integrating UAE into the global political economy (Davidson 2009).

SOCIAL, LABOUR MARKET AND GOVERNMENT INSTITUTIONS IN THE UAE

The United Nations Development Programme (UNDP), in the Human Development Report 2007/2008, placed the UAE among the 55 high income countries (GNI per capita of US$10 726 or more in 2005). Table 4.2 presents the summary of the human development index for the UAE.

In 2009 the UNDP Human Development Report placed the UAE second only to Qatar in terms of migrant population as a share of total population. Expatriate population constitutes about 80 per cent of the

Table 4.2   Human development index (2007/2008) – UAE

Item	Index
Human development index (HDI) – 2005	0.868
Life expectancy at birth (years) – 2005	78.3
Adult literacy rate (% aged 15 and above) 1995 -2005	88.7
Combined gross enrolment ratio for primary, secondary and tertiary education (%) – 2005	59.9
GDP per capita (PPP US$) – 2005	25,514
Life expectancy index	0.889
Education index	0.791
GDP index	0.925
GDP per capita (PPP US$) rank minus HDI rank	−12

Source: The United Nations Development Programme (UNDP), Report of Human Development of 2007/2008.

total, originating from, for example, the Indian subcontinent, other Arab countries and the Philippines. Expatriate labour can generally be classified in two sections: educated and skilled employees primarily recruited to occupy leadership and management positions in public and private sectors; and unskilled labour performing casual tasks such as construction labourers, office porters and caretakers. The two groups are often recruited from different nations of origin. Since high diversity of the workplace is one of the major features of the UAE labour market, organizations are in continuous search for effective strategies to manage it. According to Mr Rodney Hills (Managing Director, Hillcrest, UAE), the multiculturalism of the UAE labour market can be a competitive advantage (AMEinfo 2005a). Unlike the situation in the 1970s, from the 1990s onwards the UAE labour market witnessed a surplus of unskilled manpower. In order to reorganize the country's work force the Ministry of Labour and Social Affairs started a major campaign to monitor and regulate the labour market, aiming to discourage a further influx of unskilled employees from other countries. In both 1996 and 2007 the Government granted an amnesty to expatriate labourers working and staying illegally in the country. All affected workers were given a chance to correct their situations. Following this amnesty a considerable number of them either obtained new employment under a sponsor or left the country without being fined or subject to other sanction (Suliman 2006).

Local (Emirati) labour represents a small proportion of the work force; estimates as to the actual size vary depending on the database used, but the range is 10 to 19 per cent, most employed in administrative tasks that

Table 4.3   UAE labour force by economic sector

Labour force by economic sector(a) *Thousands*	2002	2003	2004	2005	2006
Agriculture, livestock & fisheries	163	166	169	191	193
Mining	5	5	6	5	6
Oil	27	28	30	33	33
Manufacturing industries	276	299	319	333	362
Electricity, gas & water	27	28	29	34	34
Construction	420	474	498	529	647
Trade	511	549	589	612	643
Restaurants & hotels	95	99	110	115	124
Transport & communications	131	143	148	161	174
Real estate & business services	64	67	74	77	84
Social & private services	91	99	107	114	121
Financial institutions	26	26	27	31	37
Government services	237	250	265	283	284
Household services	198	200	200	220	226
Total civilian employment	2176	2334	2461	2623	2844

Source: IMF, Statistical Appendix.
(a) Data do not include employees in the armed forces or visitors to the country.

are favoured over technical and manual roles. According to the UNDP
Human Development Report 2007/2008, the total number employed for
the period 1996–2005 was 1 779 000. Of these locals, 59 per cent work in
services, 33 per cent in industry and 8 per cent in agriculture (Table 4.3).
The majority of the employed locals work in state and semi-state sectors.
They often cite many reasons for preferring state jobs over those offered by
the private sector, for example higher salaries, greater benefits, job security and shorter working hours. According to Suliman (2006), one of the
most important issues that discourages locals from taking up employment
in the private sector is the compensation. It is not only weak compared
to the public sector, but considerable numbers of organizations in the
private sector either delay or fail to pay employees' salaries. UAE nationals are reluctant to take up employment in the private sector and they will
certainly avoid manual or unskilled jobs or those that lack status (Simadi
2006). They are less likely to seek employment in the private sector unless
they are promised managerial positions with high salary and acceptable
working conditions (Ali and Schaupp 1992; Atiyyah 1996; Wilkins 2001).
Unemployment for the period 1996-2005 was 41 000, representing 2.3
per cent of the labour force, as shown in Table 4.1. It is suggested that

Table 4.4 Emiratization programme outcomes in Dubai Islamic Bank

Item	2004	2005	2006
Staff strength	822	1204	1507
Local talent	39%	43%	47%
Expatriate Staff	61%	57%	54%
Achievement	Emiratization HR Award 2004 (Dubai, Sharjah and GCC)	Emiratization HR Award 2005 (Sharjah)	Emiratization HR Award 2006 (Sharjah)

Source: Nauman, T. (2007), A Winning Emiratization Unit, The Middle East HR Summit, 4-8 November, Abu-Dhabi National Exhibition Centere, Abu-Dhabi, UAE.

unemployment is now a significant economic factor, but no later data is available to corroborate this assertion.

The response of the UAE Government to shortages in skills, increasing numbers of expatriates and rising unemployment, especially among males of 18 to 24 years of age, has been to introduce the Emiratization, Development and Labour Growth Policy. Emiratization of the work force has been pursued aggressively by the Ministry of Labour and Social Affairs over the last two years with some success in sectors such as telecommunications and banking. This process of Emiratization aims to gradually replace the heavy dependence on foreign labour with Emiratis. Dubai Islamic Bank (DIB), for example, in collaboration with a local banking institute, introduced a new training programme called *Qiyadee* (leader). The 14-month programme targets UAE nationals to develop their skills and knowledge in order to assume leadership positions in the bank, the initial outcome of which was the appointment of 15 branch managers (Nauman 2007). Table 4.4 presents the outcomes of the DIB Emiratization Programme.

To provide the necessary support for the Emiratization Programme, many public and private organizations were developed. The majority of these organizations specialize in providing intensive and constructive training to the locals in giving them an insight into the firm's operations. One of the well-known organizations in this field is the National Human Resources Development and Employment Authority (Tanmia). Tanmia is a specialized federal organization set up by a Presidential Decree in November 1999 (Metcalfe 2010; Metcalfe and Rees 2010). It plays a major role in the preparation of locals for employment in both public and private sectors. Tanmia is engaged in varied activities and services such as providing career planning and advice and assisting with job search and interview techniques. Additionally, the Government launched the Public Authority for National Development and Employment (PANDE), an autonomous body under the supervision of the Minister of Labour and Social Affairs. Established in mid-1999, the authority is in charge of matching the real needs of employers to the qualifications of UAE nationals seeking employment (Davidson 2008a, 2008b).

To encourage the demand for non-state jobs among locals and to speed up Emiratization of the work force, the government introduced a new scheme for the provision of benefits. Begun in September 1999, the new scheme states that UAE nationals working for private companies are entitled to the same social security and pension benefits as UAE nationals working for the government. Under the new national pension and social security scheme, which took effect in the public sector in May 1999, nationals who have contributed to the scheme will be eligible for retirement benefits, disability benefits and compensation on death in service. Current end-of-service entitlements for government employees have been transferred to the new programme. Pension and social security schemes for expatriates vary from organization to organization and from job to job, but substantial government changes have assisted growth in support services for job creation and diversification (Davidson 2008a, 2009).

In summary, the UAE has benefited from strong leadership, positively associated with the inspirational leadership of the late Sheikh Zayed, in developing a strong economy, diversifying that economy and taking steps actively to manage the transition to decreased reliance on migrant labour. In the sections that follow we outline leadership characteristics in the UAE and how they can be seen in the light of dominant Western ideas and also in the context of economic development in the UAE and emerging concepts of local, specifically Arab, leadership.

LEADERSHIP OVERVIEW

Leadership research has moved on from early studies which focused on individual characteristics and simple assessments of transformational and transactional leadership. A recent trend is the examination of socio-cultural factors as they are assumed to have an impact on the leadership styles such as charismatic and spiritual leadership, specifically in Islamic states. There is a general agreement among researchers that leadership behaviour is determined culturally or socially and hence varies clearly from context to context (e.g. Alder 1991; Ali, Tagi and Krishnan 1997; Randeree and Chaudhry 2007). According to Shamim (2007), the literature on business ethics very elaborately discusses the origin, content and significance of moral values, but also admits that people do not always live up to the moral standards they hold; that is, they do not always do what they believe is morally right. He argued that the moral or immoral behaviour of people who make up a business organization is mainly influenced by four factors: the legal system under which they operate; organizational culture and environment in which they work; social setup and human relations under which they live; and individual bent of mind and preferences. Underlying these factors is the role of the leader in being able to engender a harmonious working environment, to express humility and to encourage consensual modes of social relations in the organization.

UAE is a Muslim state where the social life is highly influenced by the values and culture of Islam, the official religion of the country. The inherited Arab culture, traditions, customs and morals also play some role in influencing the daily life of UAE citizens. As in other Arab countries, the family is the cornerstone of social life in the Emirates. According to Ali (2005), 'the family and other social institutions still command the respect of almost all individuals [in Arabia] regardless of their social backgrounds'. Simadi (2006) assesses the influence of socio-demographic factors, such as gender, citizenship, income, education, occupation and family size on values. The results indicate that religious and cognitive values were prioritized by the respondents and that gender, income levels, family size and father's occupation were the most important factors influencing values. Likewise, Agnala (1998, p. 179) argued that 'the extended family, clan, tribe, village and Islamic religion play major roles in community life and interpersonal relationships'. Agnala added that family ties, sectarianism and ideological affiliation affect many work-related decisions such as recruitment and promotion.

Hendrik (1997) examined the role of tribal and kinship ties in the politics of the UAE. According to him several factors – including the small population of nationals, the relatively vast reserves of oil, the history of the region, and provisions in the federal constitution for the autonomy of the constituent Emirates – have combined to allow tribal and kinship ties to play an unusually prominent role in the politics of the country, even in comparison to similar oil-rich, traditional Arab monarchies, dominating the internal struggle for political power. Ali, Azim and Krishnan (1995) investigated work value systems and their relationships to decision styles across indigenous and expatriate managers in the UAE. They found that outer-directed values are the primary work values in the Emirates. This means that 'traditional' aspects of conducting business are the norm and consequently trust, personal relationships and social networks are key to effective business development and growth and multinational corporations may therefore find it useful to recruit individuals to manage UAE businesses who display tribalistic, sociocentric or conformist values. In

Table 4.5 Aspects of value orientation – UAE society

Aspect	Characteristic
General ethical orientation	Personalistic and particularistic
Authority	Highly respected
Interpersonal relationships	Group oriented
Status and prestige	Very high concern
Social structure	High degree of vertical (kinship) and lateral (class) stratification.

Source: Suliman, A. (2006)

addition, certain personnel policies related to training and promotion should be developed to take advantage of diversity while enhancing the competitive position of MNCs in the UAE market. The value orientation of UAE society is summarized in Table 4.5 which shows that familial and tribal affiliation tends to occupy the priority in most Emiratis' identification hierarchy.

LEADERSHIP RELATIONS AND PROCESSES IN THE UAE

While the previous discussion explored the effect of tribal and family relationships on all aspects of home and organizational life, there is surprisingly little literature (at least in English) that examines the unique characteristics of UAE leadership. For example, 'there has been no previous empirical evidence to examine the relationship among transformational and transactional leadership, knowledge sharing and organizational effectiveness in Dubai' (Behery 2008, p. 227). Likewise, Politis (2003) stated that unlike the Western world, no studies in the Arab world had examined the relationship between various leadership styles and Quality Function Deployment (QFD).

In their study of value systems as predictors of the managerial decision styles of Arab executives, Ali and Schaupp (1992) found that the consultative style was predominant in their sample. Ali (1993) also found that Arab executives are highly committed to a consultative style. Ali, Azim and Krishnan (1995) investigated the decision styles among expatriate and indigenous managers in the UAE. They found that Arab expatriates and national managers display a high preference for participative and pseudo-consultative styles, whereas foreign expatriates show a high commitment to consultative style. Yousef (1998a) tested organizational culture and level of technology used in the organization roles in predicting decision-making styles in the UAE. Results showed that organizational culture and level of technology used in the organization, and the decision maker's education and management levels, are good predictors of decision-making styles. Findings also indicate that a tendency towards the participative style prevails among Arab, young, middle management and highly educated managers. Yousef (1998b) studied the prevailing leadership style in the UAE, explored the correlates of perceived leadership style, and determined the most effective leadership style in the Emirates. He argued that leaders should adopt a leadership style that accommodates subordinates' personal attributes as well as organizational factors in order to achieve organizational goals and objectives effectively. Yousef found that the most common and effective leadership style in a non-Western, culturally mixed environment such as the UAE is a consultative leadership style. Moreover, leaders' personal attributes and organizational factors were found to have a significant correlation with leadership style. This was ultimately congruent with authority structures prevalent in ruling tribes.

Behery (2008) examined leadership, knowledge sharing and organizational benefits within the UAE. His results revealed that the two components of active exception and passive avoidant leadership were negatively correlated to service quality. Moreover, Jabnoun and al-Ghasyah (2005) attempted to identify leadership styles that support the implementation of ISO 9000:2000. Five styles of leadership were used in the study: intellectual stimulation, charisma, empowerment and contingent reward, avoidance, and active management by exception. Each of these (except for avoidance) was found to support the implementation process. Politis (2003) surveyed 104 managers from a wide variety of UAE industries involved in quality management programmes in order to investigate the role of various leadership styles in predicting QFD. Findings indicated that open and collaborative QFD methodologies are supported by leadership styles that involve human interaction and encourage participative decision making. Randeree and Chaudhry (2007) examined employee perceptions of leadership styles within infrastructure development in Dubai. The results revealed that consensus and team management leadership were felt to be predominant in the industry and that employees have shown a preference for working under these two leadership styles.

It is clear that the findings of most leadership studies conducted in the UAE reflect the culture and values of the country and the region. As mentioned earlier, UAE is a small Muslim state that is heavily dominated by tradition, by the values and culture of Islam, and by regional culture. It is clear that the consultative, transactional and transformational styles of leadership are favoured by employees in this part of the world. In this context, Jabnoun (2005, p. 199) argued that the leader should consult his or her followers when taking important decisions that may affect them and that 'the required leadership skills are not only technical. As a matter of fact the behavioural skills are the critical ones.' It is clear that most local and non-local leaders in the country have learned some lessons from the leadership style of the founder of the UAE, Sheikh Zayed. At the horizon of the Emirates we can see the Islamic leader's role in helping and teaching with humility:

> H.H. Sheikh Zayed used to anonymously send funds to various people and organizations across the globe without any discrimination. Medicines were used to send various countries. Once it was sending it to Bosnia through Serbia. Serbian forces normally used to snatch the medicine and when it came to his attention, he said compassionately, 'Those who steal the medicines are equally needy. In the next truckload, send medicine for them too. We will not only tender help to them but also stop them from becoming thieves.' (Mustufa 19 December 2007)

This tendency to favour open, participative and consultative leadership mirrors the current call to focus on ethics and CSR and to encourage a people-centred approach to management. Significantly however, in Arab culture it is *followership* that is also significant (Western 2008; Collinson 2006). Contradicting Collinson's view, appointed leaders in Muslim cultures are accepted as heroic and exemplify characteristics that are visionary and for the greater moral good; otherwise they would not be accepted as a Muslim leader.

WOMEN AND LEADERSHIP IN THE UAE

The UAE is committed to the enhancement of the status of women and the country's Constitution guarantees equal rights for both men and women. The basic rights of women are enshrined in *Shari'a*. To encourage women to play a full role in society, the UAE Women's Federation, headed by H.H. Sheikha Fatima bint Mubarak, mother of the country's President, H.H. Sheikh Khalifa bin Zayed bin Sultan al Niehyan, was founded in 1975.

Female participation in the work force more than tripled from 16 000 workers in 1995 to 50 000 in 2003 – approximately 10 per cent and 23 per cent of the work force, respectively (UNDP 2009). This increase was the result of significant economic and social changes associated with the process of development in the UAE. These changes have culturally changed family and female attitudes toward work and solidified women's position in the domestic economy. Looking at growth in the participation of Emirati nationals in the work force, female participation grew almost three times as fast as male, 16.7 per cent versus 6.1 per cent, respectively (Khaleej Times 2005). Despite this steady growth, the participation of females in the labour force remained hampered by some socio-cultural factors. According to Suliman (2006) there are many reasons for this but three major reasons can be highlighted: UAE society remains male dominated; some organizations are still reluctant to employ women, stereotyping them as less efficient, demanding more and giving less, and unable to work under pressure; finally, some women prefer to remain job seekers than take certain jobs, for example teaching jobs are favoured over nursing. Similarly, in his study of expatriate acculturation in Arab Gulf countries, Atiyyah argued that:

> Despite an increase in the number of female graduates and calls for lifting or relaxing restrictions on female employment, their participation in the labour market of Gulf Arab countries has remained marginal. Resistance to wide-scale female employment on moral or religious grounds is still strong, especially among traditional people. (1996, p. 39)

Women are increasingly entering the work force in Arab states and rising to leadership positions in the public and private sectors (Salloum 2003). They do face barriers: while highly educated, women lack the confidence to enter previously segregated work environments, are offered few training opportunities and are encouraged to leave work if they marry. Traditional business research has neglected women and leadership in the Arab world, preferring to talk about leadership in the UAE in gender-neutral terms. Al-Lamki (1999) has challenged the stereotypical view that Arab women are overwhelmingly repressed in the Arab workplace and Arab societies in general. This repression is often attributed to the dominant Islamic culture of the UAE and Arab societies in general. Harold, in a 2006 study of the leadership attitudes of university students in Abu Dhabi, found that one of the most pervasive themes within participants' perspectives on leadership was the impact of local cultural practices and of Islamic beliefs. While the participants' personal statements identified with and endorsed many aspects of international theories on leadership they consistently did so within the framework of their own cultural context. One example of this was a participant's comment on leadership: 'I strongly believe that leadership is the art of helping others to help themselves in achieving common ends in a collaborative manner without forgetting individuals, groups and the society's needs with the moral purpose. I help others to improve their lives because I will get rewards from nobody but God in my life and in the day after' (Harold 2006).

Consequently, many women find Islam empowering and feel that their leadership contribution can be made via social and community development. At the same time, UAE's leadership realizes that in order to fulfil their vision of developing the UAE into the high-tech hub of the Middle East, they need to accept that women should be valued, not just as wives and mothers, but as potential leaders in the workplace (UN 2009). Sheikh Zayed is often quoted as saying:

> Islam gives women their rightful status, and encourages them to work in all sectors, as long as they are afforded the appropriate respect. The basic role of women is the upbringing of children, but over and above that, we have to support and encourage any woman who chooses to perform other functions. (Ministry of Information and Culture 2002)

The status of women in the Middle East in general is discussed in more detail in Chapter 13 of this volume, but with around half of the country's potential work force of nationals being women, and with thousands of young female as well as male university graduates now entering the job market, the UAE's women can be found playing an increasingly important role in commerce and the health services, in education and banking and in government and administration (Neal, Finlay and Tansey 2005).

WOMEN'S LEADERSHIP ROLE IN THE UAE

In this section we aim to illustrate the different and evolving role of women's inspirational leadership in the UAE through case studies of two prominent women leaders. A woman's role is still defined principally in accordance with her family responsibilities. However, women have been afforded enhanced opportunities in education, so that there are more female graduates than male. Women also have higher literacy levels (DWE 2009) and have actively pursued entrepreneurial business start-ups. A key development is the inclusion of women in the Federal National Council (FNC), the role of which is discussed earlier in this chapter. In 2006 seats were reserved for women and as a consequence women now account for 22 per cent of the lower house, as discussed further in Chapter 13.

The case studies presented concern two influential women in the UAE: first, the wife of the late President Sheikh Zayed, Her Excellency Sheikha Fatima bint Mubarak; second, Her Excellency Sheikha Lubna al-Qasimi. These two women are noteworthy for inspiring young women all over the UAE in different ways. Sheikha Fatima is well known for her tireless work in the establishment of the Women's Federation, which has been vital in implementing Sheikh Zayed's vision of a modern society based on Arab and Islamic traditions, recognizing that it was only by organizing women that real progress could be made. In contrast, Sheikha Lubna worked her way up from being an IT programmer to earn her title as United Arab Emirates' Minister for Economy and Planning and Chief Executive Officer of Tejari, the Middle East's premier electronic business-to-business marketplace and is now Minister for Foreign Affairs. These two women have worked tirelessly to foster the recognition of the contribution that women can make to the future of UAE society.

SHEIKHA FATIMA BINT MUBARAK

> Sheikha Fatima Bint Mubarak is a major force for development and progress in our country. Her energy, her vision and her commitment to comprehensive and sustained development have enabled all of us to appreciate the role of women as leaders in our society. H.H. Sheikha Fatima has been a role model to thousands of women across the Arab world who drew inspiration from her efforts in various societal aspects like well being of children, orphans, aged and the disabled. (Hussain al Mahmoudi, Shell External Affairs Manager)

Sheikha Fatima founded the country's first women's society, the Abu Dhabi Women's Society, in 1972. The success of the Abu Dhabi association led to the creation of the Women's Development Societies throughout the Emirates. These societies were subsequently linked together under the UAE Women's Federation which was established in 1975, again headed by Sheikha Fatima. To date, the Federation has played a highly significant role in assisting the women of the UAE to realize their full potential. Sheikha Fatima sees the activation of women's societies' role in the Gulf civil society as one of the main ways to widen women's participation in political life.

The UAE Women's Federation later became the Royal Women's Union (RWU), an autonomous body with a total of 31 branches across the six constituent societies, many operating in remote areas of the country. Activities undertaken by the individual branches include illiteracy eradication, nursery classes, housekeeping, dressmaking and handicraft classes, art classes, child care advice, health education, vocational training projects, job placement programmes, religious education, welfare assistance, family advice including mediation services, as well as a busy calendar of social, cultural and sporting activities.

Sheikha Fatima has always been a keen supporter of Emirati women and the role that they can play in modern UAE society. 'Woman in the UAE today is occupying the position of a university professor, doctor, engineer, lawyer, teacher, journalist, and taking up senior level ranks as a minister, under secretary and an active member of the Federal National Council,' Sheikha Fatima said in a keynote address at the opening of the second regional conference for woman parliamentarians and decision makers in the GCC countries (Emirates News Agency, WAM). Sheikha Fatima has been an active advocate on issues related to women's equality and women's rights. She has campaigned to increase the employment of women in Government sectors and to ensure suitable workplace conditions for working mothers. Her efforts have put women on the path to gain access and participate in the political and economic institutions of the nation.

Sheikha Fatima has shown unwavering leadership and commitment to the cause of women's empowerment, gender equality and the welfare of the community at large. Through the Women's Federation she has advanced the status of women in society and helped them to achieve their full potential. She consolidated the women's movement and gave it a sense of direction at the national level and later led the RWU into involvement in regional and global, as well as local, issues (AMEinfo 2005).

The RWU however primarily adheres to its family role and focuses on ensuring that women support community social development agendas and especially children's affairs. This ethics of care role is also demonstrated by her support of charitable organizations and relief efforts. She has directly supported the Mothers' Council of the Abu Dhabi Educational Zone in its development of the Emirate's education programme and provided financial support to the Centres for the Handicapped throughout the UAE. Beyond the country's borders, Sheikha Fatima sent relief supplies to Iraqi women and children, to Albania for Kosovar mothers and children in the refugee camp established by the UAE in Kukes, and also assisted Albanian families accommodating Kosovar refugee families.

Sheikha Fatima has also supported the people of Palestine, making donations to the Palestinian Heritage Centre, to handicapped Palestinian children and to establishing a Sheikha Fatima Centre for the Rehabilitation of Palestinian Handicapped Children in Hebron. In May 2001 Sheikha Fatima also donated Dh 300 000 for distribution to Palestinian families in the refugee camps and in August the same year Dh 2 million to Palestinian families whose houses were destroyed by the Israelis. Over more than a quarter of a century, Sheikha Fatima has also supported centres and institutes for the handicapped in the Arab world, Asia and Africa; organizations caring for women and children; victims of the conflict in Southern Lebanon; and humanitarian and relief projects in Yemen, Turkey, Saudi Arabia, Egypt and Jordan (Emirates News Agency, WAM n.d.).

Through her campaigning efforts and charitable actions, Sheikha

Fatima has played an important role in realizing her late husband's vision of the equality of men and women in terms of rights and obligations and the important role that women can play in the nation's development. She has had an inspirational role in demonstrating that Emirati women can play a significant and active part in developing a more egalitarian and supportive society and can take an active role in the region and beyond. It is important to note, however, that this role essentializes the different capabilities of male and female. Empathy, ethics, sensitivity and maternal qualities are central to Sheikha Fatima's leadership role. This in no way diminishes her contribution, as in Islamic belief, sexual difference accords balance and harmony, each of the sexes playing equal but different, complementary roles.

SHEIKHA LUBNA AL-QASIMI

I am a role model for women. I am out there as a woman who achieved so much in life. People respect us (women) highly . . . seeing us . . . what we represent for our country. . . For them, it is a phenomenal representation of our country. All they know is that ours is a very tight culture . . . very conservative society. But when we go out there, we become ambassadors for ourselves in here. (George 2001)

Sheikha Lubna holds a Bachelor of Science degree from California State University of Chico, and an Executive MBA from the American University of Sharjah. She worked with Datamation, where as she puts it: 'I was the only local, the only woman in the team' (George, 2001).

She went on to become senior manager of the information systems department at the Dubai Ports Authority. By the time she became the first woman cabinet minister in the UAE, as the Minister for Economy and Planning, she had more than 15 years of information technology management experience in the Middle East region. She was founding CEO of Tejari, the online business-to-business (B2B) marketplace launched in 2000 (Tejari n.d.). Since then she has headed the Dubai e-government executive team responsible for instituting e-government initiatives throughout the public sector (Womenone). In addition, she has accumulated numerous awards and distinctions, among them Great Britain's House of Lords: Entrepreneurship Award, 2004 and the American Business Award from the American Business Council of Dubai and the Northern Emirates, 2004.

Under her leadership Tejari has also been recognized on multiple occasions as a leader in e-commerce, for example by Business.Com/Visa: (Best B2B Marketplace Site, 2000; MEED Awards: IT Project of the Year, 2002; Gulf Marketing Review: Gulf Brand of the Decade Award (E-Commerce and IT Category), 2003; World Summit for Information Society Geneva, Best eContent Provider in e-business, 2003; UAE Super Brands Council, Super Brand of 2003; and Arab Technology Awards – Outstanding Contribution to E-Commerce.

Sheikha Lubna is aware of herself as a role model for young UAE women and in the related process of Emiritization, to which the involvement of Emirati women is vital (Metcalfe 2007). Her vision of women's work is that 20 years ago the UAE took the initiative in recruiting women in many fields of work. Like any other working UAE woman, Sheikha Lubna is caught up in trying to strike a balance between the demands of a modern liberal life and traditional culture. She respects culture and tradition in her visual presentation, wearing the *hijab* in the presence of non-blood-related males and all other men. Sometimes she wears a suit and a shawl, but that is her only concession to fashion in the business world. 'People should be judged for what they are and what they do, not the way they look,' Sheikha Lubna demands. 'Stripping off one's identity does not earn one self respect.'

Sheikha Lubna is determined to assist in building up a prosperous society that does not recognize gender discrimination, nationality, or superficial appraisal factors. She is working for the day to come where gender doesn't matter, and she does her best to have her message heard by more and more people. She believes that UAE women have enormous potential as entrepreneurs, managers, business owners and consultants: they have a wealth of options. The current generation of UAE women is well-educated and interested in developing employment skills.

For all these reasons Sheikha Lubna al-Qasimi is a perfect example of what women in leadership positions can achieve. More importantly, she is an important role model for young women in the UAE who are struggling to balance their traditional culture and beliefs with the demands of modern life as well as trying to overcome the ignorance about their culture from the perspective of the West.

CHALLENGES FOR LEADERSHIP DEVELOPMENT AND PRACTICE IN UAE

Human capital, innovation and leadership are central themes in a scenario report published by the World Economic Forum (WEF 2007). The forum suggested three scenarios designated Oasis, Sandstorm and the Fertile Gulf. Oasis is a future in which the UAE leverages regional integration to minimize the volatility caused by regional instability while upgrading its human capital to involve its national populations in a robust yet primarily

government-driven economy. Sandstorm is a scenario whereby a conflu-
ence of dramatic regional events places the UAE in a difficult situation
which leaders are only able to manage reactively. Lastly, the Fertile Gulf is
a world in which the UAE consolidates its role as a global economic player
by becoming an innovation hub and a centre for industry, with investment
and prosperity spreading across Emirates.

Creating a supportive, positive and healthy work environment that
encourages innovation, productive leader-follower relationships, a well-
trained work force and high performance is the ultimate goal of organizations and the core of survival and success in a global business environment.
The major reason behind the weak performance of most organizations in
developing countries is often assumed to be lack of successful leadership
and/or mismanagement, rather than any other technical factor (al-Faleh
1989; Kanungo and Mendonca 1994; Muna 1980).

Thus, the main problem of organizations in developing nations lies
in managing people. In this context, Mendonca and Kanungo (1994)
examined work motivation in developing countries. They argued that
many organizations in the developing countries have high levels of capital
and technological investment; however, they have failed to increase their
productivity. In Mendonca and Kanungo's opinion, this is primarily due
to a lack of management concern for the optimum utilization of human
resource potential. Furthermore, Mendonca and Kanungo argue that
these organizations have recruited many leaders and managers who play
the roles of bureaucrats and technocrats admirably, but are quite inept in
managing the human resource in organizations. In this context, Consino
(2007) argued that leadership is about exciting other people to higher
levels of performance and that there are 'seven failings of really useless
leaders:' kill emotion, kill enthusiasm, kill rewards, kill culture, kill trust,
kill engagement and kill explanation. Likewise Topping: 'Enabling your
associates to work at their very best is at the core of managerial leadership' (2002, p. 79). Nonetheless, the recent process of globalization has
directed the attention of organizations in developing nations to the
importance of leadership, strategy, productivity, quality and creativity for gaining global levels of efficiency. Hughes, Ginnett and Curphy
(2006) emphasized the importance of leadership in the success of the
organization. In their words, 'a key success factor in most organizations
today is having leaders and followers with right knowledge and skills'
(p. 530). According to Randeree (2007, p. 2), 'the qualities leaders need
to possess are also essential, since these qualities will form the basis of the
vision, effectiveness, function, productivity, development, momentum
and growth of society'. Similarly, Jabnoun (2005) argued that leadership
is vital for the success of any collective work.

Emiratization is another major challenge to leadership development in the country. As mentioned earlier, about 80 per cent of the current work force are expatriates. According to Sheikha Lubna al Qasimi, UAE Minister of Economy, during the Dubai Knowledge Village Training and Human Resources Breakfast Club meeting (7 June 2006), fundamental changes in the way nationals are educated and trained, as well as in the HR approach of the public and private sectors, can significantly reduce the unemployment rate among nationals. The country is desperately in need of local leaders who should be prepared regularly to take over the responsibilities and duties of most senior managerial posts that are currently filled by expatriates. The UAE government relies on current leaders, both expatriate and local, to train and develop citizens and meet the Emiratization quota. In the banking sector, for example, an annual 4 per cent Emiratization quota should be achieved (Cabinet Resolution No. 10 for 1998). An annual 5 per cent Emiratization quota should be achieved in the insurance sector (Cabinet Resolution No. 202/2 for 2001) and trade organizations with more than 50 employees (including branches) should achieve an annual 2 per cent Emiratization quota (Cabinet Resolution No. 259/1 for 2004). It worth mentioning that the Government is equally promoting and encouraging the recruitment of citizens with disabilities. Rule No. 275 'Article for Disabled Emirati' states that hiring a disabled Emirati National counts as hiring two Emiratis with no disability.

Across the GCC countries there is currently a 'war for talent' in which companies of all sizes and from every industry compete for staff that will make their business more viable and competitive. The fast-closing gap between remuneration packages in the Gulf and in the Indian subcontinent makes it extremely difficult for UAE-based employers to attract professionals from India, historically the main source of affordable talent for the country. Scott-Jackson (2007) argued that GCC countries and the Middle East in general are losing out in the battle to produce and attract the world's most talented workers. He called for a plan to meet strategic talent needs of business and to create a competitive advantage through differentiating capabilities. Similarly, the Gulf News argued that the Middle East needs to do more to attract international talent (Das Augustine 2008).

The state and non-state organizations seem to be aware of these challenges. The UAE 2015 Government Organizations Leaders Conference, for example, held in Dubai in 2008, addressed ten leadership development and practice challenges, namely:

- Matching global standards in terms of service delivery
- Simplification of processes and procedures at different government organizations

- Cutting the red tape and avoid internal politicking
- Encouragement to localization
- Managing the nationality mix to cater all segments of society
- Equipping and adoption of ICT solutions and most modern technologies
- Encouragement of top-down and bottom-up culture at work place for better results
- Building 2015 consultants within the Government organizations
- Skills enrichment for real 2015 leaders
- Need for Leadership Roundtable focusing on 2015 objectives

CONCLUSION

Although the UAE controls about 9 per cent of the world's oil reserves, the country is continuously seeking to reduce its dependence on the hydro-carbons sector and diversify the economic base. Indicative of this is the international prominence of Dubai, especially as a symbol of a diversified post-oil economy and of ambitious projects in construction, projecting an ascendant nationalism in this still-young nation. Subject to dire predictions of economic disaster in the global recession, the UAE has remained stable. However, the completion in Dubai of the world's tallest building, originally named the Burj al Arab, is also symbolic, with its renaming to the Burj al Khalifa reflecting the necessity of UAE oil money to the project's completion.

This strategy of diversification and integration has been the guiding principle of all major national economic initiatives. An outward-oriented development strategy, good macroeconomic management, liberal labour-entry policies and access to a talented pool of human capital and a business-friendly environment, have all contributed to high and sustained growth rates. According EIU ViewsWire (2007), UAE is expected to remain relatively prosperous through to 2030. Long-term oil supply fore-casts suggest that the world will become more dependent on Middle East oil in the next few decades, and the UAE is well placed to help meet that demand. In 2006 the UAE produced around 3 per cent of the world's crude, but was home to around 9 per cent of proven reserves.

The case studies of Sheikha Fatima and Sheikha Lubna show that it is possible for women to become prominent in the political, social and economic life of the UAE. How far these inspirational role models will enable women from other social and economic backgrounds to succeed remains to be seen and is highly dependent on the social and religious aspects of UAE culture discussed above.

REFERENCES

Agnala, A. (1998), 'Management development in the Arab world', *Education + Training*, **40** (4), 179–80.

Alder, Nancy J. (1991), *International Dimension of Organizational Behaviour*, 2nd edn, Belmont, CA: Wadworth Publishing Company.

Ali, Abbas (1993), *How to Manage for International Competitiveness*, London, and New York: Routledge.

Ali, A., A. Azim and K.S. Krishnan (1995), 'Expatriates and host country nationals: managerial values and decision styles', *Leadership & Organization Development Journal*, **16** (6), 27–34.

Ali, A. and D. Schaupp (1992), 'Value systems as predictors of managerial decision styles of Arab executives', *International Journal of Manpower, * **13** (3), 19–26.

Ali, A., A. Tagi and K. Krishnan (1997), 'Individualism, collectivism and decision styles of managers in Kuwait', *The Journal of Social Psychology*, **137** (5), 629–37.

AMEinfo (2005a), 'Hillcrest establishes Dubai office', accessed 14 October 2010 at www.ameinfo.com/55266.html.

AMEinfo (2005b), 'H.H. Sheikha Fatima bint Mubarak to be honoured at the Emirates Businesswomen Award', accessed 18 October 2010 at www.ameinfo. com/59791.html.

Atiyyah, H. (1996), 'Expatriate acculturation in Arab Gulf countries', *Journal of Management Development*, **15** (5), 37–47.

Behery, M. (2008), 'Leadership, knowledge sharing, and organizational benefits within the UAE', *Journal of American Academy of Business, Cambridge, * **12** (2), 227–36.

Bin Khirbash, M. (2005), 'United Arab Emirates special focus', *The OECD Observer, Paris, * (251), 53–6.

Collinson, D.L. (2005), 'Dialectics of leadership', *Human Relations*, **58** (11), 1419–42.

Consino, S. (2007), 'A winning emiratization unit', *The Middle East HR Summit*, 4–8 November, Abu-Dhabi, UAE.

Crystal. J. (2011), 'Eastern Arabian States', in David E. Long, Bernard Reich and Mark Gasiorowski (eds), *The Government and Politics of the Middle East and North Africa*, Philadelphia, PA: Westview Press, pp. 161–204.

Das Augustine, Babu (2008), 'Mideast losing battle for international talent', accessed 24 at October 2010 http://gulfnews.com/business/general/mid east-losing-battle-for-international-talent-1.78801.

Davidson, C.M. (2008a), 'Higher education in the Gulf: an historical background', in C.M. Davidson and P. McKenzie-Smith (eds), *Higher Education in the Gulf States: Shaping Economies, Politics and Cultures*, London: Saqi Books.

Davidson, C.M. (2008b), *Dubai: The Vulnerability of Success*, New York: Columbia University Press.

Davidson, C.M. (2009), *Abu Dhabi: Oil and Beyond*, New York: Columbia University Press.

Dubai Women Establishment (DWE) (n.d.), *Arab Women Leadership Outlook 2009 – 2011*, Dubai: DWE.

EIU ViewsWire (2007), 'UAE economy: Ten-year growth outlook', 23 Jul, New York.

Al-Faleh, M. (1989), 'Cultural influences on Arab management development: a case study of Jordan', *Journal of Management Development,* **6** (3), 19–33.

George, V. (2002), 'Sheikha Lubna's interview with Womenone'.

Hall, C. and Z. Fattah, 'U.A.E. economy to expand 3.2% in 2010 with oil at \$85 a barrel', *Bloomberg Business Week*, accessed 7 October at www.businessweek. com/news/2010-05-29/u-a-e-economy-to-expand-3-2-in-2010-with-oil-at-85-a-barrel.html.

Harold, Barbara (2006), 'UAE graduate student perspectives on leadership', accessed 18 October 2010 at www.aare.edu.au/06pap/har06550.pdf.

Hendrik, V. (1997), 'The role of tribal and kinship ties in the politics of the United Arab Emirates', unpublished PhD thesis, Fletcher School of Law and Diplomacy, Tufts University.

Hughes, R., R. Ginnett, and C. Curphy (2006), *Leadership,* 5th edition, McGraw-Hill International: Singapore.

Jabnoun, N. (2005), *Islam and Management*, Riyadh: International Islamic Publishing House.

Jabnoun, N. and H. Al-Ghasyah (2005), 'Leadership styles supporting ISO 9000:2000', *The Quality Management Journal*, **12** (1), 21–9.

Jabnoun, N. and A. Al-Rasasi (2005), 'Transformational leadership and service quality in UAE hospitals', *Managing Service Quality*, **15** (1), 70–81.

Kanungo, M. and R. Mendonca (1988), 'Evaluating employee compensation', *California Management Review*, **31** (1), 23–39.

Kawach, Nadim (2009), 'UAE economy to see sharp rebound in 2010', accessed 7 October 2010 at www.coldwellbanker-ae.com/en/newsletter/uae-economy-to-see-sharp-rebound-in-2010.html.

Kerr, S. (2010), 'Emirate shrugs off ruling family strife', *Financial Times*, accessed 6 October at www.ft.com/cms/s/0/64f881f8-cbe9-11df-bd28-00144feab49a. html.

Khaleej Times (2005), 'National female labour: participation and policy implications', Sharjah, UAE.

Al-Lamki, Salma M. (1999), 'Paradigm shift: a perspective on Omani women in management in the Sultanate of Oman', accessed 18 October 2010 at www. advancingwomen.com/awl/spring99/Al-Lamki/allamk.html.

Mendonça, M. and R.N. Kanungo (1994), 'Managing human resources: The issue of cultural fit', *Journal of Management Inquiry*, **3** (2), 189–205.

Metcalfe, B.D. (2007), 'Gender and human resource management in the Middle East', *International Journal of Human Resource Management*, **18** (1), 54–74.

Metcalfe, B.D. (2010), 'Reflecting on difference: women, Islamic feminisms and development in the Middle East', in *Diversity Management in Asia*, J. Sawad and M. Ozgilbin (eds), Cheltenham, UK and Northampton, MA, USA: Edward Elgar, pp. 140–60.

Metcalfe, Beverly D. and Christopher J. Rees (2010), 'Gender, globalization and organization: exploring power, relations and intersections', *Equality, Diversity and Inclusion: An International Journal*, **29**, 5–22.

Milton-Edwards, Beverley (2006), *Contemporary Politics in the Middle East,* 2nd edn, Cambridge and Malden, MA: Polity Press.

Ministry of Information and Culture (2002), 'Sheikh Zayed Bin Sultan Al Nahyan', accessed at www.un.int/uae/she'7.htm.

Mullins, Laurie J. (2001), *Hospitality Management and Organisational Behaviour*, Harlow: Pearson.

Muna, F.A. (1980), *The Arab Executive*, New York: St Martins Press.

Mustufa, Izzedin I. (2007), *Khaleej Times*, 19 December.

Nauman, T. (2007), 'A winning emiratization unit', Presentation to The Middle East HR Summit, 4–8 November, Abu-Dhabi, UAE.

Neal, M., J. Finlay and R. Tansey (2005), 'My father knows the minister: a comparative study of Arab women's attitudes towards leadership authority', *Women in Management Review*, **20** (7), 354–75.

Politis, J. (2003), 'QFD: The role of various leadership styles', *Leadership & Organization Development Journal,* **24** (4), 181–92.

Randeree, K. (2007), 'Inaugural International Conference on Management from Islamic Perspectives, Exploring Islamic Perspectives of Management: Paradigms, Issues and Challenges', 15–16 May, Kuala Lumpur, Malaysia.

Randeree, K. and A. Chaudhry (2007), 'Leadership in project managed environment: employee perceptions of leadership styles within infrastructure development in Dubai', *International Review of Business Research Papers*, **3** (4), 220–32.

Salloum, H. (2003), 'Women in the United Arab Emirates', *Contemporary Review*, **283**, 101–5.

Scott-Jackson, W. (2007), 'Global talent management: a key strategic resource', Presentation to *The Middle East HR Summit*, 4–8 November, Abu-Dhabi, UAE.

Shamim, A. (2007), 'Inaugural International Conference on Management from Islamic Perspectives, Exploring Islamic Perspectives of Management: Paradigms, Issues and Challenges', 15-16 May, Kuala Lumpur, Malaysia.

Simadi, F. (2006), 'The United Arab Emirates youths (UAEU) between modernity and traditionalism', *International Journal of Sociology and Social Policy*, **26** (3/4), 172–84.

Suliman, A. (2006), 'HRM in United Arab Emirates', in Pawan S. Budhwar and Kamel Mellahi (eds), *Managing Human Resources in the Middle East*, Abingdon and New York: Routledge, pp. 59–78.

Tejari (n.d) 'About us', accessed 8 October 2010 at www.tejari.com/pages/en-us/aboutus.aspx.

The Emirates News Agency (2002), 'Sheikh Zayed a real supporter of women issues – Sheikha Fatima says', accessed at www.dwc.hct.ac.ae/lrc/arab%20women/laila_abdul_hamid.htm.

The Emirates News Agency, (2002), 'Sheikha Fatima and Arab Women Media Forum: report', accessed at www.dwc.hct.ac.ae/lrc/arab%20women/laila_abdul_hamid.htm.

Topping, Peter (2002), *Managerial Leadership*, New York: McGraw-Hill.

United Nations Development Programme (UNDP) (2007), *Human Development Report 2007/2008*, Basingstoke and New York: Palgrave Macmillan.

UNDP (2009), *Human Development Report 2009*, Basingstoke and New York: Palgrave Macmillan.

Wilkins, S. (2001), 'Management development in the Gulf Arab states', *Industrial and Commercial Training*, **33** (7), 260–65.

Wilson, R. (2006), 'Islam and business', *Thunderbird International Business Review*, **48** (1), 109–23.

World Economic Forum (WEF) (2007), *The United Arab Emirates and the World: Scenarios to 2025*, Cologny, Switzerland: WEF.

Yousef, D. (1998a), 'Predictors of decision-making styles in a non-western country', *Leadership & Organization Development Journal*, **19** (7), 366–73.

Yousef, D. (1998b), 'Correlates of perceived leadership style in a culturally mixed environment', *Leadership & Organization Development Journal*, **19** (5), 275–84.

5. Leadership and organizational change in the Middle East

Christopher J. Rees, Rashid Althakhri and Aminu Mamman

INTRODUCTION

In this chapter, we explore the subject of organizational change and development (OCD) in the Middle East from a leadership perspective. The critical factor of leadership in relation to the success or failure of OCD interventions has long been recognized in OCD literature and diagnostic instruments (Weisbord 1976). Yet, despite the transitional nature of the Middle East, we highlight from the outset that there is a dearth of published research that has focused on OCD in this region from a leadership perspective. In drawing on a range of source material, the main objective of this chapter is to identify and discuss a number of key contextual factors that are associated with the leadership of OCD initiatives in the Middle East. The content of the chapter is structured as follows.

We first introduce the field of OCD from a general perspective, noting the relatively high failure rates that are reported for OCD interventions. We then explore various studies on the subject of OCD that have emerged from the Middle East. These studies consistently identify resistance to change as a key factor in OCD interventions in this context. Having emphasized the association between leadership behaviour and resistance to change, we subsequently examine how various political, cultural and economic factors are inextricably associated with the leadership of OCD initiatives in the Middle East. We draw on case study material from a public sector organization in the United Arab Emirates to highlight certain aspects of the crucial nature of leadership in OCD interventions. In general terms, our approach in this chapter is consistent with emerging literature in the field of OCD which has explored critical success factors associated with particular national and international contexts (see James 2004; Piotrowski and Armstrong 2005; Rao and Vijayalakshmi 2000; Zhou et al. 2006).

LEADING ORGANIZATIONAL CHANGE AND DEVELOPMENT (OCD)

General interest in the field of OCD has grown significantly over the past two decades. Rees (2008) associates this growing interest to global issues and trends such as privatization, public sector reform, mergers and acquisitions, the influence of MNCs, population migration, poverty, and advances in ICT. These issues and trends present major challenges to those charged with equipping people and organizations to adapt and flourish in these turbulent times. In the 1980s, organizations began to operate in environments subject to radical, sudden and unpredictable shifts, rather than in more stable and predictable situations where change is familiar and incremental (Graetz et al. 2002). Rapid technological developments and changes in political, economic and socio-cultural environments require an organization to reduce costs, improve the quality of its products or services, locate new opportunities for improvement and increase productivity in order to survive (Kotter 1995). Moreover, the requirement to respond quickly to such changes in the external environment requires organizations to manage change by achieving external adaptation and internal integration (Senior and Fleming 2006). In fact, Burnes (2003) claims that one of the most important challenges facing organizations today is managing organizational change successfully. Rees (2008) argues that, given these types of challenges, it is predictable that academics and practitioners will seek to establish how best to implement and manage change effectively at the organizational level. Effective organizational change strategies are inextricably bound to organizational performance (Meyer and Stensaker 2006) and as a result, leaders within organizations are increasingly called upon to demonstrate managerial competencies that specifically relate to OCD. Thus, it is considered essential for leaders to possess OCD knowledge and competence in order to adapt to the changing environment and succeed in the current extremely competitive and continuously evolving business environment (Todnem 2005, p. 369).

Yet we note from the outset that, despite the considerable body of literature on OCD, the leadership and implementation of change interventions has long been problematic (Hartley 2002; Waldersee and Griffiths 2004). For example, Hartley (2002) states that fewer than 30 per cent of OCD initiatives are successful. Oakland and Tanner (2007) support this observation by reporting that the success rate of change programmes can be as low as 10 per cent. Similarly, it has been estimated that fewer than 30 per cent of business process re-engineering initiatives are successful, while the failure rate of new technology change is anywhere between 40 and 70 per cent (Burnes 2003). OCD failure rates of this order are reflected in a recent survey of 1536 executives who had participated in various change programmes (Isern and Pung 2007); this survey reports that only 38 per cent of the executives considered the change programme to be successful and only 30 per cent of the executives stated that the change intervention had resulted in sustained organizational performance.

This problematic nature of OCD initiatives should not be considered to be a feature of the field that is confined to the Western world. In fact, the rather limited information available suggests that, over a prolonged period of time, OCD failure rates in the Middle East are broadly similar to those reported in the West. For example, Alkadera and Alfawori (1994) report that despite support from the political administration in Jordan for the organizational development agenda, backed by the introduction of new legislation, the process of organizational development has been unsuccessful. Similarly, al-Shihi (2006) reports that the success rate of e-government change initiatives in developing countries in the Middle East is approximately 15 per cent. At a more general level, Alqahtani (2006) argues that the absence of a strategic change and development agenda has led to various problems in the Arab world which impact upon OCD initiatives throughout the Middle East. These problems include increased numbers of foreign workers and high unemployment rates, lack of loyalty to organizations, the undue influence of the tribal system and family relationships within companies, the spread of administrative corruption, and conflict between public sector ministries in terms of their responsibilities and lack of interaction with international players. The next section of the chapter pursues these themes in more depth by focusing on literature concerning OCD that has emanated from the Middle East.

ORGANIZATIONAL CHANGE AND DEVELOPMENT IN THE MIDDLE EAST

At a macro level, the region of the Middle East has witnessed fundamental changes in political, economic and social fields due to urban expansion, population increase and the constant growth of commercial enterprises. The discovery of oil and the dramatic rise in oil prices after 1973 have had a great impact on Arab societies and created an unstable environment, especially in the Gulf Cooperation Council (GCC) countries (Ali 1990; Al-Kazemi and Ali 2002; see also Chapter 1). Before the discovery of oil, this was a generally poor region which relied on seafaring, pearling and limited trade (Abdalla 1997). It has been argued however that, despite these changes in the business environment, organizations in the Arab world have not adopted the attitudes, values and norms that are needed in the new era (Mellahi 2003). Budhwar and Mellahi (2007) indicate that Arab countries still have management systems similar to most other developing countries, favouring local cultural values, beliefs and norms. Against this background, Alqahtani (2006) emphasizes the importance of change management as a powerful strategy in order to reform organizations in the Middle East. Support for this approach comes from Alqaruni and Alanzi (2004). They assessed the efforts towards administrative reform in all the ministries in Kuwait, especially after the Iraqi invasion, and found that the achievements of management development were weak, primarily because there was no clear strategy to develop the public sector in Kuwait. Therefore, they recommended that national and organizational leaders should design a national reform change strategy in order to improve all Kuwaiti ministries. Similarly, Alfawari and Alamari (2000) surveyed a group of 200 managers to examine their attitudes towards organizational development and change in the service sector in Qatar. They found that one of the most important problems facing the process of management development in Qatar was the absence of clear strategies for organizational change and development. They concluded that leaders of organizations should develop a change-management framework which would help the service sector in Qatar to implement its strategy and action plan. Moreover, they urged that such a framework should be compatible with the organizational culture embedded in Qatari society.

As well as the work outlined above, a limited number of studies are available on OCD in the Middle East (Al Blori 2005). Table 5.1 provides an indication of the types of studies that have emerged from the Middle East on the subject of OCD.

As can be seen from Table 5.1, studies on OCD that have emerged from the Middle East in recent years have tended to identify and focus upon the subject of employees' resistance to change. Further, consistent with more mainstream Western literature, one of the most regularly cited reasons for this resistance to change is the perceived poor planning and implementation of change by leaders within organizations. Elsewhere, we summarize that this body of work indicates that the more deep-rooted underlying reasons and symptoms associated with resistance to organizational change in this region include the following: (1) managers being concerned about losing their position and power; (2) staff members fearing the loss of their jobs; (3) unclear change management objectives; (4) a lack of trust in employees; (5) ineffective communication between employees and change; (6) a lack of recognition of the need to change (Rees and Althakhri 2008). These reasons for, and symptoms of, resistance to change in organizations in the Middle East highlight the association between effective OCD interventions and leadership behaviours within this region. Further,

Table 5.1   *Summary of indicative organizational change management literature in the Middle East*

Author (year)	Objective(s)	Research method	Conclusion
Alhalawani (1990)	To investigate the role of change in management development.	Questionnaire survey.	The study found that (1) change must be planned and implemented carefully in order to be successful; (2) change should not be based on personal objectives; (3) attention should be paid to motivation systems and negotiation with employees by informal channels in order to persuade employees to accept change and (4) successful change should not be continuous, because permanent change might lead to the creation of a state of fear and suspicion among employees.
Abu-Hamdieh (1994)	To examine the impact of the participation of employees, the relationships between them and the availability of information on change processes.	Questionnaire was used with 1917 employees in 40 industrial companies in Jordan.	The author reports that participation, good relations between employees at work and availability of information have a positive correlation with effective change processes, while age and the nature of work have significant correlations with resistance to change. By contrast, sex, education and work experience were found to have no association with resistance to change.
Alzni (1994)	To examine the role of communications in organizational change	Questionnaire was used with 154 employees from the Cairo Saudi Bank.	The findings highlight the need for effective communication between employees by providing them with adequate information about change in order to implement change successfully. Managers should increase confidence in their employees and encourage them to participate in change processes.

Table 5.1   (continued)

Author (year)	Objective(s)	Research method	Conclusion
Alkadera and Alfawori (1994)	To investigate managerial attitudes towards organizational development in Jordan.	Questionnaire was used with a sample of 300 managers from all ministries and governmental institutions.	The findings show that a majority of the managers agreed that organizational development was a part of their task. Results also indicate that organizational development in Jordan was facing many challenges: recruitment was not based on employees' capabilities, the monitoring of the process of organizational development was poor, there was a lack of sufficient power for those in charge of organizational development and of qualified specialists in aspects of management development.
Allozi (1999)	To examines employees' attitudes towards organizational change.	Questionnaire was used with a sample of 603 employees from 23 public sector institutions in Jordan.	The findings indicate that employees' participation in the change process is one of the most important factors in helping to implement change The study found that change from an employee perspective is considered as a threat. On other hand, managers tend to have more positive views of organizational change.
Alamri and Alfawsan (1997)	To examine the causes of resistance to change in the public sector in Saudi Arabia.	Questionnaire was used with sample of 450 employees.	The results indicate that employees resist change for several reasons. First, managers are concerned about losing their power while members of staff fear the loss of their jobs. Second, objectives and action plans for change processes are often unclear to employees. The authors consider that the most important factor leading employees to resist change is unclear channels of communication between employees and change agents.

Table 5.1   (continued)

Author (year)	Objective(s)	Research method	Conclusion
Almuslimani (1999)	To examine the obstacles to organizational development in Jordan.	Questionnaire survey.	The study identifies specific obstacles to organizational development. They are: lack of financial support, centralization of authority, rigid procedures and regulations, and certain social values, including tribalism, family relationships and favouritism.
Alzuadat (1999)	To explore the role of training in situations where organizational change results in the creation of new jobs.	Questionnaire survey was used with a sample of 370 employees from a commercial bank in Jordan.	The study finds that training programmes should be given more attention, especially when a change requires new jobs in order to help employees to gain new capabilities and skills that are necessary for their new status. The study also reports that, in order to implement change successfully, employees should participate in decision-making.
Alomari (2000).	To identify a number of factors that impede change management a telecommunication company in Saudi Arabia.	Questionnaire was used on a sample of 350 employees.	The study found that factors which impede change include: (1) poor planning and implementation of change, (2) a lack of human and material resources allocated to the change programme, (3) change objectives which are not clear to employees, (4) a lack of participation by employees in the change process and (5) managers are anxious about losing their power and influence.
Alharbi (2002)	To examine resistance to change in public institutions in Saudi Arabia.	Questionnaire was used on a sample of 348 employees.	The study concludes that there are two main factors creating resistance to change: poor planning and management of change and the fact that managers have no confidence in their employees.

Table 5.1   (continued)

Author (year)	Objective(s)	Research method	Conclusion
	Also to identify the relationships between resistance to change and demographic variables.		The study shows that the demographic variables examined do indeed have a significant correlation with resistance to change.
Aldkasma (2002)	Investigates the factors influencing change in a government department in Jordan. Also examines the obstacles to such change.	Questionnaire.	The study found that improvement of organizational performance is the most important driver of organizational change and that among the various challenges faced by this change are: (1) poor participation by employees in the change process, (2) neglect of the monitoring of the process, (3) a failure to reinforce the new status quo and (4) a lack of financial and moral support.
Alazam (2002)	To investigate attitudes towards organizational development and change in a Jordanian communications company.	Questionnaire was used on a sample of 160 managers.	The results show that external and internal environments must be analysed carefully before any decision is taken to initiate change. The author states that the organization needs to adopt a flexible organizational structure and improve communication systems in order to implement change effectively.
Khassawneh (2005)	To investigate and identify the main causes of employees' resistance	Questionnaire was used with a sample of 600 employees from central ministries in Amman.	The findings highlight the main causes of resistance to change within this context. It is concluded that the prevalence of non-participative attitudes among top level bureaucrats makes it difficult for them to

Table 5.1   (continued)

Author (year)	Objective(s)	Research method	Conclusion
	to change in government bureaucratic organizations in Jordan.		assume vibrant leadership roles. It was also found that inadequate incentives were contributing to employees' resistance to administrative change.
Abdah (2006)	To investigate the relationship between leadership styles and organizational development in different government ministries in Jordan.	Questionnaire was used on a sample of 397 managers.	The findings show that in order to improve organizational development in the Central Ministries, attention should be paid to delegating authority to staff, simplifying work procedures, reviewing legislation and regulations, and improving communication channels between managers and staff.

Source: developed from Rees and Althakhri (2008)

they raise questions as to the contextual influences that are, for example, emphasizing the relative importance of issues such as power, fear, trust and communication styles in OCD interventions in this region.

LEADING OCD IN THE MIDDLE EAST

Previous research (Appelbaum *et al.* 1998; Chrusciel and Field 2006; Graetz 2000; Oakland and Tanner 2007; Underwood-Stephens and Cobbs 1999; Weber and Weber 2001) suggested that organizations need to address critical factors during periods of change in order to be successful. As noted above, one prominent feature of the OCD discourse to emerge in recent years is the attempt to isolate OCD-related variables that are associated with specific national and international contexts. This trend is mainly attributable to the wide-scale adaptation and transfer of Western management practices to other national settings and, specifically in relation to OCD, the absence of a universally valid model of how to manage and implement OCD successfully

(Todnem 2005, p. 370). While other chapters in this volume will provide a more detailed analysis of Middle Eastern culture, the next section of this chapter explores a number of key contextual influences that impact upon the leadership of OCD initiatives in the Middle East.

It has been argued by some writers that the characteristics of the current governance systems of countries in the Middle East are contributing to slow economic growth in these countries (Budhwar and Mellahi 2007). In this context, nepotism has been tolerated in the Arab world in order to fulfil the responsibilities of individuals towards their relatives and extended families. Nepotism is regarded as a social mechanism which determines the allocation of resources in society and the economy and is often apparent in the recruitment of upper level managers, though qualifications are stressed in the selection of middle managers and lower-level employees (see Ali 1995; Hutchings and Weir 2006; Mellahi 2003; also see the discussion of *wasta* in Chapter 8). For example, Almhdie et al. (2004) found that human resource practices in Libya are significantly affected by various factors, such as the socio-political context and a tribal system in which managers are more concerned with establishing social relationships at the workplace than in job performance itself. In that sense, nepotism in the Middle East region can be seen to cascade from the macro government level down to micro decision making by leaders within organizations. However, economic globalization has intensified the pressures in favour of reforming political systems in the Arab world (Partrick et al. 2006), although such reform will inevitably have profound implications for leadership at both macro and micro levels throughout the Middle East.

In addressing the role of governments in the Arab world, Abed and Davoodi (2003) propose that there are some key elements which prevent Arab countries from taking advantage of increasing globalization. The first element is high annual population growth rates in the region. These rates, which have exceeded 2.5 per cent over the past 20 years, have acted to depress per capita GDP and thus detract from the potential benefits of globalization. The second element is the lack of political reform which remains the main obstacle to economic improvement in some Arab countries. The United Nations states in its Arab Human Development Report (2002) that the region performs poorly in terms of political freedom and the development of human skills and knowledge. However, it should be noted that some Arab countries, for example Kuwait and the United Arab Emirates, have started to reform their political systems and introduce more democratic regimes in order to enhance their economic performance (Patrick et al. 2006). The third element is the dominance of the public sector throughout the Middle East. For example, al-Yousif (2004) reports that the public sector in GCC countries accounts for 60 per cent of GDP. This dominance of the public sector affects economic systems in a number of ways, such as imposing a high cost on revenue collection, causing delays in obtaining licences or permits to start businesses, complex court systems and the poor quality of public services. Thus, the costs of starting new businesses in the Arab region are reported to be five times as high as in East Asia and 2.5 times as high as in Eastern Europe and Central Asia (Abed and Davoodi 2003, p. 15).

While government policy can be seen to exert a key influence on the leadership of organizations throughout the world, the policies and influence of governments in the Middle East do not readily compare with the policies and influence of governments in, say, Western democracies, both in terms of style and policy content. As such, it is stressed that the policies and style of government are key contextual variables, along with others such as tribalism and the promotion of Islamic values (Rees and Althakhri 2008), which should be considered when exploring the leadership of OCD interventions in the Middle East. For example, Mellahi (2003) and Rees et al. (2007) have highlighted that, since the 1970s, oil revenue has been employed to develop and enhance the public sector in Middle Eastern countries, allowing governments to provide well-paid employment in the public sector. Consequently, the indigenous workforce generally prefers to work in the public rather than the private sector, whilst the private sector has turned to foreign workers to supply its labour needs. This situation has led Middle Eastern governments in countries such as Saudi Arabia, Oman and the UAE to adopt nationalization strategies to compel organizational leaders in the private sector to employ locals (Rees et al. 2007; Forstenlechner 2008). These nationalization strategies, which have a profound impact upon employment in the Middle East, have no obvious equivalent in the developed countries of the Western world. Nevertheless, various governments within the Middle East have adopted stringent nationalization programmes in an attempt to control employment and immigration. In theory at least, OCD initiatives within the Middle East are thus influenced by government employment policies which have no obvious parallels in Western countries.

Despite the tendency towards directive styles of leadership in the Middle East, existing literature on OCD indicates that resistance to change is a key issue that has to be addressed when leading change in organizations in the Middle East. Thus, to over-emphasize the directive nature of leadership in the Middle East is to over-simply the nature of leadership of OCD in this region. For example, taking the case of the nationalization programmes referred to above, it is becoming increasingly evident that despite the fact that these programmes originate from the policies of various governments in the Middle East, organizational leaders and employees in the private sector have, to varying degrees, resisted these programmes. This has happened for a number of reasons. First, the private sector is largely dependent on foreign manual labour, which is cheaper. Despite government efforts to minimize the hiring of foreign workers by introducing new policies and regulations such as high costs for issuing and renewing work permits, locals are still more expensive to employ. Social and cultural features are also important to locals, as they prefer not to do manual work and technical jobs, which are more likely to be available in private sector organizations. Third, expatriates are easier to control and more obedient than local workers, because of fear of termination of employment and deportation from the country. The final reason is that the locals avoid social integration into the multinational work environment in order to maintain a high social status (Mellahi 2003; Rees et al. 2007). The consideration of this interaction between contextual factors such as traditional cultures, social integration, and Islamic values highlights that leading and understanding change within the context of the Middle East is a highly complex issue that cannot be understood by simply pointing to a tendency towards directive styles of leadership in this region.

The next section of this chapter presents data drawn from a public sector case study in the United Arab Emirates. The main aim of the case study is to explore an example of how the leaders of a public sector organization, operating within the influence of the contextual variables discussed above, sought to design and implement an OCD strategy in order to bring about a sweeping transformation of the organization's systems and structures.

CASE STUDY: LEADING OCD WITHIN ABU DHABI POLICE (ADP)

Historical Background of Policing in the UAE and Abu Dhabi

After the Second World War, the British government showed an unprecedented interest in the internal affairs of the Gulf region. This engagement represented a departure from the previous longstanding strategy, which was to avoid direct involvement in the internal affairs of the countries in this region. As a direct result of this new British Government stance, the 'Oman Coast Force' was established in 1951 in what were then still known as the Trucial States. The British government also delimited the internal boundaries within the United Arab Emirates in order to tighten control of security matters and to ensure that oil exploration missions could be undertaken as safely as possible. As an element of this security strategy, the British Government also began to develop the Abu Dhabi police force, primarily by the introduction of professional police officers to undertake leadership and management functions within these police forces. In these early years, the main tasks of the Abu Dhabi Police was to guard key locations such as the Ruler's palace, government buildings, banks and shipping vessels coming from neighbouring countries. Also, in the event of disputes, the Abu Dhabi Police was responsible for bringing wanted people to the courts.

After 1966 Sheikh Zayed Bin Sultan al Nahyan (ruler of Abu Dhabi Emirate at that time) identified the need for a more professional police force to maintain security in this Emirate. Various initiatives were implemented in order to substantially enhance the efficiency of the Abu Dhabi police. These initiatives involved improving the financial and technical resources available to the ADP including the introduction of modern equipment, systems, buildings and tools. For example, due to the need for development and modernization, Sheikh Zayed invited a delegation from the Jordanian Police to work with the Abu Dhabi Police. In September 1968 the Jordanian mission composed of 41 officers reached Abu Dhabi and effectively contributed to capacity building relating to traffic police, criminal investigations, guards, and financial and administration procedures.

In 1971 the entire government structure of Abu Dhabi was reconfigured. New ministries were introduced such as the Ministry of Interior, which became responsible for implementing law, protecting the security of citizens and securing life and property. The Supreme Union Council decided to consolidate the police forces of the Emirates to work under the umbrella of the Ministry of Interior. The tasks of the Ministry included matters relating to naturalization and residency; prisons; traffic; security of oil installations, ministries and public facilities; liaison with national and international police organizations; prevention of trafficking in people and drugs; and general crime detection and prevention.

However, the responsibility for local policing was delegated to each of the seven Emirates. Thus, each local police force, such as ADP, developed their own organizational strategies and unique systems to satisfy the policing needs of their area of responsibility. In the case of ADP, this organizational strategy has been under constant review. The step-by-step approach adopted by the ADP provides a fascinating insight into how organizational change was led in this organization with reference to key factors such as vision, structure and partnerships.

Step 1: Understanding the Imperative for Change

In the post-Second World War years, the UAE witnessed fundamental social and political changes due to urban expansion, population increase, the constant growth of commercial enterprises, and above all, the emergence of terrorist attacks in neighbouring countries. It was recognized by senior government officials that the Abu Dhabi Police had to develop its capacity to tackle issues relating to terrorism and other major crimes.

Step 2: Creating ADP's Leadership Vision to Change

The Deputy Prime and Minister of Interior (Lt. General H.H. Sheikh Saif bin Zayed al Nahyan) openly stated that his vision was to make the Abu Dhabi Police the most effective operational police force in one of the safest and most secure countries in the world. This vision statement by the organization's leader went as far as to identify the characteristics that ADP should possess:

- Responsiveness to the community's needs and demands
- Abidance to moral values and integrity
- Motivation of police personnel and adequate training
- Organization, education and creativity encouragement
- Cost-effectiveness and scalability.

From the outset, the most senior person in the organization recognized that ADP faced major challenges if the aforementioned leadership vision was to be put into effect. For that purpose, the Strategic Department was established, headed by Maj. General Nasser Salim al Nuaimi Secretary General of the Office of the Deputy Prime Minister and Minister of the Interior. The Strategic Department's mission was to formulate strategic plans in order to actualize the vision statement. The remit of the Strategic Department is notably wide-ranging. For example, the tasks entrusted to it include overseeing the development of ADP, in general as well as in qualitative strategies, based on a strategic view of security conditions in the Abu Dhabi Emirate and in the UAE as a whole. Further, the Strategic Department is charged with providing technical advice to ADP functional departments, so as to prepare and design strategic qualitative plans, and integrate these plans within the main strategic plan of the Abu Dhabi Police.

In terms of leadership and management of change, the Strategic Department was given a vital role. It was given responsibility for supervising the process of conducting surveys and organizational studies, with the aim of determining the requirements of strategic development in a manner which achieves the desired organizational goals. Specifically, the department was required to identify the operational obstacles faced while applying strategic plans and, in coordination with relevant directorates, to devise strategies to overcome these obstacles. Interestingly, the development and maintenance of an advanced performance management system was placed under the auspices of the Strategic Department. Thus, the department was responsible for overall monitoring of the execution of tasks and ensuring the compliance of directorates with the requirements and standards of the quality system.

In 2002, the Strategic Department conducted various diagnostic exercises in order to identify organizational weaknesses and areas for improvement. It sought to clarify ADP's strategic plan in order to ensure that ADP achieved its stated organizational goals, that is, to ensure a secure community, maintain stability, combat crime, and contribute in the prevalence of justice, in a manner that ensures and preserves the trust of the public.

Step 3: Developing Strategic Change Plans

In 2003 the Strategic Department produced a document, known as the Seven Points Plan. This document clarified the main strategic goals of ADP for the next five years. Each point of the seven was presented as a strategic goal in itself. A 'responsible officer' was assigned responsibility for each goal and each section and directorate was requested to contribute to the realization of this plan by means of their individual annual plan. The key objectives of the Seven Points Plan are summarized below.

- Focusing all operational effort on reducing crime and disorder and promoting reassurance and safety within our communities.
- Building the trust and confidence of communities by effective consultation and effective communication.
- Improving the quality of service and overall performance.
- Achieving best value in the delivery of service.
- Developing the talents and abilities of all members of Abu Dhabi Police to achieve professional goals.
- Promoting corporate and individual honesty, ethics and integrity.
- Providing equipment, buildings and technology which promote the delivery of effective and efficient services.

Step 4: Implementing the Strategic Plans: Reconfiguring the Organizational Structure

In order for the ADP to apply the Seven Points Plan, the administrative system of the organization required major change. Consequently, the head of the Strategic Department decided to reconfigure the organizational structure in order to improve decision-making styles, eliminate conflicts between departments in terms of key areas of responsibility, improve communication between departments, and to create

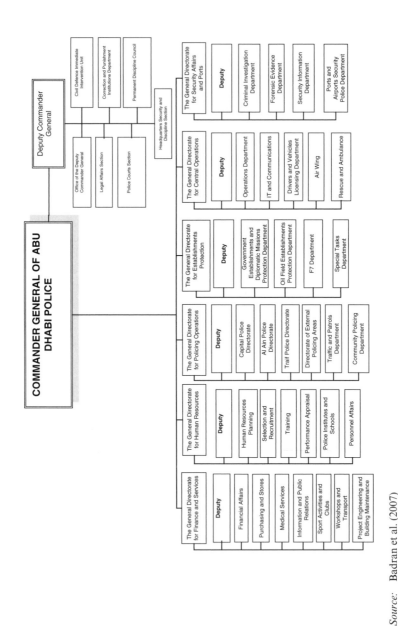

Source: Badran et al. (2007)

Figure 5.1 New organizational structure of ADP

new departments such as Community Policy and Human Resources Department. This reconfiguration was enacted in 2004 by the Minister of Interior who issued the administrative decree No. 40, which stated that a new organizational structure was to be adopted in accordance with modern crime prevention requirements. In effect, the organization was restructured into three main levels. First the Leadership and Supervisory level, which specialized in preparing annual organizational plans and formulating general strategies for the Abu Dhabi Police. Second the Logistics Support level, which contains the Human Resource directorate and the Finance and Services directorate. Third the Policing and Security level, which contains five directorates: Security Affairs, Central Operations, Police Operations, General Protection, and Information Security. This new organizational structure was designed to create effective communication paths between directorates, mainly by clarifying areas of authority and responsibility.

Step 5: Revising the Strategic Plan as a Result of Environmental Conditions

In 2005, the Gulf area experienced an increase in the scale of destructive activities by terrorist groups, particularly in relation to oil fields and diplomatic missions. These environmental conditions directly led the leadership of ADP to concentrate efforts on the protection of vital installations and also to adopt a strategic priority approach. Thus, at the beginning of 2006, the strategic priorities that every directorate was required to implement by the end of the year were unveiled. Further, in relation to these priorities, every directorate was made directly accountable to the Police General Commander. Examples of the strategic priorities are provided below:

(1) To enhance the capability of Abu Dhabi Police to respond and effectively deal with any threats to the community, government and diplomatic resources and all commercial assets, including oil fields.
(2) To develop quality of service standards for both internal and external customers.
(3) To implement the force structure and ensure all staff understand and are working to their job descriptions.
(4) To enhance the current process of establishing best value throughout the organization, and review existing processes, that could be outsourced, which distract attention away from core business.
(5) To increase the force's capability to make the road transport system safer and more efficient, targeting road traffic collisions to reduce the level of serious and fatal casualties.

(6) To implement and integrate comprehensive police station and community policing to enhance communication with local communities and increase community confidence.

(7) To enhance the ADP's investigative abilities at all levels and improve the effectiveness of the justice system.

(8) To develop and implement proactive information security system linked to tasking and coordination (teams within departments or directorates) in order to enable an appropriate response against any criminal activities.

(9) To develop an internal communication system that ensures that all staff are aware of the force priorities and that there is the opportunity for all staff to contribute to the future planning of the organization.

(10) To enhance the capability of ADP to manage and respond to any crisis (natural or man made).

(11) To develop systems that provide greater management information about incidents, crimes and traffic collisions to ensure a more effective use of resource.

(12) To increase the effectiveness and efficiency of staff through automating the HR process, in coordination with other concerned departments.

Step 6: Developing a Partnership Strategy

In order to enhance ADP's global intelligence, the Minister of Interior devised a 'partnership strategy' which involved collaborating with government agencies and police forces from outside of the Arab region. For example, with the stated aim of strengthening the principle of security partnership and cooperation between nations, the Minister of Interior signed a memorandum of understanding with the government of the UK in 2006. The remit of this agreement was wide-ranging. It covered cooperation in fighting terrorism, organized crime, drug trafficking and economic crimes such as money laundering, cyber-crime, fraud and forgery.

ADP CASE STUDY: DISCUSSION

The above case study raises a number of issues that are directly relevant to the discussion of leadership of OCD within the Middle East. First, it is notable that the OCD intervention was led and managed in a manner which resembles approaches promoted in Western academic literature. For example, the OCD intervention was holistic, based around an articulated set of vision and objectives statements, led from the top of the organization, carefully planned, informed by organizational diagnostics, and long term in outlook. In fact, references to standard definitions of Western originated Organization Development (OD) indicate that the OCD process adopted by ADP could reasonably be described as an OD intervention (Cummings and Worley 2008; McLean 2007). This observation indicates that the process of OCD can take similar paths in Western countries and countries in the Middle East, despite the contextual variations between these geographical regions. It is concluded that while there may be a specific set of values associated with the leadership of OCD in the Middle East, the process used to implement OCD strategies in the region may be drawn from more generic OCD theory and practice.

Second, it is observed that the leaders of the organization sought to establish clear lines of accountability and responsibility when implementing the organizational re-structuring. This should be considered with reference to the highly important security work undertaken by employees of ADP: arguably, this strategy can be seen as a direct attempt to negate the adverse impact of nepotism which, as highlighted in the discussion above, is prevalent in the Middle East. At a more general level, the establishment of clear lines of accountability and reporting, coupled with the creation of independent human resource functions, provide evidence of a genuine attempt to negate the influence of nepotism in organizations in the Middle East. This observation indicates that leaders within ADP were actively seeking to delegate authority and decentralize decision-making in ways that are not often associated with styles of leadership traditionally associated with the Middle East.

Third, in the case study, the creation of the Strategic Department provided both a commitment and support mechanism to manage change within ADP. This aspect of the case study provides a specific insight into the design of OCD interventions in Middle Eastern contexts: ultimately, issues of leadership, support, and commitment to change within organizations have to be considered in the light of the role and nature of government leadership in the Middle East. For example, public sector organizations may use OCD interventions as strategies to introduce government policy. At the general level, the styles of leadership evident in public sector organizations in the Middle East are likely to reflect the styles of leadership that are adopted by national leaders.

Fourth, the case study provides further evidence of the openness of some political leaders within the Middle East to work with those from outside the region who do not necessarily share their social, religious and cultural values but who can offer a positive contribution to the performance of governments and not-for-profit organizations in the region. The use of the term 'partnership strategy' in this particular OCD intervention is noteworthy as some of the partners in this case were government agencies based outside the Middle East.

CONCLUSION

In this chapter we have sought to explore issues connected to the leadership of OCD initiatives in the Middle East. At a general level, the review of literature and the exploration of case study material draw attention to issues of leadership in both the private and public sectors within the Middle East region. The study demonstrates that transformational leadership styles can exist in Arabic cultures. It also showed that leaders play a critical role in implementing change within this context by: (1) establishing a vision and a strategic plan to implement this vision; (2) giving attention to culture by building new values in order to eliminate some traditional features of Arabic culture such as nepotism; and (3) changing organizational structures in order to establish decentralization, delegation and effective communication. As such, it should not be assumed that all leadership in the Middle East region can be classified as authoritarian in nature. This point is emphasized by Rees and Althakhri (2008), who state that the cultural values of the Arab world differ from country to country and might well change over time in order, for example, to meet the standards required by the international business community. We do highlight, however, that the findings of the current study should be treated with caution especially in terms of generalization to other contexts.

Finally, we note that current research on OCD has discussed the relevance of Western OCD theories and models to organizations in the Middle East. The findings from the literature review and the case study of an organization in the Middle East lead us to stress the distinction between OCD goals and OCD processes. Further research is needed to establish the extent to which standard Western-originated OCD processes and models can be employed within the Middle East to implement OCD strategies that are based on objectives and values compatible with Middle Eastern as opposed to Western cultures. We conclude that further research is needed to examine whether the implementation models and processes (as opposed to goals) of OCD that have been developed in Western countries can be used by leaders in the Middle East to change and develop their organizations in ways that are sympathetic to the cultural contexts in which they are based.

REFERENCES

Abdalla, I. (1997), 'Construct and concurrent validity of three protestant work ethic measures in an Arabian Gulf society', *Journal of Managerial Psychology,* 12 (4), 251–60.

Abdeh, D. (2006), *Leadership Styles and Organisational Development in the Central Ministries of Jordan,* Jordan: Central Ministries of Jordan.

Abed, G. and H. Davoodi (2003), 'Challenges and growth in globalizations in the Middle East and North Africa', accessed 2 December 2007 at www.imf.org/external/pubs/ft/med/ara/abed.

Abu-Hamdieh, A. (1994), 'Employees' perspectives on organizational change and the contribution of industrial companies in Jordan', unpublished Masters dissertation, Faculty of Economics and Administration, University of Jordan.

Alamri, A. and N. Alfawsana (1997), 'Staff resistance to change in the public sector in Saudi Arabia: causes and remedy', *Public Administration Journal,* **37** (3), 17–28.

Alazam, Z. (2002), 'Managers' perspectives towards organizational development in the Jordanian communications company, unpublished Masters dissertation, University of Yarmouk, Jordan.

Aldkasma, M. (2002), 'Attitudes of managers toward organizational change in governmental departments in Irbid Jordan: an empirical study', *Administration,* **88**.

Alfawari, R. and N. Alamari (2000), 'Middle managers' attitudes toward public service: organisational development in Qatar', *Journal of King Saweed University,* **12,** (unpaged).

Alhalawni, A. (1990), 'Change and its role in management development', *Public Administration,* **67,** 45–54.

Alharbi, A. (2002), 'Resistance to change: an empirical study in public institutions in Jeddah / Saudi Arabia', unpublished Masters dissertation, University of King Abd-Alaziz.

Ali, A. (1990), 'Management theory in a transitional society: the Arab's experience', *International Studies of Management and Organization,* **20** (3), 7–35.

Ali, A. (1995), 'Cultural discontinuity and Arab management thought', *International Studies of Management and Organization,* **25** (3), 7–30.

Alkadera, B. and R. Alfawori (1994), *Attitudes of Middle Managers Towards Organisational Development in Jordan* Irbid, Jordan: Yarmouk University, Research Centre of Jordan.

Allozi, M. (1999), 'Employees' attitudes to organisational changes in governmental institutions in Jordan', *The Magazine Studies,* **2,** 338.

Almuslimani, H. (1999), *Evaluating the Effectiveness of Organisational Development in Jordan and its Obstacles from an Employee Perspective,* Jordan: Government of Jordan.

Almhdie, A., P. Iles, and R. Li-Hua (2004), 'Examining HRM aspects of knowledge transfer in the Libyan oil Industry', paper presented at the British Academy of Management Conference, St Andrews, Scotland.

Alomari, Z. (2000), 'Challenges to change and strategy for managing change: an empirical study in a Saudi Arabian telecommunication company', unpublished Masters dissertation, King Saweed University.

Alqahtani, F. (2006), 'Organisational development and reform strategies and their role in reinforcing national security', unpublished PhD thesis, University of Naife, Saudi Arabia.

Alqaruni, M. and A. Alanzi (2004), 'Efforts towards organisational development in Kuwait: an empirical study', *Public Administration Journal*, **44** (4), (unpaged).

Alzni, A. (1994), 'Communication from a behavioural perspective and its role in organisational change: an empirical study in the Cairo Saudi Bank', unpublished Masters dissertation, University of King Abd-Alaziz.

Alzuadat, K. (1999), 'Factors affecting employees' attitudes toward organizational change in Jordanian commercial banks, unpublished Master of Business Administration dissertation, University of Al Albate.

Applebaum, S.H., N. St-Pierre and W. Glavas (1998), 'Strategic organizational change: the role of leadership, learning, motivation and productivity', *Management Decision*, **36** (5), 289–301.

Badran, K., K.Alnaqbi, M. Mater and B. al Balbisi (2007), *Abu Dhabi Police: Fifty Years of Progress from 1957 to 2007*, UAE: Abu Dhabi Police.

Al Blori, S. (2005), *The Staff's Attitude Towards the Organizational Change: A Survey Study in Civil Aviation in Jeddah*, Naif Arab University for Security Sciences, Saudi Arabia.

Budhwar, P. and K. Mellahi (2007), 'Introduction: human resource management in the Middle East', *International Journal of Human Resource Management*, **18** (1), 2–10.

Burnes, B. (2003), 'Managing change and changing managers from ABC to XYZ', *Journal of Management Development*, **22** (7), 627–42.

Crusciel, D. and D. Field (2006), 'Success factors in dealing with significant change in an organization', *Business Process Management Journal*, **12** (4), 503–51.

Cummings, T. and C. Worley (2008), *Organization Development and Change* 9th edn, Ohio: Thomson Publishing.

Forstenlechner, I. (2008), 'Workforce nationalization in the UAE: image versus integration', *Education, Business and Society: Contemporary Middle Eastern Issues*, **1** (2), 82–91.

Graetz, F. (2000), 'Strategic change leadership', *Management Decision*, **38** (8), 550–64.

Graetz, F., M Rimmer, A. Lawrence, and A. Smith (2002), *Managing Organisational Change*, Brisbane, QLD: Wiley.

Hartley, J. (2002), 'Organisational change and development', in Peter Warr (ed.), *Psychology at Work*, London: Penguin Books, pp. 399–425.

Hutchings, K. and D. Weir (2006), 'Understanding networking in China and the Arab world: lessons for international managers', *Journal of European Industrial Training*, **30** (4), 272–90.

Isern, J. and C. Pung, (2007), 'Harnessing energy to drive organizational change', *McKinsey Quarterly*, **1**, 1–4.

James, R. (2004), 'Exploring OD in Africa: a response to David Lewis', *Nonprofit Management and Leadership*, **14** (3), 313–24.

Al-Kazemi, A. and A. Ali (2002), 'Managerial problems in Kuwait', *Journal of Management Development*, **21** (5), 366–75.

Khassawneh, A. (2005), 'Change resistance in bureaucratic organizations in Jordan: causes and implications for future trends of administrative reform and development', *Journal of King Saud University*, **18** (1), 15–39.

Kotter, J.P. (1995), 'Leading change: why transformation efforts fail', *Harvard Business Review*, **73** (2), 59–67.

Mellahi, K. (2003), 'National culture and management practices: the case of Gulf Cooperation Council Counties', in M. Tayeb (ed.), *International Management: Theories and Practices*, London: Prentice Hall, pp. 88–105.

McLean, G.N. (2007), *Organization Development: Principles, Processes, Performance*, San Francisco, CA: Berrett-Koehler.

Meyer, C. and I. Stensaker (2006), 'Developing capacity for change', *Journal of Change Management*, **6** (2), 217–31.

Oakland, J.S. and S.J. Tanner (2007), 'A new framework for managing change', *The TQM Magazine*, **19** (6), 572–89.

Patrick, N., E. Murphy and G. Nonneman (2006), 'Political reform in GCC London: The Foreign Policy Center, accessed 5 December 2007 at www.Fpc.org.uk/topics/civility/.

Piotrowski, C. and T.R. Armstrong (2005), 'Major research areas in organization development', *Organization Development Journal*, **23** (4), 86–91.

Rao, T.V. and M. Vijayalakshmi (2000), 'Organization development in India', *Organization Development Journal*, **18** (1), 51–63.

Rees, C.J. (2008), 'Editorial. Organisational change and development: perspectives on theory and practice', *Journal of Business, Economics and Management*, **9** (2), 87–9.

Rees, C.J. and R. Althakhri, (2008), 'Organizational change strategies in the Arab region: a review of critical factors', *Journal of Business, Economics and Management*, **9** (2), 123–32.

Rees, C.J., A. Mamman, and A.B. Braik (2007), 'Emiratization as a strategic HRM change initiative: case study evidence from a UAE petroleum company', *International Journal of Human Resource Management*, **18** (1), 33–53.

Senior, B. and J. Fleming (2006), *Organisational Change*, 3rd edn, London: FT Prentice-Hall.

Al-Shihi, H. (2006), 'Critical factors in the adoption and diffusion of e-government initiatives in Oman', unpublished PhD thesis, University of Victoria, Melbourne, Australia.

Todnem, R. (2005), 'Organisational change management: a critical review', *Journal of Change Management*, **5** (4), 369–80.

Underwood-Stephens, C. and A.T. Cobbs (1999), 'A Habermasian approach to justice in organizational change: synthesizing the technical and philosophical perspectives', *Journal of Organizational Change Management*, **12** (1), 21–34.

United Nations Development Program (2002), *Arab Human Development Report*, New York: United Nations.

Waldersee, R. and A. Griffiths (2004), 'Implementing change: matching implementation methods and change type', *Leadership and Organization Development Journal*, **25** (5), 424–34.

Weber, P.S. and J.E. Weber (2001), 'Changes in employee perceptions during organizational change', *Leadership and Organization Development Journal*, **22** (6), 291–300.

Weisbord, M.R. (1976), 'Organisational diagnosis: six places to look for trouble with or without a theory', *Group and Organization Studies*, **1** (4), 430–47.

Al-Yousif, K. (2004), *Globalization and Economic in GCC*, paper presented at American Economic Association Conference in SanDiego, CA.

Zhou, K.Z., D.K. Tse, and J.J. Li (2006), 'Organizational changes in emerging economies: drivers and consequences', *Journal of International Business Studies*, **37**, 248–63.

6. Leadership in the Sultanate of Oman

Richard Common

INTRODUCTION

Along with its Middle East neighbours, the amount of research on the topic of leadership in the Sultanate of Oman is scarce. Furthermore, 'leadership studies in the Middle East are almost nonexistent due to the inherent difficulty of conducting organizational research there' (Dorfman and House 2004, p. 64). It will also come as no surprise to anyone who is familiar with the Middle East in general that the context of Oman is such that it is difficult to conceptualize leadership as developed by theorists and practitioners in the USA, where the bulk of popular leadership theory is derived. However, as countries such as Oman are important in challenging universalist conceptions of organizational behaviour, this chapter begins by analysing the organizational context in Oman. Crucial to understanding this context is the political development of the country; when compared to its immediate Gulf neighbours such as Bahrain and Saudi Arabia, Oman's development over the last 40 years has been swift and remarkable. A discussion of societal culture follows an analysis of the political context that identifies facets unique to Oman (as opposed to generic 'Arab' characteristics). In addition, the chapter outlines the key institutional factors that shape leadership in Oman; the point that is emphasized here is that, in line with developing countries, the public sector remains the prime driver of the economy. It becomes clear from the chapter that the scope for the exercise of leadership is tightly constrained in Omani organizations. The context also presents considerable limitations for the application of theorists, such as Fiedler (1967) for instance, who argue that leaders should and can shape their context. In fact, due to the richness of the organizational environment in Oman, any manifestation of leadership behaviour, as construed by Western theorists, is highly adapted to it. This is not to say Oman lacks leadership; rather it is practised beyond the modern organizational structures that have developed rapidly within the country and exhibits behaviours that appear to be inconsistent with contemporary interpretations. The following section describes and elaborates upon the unique institutional and cultural context of Oman.

The Context of the Sultanate of Oman

Oman is a relatively small country in terms of population. In fact, Oman's population of nearly 3.5 million is spread over the third largest land area on the Arabian peninsula (exceeded only by Saudi Arabia and Yemen) (CIA 2009). Outwardly, along with rapid economic development, Oman shares many cultural characteristics with its Arab neighbours, particularly those in the Gulf Cooperation Council (GCC) (see Chapter 1). Despite some superficial similarities, the important contextual factors that make Oman unique in the Middle East are as much a product of geography and history as of culture and economic change. To examine all possible factors that shape leadership in Oman would be beyond the scope of this chapter, but we turn first to the political context of Oman, which shapes the conception of leadership in the country.

Political Context of Oman

Oman's historical development is more closely associated with overseas trade when compared to its Arab neighbours, principally with East Africa. This was largely due to the geography of its interior, which isolated it from other countries on the Arab peninsula (Riphenburg 1998, p. 3). Trade aside, relative isolation meant that Oman originally managed its own affairs, at least until the nineteenth century when the British started to exert their influence in the region. Divisions between the interior (Oman) and Muscat (the coastal region) also deepened in the early part of the twentieth century. During this period, Oman (both the coast and the interior) was particularly insular. Although its geographical isolation ensured Oman's independence long before its Gulf neighbours were created, the interior of Oman (the Imamate) and Muscat (the Sultanate) on the coast were politically divided until 1955 when the Sultanate prevailed with the assistance of British forces (Cottrell 1980). However, the unification of Oman was only completed when, following a coup against his father, the present ruler Sultan Qaboos came to power in 1970.

Halliday (2000) describes Oman as a 'traditional sultanate' transformed into a state by British support. Although the British influence in Oman and the wider Gulf has been considerable, but contrary to some opinion, the British made no direct contribution to government or administrative rule in Oman (Riphenburg 1998, p. 89; Kechichian 2000). Rather, Oman was subjected to the British 'informal empire' in the region, which effectively ended with Britain's withdrawal from Bahrain in 1971 (Smith 2004, p. 155). However, the year 1970 is seen as pivotal in the eyes of Omanis as the accession of Sultan Qaboos marked the point at which the modernization of the country began.

The political situation of Oman is extremely important when interpreting and understanding organizational leadership. As the country is a monarchical regime, where 'monarchs not only reign but rule' (Lucas 2004, p. 104), the term leadership is directly associated with the Sultan, rather than business or organizational leaders. Not surprisingly, Oman is also classified as a sultanistic regime, with its governance traditionally marked by a form of exclusionary politics derived from clan-based systems. Along with its Gulf neighbours, the Sultan has no 'popularly based legitimacy' (Sadiki 2004, p. 5; see also Kamrava 2005; Brownlee 2002). Instead, the governance of Oman relies on clan or tribal loyalties as a source of legitimation. Tradition also dictates that executive power is responsive to the monarch rather than legislative power (Lucas 2004, p. 113). Political leadership is almost exclusively concentrated in the Sultan and extends to all social and economic life.

An outcome of this political context is that when one discusses leadership in Oman, it is assumed that reference is being made to the Sultan. The personal authority of the monarch is such that any delegation of power, such as to Ministers, may diminish the ruler's position (Ayubi 1991, p. 15). If we accept Oman as an authoritarian state, the Sultan has, 'an enormous degree of discretionary power' (Lucas 2004, p. 104) over state and society. Personal rule by the monarch also overrides any wider, formal policy inputs from society to the extent that power is centralized above ministerial level. In addition, the dominance of the royal family in Oman means that they also monopolize the state and control the bureaucracy, primarily through the distribution of family members (Lucas 2004, p. 108). Tribalism is also incorporated into the state, characterized by clientelistic relationships with the royal family. Within this type of authoritarian regime there is little social or political pluralism and political parties are banned. The result is that Oman belongs to a group of relatively stable regimes in the Gulf within a wider Middle East marked by instability (Common 2008, p. 182). The authoritarian nature of the state, where ruling families populate government institutions and the bureaucracy, helps to shore up stability: Brownlee (2002, p. 496) observes that by doing so leaders are able to mould institutions, 'to support their own aims, while further restricting popular political space.' This statement holds true for Oman as well as other GCC countries.

Arguably, authoritarianism in the states of the Gulf region has been supported by the wealth accrued from oil. In line with other countries in the Gulf Region which began oil production during the twentieth century, political leadership in Oman was further consolidated by 'the possibilities of oil revenue which allowed the centralization of state power' (Gause 1994, cited in Owtram 2004, p. 198). To some extent, oil wealth has helped to immunize the Gulf States from international economic pressure. Yet, the need for economic diversification will become even more pressing for Oman with its oil reserves expected to diminish over the next two decades (Ministry of National Economy, 1999; see also Table 1.6 in Chapter 1).

Oil wealth also encouraged the rapid expansion of the public sector from the 1970s. Government remains the dominant focus of economic activity and provides attractive employment for nationals (Ayubi 1992; Sick 1998). Oil revenue also provides or subsidizes the vast majority of public services and utilities (Gause 2000, p. 172). The dominance of the state sector in the economy and the resulting high level of public sector employment for nationals constitute a form of social obligation and allow the distribution of wealth across society. In Oman, as in its Gulf neighbours, this further adds to the concentration of political power in the hands of the ruling families (Winckler 2000).

The result of Oman's centralization of political power, inclined to authoritarianism and supported by oil rents, poses an immediate dilemma for the analysis of leadership in such a context. Oman's development placed extraordinary power in the hands of the Sultan, to the extent that leadership is synonymous with the office. Any initiative relating to public policy, business enterprise or economic direction emanates from, or is attributed to, the leadership of the Sultan. Oman's political context also circumscribes the scope for leadership in the public domain beyond the office of the Sultan. Yet this is a limited view: cultural factors in Oman also suggest that the exercise of leadership is much wider and more ingrained in tradition than the rapid centralization of political power through a phase of rapid economic modernization seems to suggest.

Religion and Culture

Other contextual factors are as important in shaping organizational behaviour in Oman as the political context. The relatively recent and artificial nature of the state in Oman means that it is difficult to describe a 'national culture' when analysing management and organizational behaviour. Furthermore, al-Hajj (1996, p. 556) argues that in the West nationality determines identity and loyalty, whereas in the Muslim world it is defined by faith. Therefore, Oman is more conveniently classified as part of an 'Arab' attitudinal cluster (Ronen and Shenkar, 1985), and as a consequence Oman's culture is subsumed in assumptions about regional culture. While writers following Hofstede (2001) tend to group the Middle East within Arab culture, there is sufficient cultural heterogeneity within its national boundaries to consider Oman separately from other Arab Gulf states. In addition, Omanis along with Saudis 'tend to hold onto their deeply seated values throughout the transformation of their economy and lifestyles' (Al-Khatib et al. 2004, p. 311). Furthermore, Omanis themselves are more ethnically diverse, with many originating from East Africa or Baluchistan (a region which now straddles Afghanistan, Iran and Pakistan). Thus, it is also claimed that Oman's cultural diversity is much greater than that of its Arab neighbours given its historical expansion to East Africa and the Indian Ocean (Al-Lamky 2007, p. 57).

Islam is the official religion, although its society is diversified among different Islamic sects and ethnicities. Omanis practise two forms of Sunnism (Ibadhism in the interior; mainstream Sunnism on the coast). Unlike the other Gulf States, Ibadhism is the dominant sect and is a form of Islam distinct from other sects which is only found outside Oman in parts of North Africa (Risso 1986, p. 89). Riphenburg (1998, pp. 26–9) argues that Ibadhism has shaped Oman's context significantly, and has provided further insulation from the influence of other Arab states. However, Ibhadhism declined in the nineteenth century following the accession to power of the Al Bu Said dynasty, which led to the division of the country in 1869 between Muscat and the Ibadhi Imamate in the interior, based at Nizwa (Wilkinson 1987). As was noted earlier, this situation persisted until 1955. In addition to Ibadhis and Sunnis, Shi'a have representation in Oman. The Basic Law, Oman's constitution, promulgated in 1996, does not ascribe any ascendancy to any particular sect, while at the same time providing for Islam as the foundation of the state.

Despite this influence over the governance of society in Oman, Ibadhis only comprise around 45 per cent of the population, with Sunnis in the slight majority (Riphenburg 1998, p. 61). In some ways, the tenets of Ibadhism contradict the centralization of politics in Oman around the Sultan. Al-Ghailani (2005) notes that Ibadhi leaders considered that power should not be in the hands of a single person and that tribal balance was considered more important. Ibadhis believe that leaders should be chosen by religious scholars and tribal leaders, and then presented to the public for acceptance. Al-Ghailani's argument is that, although the merit principle is strongly established in Omani culture, it also served as an obstacle to the establishment of a modern state in Oman. However, the rapid modernization of the country from 1970 onward appeared to require the kind of power vested in the leadership of Sultan. As Kechichian (1995, p. 25) notes: 'the Ibadhi political-religious ideology proved to be an impractical basis for the permanent development of a state in Oman.'

LEADERSHIP IN OMANI CULTURE

While 40 years of development have centralized political leadership in the country, Oman appears to have a culture that is potentially supportive of participative leadership. For instance, although the above discussion of Ibadhism in relation to leadership appears to be a narrow religious aspect of the cultural context of Oman, it is clear that the concept of the, 'people of consultation', as the Ibadhis refer to themselves, does have consequences for conceptualizing leadership in modern Oman (Eickelman 1987, p. 32). Although a full discussion of the influence of Ibadhism in Oman is beyond the remit of this chapter, it is worth reiterating that Ibadhism supports the notion of leadership by merit rather than succession. A fuller discussion of the influence of Ibhadhism on Omani society can be found in Riphenburg (1998).

The selection of leaders by priests and tribal representatives, rather than inheritance, remains influential when addressing organizational behaviour in Oman. Culturally, the persistence of tribal allegiances also continues to have an important influence. The use of social criteria for selection, recruitment and promotion is still widespread in apparently modernizing institutions such as the civil service, which at the same time are attempting to operate good human resource management practice (Al-Ghailani 2005). For instance, tribal members will personally petition public officials in an effort to obtain employment for family members: nepotism remains a common practice. In effect, two systems work in parallel. There are formal systems based on the merit principle, while it is clear that ascriptive or social criteria are still used when making judgements about selection, recruitment and promotion.

If leadership is conceptualized as situational (in other words, the environment in which it is exercised determines leadership), then the evidence so far appears to demonstrate that Oman, like other countries in the Gulf States, offers an unpromising context for the development of contemporary interpretations of leadership. For instance, situational leadership models such as Hersey and Blanchard's (1998) would suggest a high emphasis on participation in Oman, given the emphasis placed on social relations. However, such relationship behaviour is likely to be very different from that experienced in a British or American company. There is an exploration of this aspect of Arab management culture below in relation to the characteristics of 'in groups'. Of course, the exercise of leadership depends on the interpretation of leadership on offer, but the implicit assumption here is that it is the heroic version of leadership, as found in the mainstream management literature and which dominates thinking about leadership development, which is under discussion (House at al. 2004). Schieffer et al.

(2008) emphasize the 'human-social dimensions' of management in what they refer to as the 'Arabic-Muslim' region which they present as having the potential to complement Western concepts rather than simply 'adapt'.

Although Western commentators and practitioners have come to acknowledge how the concept of leadership is culture bound, leadership can be alternatively conceptualized in terms of competing elites or social groups (House and Javidan 2004). Therefore, to be able to analyse leadership in Oman, one needs to understand the nature of its elite. If we narrowly interpret Oman's elite as the leading commercial families, even here Oman differs sharply from its Gulf neighbours in that its prominent families have benefited from other commercial deals rather than the oil market. In addition, the size of the royal family is relatively small when compared to others in the Gulf region (Quilliam 2003, p. 47). Thus, in the case of Oman, the centralization of leadership is such that the Sultan will act with the tacit approval of the social and business elite.

Given the cultural context of Oman, it is possible to emphasize the features of Omani (rather than generic Arabic) culture in relationship to leadership. The extent to which cultural diversity in Oman is important in relation to leadership development in the face of universal Arab cultural values and Islam is debatable and inconclusive. Neal et al. (2005, p. 484) argue that the similarities were more important than the differences for explaining attitudes to leadership in the Gulf countries. However, as Schieffer et al. explain, Oman's history as a trading nation, along with the model of leadership based on the high visibility of the Sultan's form of participative consultation and rooted in local tradition, has also contributed to the relative success of the country (2008, p. 340). Ibadhism partly accounts for Oman's distinctive character within the Gulf and although the emphasis this sect of Islam places on communal consensus when ascribing leadership roles, this collectivist approach became increasingly subsumed by rapid economic modernization and development. Consequently, leadership remains synonymous with the Sultan.

What are the implications of culture for leadership and its development in Oman? As noted earlier, wider Arab management studies subsume generalizations about organizational culture in Oman, which may not be accurate. One concept that is applicable in relation to general Arab cultural characteristics is the importance of 'in groups'. The 'in group' consists of the extended family and friends, further embedded by a shared place of origin, such as a village. According to Tayeb (2005, p. 76), the importance of the 'in group' is emphasized by reinforcing 'consultation, obedience to seniors, loyalty, face-to-face interaction and networks of personal connections'. An 'out group' consists of any group outside this. The modification of leadership behaviour is dependent on the status of the group. Thus, managers tend to emphasize tasks over relationships with 'out groups' (non-kin and guest workers) but within the 'in group', while relationships are more directive, they are also welfare-oriented or paternalistic (Mellahi and Wood 2001, cited in al-Hamadi et al. 2007, p. 111). This dichotomization between in and out groups has enormous ramifications for the potential of leadership development in the country, particularly where the use of expatriate labour is prevalent.

Hence, leadership in Oman will appear more 'traditional' through the use of power or coercion by senior managers, supported by the high power distance of Hofstede's classification of cultural dimensions ascribed to Arab countries (Carl et al. 2004). However, this is a rather narrow interpretation of the effect of culture on leadership in Oman. In a rare study of leadership in Omani culture by Neal et al. (2005), who also looked at Lebanon and the United Arab Emirates, it was found that Omani leadership values are based on a combination of charismatic, interactive and rational legal authority. Charismatic and rational legal authority is based on Weber's ideal types (Roth and Wittich 1968). Interactive authority is a fourth category (in addition to traditional authority) added by Neal et al., 'to capture those residual non-Weberian ideas about authority centered primarily on embedded contingent social interactive processes such as participation and consultation' (p. 482). Neal et al. were unsurprised at the approval for charismatic authority in Oman. In relation to interactive authority, the study showed that, 'an effective leader in Oman considers the personal welfare of all employees' (ibid. p. 489), which suggests that Oman is closer to Western style participative leadership than is often assumed. The value placed on rational legal authority also came as no surprise given the dominance of the bureaucracy in Omani society, although Neal et al. wrongly attribute this facet to British administration, which was never direct in Oman (see above). This aspect also supports the cultural dimension of high power distance as a contextual influence (Quigley et al. 2005, p. 375). Neal et al. expected traditional authority to be given a higher value in Oman. While they found that religiosity was important in Oman, the emphasis was only moderate.

The cultural context in Oman appears to make it difficult to conceptualize leadership within organizations. For instance, in Western theory, great emphasis is placed on leadership and team management in relation to transformational leadership (for instance, Alimo-Metcalfe and Alban-Metcalfe 2004). However, a British consultant in Oman made the observation that 'people do not work in teams' (Plummer 2005, p. 69). This was due to rigid hierarchical structures and to a culture where employees who showed leadership 'were targets for disapproval' (ibid p. 70). It is possible that this is a slightly dated perspective given the attention to leadership and team working in Oman's corporate sector, within a wider approach to competency development. For example, Omantel, Oman's national telecommunications provider, is a leading public enterprise which addressed the development of leadership competencies. This was the result of a 2004 market restructuring and the introduction of competition. However, it remains a bureaucratic organization, where traditional approaches to compensation are still practised (Tremmel 2007). The idea that teams and leaders can operate across horizontal layers of management is also difficult in a context where there is more reliance on superiors rather than on subordinates (Smith et al. 2006, p. 15).

Although leadership in Oman is not readily associated with organizational status, but determined by tribal or group affiliation rather than individual merits (Kazan 1993, p. 190), it would also be wrong to suggest that this is prevalent. In addition to assumptions of authoritarian styles of leadership, leadership in Oman is also a function of intuitive decision making, which clashes with the rational assumptions of Western management. There is an aversion to professional management and organization reinforced by group loyalties (Tayeb 2005, p. 76–7) and face-to-face interaction is valued above written documentation and consultation. In their study of HRM in Oman, Al-Hamadi et al. (2007, p. 102) conclude, 'the tribe and the family are second top authorities after Islam in formulating the culture of the country and organizations to a great extent'. Omani culture thus produces a combination of extremes: authoritarian leadership styles within hierarchical settings and with 'out groups', and democratic group consensus making with the 'in groups' of tribe and family.

The Public Sector and Leadership in Oman

Oman's relative isolation until very recently has also had a lasting influence on the organizational culture of the country. Despite rapid modernization, Oman is part of a wider group of Gulf states where the public sector has driven economic development. Thus the public bureaucracy may prove resistant to the types of change demanded by human resource theorists. For instance, despite the conscious adoption of Western management techniques in general, Jabbra and Jabbra (2005, p. 139) argue that this has been unsuccessful in the Gulf region because of the 'pervasive and powerful traditional administration culture'. This is supported by the centralized nature of the state, which assumes that the top leadership has 'full knowledge' of governance, and 'therefore knows the problems and the changes required to solve them'. Authority to reform and make changes is vested in them, plus having the financial capacity to fund and implement the necessary changes (Farazmand 2006, p. 548).

Another key constraint on organizational leadership in the Gulf is extensive government regulations. Within a rentier state, such as Oman, the regulatory environment may be a limiting factor on business leadership and entrepreneurial behaviour (Yusuf 2002). In addition, in line with other countries in the region, Oman is attempting to diversify and privatize much of its economy, which presents both challenges and opportunities for leadership. Fundamental to developing its human resources is the long-term development plan, Vision 2020. Apparently modelled on similar plans in Malaysia (also a source of policy inspiration to other Gulf states), human resource development in Oman is very much public sector led. Moreover, in line with other Arab Gulf states, public sector employment for nationals is preferable to private sector employment. An indigenization policy, known as 'Omanization' is aimed at eradicating this through human resource development. Although Oman does not have a significant private sector, its economy is dominated either by public sector organizations or state-owned enterprises (Budhwar et al. 2002, p. 200). This and the similar nationalization policies of countries in the region are discussed in Chapter 1.

The result of the pervasive influence of the public sector on Oman's economy, accompanied by rapid economic expansion, is a formal system of public administration that operates side-by-side with traditional forms of governance. The traditional system continues with the Sultan whose leadership influences the corporate sector. More specifically, within the wider sheikhdom (or tribal leaders), leadership depends on loyalty and support. This is conditional on the accessibility of the leader, particularly through the *majlis* or council which provides a forum for people to air their opinions. Leadership authority relations are thus maintained through family succession planning and loyalty to established tribal-familial networks. This remains an important part of the political life of Oman, and traditional channels of participation have allowed stability and continuity during a period of rapid economic growth.

However, if we consider public sector perspectives on leadership, such as the politics/administration dichotomy and bureaucratic leadership, these are also difficult to apply in the Omani context. The dichotomy between politics and administration firmly vests power with political leadership, and this view has a long tradition in European administrative thought (Rugge 2007). In Oman, it can be argued that the Sultan stands on one side of the dichotomy and the rest of the government on the other. Political power in Oman is heavily concentrated in one person, particularly in comparison with other Gulf States such as Bahrain and Saudi Arabia (Common 2008). However, early administrative theory also maintains that leadership was concerned with organizational efficiency and effectiveness, although management in the Middle East does not lend itself readily to the assumptions of 'classical' management. Such classical notions of public leadership, developed within the context of Western democratic administration, are also difficult to apply.

More recent models of public leadership follow the work of Terry (1995) and Denhardt (1993). Terry's concept of the role of the leader is to protect the integrity of the organization and the leader is guided by constitutional principles. The role requires professionalism, political skills and an understanding of participation in governance. Denhardt discusses how leaders meet the needs of users, ensure quality and reduce waste and inefficiency. The emphasis is on public service and employee empowerment. Of course, both perspectives were developed in the context of American-style democratic administration and are unlikely to be adapted in the Omani context. The bureaucratic nature of Oman's public sector is such that it is difficult to equate leadership with organizational position, although this is done in a rare study of women and leadership in Oman (Al-Lamky 2007). Hence, leadership is likely to be directive and authoritarian, and accepts hierarchy and structure. For instance, Budhwar et al. (2002, p. 209) found that the main method of communication for Omani managers was through their immediate superior. Employees expect managers to lead and are uncomfortable if discretion or decision making is devolved to them. Yet more traditional forms of leadership, beyond the formal structures of government, continue to rely on participation.

Given that leadership in Oman is essentially public service driven, how can leadership be developed? As Halligan argues (2007, p. 68), the significance of leadership development 'depends on state traditions, institutional structures and the extent of reform'. Furthermore, citing an OECD report (2001), Halligan also notes leadership development is more important in a diversified society with a decentralized government, where public administration is less traditional, and where comprehensive reform has succeeded incremental change. Given these parameters, it is unlikely that leadership development is on the agenda of the Omani government. Human resource development (HRD) has been identified as a main component of economic development in Oman for over ten years, yet the reality is that Oman's traditional, highly centralized bureaucracy identifies members of the country's elite for development, despite the outwardly rational process in terms of selection. In short, the scope for leadership in Oman's public sector remains constrained unless it is exposed to the kind of managerialist reforms that reorganize the public sector, expose it to the market and emphasize the delivery of outcomes. Of course, the introduction and acceptability of managerialism in general is questionable within the administrative culture and context of Oman.

CHALLENGES AND PROSPECTS FOR LEADERSHIP DEVELOPMENT IN OMAN

The concept of leadership in an organizational sense is relatively new in Oman. The lack of a developed market sector, in addition to the dominance of the private sector by expatriates, inhibits young Omanis from developing leadership skills in a business and administrative context. Politics, culture and institutional factors continue to inhibit the scope for leadership. This may change in the near future for a number of reasons, including pressure for economic diversification which includes encouraging a market-led economy, and cultural changes to reduce the reliance on public sector employment. Politically, the succession of the present Sultan is still unresolved, which may force a constitutional review or even political instability in years to come.

Oman's clientelistic business culture, which also allows civil servants to undertake private business, within certain legal parameters, hinders the scope for organizational leadership. The result is that the relationship between government and contractors is extremely close and comfortable for both parties (Skeet 1992, p. 151). Accession to the World Trade Organization (WTO) in 2000 is likely to have challenged 'tradition' in this sense and will expose Oman to standards supportive of trade and investment more in line with the West. In the case of Omantel, mentioned earlier, the change in its business environment was necessary to meet WTO requirements regarding deregulation, moving leadership onto its corporate agenda in order to meet the change agenda.

Leadership is in fashion and, in turn, reflects management thinking. The question for Oman is therefore, what sort of leadership is appropriate to its unique context? Given the challenges that the country will face in the near future, it is clear that meeting economic goals determined by the political leadership will be one way of directing leadership development. However, abandonment of the larger formal systems of government, the extension of the very socio-cultural barriers to leadership, is as unlikely in the near future in Oman as it is in most of its neighbouring countries. Adoption of US or European development packages will lack the cultural sensitivity to make any difference, although it is clear that Arab executives are keen to learn from expatriate managers. Given that leadership is the result of human activity and not dependent on applied techniques, harnessing and making explicit the cultural attributes of leaders in Omani society is an alternative to adoption of Western techniques. For instance, Omani organizational culture is more participative and consultative than it first appears, which takes it closer to Western theorization. At the same time, social connections are valued over loyalty to the firm, which conflicts with Western assumptions that leadership will improve organizational performance.

At present, it is not surprising that the overall drive in Oman to develop the nation's human resources does not explicitly address leadership. However, attempts to diversify the economy given dwindling oil reserves, to reduce the social reliance on public sector employment and to stimulate a genuine private economy will increase the demand for leadership skills within Omani organizations. Within high power distance cultures such as Oman there is high uncertainty avoidance which means security is more likely to motivate than the potential for the type of self-actualization implicit in Western-derived leadership theory. This will continue to reinforce the preference for public sector employment. Limited evidence is emerging that Omani organizations (both public and private) are taking HRD seriously (Budhwar et al. 2002), which will encourage organizational leadership and development. Yet the gradualist and cautious mode of reform favoured by Oman is unlikely to predicate the type of continuous and transformational change typified by the dynamic, market-driven environments of the West that produces organizational leaders.

CONCLUSION

It is clear that considerable barriers remain to leadership development in countries such as Oman. Although leading international leadership studies such as the 'Globe Study' (House et al. 2004) do not include Oman in their range of societies, their other findings from the Arab Middle East are largely consistent with the findings of this chapter. Dorfman and House (2004, p. 63) refer to the 'heroic' status accorded to leadership in Arab countries and support the importance of the other traditional influences discussed in this chapter. The sum total of these influences on the leadership style is characterized as 'sheikocracy', which is consistent with hierarchical authority, an emphasis on interpersonal relations and low observance of formal rules and regulations (Dorfman and House 2004, p. 62–3). Thus the conceptualization of leadership in countries such as Oman appears to reveal some awkward contradictions.

At least as far as leadership development from a Western cultural perspective is concerned, the main barrier in Oman appears to be that tribal and familial interdependence remains deeply rooted and this extends into organizations, both public and private. The classical management preoccupation with efficiency remains compromised by traditional attitudes that place kin and tribal allegiances above all else. Initiative, organizational transformation and team work are stifled by the richness and the enduring nature of these attitudes. Strong political centralization in the office of the Sultan acts as a further check on the development of leadership attributes. The centralization of personal power in the monarch reinforces elite dominance in both corporations and the public sector. Leadership development continues to be checked by high power distance, leading to a lack of genuine team management and intuitive decision making.

Despite the rapid economic transformation of Oman since the discovery of oil, cultural change has occurred much more slowly. Such change will require time; as Foster argues (1983), a 'reconciliation period' is necessary before real change occurs. As a developing country, Oman is in a state of transition between material and non-material change. The following quotation is from the Omani government, and emphasizes the continued importance of cultural values in the face of demands for modernization:

> For the leader of any developing nation there is always the problem of combining progress with conservatism. His Majesty maintains a delicate balance between preserving the traditions and culture of his country and introducing the modernization needed to keep pace with the changes taking place in the rest of the world. (Ministry of Information 2000, p. 15)

Given the determination to hold on to traditional values in the face of rapid modernization, a synthesis of traditional conceptions of leadership, rooted in Omani culture, can be encouraged. This will defy Western management consultant strategies but traditional approaches to leadership, based on a contemporaneous interpretation of the merit principle, may be more suited to Omani organizations. At the same time, the persistence of social criteria (based on tribe, etc.) and authoritarian leadership styles related to 'out groups' has continued to act as a brake on genuine leadership development. Although leadership will still differ from the prescriptions of Western commentators, the emphasis on what Schieffer et al. (2008) termed the 'human-social dimensions' of management may have some complementarity with participatory styles of leadership. While such adaption may look feasible, for high power distance cultures such as Oman, the expectation that managers 'lead from the front' may continue to be a source of frustration.

REFERENCES

Alimo-Metcalfe, B. and R. Alban-Metcalfe, (2001), 'The development of a new transformational leadership questionnaire', *Journal of Occupational and Organizational Psychology*, **74** (1), 1–27.

Ayubi, N. (1991), *Political Islam: Religion and Politics in the Arab World*, London: Routledge.

Ayubi, N. (1992), 'Withered socialism or whether socialism? The radical Arab states as populist-corporatist regimes', *Third World Quarterly*, **13**, 89–105.

Brownlee, J. (2002), 'Low tide after the third wave: exploring politics under authoritarianism', *Comparative Politics*, **34**, 477–99.

Budhwar, P., S. Al-Yahmadi, and Y. Debrah (2002), 'Human resource development in the Sultanate of Oman', *International Journal of Training and Development*, **6** (3), 198–215.

Carl, D., V. Gupta, and M. Javidan (2004), 'Power distance', in R. House, P. Hanges, M. Javidan, P. Dorfman and V. Gupta (eds), *Culture, Leadership and Organizations: The GLOBE Study of 62 Societies*, Thousand Oaks, CA: Sage.

CIA (2009), *World Factbook: Oman*, accessed 18 January 2010 at www.cia.gov/library/publications/the-world-factbook/geos/mu.html.

Common, R. (2008), 'Administrative change in the Gulf: modernisation in Bahrain and Oman', *International Review of Administrative Sciences*, **74** (2), 193–211.

Cottrell, A. (1980), *The Persian Gulf States: A General Survey*, Baltimore, MD: Johns Hopkins University Press.

Denhardt, R. (1993), *The Pursuit of Significance*, Fort Worth, TX: Harcourt Brace.

Dorfman, P. and R. House (2004), 'Cultural influences on organizational leadership', in R. House, P. Hanges, M. Javidan, P. Dorfman and V. Gupta (eds), *Culture, Leadership and Organizations: The GLOBE Study of 62 Societies*, Thousand Oaks, CA: Sage.

Eickelman, D. (1987), 'Ibadism and the sectarian perspective', in B. Pridham (ed.), *Oman: Economic, Social and Strategic Developments*, London: Croom Helm.

Farazmand, A. (2006), 'Public sector reforms and transformation: implications for development administration' in A. Huque, and H. Zafarullah (eds), *International Development Governance*, Boca Raton, FL: CRC/Taylor and Francis.

Fiedler, F. (1967), *A Theory of Leadership Effectiveness*, New York: McGraw-Hill.

Foster, G. (1983), *Traditional Societies and Technological Change*, New York: Harper and Row.

Gause, F. (1994), *Oil Monarchies: Domestic and Security Challenges in the Arab Gulf States*, New York: Council on Foreign Relations Press.

Gause, F. (2000), 'The persistence of monarchy in the Arabian Peninsula: a comparative analysis', in J. Kostiner, (ed.), *Middle East Monarchies: The Challenge of Modernity*, London: Lynne Rienner, pp. 167–86.

Al-Ghailani, R. (2005), 'Equal opportunity in public office in principle and practice: an empirical study of the Omani civil service', PhD dissertation, University of Hull.

Al-Haj, A. (1996), 'The politics of participation in the Gulf Cooperation Council: the Omani Consultative Council', *Middle East Journal*, **50**, 559–71.

Halliday, F. (2000), 'Monarchies in the Middle East: a concluding appraisal', in J. Kostiner (ed.), *Middle East Monarchies: The Challenge of Modernity*, London: Lynne Rienner, pp. 289–303.

Halligan, J. (2007), 'Leadership and the senior service from a comparative perspective', in B. Peters, and J. Pierre (eds), *Handbook of Public Administration*, London: Sage, pp. 63–74.

Al-Hamadi, A., P. Budhwar and H. Shipton (2007), 'Management of human resources in Oman', *International Journal of Human Resource Management*, **18** (1), 100–113.

Hersey, P. and K. Blanchard (1998), *Management of Organizational Behaviour: Utilizing Human Resources*, Englewood Cliffs, NJ: Prentice Hall.

Hofstede, G. (2001), *Culture's Consequences: Comparing Values, Behaviors, Institutions and Organizations Across Nations,* Thousand Oaks, CA: Sage.

House, R., P. Hanges, M. Javidan, P. Dorfman and V. Gupta (eds) (2004), *Culture, Leadership and Organizations: The GLOBE Study of 62 Societies,* Thousand Oaks, CA: Sage.

Jabbra, J. and N. Jabbra (2005), 'Administrative culture in the Middle East', in J. Jabbra, and O. Dwivedi (eds), *Administrative Culture in a Global Context*, Whitby, ON: de Sitter.

Kamrava, M. (2005), *The Modern Middle East*, Berkeley and Los Angeles, CA and London: University of California Press.

Kazan, F. (1993), *Mass Media, Modernity, and Development: Arab States in the Gulf*, Westport, CT: Praeger.

Kechichian, J. (2000), 'The throne in the Sultanate of Oman', in J. Kostiner (ed.), *Middle East Monarchies: The Challenge of Modernity*, London: Lynne Rienner, pp. 187–212.

Al-Khatib, J., M. Rawwas, and S. Vitell (2004), 'Organizational ethics in developing countries: a comparative analysis', *Journal of Business Ethics*, **55**, 309–22.

Al-Lamky, A. (2007), 'Feminizing leadership in Arab societies: the perspectives of Omani female leaders', *Women in Management Review*, **22** (1), 49–67.

Lucas, R. (2004), 'Monarchical authoritarianism: survival and political liberalization in a Middle Eastern regime type', *International Journal of Middle Eastern Studies*, **36**, 103–19.

Ministry of Information (2000), *Oman 2000, Thirty Years of Dedication*, Muscat: Establishment for Press.

Ministry of National Economy (1999), *Monthly Statistical Bulletin*, **4** (21), Muscat.

Neal, M., J. Finlay and R. Tansey (2005), ' "My father knows the minister": a comparative study of Arab women's attitudes towards leadership authority', *Women in Management Review*, **20** (7/8), 478–98.

Organisation for Economic Cooperation and Development (2001), *Public Sector Leadership for the 21st Century*, Paris: OECD.

Owtram, F. (2004), *A Modern History of Oman: Formation of the State since 1920*, London: I.B. Tauris.

Plummer, G. (2005), 'Beyond the doorstep. Arabian (k) nights and personal nightmares: a working life in Oman', *Changing English*, **12** (1), 63–72.

Quigley, N., M. Sully de Luque and R. House (2005), 'Responsible leadership and governance in a global context: insights from the GLOBE study', in J. Doh and S. Stumpf (eds), *Handbook of Responsible Leadership and Governance*, Cheltenham, UK and Northampton, MA, USA: Edward Elgar.

Quilliam, N. (2003), 'The states of the Gulf Cooperation Council', in T. Najem and M. Hetherington (eds), *Good Governance in the Middle East Oil Monarchies*, New York: Taylor and Francis, pp. 29–59.

Riphenburg, C. (1998), *Oman: Political Development in a Changing World*, Westport, CT: Praeger.

Ronen, S. and O. Shenkar (1985), 'Clustering countries on attitudinal dimensions: a review and synthesis', *Academy of Management Review*, **10**, 435–54.

Roth, Guenther and Claus Wittich (eds) (1968), *Max Weber: Economy and Society: An Outline of Interpretive Sociology,* reprinted 1978, Berkeley, CA: University of California Press.

Rugge, F. (2007), 'Administrative traditions in Western Europe', in B. Peters and J. Pierre (eds), *The Handbook of Public Administration*, London: Sage.

Sadiki, L. (2004), *The Search for Arab Democracy*, London: Hurst.

Schieffer, A., R. Lessem and O. Al-Jayyousi (2008), 'Corporate governance: impulses from the Middle East', *Transition Studies Review*, **15** (2), 335–42.

Sick, G. (1998), 'The coming crisis in the Persian Gulf', *Washington Quarterly*, **21**, 195–213.

Skeet, I. (1992), *Oman: Politics and Development*, Basingstoke: Macmillan.

Smith, P., M. Achoui and C. Harb (2006), 'Unity and diversity in Arab managerial Styles', University of Sussex working paper, Brighton.

Smith, S. (2004), *Britain's Revival and Fall in the Gulf*, London: RoutledgeCurzon.

Tayeb, M. (2005), *International Human Resource Management*, Oxford: Oxford University Press.

Terry, L. (1995), *Leadership of Public Bureaucracies*, Thousand Oaks, CA: Sage.

Tremmel, L. (2007), *Workforce Diversity in the Middle East*, accessed 3 December 2007 at http://tremmel.com/Diversity%20White%20Paper.doc.

Winckler, O. (2000), 'Gulf monarchies as rentier states: the nationalization policies of the labor force', in J. Kostiner (ed.), *Middle East Monarchies: The Challenge of Modernity*, London: Lynne Rienner, pp. 237–56.

Yusuf, A. (2002), 'Environmental uncertainty, the entrepreneurial orientation of business ventures and performance', *International Journal of Commerce and Management*, **12** (3-4), 83–104.

7. Leadership development philosophy and practice in Saudi Arabia

Fouad Mimouni and Beverly Dawn Metcalfe

INTRODUCTION

That the Middle East is at the centre of international focus and concern at the end of the first decade of the twenty-first century is without question. The reasons for this can be found in energy wealth – in the form of oil – and geopolitical considerations (Ali 1999). Saudi Arabia, with an estimated 20 per cent of the world's known oil reserves (Energy Information Administration 2009) and a unique religious and cultural position as the home of Islam's two most holy sites of Makkah and Madinah, is a nation central to the understanding of the politics and international relations of the Middle East. Yet dealing with the Middle East can be a challenging task for transnational companies, for consultants and academicians, and for the policy makers both of the West and of the Far Eastern nations which are increasingly concerned with the geopolitics of the area (Bilgin 2004).

Such global participants, in encountering the Middle East, are more aware than ever of the subtle differences in thinking and worldview between their national cultures and those of the Middle East (Said 1981, 2001). As this chapter will argue, one discipline that has become crucially important is leadership development theory and practice. This arises from this discipline's deep underlying universal philosophies concerning decision making, people behaviour in organizations, and business development across cultures (Ali 1996). Many Arab writers during the twentieth century and at the beginning of the twenty-first century have argued the necessity for a theory and practice of leadership that reflects the embedded cultural specificities and value system of the region (al-Banna and al-Anani 1982; al-Burai and Mursi 1995). Human resource theory and practice will be more meaningful when they reflect the indigenous heritage of a specific culture (Abu Sinn 1984; al-Aliyy 1985; Beekun and Badawi 1999; al-Baqri 1987; al-Dhahyan 1986; al-Ibrahim 1988; al-Jabiri 1994; Kanaan 1985; Mellahi and Budwhar 2006; Metcalfe 2006, 2007, 2008; al-Omar 1999; al-Talib 1991).

Today, most Arab countries need further development in their administrative and governance systems. The World Economic Forum (WEF) has looked into structural issues in the region. In the preface to *The Arab World Competitiveness Report 2005* Klaus Schwab, Executive Chairman of the WEF, echoing Ali (1998), stressed the scrutiny placed by the world community on the region and how this emphasizes political and security issues (Lopez-Claros and Schwab, 2005). He proceeded to ask:

> What will it take to revitalize growth? What are the priorities for authorities and policymakers, as they seek to unleash a process of modernization that will release the vast, unfulfilled potential of the Arab world? What are the sorts of inertia and inaction?. (WEF 2005, p. v)

Looking at data on GDP, growth rates for the period of 1990–2004, and a Growth Competitiveness Index for Arab countries, the authors conclude that:

> the Arab world finds itself at a critical crossroads. Demographic trends have pushed unemployment rates to some of the highest levels in the world and brought into sharp relief the urgent need for a reorientation of economic policies. Reforms are needed to engender a process of sustained job creation, well into the next decade, if the region is to avoid the inefficiencies associated with poor utilization of human resources, to say nothing of the social and political costs. (WEF 2005, p. 167)

A report by the World Bank (2007) shows some progress in public administration improvement while acknowledging that not all Middle East and North Africa (MENA) countries are at the same level. As the World Bank states, some Gulf Cooperation Council (GCC) countries have made continued progress in reforms including the reduction of corruption. However, 'Resource-rich, labor-abundant economies . . . have not kept pace with worldwide progress in public administration reform, ranking on average in the bottom third worldwide with respect to improvements in the mechanisms for the delivery of quality public service' (World Bank 2007, p. 129). This has serious implications for human resource development and leadership capabilities in respect of managing public administration reform programmes.

As the report states, and as this chapter will argue, employment issues are the key challenge to development in Saudi Arabia. An updated and expanded version of *The Arab World Competitiveness Report* (WEF 2007) went further in answering the question of future competitiveness in the region:

the future of competitiveness for the GCC countries relies heavily on invest-ment in education and innovation, supported by an enabling business environ-ment and well-functioning institutions . . . current competitiveness bottlenecks related to workplace skills, access to credit, and innovation must be resolved with effective investment and better incentives for increased productivity as well as improved labor force participation.

An important piece of original research included in the 2005 WEF report is the Executive Opinion Survey. Chief Executives represent-ing a cross-section of industries identified in their responses significant weaknesses in areas such as staff training (ibid). As the Arab Human Development Report puts it, 'Training in Arab countries is generally driven by supply rather than demand and the focus is on quantity, not quality' (UNDP 2003, p.71).

It is thus apparent that the administrative system in most Arab coun-tries suffers from underdeveloped governance practices characterized by a lack of transparency in decision making, absence of professional human resources and leadership development systems and an overall lack of sys-tematic management processes and procedures. However, when solutions are brought in to 'fix' this situation, they are usually imported from the West and incorporate a different set of underlying values and assump-tions about human behaviour, motivation and leadership dynamics, and have little knowledge of the cultural nuances peculiar to the region. Hence the pivotal importance of a culturally appropriate model of leadership development in most Middle East countries.

In this chapter, we shed light on the current leadership development practices in Saudi Arabia. We begin by outlining the economic, social and cultural context of Saudi Arabia. We then explore the implications of this particular context for leadership development practice, and through a case study, we illustrate an example of positive progress in the creation of a culturally appropriate model of leadership development in Saudi Arabia.

THE ECONOMIC, SOCIAL AND CULTURAL CONTEXT IN SAUDI ARABIA

General Situation

The current religious, cultural and political situation of Saudi Arabia can best be understood in the context of its geography, natural reserves of oil and the position of the al Sa'ud dynasty politically and, in religion, the Wahhabi interpretation of Islamic law (Morgan 2008; Tibi 2001).

The Kingdom of Saudi Arabia occupies most of the Arabian Peninsula, with borders to Jordan, Iraq, Kuwait, Qatar, the United Arab Emirates, Yemen and Oman, and coastlines on the Persian Gulf and the Red Sea (see Chapter 1, Figure 1.6). Riyadh is the capital and Jeddah the principal port. There are five major physical regions (see Figure 7.1): Rub al-Khali (the Empty Quarter), a sand desert occupying the entire south and southeast; Nejd, the centre of the country and the location of Riyadh, the capital city; Hejaz which consists of Makkah, Madinah and Jeddah, and Asir, along the Red Sea, with mountains rising from an arid coastal plain; and Eastern Province, site of the country's rich oil resources.

The overwhelming majority of the populations are Muslim Arabs, with 27 per cent of a population of 24.8 million consisting of resident foreigners (Ministry of Economy and Planning 2009) including populations from Egypt, North Africa, Yemen, Syria, Lebanon, Sudan, Pakistan, Bangladesh, Philippines and Malaysia. The currency is the Saudi Real (SR).

Saudi and Arab History and Culture

The Saudi Arabian culture is a natural extension of Arab culture, with a special status accorded as host of the Holy Mosques in Makkah and Madinah, making the country the spiritual centre of the Muslim world, receiving millions of pilgrims from around the globe. Saudi Arabia has important cultural affinities with the Arab states of the Gulf – Bahrain, Kuwait, Qatar, the Kingdom of Saudi Arabia, the Sultanate of Oman and the United Arab Emirates. The regional culture shared by these states is sometimes referred to as '*khaleeji*' (Gulf) culture. It is argued that *khaleeji* culture has turned into an identity with which the Gulf states consciously and deliberately define themselves compared to the other Middle Eastern countries (Patrick 2009). These states are also members of the Cooperation Council for the Arab States of the Gulf, more commonly known as the Gulf Cooperation Council (GCC), founded in 1981.

Early civilization in the Arabian Peninsula depended on economic and cultural interaction with communities in the Fertile Crescent, from contemporary Iraq to Turkey, as well as Egypt and, later, the Roman Empire. The lifestyle of the early Arabs was fundamentally influenced by the desert, an environment that required a strong sense of independence and ability to adapt. Some Arabs turned to agriculture, forming settlements around a water source, while others became nomads, travelling with their flocks in search of water and grazing land. From this duality evolved a distinctive culture of nomadic tribes and scattered oasis settlements, as well as the caravan cities that formed along the Red Sea coastal region. Although the

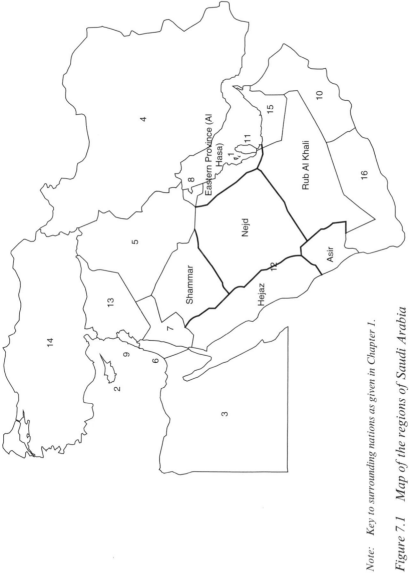

Note: Key to surrounding nations as given in Chapter 1.

Figure 7.1 Map of the regions of Saudi Arabia

desert environment was difficult to endure, it provided isolation and protection for the Arabs throughout the centuries (Esposito 2005; Tibi 2001).

Around 600 CE the Prophet Muhammad proclaimed his prophetic
message of the oneness of Allah. This, and the establishment of an Islamic
government with its capital at Madinah, united the countries of the Middle
East for the first time. Arabia lost much of its importance after Ali, the
fourth ruler, moved the capital to Iraq, although Makkah and Madinah
continued to play significant roles in the religious life of the region. The
later rulers in Damascus and Baghdad lost control of the united Muslim
world and most of Arabia reverted to tribal rule (Esposito 2005).

During the mid-fifteenth century the Sa'ud dynasty controlled a small
area around the town of Diriyah, near the present day capital of Riyadh in
Nejd (see Figure 7.1). In the eighteenth century the Sa'ud rulers strengthened their political power through an alliance with Muhammad ibn Abdul
al-Wahhab, a religious reformer who called for the return to pure monotheism (*tawhid*) (International Crisis Group 2009). This movement, calling
themselves *Muwahaddin* or monotheists but known to outside detractors
as *Wahhabis*, spread throughout most of Arabia with the support of the
Sa'ud armies and by the nineteenth century, the al-Sa'ud family ruled most
of the Arabian Peninsula.

In 1927 ibn-Sa'ud, having forced out the Hashemite rulers of Nejd, was
enthroned as King of both the Hijaz and Nejd regions. On 23 September
1932, the country proclaimed itself an independent Islamic state with
Arabic the national language and the Holy Qur'an as its constitution
(Madawi 2002). The family of King Abdulaziz bin Abdelrahman al-
Sa'ud remains the ruling monarchy of Saudi Arabia. The Wahhab family
remains responsible for religious matters and the 'Wahhabi' movement
has continued strongly to influence leadership, governance, and social and
gender relations (Chapra 1993; Esposito 2005).

Saudi Cultural Values

The complex set of historical developments outlined above has contributed to the making of the Arab mindset and behaviour: pride in a history
of developed civilization versus a perceived contemporary backwardness;
a religion essentially based on peace, yet a history of conflict; a religious
system that touches every aspect of life, yet an epistemological and ontological disconnect between how a Muslim ought to be and how he is
perceived in the world (Sardar 1985, 1987).

Several authors have attempted to define a typology of the Arab individual. Ali (1998) sums up this research. Findings by researchers like
Ali (1984) and Barakat (1993) reveal that an Arab individual's typology

ranges between to such extremes as idealistic-pragmatic, conservative-progressive, and traditionalist-progressive. However, Ibrahim (1982) has developed a different Arab profile in more practical terms such as the Mechanized Bedouin, the Semi-Capitalist, the New Middleman, the Sponsor, the Egyptian Fellah, the angry Muslim Militant, etc. (Ali 1990; Almaney 1981; Baali and Wardi 1981; Hamady1960).

Based on this research, 12 years of empirical studies in the Arab world and extensive research in the literature on Arab culture, Ali (1998) postulates eight types of individual: *Traditionalist, Spectator, Idealist, Illusionist, Traditional Revivalist, Manipulator* and *Existentialist.* 'The typology evolves around political, social and economic shifts taking place in the Arab society' (ibid., p. 4). So, for instance, a traditionalist would value stability and avoid change, an idealist would adopt change as long as it serves ideological goals, and a manipulator would accept change that maximizes personal interests and rewards. When it comes to motivation, a traditionalist is motivated by recognition from the boss, and from social relations and the opportunity to get paid for helping others (Metcalfe 2008a). The idealist is motivated by group recognition and intellectual commitment, while the manipulator is motivated by high achievement, hierarchical advancement and material gain.

The categorization of cultures according to specific tendencies or dimensions has been the subject of many studies (Hofstede 1980, 1991; Trompenaars and Hampden-Turner 2000). The Arab culture has been described as high power distance, high context, collective and poly-chronic (al-Omari 2005; Nydell 2002). In such cultures, high power distance is manifested through bureaucratic systems with unnecessary organizational layers, favouritism and exclusive privileges (Metcalfe 2008a). As high context, the Arab culture is characterized by collectivism and depends heavily on personal relationships. When people communicate, they resort to both explicit as well as implicit means of conveying the message. Special attention is given to saving others' face in public. Being collectivist as opposed to individualist, Arab culture gives more priority to the family and the community and less to the individual. The honour of the whole is to be preserved even at the expense of one's personal interest (House et al. 2004).

The community values are the guiding principle of the individual's attitudes and behaviour. In decision-making, collectivist behaviour tends more toward consensus rather than resorting to voting. Consequently, decisions can take a long time. Finally, in a polychronic culture such as the Arab culture, it is acceptable to have multiple tasks at the same time. When faced with urgent matters, prioritization is critical, rather than how much time is given to a certain task. Resort to diplomacy, rather than focus on the time constraint, is always a wise tactic to follow (Al-Omari 2005).

Amidst the diversity, richness and contradiction of the Arab culture, the single unifying thread that gives each Arab Muslim person a sense of identity and dignity is Islam. Islam plays a pivotal role in the socio-cultural and economic dynamics of the Arab world (Sardar 1983; Chapra 1993). For most practising Arab Muslims, Islam is a way of life that governs not only the esoteric aspects of life but worldliness in its large sense (Ali 2005).

In Saudi Arabia, the dominant social norms stem from the Wahhabi interpretation of Islamic texts, stricter than in most of the Islamic world (Esposito 2005). These norms include men and women typically dressing in traditional cultural and religious dress. Women must cover their heads and bodies; mixing of the sexes in public areas is strongly discouraged; men are not supposed to talk to the opposite sex except out of necessity. Women are not, despite increasing pressure for reform, allowed to drive cars or ride bicycles on public roads (Asharq al-Awsat 28 May 2010). Adult men and women may not mingle in public, unless they are married or close relatives.

The position of women in Islamic society in general and in Saudi Arabian society in particular is a complex issue and a frequent source of misunderstanding between Muslim and Western cultures. From the beginning of Islam, women have been legally entitled to inherit and bequeath property, holding their wealth in their own names even after marriage, without obligation to contribute that wealth to their husband or their family.

Under Islam, a woman is enjoined to behave modestly in public and, as in the West until recently, is generally expected to give a full commitment to making a family home – a home within which, incidentally, she enjoys a pre-eminent role (Metcalfe 2008b; Pharaon 2004). However, it would be a mistake to think that the role of women in Saudi Arabian society is confined to home making. The development of the Kingdom of Saudi Arabia has brought with it increasing opportunities for women in both employment and education (Metcalfe 2008a). A national education programme for girls was introduced in 1960: by the mid-1970s, about half of all Saudi Arabian girls were attending school. Five years later, education was available to all Saudi girls.

Culture, Heritage and Islam

The accelerating pace of development in the 1970s, exemplified by the Development Plans discussed below, led Saudi leaders to acknowledge the threat to and need to protect the nation's cultural and artistic heritage. The General Presidency of Youth Welfare (GPYW) was established in 1974: one of its main functions was to strengthen an understanding and respect for the nation's culture and arts among young people, a function later taken over by the Ministry of Culture and Information. Also in 1974, the Department of Museums and Antiquities was formed in the Ministry of Education and now oversees the National Museum in Riyadh, major museums in each of the Kingdom's 13 provinces, and many smaller ones, some of them privately owned. The Kingdom also organizes annually one of the most important cultural festivals in the Arab world, the National Festival of Heritage and Culture in al-Janadriyah region, Riyadh. The festival has become a crossroads where poetry, intellect, culture, art, theatre, heritage and history meet (Ramadan 2009; Sakr 2008).

The culmination of this emphasis on cultural development in the context of a rapidly developing and modernizing nation is a vibrant twenty-first century culture in which contemporary Saudi writers look to the past for inspiration, popular musicians incorporate ancient rhythms and instruments into their modern music and painters interpret traditional scenes.

Historically, the revelation of Islam had a profound influence on its followers. It had an impact on the economic, political, social and cultural dynamics of Arabia (Chapra 1993; Ahmed 1992). It opened Arabia to the world and opened the Arabs' minds to new lands and civilizations. The Qur'an explicitly instructed Muslims to explore what lies beyond their immediate environment: *'disperse through the land and seek of the bounty of God'* (Qur'an 62:10). The Prophet Muhammad gave a special status to traders as actors in the socio-economic fabric of society: 'I commend the merchants to you, for they are the couriers of the horizons and God's trusted servants on earth and the honest, truthful Muslim merchant will stand with the martyrs on the Day of Judgment' (Ali 2005; Chapra 1993; see also Morgan 2008).

Islam preserved and further enhanced the sense of belonging to the community and responsibility for self and the larger society. Thus, every member of the community is a leader and a guardian in his or her local context. The sense of responsibility and accountability is a shared one. In the Prophet's words:

> Each one of you is a guardian, and each one of you will be asked about his subjects. A leader is a guardian over the people and he will be asked about his subjects; a man is a guardian over the members of his household and he will be asked about his family members; a woman is a guardian over the members of her family . . . Each one of you is a guardian and each one of you will be asked about his subjects. (Al-Omari 2005)

Similarly, it is everyone's responsibility to correct the wrong, especially if it comes from the people in authority and power. Abu Bakr, the first successor of the Prophet, said: 'I have been given authority over you and I am not the best among you; if I do well, help me and if I do wrong put me right' (Al-Omari 2005).

It is apparent that culturally, in the Wahhabi context, Islamic values stress the importance of the community in maintaining both good governance and a strong Islamic state. This also requires that leaders both in organizations and in public governance roles assume responsibility to serve and develop the community. Indeed, this reflects the ideologies of servant leadership literature (Greeenleaf 2002).

ECONOMIC OVERVIEW

Saudi Arabia has approximately one-fifth of the world's proven oil reserves (Energy Information Administration 2009) and the oil industry dominates the economy. Huge revenues from oil exports have been used to diversify the industrial base; metals, chemicals, plastics, cement and fertilizers are now produced. Irrigation projects have reclaimed many acres of desert, and grains, dates, citrus fruits and vegetables are grown. Nomadic Bedouins raise camels, sheep, goats and horses. Income is also derived from Muslim pilgrims who travel from all parts of the world to the holy cities of Makkah and Madinah (Ministry of Pilgrimage 2010).

Since 2002, the Saudi economy has been aggressively expanding on the back of record oil prices and production levels. Robust global economic growth perpetuated the current economic boom in the kingdom as external demand for commodities and energy fuelled the ongoing rally in oil prices. Between 2002 and 2006 nominal GDP grew at an annual rate of 13.6 per cent (Saudi Arabian Monetary Agency Report 2006). By 2008, year-on-year growth of GDP per capita was 18 per cent with a per capita income of SR 70 859 million (Ministry of Economy and Planning 2009).

In contrast to previous oil booms, much of the windfall oil revenues earned during the last few years have remained within the Saudi economy. It is estimated that over SR 1.3 trillion worth of projects, in various implementation stages, are to be executed in the Kingdom by 2014 (Middle East Economic Digest 2007). These include mega-projects in energy, utilities and infrastructure. With both the public and private sectors flush with cash, investment expenditures over the medium-term will be a major contributor to economic growth and, in turn, employment creation. Furthermore, acceleration of economic reforms stimulated by the Kingdom's accession to the World Trade Organization (WTO) in December 2005, coupled with rising foreign direct investment (FDI) inflows, are further adding to the depth and sustainability of the current economic boom. An important mechanism for directing the development of the Saudi economy has been the nation's Development Plans, which are discussed below.

Economic Development Planning in Saudi Arabia

There is a shortage of workers, both skilled and unskilled, in Saudi Arabia. This is the most serious obstacle to economic development in the Gulf region (Achoui 2009). Saudi men prefer management careers, which are high paying and offer the best opportunities for advancement. The rapid growth of the Saudi economy and the severe shortage of skilled people have contributed to the presence of a large number of foreigners in the workforce. Foreign workers are brought to Saudi Arabia on contract for blue-collar jobs. Expatriates are concentrated mainly in manufacturing industry and construction and some service sectors. Saudi nationals work in the service and trade sectors, although the government is currently training nationals for skilled work.

Saudi Arabia's Development Plans

The Kingdom's Development Plans have considered every aspect of the economy (Ministry of Economy and Planning 2009), identifying its infrastructural, agricultural, industrial and commercial needs and future national priorities. The first two development plans, covering the 1970s, emphasized infrastructure. In the third plan (1981–85) education, health and social services were the top priorities, beside expanding manufacturing industry.

In the fourth plan (1986–90), emphasis moved to education and training. Private enterprise and foreign investment were encouraged. The fifth plan (1991–5) emphasized consolidation of the country's defences, focused on government social services improvement, and created greater private sector employment opportunities for Saudi nationals by reducing the number of foreign workers.

The sixth plan (1996–2000) focused on lowering the cost of government services without cutting them and sought to expand educational training programmes. The seventh plan (2001–5) focused more on economic diversification and a greater role of the private sector in the Saudi economy.

The eighth plan (2005–10) transformed the five-year plan into a long-term development strategy (to 2024), with emphasis on full utilization of the nation's workforce. The ninth plan will be a continuation of this programme, with the objective of improving the living standards of

Saudi citizens, boosted by high oil prices and increased output (Kawach 2009).

It is clear that oil revenues, controlled through government, have been the driving force behind the Saudi economy. Through the sequence of five-year plans, essential infrastructure has been put in place on top of which the economy can mature. Vital to continuing development is a market economy in which free enterprise can flourish. The country's agricultural and industrial base will expand, leading to the growth in importance of the private sector, and a commensurate reduction in the economic role played by government.

So far, this chapter has illustrated the complex social, economic, cultural and religious heritage of Saudi Arabia, as custodian of the two holy mosques and a stronghold of conservative Wahhabi Islam. The issue of how an Islamic state collaborates and integrates economically with other nations with different value systems while maintaining its own heritage, both Islamic and, in the case of Saudi Arabia, distinctly Arabic, is one of the country's challenges for future competitiveness. It is this interrelated dynamic between economic development, governance, Saudi Arabian heritage and Islamic values that is key to understanding leadership development practice in Saudi Arabia (Davis and Robinson 2006; Lewis 2002; Metcalfe 2008b; Morgan 2008).

LEADERSHIP DEVELOPMENT RESEARCH AND PRACTICE IN SAUDI ARABIA

There is a remarkable scarcity of solid studies on leadership theory and practice in Saudi Arabia. The dominant literature focuses on issues related to the impact of Arab culture and Islamic values on Saudi managers, human resources development and Saudization as a national development strategic imperative, women's participation in the work force and various comparisons between Saudi managers and expatriates.

In the following, we will try to provide a brief review of the available literature on leadership and management that is directly related to Saudi Arabia or is relevant to the Saudi organizational and cultural context.

Organizational development and management practices, in most Arab countries, are unique and have been conditioned by specific historical and social circumstances. Arab societies have moved to the industrial stage of development without establishing the sound foundations necessary for coping with the demands of modern institutions (Koontz et al. 1980).

According to Ali (1990), Arab management thought is fragmented and suffers from an identity crisis. Four major forces underpin its development and current state. *Authoritarianism* has led to centralized structures, whether in the public or private sector; *colonization* has led to bureaucratic structures and systems (Ali 1984); *tribal perceptions* influence approaches to creativity and problem solving; and oil revenues, in leading to improved lifestyle and interaction with industrial cultures, have strengthened the influence of pragmatic values and approaches (Ali 1999).

Ali (1988) contends that in Saudi Arabia, managers are highly committed to the Islamic work ethic and show a moderate tendency towards individualism. This echoes previous research that people with a high work orientation do appear to place strong emphasis on self-reliance and individualism (Goldstein and Eichhorn 1961; Furnham 1982). In another study, Robertson et al. (2002) identified that strong work beliefs such as humanistic, organizational, and participative decision-making were commonly held among many Arab countries. According to the authors, one of the major sources of cultural values in the Arab world is the Islamic work ethic.

In another study, Ali (1995) contends that values associated with the work environment are a critical influence on organizational efficiency and effectiveness. Saudi managers, like managers from Kuwait and Qatar, are conformist and thus oriented towards duty and loyalty. They have a high respect for written work, policies, procedures and work duties. They show a need for charismatic leaders.

Several authors have found in the Arab manager a 'split personality' (Ali 1982; Baali and Wardi 1981; Berger 1964; Hamady 1960). Al-Aiban and Pearce (1993) state that in contrast to the organizational assumptions of Americans, the Kingdom of Saudi Arabia is governed by a structure akin to what Weber (1947) characterized as a traditional authority structure. They also point out that as the values of members of society shift, we would expect pressures on organizations, and especially on governmental organizations, to adopt different practices.

Earlier studies have focused on Saudi bureaucracy and its efficiency, or lack of it. Saud al Nimir (1982) finds low levels of innovative behaviour among Saudi bureaucrats. However, al Awaji (1989) argues that despite these shortcomings, the Saudi local administrative system has been strengthened by national development plans which emphasize the development of the Kingdom's geographic regions through the establishment of regional development centres.

The establishment of the Institute of Public Administration in 1961 was meant to upgrade the efficiency of civil service personnel and improve the management standard, and thereby support the development of the national economy. However, no serious attempts have been made to date to establish specialized national institutes for developing future leaders.

LEADERSHIP DEVELOPMENT PRACTICE IN CORPORATE SAUDI ARABIA

Leadership development practice in the Saudi private and, to some extent, public sector is primarily dominated by strategic partnerships with world class business schools such as the London Business School, INSEAD and Ashridge and Wharton, among others. Executives are sent to these institutions to upgrade their knowledge and hone their leadership skills. This practice is driven by the need to develop existing executives and potential talent for the future. The maturity in implementing such programmes varies from one organization to another; however, such programmes are mainly in leading companies and banks such as Aramco, SABIC, Xenel Group, Saudi French Bank and multinationals such as Unilever and Procter and Gamble.

It is also common in many private sector institutions to establish development programmes for the young graduates from whom future leaders are identified and further developed.

However, up to now there is no leadership institute at the national level that is dedicated to leadership development, especially for the public sector. This is an essential strategic imperative for the country. This will also substantiate the current government efforts to invest in education through the visionary King Abdullah scholarship programme for higher studies.

In Search of a Culturally Sensitive Leadership Model

Some researchers have attempted to devise a leadership model based on the cultural specificities of Muslim countries. Both Khadra (1985) and Hawi (1982) advocate a leadership model that is inspired by the prophetic leadership image: Arabs need a great man to show them the way and rally them to achieve their potentials.

Sharafuddin (1987) proposes that the Islamic theory of organization integrates the socioeconomic needs of the employees with their humanistic and spiritual needs. Kalantari (1998) advocates that core Islamic values have to be part of the administrative culture in the Middle East in order to bring about an overhaul of public institutions in the area. He also argues that despite its rich culture and long history of administration, most Middle East countries have failed to maintain viable, effective and efficient public organizations.

Samir Abuznaid (2006) argues that the Islamic five pillars – faith, prayers, giving alms, fasting and pilgrimage – have a direct, positive impact on Muslim managers' behaviour and practice. He also adds that God's Divine Names are a strong source of inspiration for Muslim managers.

Abbas Ali's model of leadership (2005) focuses on the attributes of a Muslim leader in an ideal cultural context. In his words:

> since both the Quran and the Prophet's teaching place emphasis on social coop-
> eration and idealism, there is a need for a model that reflects the essence of the
> Islamic message, while capturing the nature of leadership in the Muslim world
> . . . The suggested model explains how two primary types of leaders come to
> exist. The model has four elements: personalism, idealism, great expectation,
> and culture. (Ali 2005, p. 148)

For Ali, personalism is a characteristic of Muslim society whereby individuals relate to each other in a personal and warm manner. As such, it needs to be encouraged and promoted. Idealism, on the other hand, is what a Muslim social community aspires to attain, an ideal character informed by the teachings of the Quran and the Prophet's conduct. Great expectation refers to the desired state characterized by improved societal conditions and a higher cultural identity. Finally, the culture that is healthy for sustainable development is the one that is based on the prophetic model of leadership, epitomizing the ideal human characteristics and attributes, rather than a caliphal model that is based on the will of the leader and a lack of institutionalism.

Ali succinctly links personal leadership characteristics to social dynamics and the interplay where each influences and is influenced by the other. In the context of the organization, he does not provide an integrated approach that leads to organizational effectiveness. In other parts of his research, he deals with such issues as power and decision making in contemporary Arab societies, and reflects on the teachings of the Qur'an and the tradition of the Prophet, and highlights the gap between a glorious past and a backward present. On the basis of this analysis, he theorizes about the potential of basic Islamic principles and the core values of Islam in establishing healthy societies where justice and happiness become the norm.

While Ali's scholarship represents a major source of knowledge on Islamic perspectives of management and organizational dynamics, his focus tends to be more on the psychology of leadership and the individual characteristics of leaders. He often critiques the political and societal causes of leadership behaviour in Muslim rulers in the historical and the modern world, and draws conclusions that often justify, from his perspective, the necessity of upholding the core Islamic values and work ethic that will help the Muslim world to transform itself into a nation on a par with the developed world.

It can be argued that Noor (1999) is among the first modern Muslim management writers who have proposed an integrated model for organizational effectiveness based on the Prophet Muhammad's leadership paradigm. The major dimensions of this paradigm are: alignment, which takes its roots from *Tawhid* and thus inspires a sense of mission and purpose; attunement to the systemic purpose and mission, which incorporates the shared communal values such as commitment, trust, mutual respect and working for the overall good; and empowerment, which induces the leader with more responsibility and accountability for the community, thus embodying the role of the vicegerent (*khalifah*) of God on earth: 'When all these three elements have been addressed, then we have al-falah, which gives synergy – the total convergence of the elements into a symbiotic whole. Synergy entails the attainment of success and prosperity for all who share the common vision of greatness' (Noor 1999, p. 3).

Within the integrated model for leadership effectiveness, Noor proposes a set of competencies and behavioural conduct that assist leaders in managing their teams and achieving effective results. These competencies are: mutual consultation, justice, freedom of expression, personal integrity, enhancement of relationships, leadership efficacy, ethical conduct, and moral uplift through spiritual knowledge. Noor presents a series of events and landmarks in the history of Islam where leaders embodied, through their decisions and behaviours, some of the competencies that are in harmony with the Muslim worldview and which, at the same time, led to positive outcomes for the Muslim community at large.

A major feature of Noor's leadership model, like Ali's, is the predominance of behavioural competencies and the core values of Islam. It always takes the ideals of the Qur'an as a reference and theorizes on their relevance and potential impact on today's organization. Noor, however, talks about the importance of cascading the organizational vision by the leaders and the process of continuous evaluation. To demonstrate his points, Noor dwells on historical events since the time of the Prophet Muhammad and the later periods of Islamic history.

Away from the Middle East, but from an Islamic country, Mazilan bin Musa belongs to a movement (to which Noor Ismail above also belongs) that attempts to offer an interpretation of modern social sciences from an Islamic perspective. He looked at the concept of total quality management and proposed an alternative Model of Islamic Total Quality (Musa 2005). The model consists of nine elements categorized in three dimensions: process and design fall under the Process dimension; management and employee fall under the Implementers dimension; and rules/regulations, clients, public, environment fall under the Guidance dimension.

The assumption behind the total quality model above is that an Islamic organization has to have a strong internal system and a systemic responsibility for its external environment. The model does not, however, provide the practical tools to achieve this. It dwells on the importance of religious understanding which is a pre-requisite for the Guidance dimension, as well as the concept of work as an act of worship. It remains however an important reference for some management aspects in the Islamic thought system.

Beekun and Badawi (1999) have attempted to approach the theory and practice of leadership from the perspective of Islam (1999). Their main focus is on the moral and ethical aspects of leadership practice. Hence their focus on such core values as *Birr* (fair dealing), *Amanah* (trust), *'Adl* (justice), *Mujahadah* (self-improvement), and *'Ahd* (integrity and keeping one's word).

The authors argue that just as these core values helped the Muslim leaders establish the Muslim state at the time of the Prophet Muhammad, we can manage our institutions guided by the same principles and values. It is very interesting to note that Beekun and Badawi approach leadership from the perspective of Islam, but take into account the context or the situation where a leader is in action. They talk about a leader's characteristics, the followers' characteristics, and the situation characteristics. When these three areas match and harmonize, as if in a 'locus of three circles' (Beekun and Badawi 1999), the leader acts in a more effective way.

Beekun and Badawi present their views on leadership in the absence of an integrated framework for organizational effectiveness. In their analysis of a leader's characteristics, they refer back to the ideal types of men and women that the history of Islam has witnessed. Their research remains an important reference for researchers on the implications and relevance of Islam to management studies and practice.

CASE STUDY: ARABIAN STAR

In the following case study, we focus on one example of a successful company in contemporary Saudi Arabia that exemplifies a model of leadership, the success of which has been the result of strong visionary leadership inspired by models of Islamic leadership as discussed above, and supported by a flourishing economy.

Arabian Star, a subsidiary of a larger mother company, is engaged in manufacturing, marketing and selling edible oils. Arabian Star's mission is to manage and grow a portfolio of successful edible oils and fat brands in the Saudi and Gulf markets and to be the role model of a successful company while striving to create an enjoyable workplace compatible with

Arabian Star's high work ethics (Arabian Star 2006). In this context, *role model* means achieving the highest return on shareholders' equity, while leading innovation, fulfilling local needs, and becoming a world-class user of leading-edge systems and processes.

Arabian Star was founded in Saudi Arabia in the 1970s as a manufacturer of edible oils. At the beginning of the 1980s, the Company started commercial production of commodities such as soya and corn oil. Today, the company produces a variety of brands of corn oil, palm oil and sunflower oil in Arabia. It is enjoying a stable and steady market share in Saudi Arabia and the Gulf countries of about 71 per cent, with products distributed in 99 per cent of Saudi Arabian outlets and exports to many other countries.

Arabian Star has some distinguishing strengths; however, it faces some challenges. It boasts a highly qualified management team and employees, core competencies in marketing and market research; commodity research and raw materials purchasing; new product development; operational excellence; and world-class, sophisticated management techniques, all combined with strong ethical values. However, the company faces major external challenges such as raw material price volatility, increased competition, World Trade Organization regulations, economic stability (both regional and worldwide) and changes in consumer preferences. Internally, the company faces the challenge of recruiting and retaining highly qualified management and operational staff (Author's interview report).

Brief Description of Sample Respondents

In Arabian Star, the total number of employees is around 1000. Of these, 65 were interviewed. The respondents represent seven nationalities, mostly from Arab countries, and between them spoke three first languages; Arabic, English and French. Most are married and their age range is 26 to 43.

In the process of communication with the company for access, the author requested that the selected respondents cover the various levels in the company hierarchy. Thus eight respondents are at senior management levels, 20 at middle management levels such as line supervisors, and 37 are individual contributors. They cover three areas of activity; sales, marketing and information technology.

It is worth mentioning that all respondents are Muslim men. This is due to the fact that at the time this study was conducted, Arabian Star was not yet employing women. This was not limited to Arabian Star: at the time of the research, most companies in Saudi Arabia did not allow men and women to work together. Therefore, access to female employees usually proved difficult except in the case of a female researcher.

Additionally, all respondents are Muslims, although Saudi labour law does not prohibit employing people of other faiths. Had there been non-Muslim employees, it would have been interesting to explore with them their experience in an organizational context where employees adhere to a given set of values and get inspired and motivated by working for a higher purpose. In what follows, I will summarize the major issues covered during the interview.

Values and Corporate Culture

The intent here is to explore how the respondents view the impact of their value system on the way they behave and deal with each other. The issue of the dynamics of values and corporate culture is well researched (Argyris 1994; Collins and Porras 1994; Csikszentmihalyi 2003; Goleman, Boyatzis, and McKee 2002; Kotter 1996; Kouzes and Posner 2002; al-Omar 1999; Raghib 1995; Schein 1992; Spitzer 2000). In the course of the interviews, attention is also given to the difference between the espoused value system and the way people actually behave (Schein 1992).

Muslim values inform the social and work relations of the respondents and are likely to drive their behaviour. Understanding these values is essential to understanding the survey responses. The disconnect between the belief system espoused by the individual and the belief system in use, in this case in the organization, is at the heart of a Muslim's integrity or lack of it (Qur'an 61:2–3). Muslim scholars have written extensively about this issue and argued that the history of the rise and fall of the Muslim civilization lies, among other things, in the level of people's integrity; in whether their actions do match what they declare as their belief system (Al-Faruqi 1986; Qutb 1991).

Another aspect of the dynamics of values and corporate culture is related to the way the espoused Islamic values influence the way people work together in teams, how knowledge is shared to achieve corporate goals, whether feedback on performance is shared, and how power relations are played out.

Purposefulness, Tawhid and Corporate Strategy

Another aspect that the interviews explore is the implication of *Tawhid* on strategic thinking. A Muslim's basic belief is that creation, and man's existence in life, are not essentially without a purpose (Al-Faruqi 1986; Chapra 1993). A strong sense of purposefulness engenders a high level of energy and hope that life is worth exploring and living. The interview seeks to find out whether respondents perceive that their sense of purposefulness in life has any relevance to their corporate strategy and whether they feel engaged by their sense of purpose to achieve the organizational goals.

Besides purposefulness, a Muslim is driven by the unity of purpose in life: to play the dual role of God's servant and God's trustee in life (Al-Faruqi 1986). This unity of purpose is deeply rooted in the concept of *Tawhid* (unity of God) that is at the heart of the Muslim belief system. Some Muslim researchers have written on the implications of *Tawhid* on the organizational dynamics and people's behaviour at work (Abdullatif 2002; Ali 2005; Beekun 1997; Jabnoun 2005). In this study, the interviews explore how the respondents perceive the implications of *Tawhid* on their strategic thinking and practice in their organizations.

Tawhid, Values, Purposefulness and Human Motivation

Another aspect related to purposefulness is the issue of motivation. Human behaviour is driven and directed by a number of motivators such as the need for achievement (Atkinson 1964), the need for power and affiliation (McClelland 1951), internal and/or external factors (McGregor 1960), a hierarchy of needs (Maslow 1954, 1962) and intrinsic rewards out of interesting and challenging work (Hertzberg 1959).

The interviews are meant to explore whether the employees' belief system, their shared values, their unity of purpose and their sense of purposefulness are strong motivators that drive their behaviour (Jabnoun 2005; Mohammed O al-Ibrahim 1988; Qassem in al-Burai and Mursi 1995). Many Muslim writers have theorized about the potential motivating power of *Tawhid* and consistent values (Ali 2005; al-Attas 1995; Chapra 1993; al-Faruqi 1995; Izutsu 2004; Noor 1999).

The Organizational Value System and General Philosophy in Arabian Star

To maintain its market position, especially in a region considered politically high risk, the company has adopted what every employee knows as the 'Arabian Star Way'. This is the company's phrase to capture the employees' aspiration to become one of the most successful food companies in the region. This is achieved through the 'Arabian Star Process': to be the most ethical and committed in behaviour and actions, and the most sophisticated in system and management style. A distinctive feature of this process is to become satisfied spiritually, intellectually and financially for the company employees as well as the shareholders, customers, communities and all other stakeholders.

The process requires a commitment to a unique blend of values, attitudes, and styles. It also requires a mindset of persistent drive toward scientific sophistication in methods and practices of management.

Arabian Star has striven to institutionalize these ideals by creating a culture that enshrines such Islamic ideals as honesty, responsibility, justice, and self-discipline. A very important objective is to become an ethical company. Specifically, the Company espouses four values drawn from the Islamic heritage. The terms used to refer to these values are kept and used in Arabic even among the non-Arabic speaking employees. As such, the core meaning of these values is preserved and its spiritual significance is echoed as it occurs in its original context, the Qur'an and the *hadith*.

These values are: *amanah* (honesty), *taqwa* (conscientiousness), *birr* (caring justice), and *mu'azarah* (team work with care) – although it is important to note that the English translation captures only some aspects of the original terms. Arabian Star management has pursued rigorous steps to make these values common knowledge to all employees. New recruits attend focused induction sessions during which they learn the organization's values and how they are applied in practice. The performance system assigns a high priority to behaviour reflecting corporate values. They are posted on boards ubiquitously on company premises and the information technology department has introduced a 'saying of the day' screen, which is seen by every employee when they first access their computers and reflecting corporate values.

PURPOSEFULNESS, STRATEGIC INTENT AND EMPLOYEE MOTIVATION

Almost all respondents agreed that the clarity of purpose of Arabian Star pulls everyone's energy together. They have developed a unique sense of belonging to that purpose. Some of them have said that in the case of launching a new product, everyone feels that it is a matter of 'life or death' for the company. Several respondents have agreed that in such circumstances, almost everyone spends extra hours at work, information is shared instantly, and everyone feels they are being challenged. This collective challenge increases the level of team spirit and loyalty to the company (Ali 2005; al-Attas, 1995; Chapra 1993; al-Faruqi 1995; Hertzberg 1959; Izutsu 2004; Noor 1999). One respondent said:

During the religious holidays, one client – a major Superstore – desperately needed edible oil. I received a phone call from the purchasing department. It was seven o'clock in the morning. I immediately made it to the company, called a colleague from Sales, and a driver. The security people were already there. Within three hours, the required quantity of edible oil was packed in boxes and on its way to the Superstore.

Shared Values and Corporate Culture

Two important factors have contributed to the impact of the shared values and employees' adherence to them in Arabian Star. The first is the fact that the adopted values stem from the very religious beliefs of the employees. The second is that the company has wisely chosen to keep the terms in their original Arabic form. All respondents confirmed that they felt proud of belonging to their company. Some used the metaphor of the 'family' to describe the relationships binding employees. Some said they feel secure in a work environment without threats of back-stabbing.

Motivation

Respondents shared interesting thoughts on the impact of the individual's motivation on the overall team dynamics (al-Ibrahim 1988; Jabnoun 2005; Qassem 1995). Some respondents argued that without the individual's involvement, the organization's purpose comes to a crisis, and the shared values become a mere organizational narrative devoid of any meaning. They have shared instances, either in the office or during field missions, that illustrate their point. One common feature of these accounts is the extent to which a weakness in one individual systemically influences everyone else. Among the indicators for such systemic influence are: a low level in information flow, conflict over decisions, miscommunication, and lack of trust among team members.

Arabian Star employees have become part of an overall purpose. Achieving the target objectives is the central focus of their activities. Their individual engagements become aligned to the bigger purpose and the common language of the company's shared values.

Sharing values mean that employees actually speak the same language and understand each other's frames of reference. Respondents agree that most conflicts are a result of differences in values. Respondents come from different ethnic backgrounds, hold different education degrees from various places in the world, and speak different languages. However, none of the respondents has indicated that these differences have had a noticeable impact on the work dynamics. These differences have become neutralized given the power of the shared values which borrow their impact and legitimacy from the religious tradition. In fact, this cultural and ethnic diversity has induced a sense of unity around an ideal.

None of the respondents have indicated that employees disagree about the organization's purpose. However, their responses have revealed disagreements arising from differences in how individuals reconcile commitment to organizational values on one hand, and their individual level of engagement and commitment to the overall best interest of the organization on the other.

When conflict arises because of non-adherence to the shared values, employees have a tendency to create personal goals to work for. Instead of being part of a common purpose, they become each other's hostile environment. They start competing instead of cooperating. Eventually, the overall purpose is harmed (Ahmad 1995; Al-Aliyy 1987; Al-Baqri 1987; Al-Jabiri 1994; Beekun and Badawi 1999; al-Dhahyan 1986; Noor 1999; Raghib 1995; al-Talib 1991).

Individual motivation constitutes the organizational space wherein the webs of connections and relationships between employees take place. In their exchanges, employees display different levels of willingness to contribute. These exchanges influence the transformation process at the individual and organizational levels. This can take the form of readily providing information, sharing a relevant experience, or giving feedback. The higher the level of intentional willingness, the stronger the transformation process. The more people willingly share, the more they develop and grow. A low level of motivation influences the level of exchange in the system. This in turn impacts the confidence in the shared values and adherence to the company purpose (al-Ibrahim 1988; Jabnoun 2005; Qassem 1995).

As for the shared values, they help leaders better understand how to manage conflict and differences, and how to benefit from aligned teams around shared values. At the level of individual motivation, leaders have an opportunity to capitalize on the individuals' energy and motivate them to create a collective power. In communitarian social contexts, such as in Islam, engaging the spiritual aspirations and religious ideals is a powerful source of energy and motivation for people.

As revealed by several responses, people in Arabian Star find themselves engaged in complex networks of relationships. They no longer see themselves as separate entities, independent of the others. They realize that it is only through others that they can sustain the overall system of which they are part. Consequently, a new organizational narrative emerges among them. They start thinking in accordance with this new narrative which emphasizes a 'we' and 'us', rather than 'I' and 'me', attitude.

Thinking through a network-based narrative, people in Arabian Star realize that just as the others' behaviour has an impact on them, so their behaviour impacts others. As they interact through networks, they realize that one small input on their part can have a huge impact throughout the system. Consequently, a behaviour which is informed by a shared value impacts not only the group dynamics but also has long term effects. As testified by several interview responses, communication flow increases and team members wish to join similar teams with similar relationships.

Leaders in Arabian Star have created the necessary conditions conducive to the emergence of behaviour patterns guided by shared values and inspired by a strong sense of purposefulness and motivation. These same conditions provide the leaders with a management framework to guide their continuous efforts to improve the effectiveness of their organization. In other words, organizational development interventions can benefit from these conditions as a basis to design solutions for a better organizational alignment.

CONCLUSION

Studies on leadership development and practice in Saudi Arabia are still in their early stages. Extensive research is needed. The existing literature focuses mainly on the impact of the Islamic value system and local culture on leadership behaviour. However, the country is witnessing many changes to cope with the demands of globalization and regional and international challenges. Institutions, both private and public, are now reforming to implement the latest up-to-date management and governance systems. It would be useful for new research to focus on the current organizational dynamics in which current managers and organizational leaders are catching up with modern trends in human resources development and corporate excellence.

Western management researchers and practitioners would benefit greatly by studying the nuances of Saudi Arabian culture and the impact of the Islamic heritage if they are to understand Saudi managers' and leaders' behaviour. The case study in this chapter illustrates an example of an organization whose leaders have consciously shaped their corporate culture on the basis of Islamic values. Many managers would see value in the model followed by this organization; however, not all of them would take the necessary steps to implement it.

It needs to be highlighted that many Saudi managers, and many Arab managers more generally, would live these values in their private lives. However, not many conscious efforts exist to apply them to the way they manage their organizations. It was the contention of this study that management and leadership practices would be more effective and yield lasting results if they are rooted in the cultural and value systems of local people.

REFERENCES:

Abdullatif, S. (2002), *The Mind al-Quran Builds*, Kuala Lumpur: Islamic Book Trust.

Abu Sin, Ahmad Ibrahim (1984), *Al-Idarah fi al-Islam* [*Management in Islam*], Cairo: Maktabah Wahbah.

Al-Aiban, M. Khalid and J.L. Pearce (1993), 'The influence of values on management practices: A test in Saudi Arabia and the United States', *International Studies of Management and Organization*, **23** (3), 35–52.

Ali, Abbas J. (1990), 'Management theory in a transitional society', *International Studies of Management and Organization*, **20** (3), 7–35.

Ali, Abbas J. (1995), 'Cultural discontinuity in Arab management thought', *International Studies in Management of Organization,* **25** (3), 17–30.

Ali, Abbas J. (1996), 'Organizational development in the Arab world', *Journal of Management Development*, **15** (5), 4–21.

Ali, Abbas J. (1998), 'The typology of Arab individual: implications for management and business organizations', *International Journal of Sociology and Social Policy*, **18** (11–12).

Ali, Abbas J. (1999), 'Middle East competitiveness in the 21st century's global market', *The Academy of Management Executive*, **13** (1), 102–8.

Ali, Abbas J. (2005), *Islamic Perspectives on Management and Organizations*, Cheltenham, UK and Northampton, MA, USA: Edward Elgar.

Al-Aliyy, M. Mohammed, (1985), *Al-Idarah fi al-Islam* [*Management in Islam*], Jeddah, Saudi Arabia: Al-Dar Assaoudiah li Annashr wa Al-Tawzi'.

Almaney, A. (1981), 'Cultural traits of the Arabs', *Management International Review*, **21** (3), 10–18.

Arab Human Development Report (2002), *Creating Opportunities for Future Generations*, Amman: National Press.

Arab Human Development Report (2003), *Building a Knowledge Society*, Amman: National Press.

Arabian Star (2006), internal publication.

Argyris, C. and Schon, D.A. (1978), *Organizational Learning II: Theory, Method and Practice*, Reading, MA: Addison-Wesley.

Arnold, T. (2003), *The Spread of Islam in the World: A History of Peaceful Preaching*, New Delhi: Goodword Books.

Atkinson, J.W. (1964), *An Introduction to Motivation*, Princeton, NJ: Van-Nostrand.

Al-Attas, S.M.N. (1995), *Prolegomena to the Metaphysics of Islam*, Kuala Lumpur: ISTAC.

Baali, F. and Wardi, A. (1981), *Ibn Khaldoun and Islamic Thought Style*, Boston, MA: G.K. Haland Co.

Al-Banna, J. and H.S. al-Anani (1982), *Alhall Alislami Liazmat Alidara fi Alasr Alhadith* [*The Islamic Solution to Management Crisis in Contemporary Times*], Cairo: The International Institute for Banks and Islamic Economics.

Al-Baqri, M. Ahmed (1987), *Al-Qiyadah wa Fa'aliyatuha fi Daw' al-Islam* [*Leadership and Its Effectiveness in Islam*], Alexandria, Egypt: Muassasat Shabab Al-Jami'ah.

Barakat, H. (1993), *The Arab World*, Berkeley, CA: University of California Press.

Beekun, R.I. (1997), *Islamic Business Ethics*, Virginia, USA: IIIT.

Beekun, R.I and J. Badawi (1999), *Leadership: An Islamic Perspective*, Bettsville, USA: Amana Publications.

Bilgin, Pinar (2004), 'Whose "Middle East"? Geopolitical inventions and practices of security, *International Relations*, **18** (25), 25–41.

Bin Musa, M. *et al.* (2003), 'The concept of total quality in Islam', in M. Abdullah, N. Husain, N. M. bin Hj. Nik Hassan and M. Musa, *Essays on Islamic Management & Organizational Performance Measurements*, Kuala Lumpur: Institute of Islamic Understanding.

Budhwar, P. and K. Mellahi (eds) (2006), *Managing Human Resources in The Middle East*, Oxford: Routledge.

Al-Burai, M.A. and Mursi, M.A. (eds) (1995), *Alidara fi Al-Islam* [Administration in Islam], Jeddah, Saudi Arabia: Islamic Research and Training Institute.

Chapra, M.U. (1993), *Islam and Economic Development*, Islamabad: IIIT & IRI.

Collins, J.C. and J.I. Porras (1994), *Built to Last: Successful Habits of Visionary Companies*, New York: Harper-Collins.

Csikszentmihalyi M. (2003), *Good Business: Leadership, Flow, and the Making of Meaning*, New York: Penguin Group.

Al-Dhahyan, I. Abdurrahman (1986), *Al-Idarah fi al-Islam: al-Fikr wa al-Tatbiq* [*Management in Islam, Theory and Practice*], Jeddah, Saudi Arabia: Dar al-Shorouq.

Al-Faruqi, I.R. (1986), *Al Tawhid: Its Implications for Thought and Life*, Herndon, VA: The International Institute of Islamic Thought.

Furnham, A. (1982), 'The protestant work ethic and attitudes toward unemployment', *Journal of Occupational Psychology*, **55**, 277–86.

Goldstein, B. and R. Eichhorn (1961), 'The changing protestant ethic', *American Sociological Review*, **26** (2), 557–65.

Goleman, D., R. Boyatzis and A. McKee (2002), *Primal Leadership: Realizing the Power of Emotional Intelligence*, Boston, MA: Harvard Business School Press.

Hamady, S. (1960), *Temperament and Character of the Arabs*, New York: Twayne Publishers.

Hertzberg, F.A., B. Mausner and L. Sherwitz (1959), *The Motivation to Work*, New York: John Wiley.

Hofstede, G. (1980), *Cultures' Consequences*, Beverly Hills, CA: Sage.

Hofstede, G. (1991), *Cultures and Organizations: Software of the Mind*, New York: McGraw-Hill.

Holy Quran, English Translation of the Meanings and Commentary (1991), Medina, Saudi Arabia: King Fahd Holy Quran Printing Complex.

Human Resources Development Strategy (2005), Saudi Arabia: Central Department of Statistics, Ministry of Economy and Planning.

Al-Ibrahim, M.O. (1988), *Hawafiz Al-Amal bayna Alislam wa Annadariyyat Alwadiya* [*Work Motivation between Islam and Secular Theories*], Jordan: Maktabat Alrisala Alhaditha.

Ibrahim, S. (1982), 'Arab social change: six profiles', *Jerusalem Quarterly*, (23) (Spring), 13–23.

Izutsu, T. (2004), *Ethico-Religious Concepts in the Quran*, Kuala Lumpur: Islamic Book Trust.

Al-Jabiri, S. Bashir (1994), *Al-Qiyadah wa al-Taghyir* [*Leadership and Change*], Jeddah, Saudi Arabia: Dar Hafidh Publishers.

Jabnoun, N. (2005), *Islam and Management*, Riyadh: IIPH.

Jeddah Chamber of Commerce and Industry (2006) *Economic Report*.

Kalantari, B. (1998), 'In search of a public administration paradigm: is there anything to be learned from Islamic public administration?', *International Journal of Public Administration*, **21** (12), 1821–61.

Kanaan, Nawaf (1985), *Al-Qiyadah al-Idariyah* [*Administrative Leadership*], Cairo, Egypt: Dar Al-Oloum.

Koontz, H., C. O'Donnell and H. Weihrieh (1980), *Management*, New York: McGraw-Hill.

Kotter, J.P. (1996), *Leading Change*, Boston, MA: Harvard Business School Press.

Kouzes, J.M. and B.Z. Posner (2002), *The Leadership Challenge*, San Francisco CA: Jossey-Bass.

Maslow, A.H. (1954), *Motivation and Personality*, New York: Harper & Row.

Maslow, A.H. (1962), *Toward a Psychology of Being*, New Jersey: D. Van Nostrand.

McClelland, D.C. (1951), *Personality*, New York: Holt, Rinehart & Winston.

McGregor, D.M. (1960), *The Human Side of Enterprise*, New York: McGraw-Hill.

Metcalfe, B.D. (2006), 'Exploring cultural dimensions of gender and management in the Middle East,' *Thunderbird International Business Review*, **48** (1), 93–107.

Middle East Economic Digest (MEED) (2007) **51** (25), accessed at www.meed.com.

Musa, Mazilan and Shaikh Mohd Saifuddeen Shaikh Mohd. Salleh (eds) (2005), *Quality Standard: From the Islamic Perspective,* Kuala Lumpur: Institut Kefahaman Islam, Malaysia.

Naquib al-Attas, S.M. (n.d.), *Prolegomena to the Metaphysics of Islam: An Exposition of the Fundamental Elements of the Worldview of Islam*, Kuala Lumpur: International Institute of Islamic Thought and Civilization.

National Commercial Bank (2006), 'Semi-annual report August/September 2006', Jeddah, Saudi Arabia: National Commercial Bank.

Noor, Ismail (1999), *Prophet Muhammad's Leadership: The Paragon of Excellence, Altruistic Management*, Kuala Lumpur: Utusan Publications and Distributors.

Nydell, M.K. (2002), *Understanding Arabs: A Guide for Westerners*, Boston, MA: Intercultural Press.

Al-Omar, F.A. (1999), *Akhlaqu al-Amal* [*Work Ethics*], Jeddah, Saudi Arabia: Islamic Research and Training Institute.

Al-Omari, J. (2005), *The Arab Way: How to Work more Effectively with Arab Cultures*, Oxford: Howtobooks.

Raghib (1995), in M.A. al-Burai and M.A. Mursi (eds), *Alidara fi Al-Islam* [Administration in Islam], Jeddah, Saudi Arabia: Islamic Research and Training Institute.

Robertson, C., M. al-Khatib, and J.A. al-Habib (2002), 'A three-country study of beliefs about work in the Middle East', *Thunderbird International Business Review*, **11**, 91–111.

Said, E.W. (1978), *Orientalism*, New York: Vintage Books.

Said, E.W. (1981), *Covering Islam: How the Media and the Experts Determine How We See the Rest of the World*, New York: Pantheon Books.

Said, E.W. (1993), *Culture and Imperialism*, New York: Vintage Books.

Said, E.W. (2001), *Power, Politics, and Culture: Interviews with Edward Said*, New York: Vintage Books.

Sardar, Z. (1985), *Islamic Futures: The Shape of Ideas to Come*, London: Mansell.

Sardar, Z. (1987), *The Future of Muslim Civilization*, London: Croom Helm.

Sardar, Z. (1983), 'The Future of Islamic Studies', *Islamic Cultures*, **57** (3), 193–205.

Saud Mohammed al-Nimir (1982), *Present and Future Bureaucrats in Saudi Arabia: A Survey Research,* Tallahassee, FL: Florida State University.

Saudi Arabian Monetary Report (2006), accessed at www.sama.gov.sa/ newreports/annual/en/section9/indexe.htm.

Schein, E.H. (1992), *Organizational Culture and Leadership*, San Francisco, CA: Jossey-Bass.

Sharafuddin, I. (1987), 'Toward an Islamic administrative theory', *The American Journal of Islamic Social Science*, **4** (2), 229–44.

Spitzer, R.J. (2000), *The Spirit of Leadership: Optimizing Creativity and Change in Organizations*, Provo, UT: Executive Excellence Publishing.

Al-Talib, Hisham (1991), *Training Guide for Islamic Workers*, Herndon, VA: The International Institute of Islamic Thought.

Trompenaars, F. and C. Hampden-Turner (2000), *Building Cross-Cultural Competence*, New Haven, CT and London: Yale University Press.

8. Leadership in Jordanian organizations: how does it differ from leadership in Western organizations?

Samir Abuznaid and David Weir

INTRODUCTION

Jordan is a small country, relatively poor in natural resources, with a political history marked by its central position in the long-running conflict between Israel and its Arab neighbours. The kingdom, in common with many of the others in the region, has largely artificial boundaries deriving from the division of former Ottoman territories between Britain and France after World War I and, in particular, in the creation of the states of Palestine, Transjordan and Iraq out of the lands of the British mandate (Ryan 2011). However, the country has developed a strongly integrated political sense in which the lack of natural resources is balanced by a very strong sense of national identity and social culture. The monarchy, especially as embodied by the late King Hussein, has been a defining influence on this identity and culture in this Arab and Muslim (predominantly Sunni) state.

In this chapter we first characterize the economic situation of Jordan, and then describe some general features of the organizational structure and leadership behaviours and styles in the region of the Arab Middle East. We then discuss some recent empirical research studies on leadership and management in Jordan. Although the unique style of leadership in the country owes much to the continuing influence of the military, the relative lack of corruption is also an influence, with Transparency International stating: 'countries such as Bhutan, Botswana, Cape Verde, Chile, Jordan, Uruguay and some Caribbean islands continue to exhibit relatively low levels of perceived corruption despite being relatively low-income' (Transparency International 2009, p. 396), although there remains a palpable tension between the older, family and network-based models of organization and the aspirations of younger managers with stronger grounding in education, skills and higher level qualifications. Finally, we discuss the unique position of women, noting especially the influence of specific role models like queens consort Noor and Rania, and the findings of studies that imply a suppressed desire for stronger representation of women in public leadership roles. The chapter concludes with some remarks on likely future trends in leadership skills development.

HISTORICAL AND ECONOMIC BACKGROUND

Jordan is a kingdom, in full the Hashemite Kingdom of Jordan, with the monarch, His Majesty King Abdullah II, claiming descent over 40 generations from the Prophet Muhammad. The full history of global politics and colonial nation building which led to the formation of the states of Iraq, Jordan and Israel, as well as the nations of the former French mandate (Syria and Lebanon), and the role of the Hashemites in each, is beyond the scope of this volume. The British Mandate of Transjordan was established in 1921 in an attempt both to placate Britain's allies of the Arab Revolt in World War I and to establish a stable regime in an underdeveloped and neglected area of the former Ottoman Empire (Cleveland and Bunton 2009; Ryan 2011). Thus the Emirate of Transjordan was established under its first ruler, Abdullah. Further support given to the British through Word War II led to independence in 1946 with Abdullah as King (Cleveland and Bunton 2009).

The defining action of Abdullah's new Kingdom of Transjordan was the first Arab-Israeli War of 1948 in which his army, the Arab Legion, was the most successful of the disunited Arab forces (Cleveland and Bunton 2009), occupying, and later annexing, the area of Palestine known as the West Bank, including East Jerusalem (Ryan 2011). Although Abdullah extended full citizenship rights to the Palestinians, there was widespread resentment and in 1951 the King was assassinated by a Palestinian nationalist (Ryan 2011).

Abdullah was succeeded briefly by his son Talal until his abdication in favour of his own son Hussein who, after a period of regency, was to rule from 1953 until his death in 1999 (Ryan 2011), becoming almost indistinguishable in his person from the Kingdom itself, steering the nation through threats of military insurrection; further Arab-Israeli wars; the Iran-Iraq war; and the Iraqi occupation of Kuwait; all of which would have enormous economic implications for the state. Hussein died in 1999, succeeded by his son Abdullah II, who has been in power throughout the economic developments discussed in this chapter.

In the United Nations Human Development Index, which classifies the countries of the world against a range of indices including life expectancy, literacy, education and living standards, Jordan appears in the middle group of developing nations. Compared to other Middle East countries it is behind Turkey and ahead of Lebanon and Tunisia. In many other indices Jordan also appears in the 'middle' group as can be seen in Table 8.1 (UNDP 2009a; 2009b).

Geographically, Jordan is located to the East of the River Jordan. It has a scarcity of natural resources, suffering endemically from inadequate supplies of water and, compared with many of its Middle East neighbours, shortages of other natural resources such as oil (Said 1995). Fourteen per cent of the population are estimated to be below the poverty line (UNDP 2009b). Further, literacy rates are low compared to other states in the region such as Kuwait, Qatar, UAE and Bahrain (UNDP 2009b). In terms of population origin there is a strong connection between the people of Jordan and those of Palestine that dates back to the partition of the British mandate of Transjordan as discussed above, and familial ties are very strong between Jordanian families and those who live in what is currently the Occupied West Bank of the Jordan. Studies of attitudes, leadership philosophy and behaviour in Jordan are likely to be relevant to Palestine, and vice versa, making allowances for evident political and economic differences.

Debt, poverty and unemployment continue to be fundamental problems in the economy, but in the past few years broad economic reforms and a programme of economic privatization have formed part of a long-term effort to improve living standards (National Agenda 2006). The government of King Abdullah has liberalized the trade regime sufficiently to secure Jordan's membership of the WTO (2000), a free trade accord with the US (2000) and an association agreement with the EU (2001). These measures have helped improve productivity and have increased the visibility of Jordan to international investors.

Political events in the Middle East region have, however, not been favourable to the Jordanian economy. In particular, the US-led invasion of Iraq in 2003 dealt a considerable economic blow to Jordan, which had been dependent on Iraq for an economic advantage, worth $300-$600 million a year, by way of discounted oil and as a market for Jordanian exports, for which Iraq was by far the largest export market (Morgan 2007). Several Gulf nations provided temporary aid to compensate for the loss of the oil subsidy; the long-term effect, however, was a rise in the cost of Jordan's fuel and petroleum imports from JD 540 million in 2002 to JD 1.7 billion in 2005 (Saif and DeBartolo 2007). There was also a significant economic effect of the influx of an estimated 800 000 Iraqis to Jordan and an economic change where, although exports to Iraq more than recovered their previous value, the USA has become a far more important export market (Saif and DeBartolo 2007).

The economy is largely service based. In 2003, 3.6 per cent of the total working population were employed in agriculture, 21.8 per cent in industry and 74.5 per cent in services (World Bank 2010). There has been an acceleration of growth in the economy from a base of around 3 per cent per annum in the previous decade to around 8 per cent annually (adjusted for inflation, which has become an issue) from 2005 to 2008 (Economist Intelligence Unit 2005). Unemployment is officially around 13 per cent (World Bank 2010) but informed estimates put it closer to 30 per cent (CIA 2009).

The overall picture of the Jordanian economy which may be drawn from the rankings set out in Table 8.1 is of one that is in the stage of medium economic development, or somewhere below it, on a range of metrics that do not show the country in any way as a 'leader' or one that has had a tradition of being in the forefront of world events. Despite this, most visitors come away with a sense that Jordanians are proud of their country, see it as playing an important role in the politics of its region, and view Jordan as having several characteristics that distinguish it from its neighbours. It is equally evident that not everything in the contemporary economic scene in Jordan is positive. The economic base of a country in this region that is attempting a comprehensive programme of modernization without the benefits of oil revenues may be vulnerable. There are unique demands on the Jordanian economy and society to remain responsive to the continuing socio-political instability in the region without opting irrevocably for one type of extremism or another. This includes demographic and political pressures exerted by the situations of Palestine and Iraq that are not shared by all of Jordan's neighbours.

Brynen characterizes the overall political situation in Jordan thus:

> in many Arab countries the political economy of regional petroleum wealth has served to inhibit democratization. In the particular case of Jordan, petrodollar foreign aid and workers' remittances long served as a critical aspect of political stability, supporting regime neo-patrimonialism and blunting pressures for greater participation. Equally, the decline of those revenues in the late 1980s spurred the eventual collapse of the foundations upon which the old economic and political order had been built. With this came the need to negotiate a new social contract, resulting in a far-reaching process of political liberalization and partial democratization after April 1989. (Brynen 1992, p. 69)

The economy of Jordan faces a continuing demographic challenge as 23 per cent of the population will reach working age in next few years

Table 8.1 Economy and development ranking factors

Measure	Dataset Date	Jordan Ranking	Number of countries ranked	Source
Index of Economic Freedom	2010	52 out of 157 countries	179	The Heritage Foundation 2010
GDP per capita	2007	107	182	UNDP 2009a
Human Development Index	2007	96	182	UNDP 2009a
Gender-related development index (GDI) as % of HDI	2007	145	155	UNDP 2009b
Global Competitiveness Index 2009–2010	2009	50	133	World Economic Forum 2009
Environmental Performance Index 2010	2010	97	163	Yale Center for Environmental Law & Policy and CIESIN, Columbia University
Globalization Index 2007	2005	9	72	A.T. Kearney/Foreign Policy Magazine 2007
Corruption Perceptions Index 2009	2009	49=	180	Transparency International
Worldwide press freedom index 2009	2008 – 2009	112	175	Reporters Without Borders
e-readiness rankings 2009	2009	50	70	Economist Intelligence Unit
Quality-of-life index 2005	2005	75	111	Economist Intelligence Unit

Source: Jordan Economy: CIA Factbook: 2006, updated and expanded.

(UNDP 2006). However, the Jordanian economy does not at present have the capacity to absorb the annual inflow of job seekers. The official unemployment rate in Jordan could reach 20 to 30 per cent by 2015 if present conditions continue (National Agenda 2006, p. 25). The problem is especially severe amongst women, since the official unemployment rate of males is 11.9 per cent while the female rate is 25 per cent (UNDP 2006).

According to the profile published by the Department of Statistics, 22.3 per cent of the unemployed in Jordan are bachelor degree holders (Department of Statistics, 1996). This is the second largest grouping, second only to those with less than secondary education (55 per cent). However, a significant proportion of unemployed women are educated to degree level – in fact 49.7per cent are BA holders, constituting the largest segment of the female unemployed (UNDP 2006).

EDUCATION, SKILLS AND DEVELOPMENT

In addition to the demographic and unemployment issues discussed above, the UNDP report (2006) identified structural weaknesses in other sectors. As it states:

> There is no systematic provision of labour market information which limits the decision-making ability of universities when revising, redesigning or restructuring course majors.

- Significant gaps exist between academic institutions and the private sector both in terms of structures and programmes and the links remain inconsistent and unregulated.
- Guidance for school and university graduates in their choice of career path is limited.
- Lack of University specializations; positioning and proper information on their rating.
- Employers use their experience to build their own perception about graduates without referring to statistical information.
- Gender stereotyping exists in the choice of specializations, such as IT.

(UNDP 2006)

In common with other states, education provision is not matched to market needs, especially in engineering, accounting and architecture, as well as in other professional disciplines including the areas of organizational behaviour and leadership in much of the country's business administration provision (ILO 2008; Abu Doleh 2004). The government has been slow to transform curriculum and education provision in response, and gaps have often been filled through interventions by international organizations such as the International Labor Organization. The ILO has supported a wide ranging programme of vocational training including creating a Vocational Training Institute and a Training and Development Institute but these institutions will clearly take time to make an impact

(ILO 2008). International agencies are also engaged in other initiatives, for example in micro-finance, to empower the poorest sections of the community, especially in rural areas (UNDP 2005).

Despite these interventions, some sectors remain chronically short of leadership skills. For example, a recent study of management capabilities in agriculture (a key sector in Jordan) found that:

> Operators appeared to be largely commercial, but they did not highly rate the significance of farming as a business, or their level of management skills. Two-thirds of respondents perceived technical skills as the key to success. Poor management skills limit the operators' ability in making informed decisions, planning and analyzing the financial performance of their operations. Farm management extension enhances farmers' willingness and ability to make successful changes to their management practice. Improvement programs have to be targeted to the groups of operators who are more favourable to management extension, that is, full-time farmers, renters, the more experienced, the educated and the more dependent on farm income. (Al-Rimawi, Karablieh, Al-Qadi and Al-Qudah 2006, p. 125)

In the education sector, a British Council Report on a project that ran from 1998 to 2003 claimed success for a complex programme of change focused on five strands: the management of schools; the dissemination of good practice and the improvement of teaching; the development of management skills within the central and governate system; the development of educational training, certification and supervisory management; and the development of the leadership role of women (British Council 2003). In respect of the last factor, the report claimed that the percentage of women in leadership positions increased by 5 per cent over a three-year period. Likewise, there is a small but increasingly significant representation of women in the political life of the country. A pioneer in this respect was Tujan al-Faysal who was elected to the parliament of 1993 on a platform of democracy and human rights, and made an impact through the professionalism that she brought to her role, her balanced stance on democracy and human rights, and her leading role in exposing corruption, all combined with the ability to demonstrate deep knowledge of Islam and its evolution. She famously declared: '. . . women who find it difficult must not say that it is difficult. The lesson to be learned is that a woman can choose not to give up and not to be underestimated just because she is woman' (Abu-Zayd n.d.).

The overall picture is of a society that is solidly based and which, having surmounted a decade or more of enormous challenges in its establishment and maintenance in a highly charged political and military situation, where international tensions and resource limitations have from time to time appeared likely to become overwhelming, is nevertheless pursuing governance and social reform agendas. The success of these reforms can be seen in two recent measures. Inequality between social groups as measured by the Gini index, at 37.7, is on a par for the region and not too far distant from that of the United Kingdom (36.0) (UNDP 2009a). This, and similar progress against Millennium Development Goals, has produced a strong sense of national identity and a perceptible organizational and civic style.

LEADERSHIP CULTURE IN THE ARAB WORLD

In this section we provide an overview of Arabic leadership and frame the dynamics of leader-follower relations. We then make connections to more recent leadership works, and then examine in detail concepts that underpin the operation of Middle Eastern Arabic leadership: *wasta*, Islam and family.

Wasta relations are of central importance in networks that can be described as essentially tribal-familial, although we note that in Jordan these networks represent a value-terrain increasingly contested by younger, more professionally qualified managers. Islam is an essential continuing influence in a country that is strongly Muslim but where Anglo-Saxon influences, through the military and civil administrative histories, have mediated practice in special ways. Family remains an overriding force of social integration and potential for business opportunity.

These three factors interweave and help to shape the unique dynamic of leadership processes and behaviours that are central to business and society in most Arab countries.

An Overview of Arab Leadership

We argue that the Middle East region will achieve sustainable economic and social growth only by studying what it does well rather than by trying to copy the paths followed by other economies. It may be helpful to regard leadership in Jordanian organizations as *sui generis* and neither as a failed attempt to copy Western models, nor a hangover from a decaying traditionalism.

Undoubtedly, every set of economic practices will make evident, in its business activity and management practices, a recognizable pattern of beliefs and processes that relates in a functional and supportive way to the generic culture in which it is embedded. Organizational leadership has to occupy a position within its culture rather than to be in opposition to the main trends of thought in society and the major axes of societal configuration (Abdulla and al Homoud 2001, p. 506).

The literature on the relation of religious belief to organizational theory has expanded recently in an attempt to search for alternate ways of organization, communication and team development. This can incorporate transcendent views of authority as well as reflecting a human-centred orientation (Fry 2003; Sdendjaya 2007).

An important text that has strong relations to Islamic principles is the account by Greenleaf (1977) of servant leadership. The text outlines his disillusionment with Western hierarchical and material social structures, and looks to the East, especially Buddhism, for a more holistic and humanistic way of organization. Greenleaf views leadership as a process of serving others (primarily in a Christian context). This reflects the ethical stance of much scholarship in the corporate world that examines the ethical dimension of leadership (House and Aditya 1997; Kanungo and Mendonca 1996). Some of these works built on Greenleaf's insights, for example, transformational leadership (Bass 1998). Thus, there is much literature in Western scholarship that has explored leadership in a religious context.

Sarayah's study (2004) examines the nature of leadership in Arab culture, based on Greenleaf's servant leader model (Spears 1988), and is relevant to understanding the development of Jordanian leadership behaviour. Sarayrah selects two Muslim leaders: Umar, the second caliph, who lived in the middle of the seventh century; and Hajj Ali, a tribal leader from the late twentieth century. This selection allows Sarayrah to assert that Muslim leadership characteristics have altered little over the intervening centuries.

Islamic communities used *shurah* to elect the first four caliphs. As Kriger and Seng argue (2005, p. 777), leadership in Islam emphasizes spirituality in the human condition and, importantly, that leadership is not sought with ambition. Thus *shurah* very much rests on the assumption of community consensus and decision making with respect to the selection and approval of the leader. Once endowed with leadership authority, followers follow.

A key feature of an effective leader in an Islamic context is one who displays humility and compassion and who values consensus-oriented decision making. However, the leader is the guardian, one who presides over the spiritual, moral and intellectual development of his community. Loyalty, commitment, and high trust relations are valued and reciprocated. As we will argue, wasta viewed through an Islamic lens is associated with support and nurturing, although as we further suggest, the concept is increasingly debated in Jordan. We will expand further on leadership authority relations, and issues of trust and valuing connections, in the following sections.

Wasta

This all-pervasive concept of business networking is the first aspect of leadership that Westerners typically come into contact with when they do business in this region. *Wasta* involves a social network of interpersonal connections rooted in family and kinship ties. Involving the exercise of power, influence and information sharing through social and politico-business networks, wasta is intrinsic to the operation of many valuable social processes and is central to the transmission of knowledge and to the creation of opportunity. Just as, in China, *guanxi* has both positive connotations of networking and negative connotations of corruption, so too does wasta (Hutchings and Weir 2006). The term is politically and socially contentious and many younger professional managers are very critical of wasta. Although they believe that it will continue to form the basis of business for them and for their children, they tend to perceive that wasta is the use of connections for personal gain and thus stands for nepotism, cronyism and corruption; and that this is a deeply rooted practice among all segments of society and in all sectors. Some distinguish frankly between 'bad wasta', with its connotations of nepotism, corruption and the undue influence of shadowy middlemen, and 'good wasta' that is perceived as central to effective business and alumni networking (Weir 2003). Others argue that the concept is also gendered, since wasta often operates through male networks (Metcalfe 2007).

In contrast, older managers argue that this was not the original meaning, which comprises intercession or mediation. Traditionally, the head of the family was expected to perform wasta services at a familial level, but in recent years the term has come to imply the seeking of benefits from government. Although wasta pervades the culture of all Arab countries and is a force in all significant decision making, it is not usually mentioned by most academic writers nor is it often openly discussed in a business context. Nonetheless, its impact is very pervasive (Metcalfe 2007; Weir 1999, 2000).

The basic rule of business in the MENA region is to establish a relationship first, then to build on that relationship. This process is very time consuming, yet once a relationship has been established verbal contracts are regarded as absolute and an individual's word is held to represent his/her bond. Failure to meet obligations may terminate a business relationship (Ali 1990).

The principal perceived objectives of wasta have changed over time and its main goal has shifted from conflict resolution to intercession, and the term may denote the person who mediates or intercedes as well as the act of mediation or intercession. Intermediary wasta endeavours to resolve inter-personal or inter-group conflict and can therefore also imply mediation to bind families and communities for peace and well-being in a hostile environment. This benefits society as a whole as well as the parties involved. Intercessory wasta involves a protagonist intervening on behalf of a client to obtain an advantage for the client such as a job, a tax reduction, or admission to a prestigious university (Weir 2003).

The exchange of gifts in the context of business relationships often puzzles or offends Western managers, but should not necessarily be construed as an attempt to influence the judgement of a recipient, but may rather be interpreted as a mark of respect, signifying reciprocal acceptance of status and marking the initiation or honouring of an agreed bond. However, managers themselves are increasingly concerned that favours are being interpreted as an attempt to change the behaviour of the recipient (Al-Shalalfeh 1993). In an opinion poll carried out by the Arab Archives Institute in 2000, 87 per cent of respondents stressed the need to eradicate wasta, viewing it as divisive and symptomatic of corruption, even though more than 90 per cent also responded that they believed they would be using it at some point in their lives (Arab Archives Institute, 2000; Al Kharouf 2000). This ambivalence is typical.

Islam

The underlying dimension of leadership that is universally applicable is the all-pervading influence of Islam within the Arab world and wherever Arabs are to be found. To be effective, wasta requires a supportive framework of generally honourable dealing, and throughout this region that framework is based on Islam. In principle Islam represents a pattern of behaviours and beliefs which affect the whole of human life, no segment being exempt. Thus, to a believer, economic and business life are governed by the practical obligations of the five pillars of Islam (testimony of faith, duty of prayer, alms giving (*Zakat*), self-modification and purification – including duty of fasting during Ramadan and obligation to make the Hajj to Mecca) that contain the structural foundations of the ethical basis of all behaviour for a believer, including the beliefs and practices of management and business life. Behaviours which are incompatible with these foundations cannot be *halal* or acceptable; they are *haram* or unacceptable.

The ideal of the 'just ruler' informs all Islamic thinking (see Metcalfe in the introduction to this volume). Leaders in the Arab world can be expected to be respected and obeyed but nonetheless, 'people are expected to follow their leaders' orders only if they are in line with God's orders'. Such a ruler must 'follow God's law, ensure justice amongst all his peoples, provide economically for them in a fair manner and as personal attributes be moderate, consultative, forgiving, honourable, abiding by his promises, honest, humble, respectable in appearance, patient, and hold non-materialistic and ascetic values' (Abdulla and Al Homoud, 2001, p. 509; Mizel 1994).

Family

The third dimension that influences leadership behaviour is that of family. Family forms the basis of all social and business relationships in the region. The formalities of social, family and political life are carried through into managerial settings (Moghadam 1993; Abu Doleh and Weir 2007; Al-Faleh 1987). It is impossible to undertake any kind of meeting in an Arab organization without the ubiquitous coffee or tea rituals associated with the *diwan*. The family in the Arab world is the primary channel and model of wasta. The traditional tribal leader, the sheikh, was publicly validated as a person of honour, whose word was his bond and who would assume responsibility for those under his trust, and contemporary business relationships can still be expected to conform to this model.

Although originally based upon family loyalty, wasta relationships expand to encompass the broader community of friends and acquaintance and wasta-based recruitment and allocation of benefits reinforce family ties, thereby connecting the individual to the economy and polity, and it is still widely regarded as improper for the demands of organizational hierarchy to take precedence over the obligations due to family.

The role models of business leadership are found in family structures. This at first seems to imply that, for women at least, the leadership role models available in the organizational sphere must be closely patterned on the woman's role in the family. In the Jordanian context matters are more complex and subtle, and in many ways Jordan emerges as an interesting meld of traditional and modern ideas. But in the field of leadership not all the tradition implies masculine leadership and not all of the modernization is based on Western models. In this region leaders have traditionally been those who have age, rather than qualifications, as the basis of seniority and employees will take their cues from leaders accordingly. But this does not mean that these leaders have inevitably lacked legitimacy.

The spatial framings of social, family and political life are replicated in managerial settings with the *diwan* style of decision making. Diwan is a room with low seats around the walls, found in many homes where it is a place of decision as well as of social intercourse. In diwan, decisions are the outcome of processes of information exchange, practised listening, questioning and the interpretation and confirmation of informal and formal meanings. Decisions of the diwan are enacted by the senior people, but can come to be owned by all, ensuring commitment based on respect for both position and process. In diwan decision making, both seniority and effectiveness are significant, but to be powerful, the concurrent consent of those involved has to be sought, and symbolized in the process of the diwan.

Servant Leadership and Authority Relationships

Sarayah has traced the prevailing styles of leadership to the cultural practices of leadership among the Bedouin and established similarities with contemporary 'servant-leadership' styles (Sarayah 2004). In this style, listening skills are central to the legitimate leader. Sarayah sees wasta as in some ways more characteristic of a slightly deformed leadership pattern that has been influenced by weak bureaucracy (Sarayah 2004, p. 76).

Business organization structures may tend to appear flat even though authority is strongly identified at the apex of the organization. Nonetheless, many Jordanian organizations appear to have vague authority relationships and show evidence of substantive employee participation despite this. In specific respect to human resource management (HRM), international managers may also encounter personnel and human resource departments, where they exist formally, that deal solely with payroll, recruitment, remuneration and discipline within quite explicit constraints, rather than the more strategic, global focus that is the trend in HR in the developed world.

Moreover, though formal organizational structures may exist on paper, in practice they may be quite ill defined, and commonly the general manager will assume responsibility for HR issues, as the father of a large extended family assumes general and residual responsibilities for the kin-folk. With respect to training and development, mentoring is an understood and welcomed practice, as it can be construed as respect for seniority, age and experience, but this often co-exists with an emphasis on job-related training based on improving qualifications (Metcalfe 2007).

In common with the observations of other scholars, Abdulla and al Homoud (2001) found that even Arab scholars have 'paid little attention to the study of leadership and organizational practices in the Arabian Gulf region' (op. cit., p. 507) and quote Ali's (1990) distinction between the 'Westernized, Arabized and Islamicized' approaches to leadership studies. That is, there has been a tendency to replicate Americanized knowledges and texts simply by translation. This view is being challenged across all Arab nations as modernization programmes are being planned with a strong commitment to Arab knowledge and values and the significance of each country's heritage.

Abdulla and al-Homoud's own findings illustrate the mixed tendencies in contemporary organizational leadership in the Gulf region, as managers, driven by countervailing tendencies for change and stability, see themselves as caught between the forces of old and new and conclude that: 'in socially oriented societies what is right for better work performance and for the wider society takes lower priority than what appeases significant social groups' (op. cit., p. 528).

While it is common in the West to characterize the economies of this region in such terms as 'conservative' or 'traditional', this is far from accurate and may often mislead the Western manager or scholar. These are dynamic societies which have known indeed suffered much change in the past 50 years. Jordan has moved further than most societies since 1945 (Saud 1995).

SPECIAL FEATURES OF LEADERSHIP IN JORDAN

While leadership behaviour is influenced by wasta, Islam and family, there are additional factors that significantly influence the type of leadership characteristic of Jordanian organizations. They are first, the legacy of British imperialism, and in particular its influence on the leadership style of the monarchy; second, the education and training background; and third, the role of women in Jordanian society.

Monarchy and Leadership Culture

Jordan was, for most of the period up until the establishment of the Kingdom of Jordan, heavily influenced not just by the effects of the political and military history of the region but by the impact of a style of leadership that owed much to British military and civil administrative models and by the specific interpretation of the monarchical leadership role developed by King Hussein and continued by his successor, King Abdullah II (Sharabi 1988a, 1988b, 1990).

It is commonplace to refer to the military background and Sandhurst training of King Hussein. This is not untypical, as across Middle East states, leaders have continually looked to the West, particularly British institutions, for inspiration in moulding societies and projecting modernity (Ahmed 1992). However, in Jordan there is a genuine and pervasive influence of a royal style, continued through the British education, Sandhurst training and military career of King Abdullah, that almost consciously embodies some of the styles of the British monarchy as well as those of the traditional Arab ruler (Massad 2001): a distinctive royal style that was largely defined by the background and career of the present King's father, King Hussein, who assumed office at the age of 16 after his father became ill. However, the defining incident in his formative years was the assassination in his presence of his grandfather King Abdullah at Friday prayers in al-Aqsa mosque in Jerusalem. Hussein pursued the gunman and narrowly escaped death himself when a bullet was deflected by a medal. He was educated at Harrow and Sandhurst and later trained as a professional pilot, kept up his licences and flew his own aircraft, notably flying to a meeting at Beth Gabriel on Lake Galilee to reconfirm the Jordan-Israel Peace Treaty with Israeli Prime Minister Yitzhak Rabin. He was an enthusiastic radio amateur and communicated regularly with radio hams all over the world. He was well-informed, professional and personally unassuming. In 1991 King Hussein created the National Charter which reaffirmed democratic principles, also legalizing opposition movements and political parties and confirming press freedoms. His style became the style of government and its influence became pervasive in Jordanian organizations (Al Faleh 1987).

These personal comparisons are neither superficial nor insignificant because the distinctive style of the monarchy has been pervasively influential throughout Jordanian organizations, transcending temporary political considerations. In Jordan, the comparatively public presentation of leadership by the ruling elite, and especially the royal family, provides a consistent and ongoing model for a leadership style that consciously attempts to offer a meld of traditionalism and modernity (Massad 2001).

Leadership and the Colonial Legacy

The influence of British military models on the army and air force in Jordan survived the political and diplomatic implications of the dismissal of Sir John Glubb (Glubb Pasha), the commander of the Arab Legion and founder of the Jordanian Army, in 1956. Glubb Pasha was personally influential in creating the first cadre of professional leaders in Jordan, the officers and men of the Arab Legion, and this influence has persisted in leadership styles and behaviour. It has been claimed that, 'Glubb developed the Arab Legion from little more than a gendarmerie into the best-trained, most disciplined, and most efficient of all the Arab armies (Sharabi 1990). His most distinctive contribution, however, was the recruitment of Bedouins and their transformation from unruly nomads into disciplined soldiers and loyal citizens' (Massad 2001). Glubb Pasha's son Godfrey became an important journalist and historian in the region, having converted to Islam as soon as he was of mature age, taking the name Faris.

King Abdullah is of course half British by parentage and partly British and American by education. He served in the Royal Hussars regiment and it is sometimes remarked that his Arabic is less assured than his English. This style of monarchy gives symbolic meaning to an approach to management and leadership that has been widely influential in Jordan, embodying ideals of public service, trans-nationalism and professionalism that are met with in many sectors of public and private leadership.

His Majesty King Abdullah has a quite openly publicized social and political agenda that is clearly articulated in this quotation from his personal website:

> King Abdullah II is committed to building on the late King's legacy to further institutionalize democratic and political pluralism in Jordan. He has exerted extensive effort to ensuring sustainable levels of economic growth and social development aimed at improving the standard of living of all Jordanians. (Abdullah 2008)

And:

> The King has also been involved in the drive for national administrative reform, as well as governmental transparency and accountability. He has been working on the advancement of civil liberties making Jordan one of the most progressive countries in the Middle East. Also, he has been involved in enacting the necessary legislations that guarantee women a full role in the Kingdom's socio-economic and political life. (ibid.)

Education Leadership in Jordan

A further strong influence on the contemporary traditions of leadership in Jordan is the profound impact of policies towards education and the involvement of educational leaders in the public life in the country. Jordan has given particular attention to education in particular. In general literacy rate it is ranked 82nd in the world, with a male rate of 96 per cent and female of 84 per cent, and ranks first in the Arab world. The secondary education system produces students with leaving qualifications that are accepted in world-class universities.

The university sector has also developed significantly in recent years and there are eight public universities, plus two newly licensed ones, together with 13 private universities plus four newly licensed ones. The two leading universities of Jordan, in Amman and in Yarmouk (Irbid governorate), are well established and both have important business and management schools of international standing (ILO 2008). All post secondary education is the responsibility of the Ministry of Higher Education and Scientific Research. The Ministry includes the Higher Education Council and the Accreditation Council. The major universities have also expanded their interests into the international stage.

Senior managers within key industries including finance, pharmaceuticals and engineering are now being taught in Jordan by business school experts on the school's overseas Enterprise Management Programme. The Durham Business School won an EU contract to help tackle Jordan's deficit in management development and boost the country's business SME infrastructure following the difficulties in the Middle East. Durham has built a partnership with the University of Jordan based in Amman to co-accredit the qualification through their Higher Education Ministry. This partnership has also led to the creation of the European Jordanian Advanced Business Institute (EJABI) based in Amman, Jordan.

Several universities have established recruitment from other countries in the region and have created good reputations in business and management education. An important feature has been the recruitment of women students from other countries in the region, especially the Gulf states. There is also a network of community colleges offering two to three year programmes in many fields, such as arts, science, management, business administration and engineering. After the invasion of Iraq by Western forces in 2003, there was a great influx of refugees from Iraq into Jordan, and an increase of Iraqi students in Jordanian schools. In 2007 Jordan allowed all Iraqi refugees, regardless of immigration status, to attend free state operated schools in Jordan and these incomers to Jordanian society have brought with them the high expectations of education that had to some extent been suppressed by the effect of economic sanctions during the years since the first Iraq war. These refugees from Iraq will in due course contribute in their own way to Jordanian society and will influence future patterns of leadership in Jordan.

An increasing supply of trained managerial talent is becoming available to Jordanian society, however, frustrations exist among these cadres as the traditional regimes of authority, seniority and inter-familial networking are not always perceived by them as providing the opportunities their qualifications fit them for. In this respect they are not unusual in the region.

Leadership Development in Jordan: a Summary

Although there is no massive tradition of empirical studies of leadership, there is nonetheless a growing body of empirical research on leadership in Jordanian organizations from which some tentative generalizations can be drawn. Baseline studies including Al Faleh (1987) reviewed the field of management development in Jordan and identified its unique constellation of cultural features.

Durra and Buera (1988) pointed to the changing nature of HRM in Jordan and the requirement for management development to move from the traditional lecture mode to more modern methods including role playing, and to the building of skills and developing of attitudes. Mizel (1994) found that most managers had autocratic leadership styles. Leaders tend to stick to the rules and regulations and to see rewards and punishment as the best method of control, and managers' involvement of employees in decision making is implicit and indirect rather than overt. There was a close relationship between organizational dimensions and leadership style, participation and organizational effectiveness.

Al-Kilani (1988) studied leadership styles among directors of directorates of education in Jordan and his results indicate the emergence of what is called a *convincing* leadership style, in which attempts were made to persuade subordinates. These results also indicated that leadership style changes with work experience.

Abuznaid (1990) studied managerial attitudes among Palestinian managers in the West Bank, and his findings may be taken as partially indicative of the Jordanian pattern as many Jordanian managers are Palestinian by family background. Almost half of the managers surveyed used a consultative leadership style and West Bank managers are more willing to let their subordinates share in the decision making process. Twenty-three per cent used the participative style while 22 per cent used the pseudo consultative style. Only 5.6 per cent used an autocratic style.

These findings also indicate that managers' attitudes toward leadership were influenced by size of organization, educational level, and age of managers. In large organizations managers found it more appropriate to delegate authority to subordinates.

Managers with a higher educational level were believed to have gained a broader knowledge of the way business should be conducted and managers with higher education are more consultative (Abuznaid 1990).

Age also has an influence on the attitude of managers towards leadership, reinforcing the view that in the Arab world older managers are more respected because of their age, perceived as reflecting wisdom through knowledge and practice. As a result, older managers in the Arab world take it for granted that they will be respected. Muna, in his benchmark study, indicated that older managers in the Arab world tend to be more autocratic (Muna 1986).

Al Khatib and Abu Farsakh (1996) studied the leadership style at Yarmouk University and the School of Science and Technology from the perspective of teaching staff and found that Yarmouk University paid more attention to status while the School of Science and Technology paid more attention to work framework.

Abu Hantush (1989) in his study in community colleges in Jordan found that employees with higher educational levels were less satisfied. Al Omari (1994) found that appropriate work environment, manager-employee relationship and job security all played a major role in employee job satisfaction.

Al Shalalfeh (1993) also studied leadership styles in a school setting, finding that the majority of principals and teachers perceived the leadership style of principals as considerate. There were significant differences between principals' perception of the two dimensions of leadership behaviour (consideration and initiation structure). There were no significant differences in principals' perception level of their leadership style by sex. Sixty per cent evidenced high task and high people orientation, while half demonstrated high task orientation coupled with low concern for employees.

Business Leadership in Jordan

While there has been considerable progress in developing more systematic methods of developing leadership and managerial skills in Jordanian organizations, studies by Abu Doleh indicate that there is still some way to go. Abu Doleh reviewed the current plans, procedures and practices of management training and development (MTD) needs assessment in Jordanian private and public organizations. Self-completion questionnaires were distributed to 64 training managers evenly divided between the private and public sector. The major research findings include the fact that only one third of the investigated organizations had a formal and systematic plan for the analysis of their managers' MTD needs. The study shows that in few of the organizations do training managers report having MTD needs assessment procedures linked with managers' job descriptions and management performance appraisal schemes. Abu Doleh recommended that training managers should monitor effectively their MTD needs, assessment plans, and procedures (Abu Doleh 2004).

Subsequently, Abu Doleh and Weir explored the attitudes of human resource managers in 74 organizations towards their performance appraisal systems, and the ways in which performance appraisal systems were implemented. The results of the study revealed that private organizations' performance appraisal had significantly greater impact than their counterparts in the public sector on promotion, retention and termination, lay-offs, identifying individual training needs, transfers and assignments (Abu Doleh and Weir 2007).

In a number of studies also based on empirical fieldwork, Al Rasheed (1996, 2001) has attempted to build a 'balanced' picture of Arab management and organization. He concludes that despite continuing efforts at modernization of management practice, leadership in Jordan is still largely traditional in terms of many specific features including limited future orientation and excessive lack of delegation of authority.

Al-Shaikh (2003) has investigated the degree to which business managers in developing countries adhere to business ethics, with special reference to the case of Jordan. He applied practical reality theory in a survey to assess whether business managers in different countries make compromises in their ethical stance under the pressure of practical reality and explored the links (if any) between each of the company's features, the manager's characteristics, and ethical orientations of business managers. He found that the ethical orientations of Jordanian business managers are positive on certain aspects and negative on others.

Respondents were asked to rate a number of scenarios on a scale of one (always acceptable) to seven (never acceptable). For instance, the scenario of inflating an expense account was considered broadly unethical with a mean response of 5.30. By contrast, giving gifts to purchasing agents was not perceived unethical, registering a mean response of 3.29. The findings seem consistent with previous studies in the region and indicate that it is dangerous to apply expectations derived from Western understandings of business ethics uncritically to such activities as offering gifts in a business context (Al-Shaikh 2003). This reinforces what Hutchings and Weir describe as the still pervasive influence of business networking building on shared participation in wasta processes (Hutchings and Weir 2006).

The rapid growth of IT is making an impact on traditional leadership practices. Al-Ahmad and Zink in 1995 researched a sample of 44 Jordanian public agencies, examining the adoption and uses of IT in the Jordanian public sector. The findings showed that by this date the vast majority of Jordanian public organizations had access to computers, and most of the agencies had 'in-house' systems (as opposed to shared use with another public organization or outsourced IT provision).

Microcomputers were found to be the most common computer platform, and agency use of IT was consistently intense in the area of financial management. Most public organizations with in-house computers employed one to four staff programmers (Al-Ahmad and Zink 1998). Within the economy generally, the public sector still dominates in terms of attitudes and values, although the private sector is taking the lead in introducing modern management practices (Abu Doleh and Weir 2007).

Allinson and Hayes included some Jordanian subjects in their sample of 394 managers from six nations and 360 management students from five nations who completed the Cognitive Style Index, a self-report measure of the intuitive-analytic dimension and concluded that Arab managers tended to be more 'analytic' as compared to the more 'intuitive' European managers (Allinson and Hayes, 2000).

THE POSITION OF WOMEN

The position of women as leaders in Jordanian organizations also requires comment and once more we have to transcend the generic and to some extent over-arching explanations given in the literature to understand the special situation of Jordan. One of the most influential characterizations of gender and dependency issues is that of Hisham Sharabi, who coined the term 'neo-patriarchy' to describe the social structures of the contemporary Arab world, arguing that over the last one hundred years the patriarchal structures of Arab society, far from being displaced or truly modernized, have been strengthened and deformed. A central psycho-social feature of this kind of society, whether conservative or progressive, is the dominance of the Father (patriarch), the centre around which the national as well as the natural family are organized according to this analysis (Sharabi 1998a and 1998b; see also Chapter 13).

The neo-patriarchal society is seen by Sharabi as a dependent, non-modern socio-economic structure that represents the quintessentially underdeveloped society. Its most pervasive characteristic, he finds, is a kind of generalized, persistent, and seemingly 'insurmountable impotence': it is incapable of performing as an integrated social or political system, as an economy, or as a military structure, for, possessing all the external trappings of modernity, this society nevertheless lacks the inner force, organization and consciousness which characterize truly modern formations. Thus whatever the outward ('modern') forms – material, legal, aesthetic – of the contemporary neo-patriarchal family and society, their internal structures remain rooted in the patriarchal values and social relations of kinship, clan, religious and ethnic groups. Familial patriarchy thus provides the grounds for a dual domination of the father over the family household, and of the male over the female. The precondition for emancipation is access to work. If correct, Sharabi's analysis would contain a powerful indictment of contemporary Arab society and the basis for a comprehensive explanation of the relative lack of economic and social development of Arab society (Sharabi,1990).

Several writers from feminist and other perspectives have adopted this terminology relatively uncritically, and some Western commentators, for example, appear to believe that women are universally barred from the labour market or face implacable obstacles to undertaking paid employment outside the home.

Royal Women Leaders

In relation to Jordan, the patriarchal model discussed above is partial and even misleading. Jordanian civil society shows several examples of powerful women leaders and in principle the policy of government and official agencies in Jordan is favourable towards a strong role for women in the labour market. Her Majesty Queen Noor of Jordan, the last wife and now widow of King Hussein, and daughter of a Lebanese-American businessman, once publicly emphasized the importance of the pivotal role of women as 'the anchor of society' and of the need to 'evolve that role naturally by building on traditions and social values to develop economic and political awareness and opportunities for women' (NIC 1997).

As in all Muslim societies, the theoretical position of woman in Jordan is that they are not judged to be inferior to men (Metcalfe 2007). An important aspect of the juridical systems of all countries influenced by Islam is that the rights of women are protected. Divorce is less common than in the West, but in the case of divorce, a woman can expect to obtain full financial support from the man. A Jordanian woman may own property, inherit wealth and her individual possessions are protected.

Jordan is in some respects socially more liberal than some of the GCC countries for instance and women are not normally subject to the extreme aspects of seclusion. The educational system in Jordan is especially attractive to young women from other Arab countries, especially from the Gulf region, and several higher education institutions cater strongly for these students.

While in many respects this conforms to generally understood models of women's role in other Middle Eastern societies, in others it differs markedly from the stereotypical portrayals of women's role as depicted in media in Western countries. Over the last few decades Jordan has made steady progress in the field of the education of women. This has had a considerable impact not just on the skill base available to the Jordanian economy, but also in attracting the development of educational and training institutions oriented towards providing programmes for women from other countries in the region and, more generally, from other countries with similar cultural backgrounds. The extensive inter-penetration of Jordanian and Palestinian families discussed earlier means that many Jordanians are in fact originally from west of the Jordan and several studies, including those of Abuznaid and Salman, have identified the continuing importance of women in leadership roles in the Palestinian state as well as in the Palestinian diaspora (Abuznaid 1992; Salman 1996).

The royal family, in particular the present Queen Rania, have taken a vanguard role in promoting the interests of women leaders in Jordan and throughout the region. The Queen's website contains very strong messages on these themes. Thus:

> The best advertisement for empowering women is an empowered woman. Jordan's towns and villages, I am proud to say, boast numerous examples of women who have overcome challenges and redefined what it means to be a woman in Jordan in 2007. Talented, resourceful and hard-working, these women have transformed their lives and those of their families and their communities. As women look around, they see their friends and neighbours standing tall and often decide that it is time to invest in themselves. Success, as you know, breeds success.
>
> To my husband, King Abdullah and me these women represent a vital component in our country's growth and development. We both firmly believe that Jordan's economy will only flourish when all of its population actively contributes to the employment market.
>
> With a view to achieving that, we are resolutely improving educational standards and already reaping great dividends. For example, female literacy rates in Jordan currently stand at 86 per cent; recent High School competency tests this year saw girls score better than ever before, and female enrolment rates at university are at their highest levels in history.
>
> Following logically upon enhanced academic achievement and rising literacy scores, women's participation in the political sphere is also increasing. Jordan's Government currently contains a minister and representatives in both the upper and lower houses of Parliament. Additionally, Jordanian women are moving front and center in the private sector, taking advantage of enhanced business opportunities and public sector initiatives designed to encourage female entrepreneur. (Rania 2008)

Women and the Labour Market in Jordan

Amal El Kharouf, a Professor of Women's Studies in the University of Jordan, has produced interesting findings that challenge the stereotypical portrayal of Arab women in the employment market. She found that employment status for women correlates not only with personal education level, but also the educational attainment of her mother, father and husband (El Kharouf 2000). Her studies also indicate that among women of the older generation there is a set of values that is strongly supportive of the leadership aspirations of their daughters. Professor El Kharouf herself is indicative of the new patterns of upward mobility for Jordanian women. From a family background in the Palestinian community she rose from graduate statistician in the General Directorate for Planning, Research and Educational Development Department of the Ministry of Education to be appointed in 2003 as the Coordinator for the Jordanian Executive Committee for the Arab Women Summit, a part-time assignment in the Royal Hashemite Court.

In terms of most Western societies there would be seen to be nothing especially remarkable about this talented woman's personal ascent of the *cursus honorum*, but what is exceptional about it is that it exemplifies rather precisely the characteristic inter-penetration of education, qualification and achievement of internationally-relevant qualifications that is found in the typical post-modern society, rather than the persistence of Sharabi's pattern of neo-patriarchy. The institutions of Jordanian civil society can definitely produce strong women leaders who can function as role models for the next generation.

The latest EUI survey data indicates that the range of occupational choice available to women in Jordan remains relatively narrow, being heavily concentrated in the teaching, secretarial and health professions. In some sectors, including transportation, sales and agriculture, there is very little female participation (EUI1996).

The pattern appears to bear out the conclusions of UNICEF that there are pressures on women to choose forms of employment which are consistent with their generic social roles as 'carers' and 'nurturers' (UNICEF 1994). Thus 14 per cent of the female labour force is in the health and social sectors and 41 per cent in the teaching profession.

Women are more heavily represented in the public than the private sector (49 versus 33 per cent) in Jordan. However the female work force is in general better educated than the male, with more than 65 per cent possessing a diploma or higher level, compared with only 62 per cent of their male counterparts.

However, as discussed above, the unemployment rate among women available for work is higher than for men and these unemployed women have a high level of educational attainment, two-thirds possessing a community college degree or higher qualification, almost a hundred per cent having a secondary certificate and only 2 per cent being designated as illiterate. Only 20 per cent of unemployed men have a secondary certificate with 10 per cent designated illiterate. Women are also unemployed for longer, more than two years on average, twice the time period for men.

These disproportions represent a failure to capitalize on a significant investment in human capital and a waste of skills potentially available to the labour market. Other social factors bear on the equation. The average age of marriage for women has, since 1979, risen from 21 to almost 25, while the average age differential between women and their husbands has fallen to three years. These statistics, far from reinforcing stereotypes of neo-patriarchy, appear to presage some convergence towards Western patterns (El Kharouf 2000).

Attitudes towards income, and family income in particular, are affected by marital status, with married women more likely to regard their income as a contribution towards 'family income' (Ahmed 1982, 1986). Women's employment status was also found to be related to the employment status of husbands and fathers. Some other more general factors are associated with women's attitudes. Household living conditions affect a woman's chances of employment and the presence in the home of a dependent relative is a negative indication.

The majority of employed women stated that they would not stop working while they were capable of undertaking work. Some stated that they could anticipate working on their own account, as entrepreneurs and there are significant role-models for this in Jordanian society.

Most women in Jordan believe that, in principle, there should be no difference between women and men in their rights to education and their rights to work. They perceive that these rights, within the framework of an Islamic constitution, will improve their position in society, their level of social life, their knowledge and skills, and family income. They also believe that their involvement in the labour market will be of benefit to their children. Women seek both protection and independence as consequences of their involvement in work (Mernissi 1987, 1991, 1992).

These beliefs are supported by the perception that for those women who do not enter the labour market, there are strong positive advantages to their family and children from their obtaining an enhanced educational level.

Most of the women surveyed by El Kharouf expressed a belief that it is possible to meet the demands of domestic management and the requirements of the workplace with good time management. All women rated very highly their expectations for their daughters to obtain high educational qualifications and satisfying work: 'a good qualification, a good job and a good life'.

Women, as reported in these survey results, have characteristic ideas about what constitutes 'a good job' and in order of preference they rated: important work for society; good promotion prospects; and interesting work, which were all rated ahead of: close to home; good holidays; pleasant people to work with; flexible hours; good health insurance; and good pay. Last of all was rated 'a job where they can obtain new skills' (El Kharouf 2000).

We argue that these findings are not consistent with simplistic explanations in terms of 'neo-patriarchy', nor indeed with cultural explanations, predominant in many other studies (Sharabi 1988a; Weir 2000) that depend on out-dated stereotypical understandings. Rather they challenge stereotypical images of Arab women as being primarily concerned with family issues.

One interpretation is that women represent a considerable latent potential for leadership in Jordanian organizations. But the crystallization of this potential into actual opportunities to exercise leadership is inhibited by other social factors: that said, this conclusion is consistent with the situation in many other societies, including those of the 'developed world'.

CONCLUDING REMARKS

There is an almost tangible frustration among many young managers in Jordan and throughout the region at not being called upon to apply their cutting-edge knowledge and skills in the service of responsive enterprises. Inflated state bureaucracies offer too easy a route for the absorption of energies rather than the creation of social wealth.

Enterprise structures are moving from command organizations, with their persistent and obstructive hierarchies, to smaller, networked organizations, with both latent and active elements, based on the familial models prevalent in the Arab world rather than on juridical composites linked by shareholder and stakeholder obligations that generate purely legal obligations and an army of corporate lawyers to soak up the intermittent profit streams.

Knowledge economies depend on educated and trained entrepreneurs rather than on conformant management cadres and this expectation is increasingly being adopted as a substantive responsibility of national government institutions. Centralist state control is not the obvious answer to creating social wealth through business activity, but neither, we argue, is the ethic of selfish individualism.

Leadership in Jordan is an evolving phenomenon but its roots are deeply located in the social structures and belief patterns of the region and its ways of life, even in modern industries like IT (Al-Shaikh and Abbas 2006; Sharabi 1990). Leadership is closely associated with the social forces of reputation. Arab cultures, in common with those of the Mediterranean regions, have been characterized in terms of 'shame' rather than 'guilt'. This governs relations in all areas of social life. A good leader is one who arranges matters so as to protect his dependants from shame. If a leader performs at this level, he or she will be forgiven much that, in other cultures, would be seen as evidence of failure.

Leadership is a fundamental aspect of organizational life but its connotations are not necessarily the same as those in the West. The 'leader' is one who has to be acceptable to peers or colleagues to guide activities, ensure progress towards some agreed goals and to coordinate disparate efforts. There is not necessarily an agreed formula for deciding who will lead: in ruling families it is not necessarily the eldest male who inherits the crown and the succession in the Jordanian Royal Family has exemplified this practice. But leaders, once agreed upon, can expect to be followed, unless they transgress severely.

This is not to elevate 'traditionalism' and 'conservatism' as master explanatory categories but to establish the generic context from which leadership models in this country are continuing to evolve, for this is a fast changing landscape (Said 1978). Decision making follows different rules in the network economy of the Information Society to that of 'traditional' organizations in which the strategic judgements of highly-paid executives, remote from customers and suppliers, are hierarchically imposed on unwilling or ill-informed operatives. Informed consent will be required: perhaps it is the model of the family *diwan* or *majlis*, with its balance of consultative and autocratic processes, that will provide a better guide to the 'loose-tight' properties of effective decision making in the Jordanian context than does the model of the Western 'corporate boardroom' (Ashfari 2005).

The dual pull of tradition and modernity is evident in the characteristic responses of Jordanian managers, especially the young and well-qualified ones, to the problems of managing authority and relationships in organizations. The personalized concept of power may lead to feelings of uncertainty and loss of autonomy among lower-level organizational participants. Conversely, when problems occur, they tend to be ascribed to personal failure rather than to organizational or administrative shortcomings.

It is also clear that Jordan now has the capacity to offer leadership on the basis of its continuing production of a trained and competent management cadre emerging from its educational institutions and to continue to develop its ability to offer a model of a modernizing state that can meld the best of Western and Arab models.

Important considerations remain that lead to anxiety for the future in Jordan. The political and social stability of the region is still fragile, the demographic projections, both endogenous in terms of population growth and exogenous in terms of inward migration, are unfavourable and the economic future for a non-oil producing state in this region is unpredictable. Yet Jordan has demonstrated great internal vitality during the last 30 years, its people are resilient and confident and the ruling political elites are well-informed and collectively motivated.

In Jordan, as in many countries in the Middle East, the evolution of trained managers is presenting organizations with opportunities that did not exist a generation ago. Undoubtedly there exists in Jordan a cadre of professional managers and especially well-trained younger people of both genders who are capable of offering sustained and competent leadership in a variety of contexts. Whatever happens, it will not necessarily be in ways that conform to Western models of leadership and management.

REFERENCES

Abdulla, I.A. and M.A. Al-Homoud (2001), 'Exploring the implicit leadership theory in Arabian Gulf states', *Applied Psychology: An International Review*, **50** (4), 506–31.

Abdullah (2008), 'His Majesty King Abdullah II King of the Hashemite Kingdom of Jordan', accessed 21 July 2010 at www.kingabdullah.jo/main.php?main_page=0&lang_hmka1=1.

Abu Doleh, J. (2004), 'Management training and development needs assessment practices in the Jordanian private and public sectors: integrated or isolated?', *Journal of Transnational Management Development*, **9** (2–3), 107–21.

Abu-Doleh, J and D.T.H. Weir (2007), 'Dimensions of performance appraisal systems in Jordanian private and public organizations', *The International Journal of Human Resource Management,* **18**, 75–84.

Abu Hantush (1989), 'Job satisfaction among employees of community colleges in Jordan', Masters thesis, Jordan University.

Abu-Zayd, G. (n.d.), 'In search of political power – women in parliament in Egypt, Jordan and Lebanon', accessed 23 July 2010. at http://archive.idea.int/women/parl/studies1a.htm.

Abuznaid, S. (1990), 'Aspects of management attitudes, beliefs and business culture on the west bank', PhD thesis, Glasgow University.

Abuznaid, S. (1992), 'Palestinian women: from followers to leaders', paper presented at the British Academy of Management Conference, Bradford, UK.

Afshari, R. (2005), 'Egalitarian Islam and misogynist Islamic tradition: a critique of the feminist reinterpretation of Islamic history and heritage', *Middle East Critique*, **3** (4), 13–33.

Ahmad, Alaa-Aldin A. and Steven D. Zink (1998), 'Information technology adoption in Jordanian public sector organizations', *Journal of Government Information*, **25** (2), 117–34.

Ahmed, A.S. (1992), *Postmodernism and Islam*, London and New York: Routledge.

Ahmed, L. (1982), 'Western ethnocentrism and perceptions of the harem', *Feminist Studies*, **8** (3), 521–34.

Ahmed, L. (1986), 'Women and the advent of Islam', *Signs: Journal of Women in Culture and Society*, **11** (4), 665–91.

Ahmed, L. (1992), *Women and Gender in Islam: Historical Roots of a Modern Debate*, New Haven, CT: Yale University Press.

Ali, Abbas J. (1990), 'Management theory in a transitional society', *International Studies of Management and Organization*, **20** (3), 7–35.

Allinson, C. and J. Hayes (2000), 'Cross-national differences in cognitive style: implications for management', *International Journal of Human Resource Management*, **11** (1), 161–70.

Arab Archives Institute (2000), Wasta in Jordan Arab Archives Institute and Transparency International, *Towards Transparency in Jordan*, Amman, Jordan, May 2000, accessed 10 August 2010 at www.alarcheef.com/reports/englishFiles/wastaOpinionPoll.pdf.

Ashfari, R. (2005), 'Egalitarian Islam and misogynist Islamic tradition: a critique of the feminist reinterpretation of Islamic history and heritage', *Middle East Critique*, **3** (4), 13–33.

British Council (2003), 'Report on capacity building', accessed 2 February 2010 at www.britishcouncil.org/development-capacity-building-in-management-educational-services-jordan.pdf.

Brynen, R. (1992), 'Economic crisis and post-rentier democratization in the Arab world: the case of Jordan', *Canadian Journal of Political Science*, **25** (1), 69–98.

CIA (2009), The World Factbook 2009, Washington, DC: Central Intelligence Agency, accessed 9 August 2010 at www.cia.gov/library/publications/the-world-factbook/index.html.

Cleveland, William L. and M. Bunton (2009), *A History of the Modern Middle East*, Boulder, CO: Westview Press.

Durra, A.B. and A.M. Buera (1988), 'Administrative education and training in the Arab world: an empirical study', *International Journal of Manpower*, **9** (6), 22–7.

Department of Statistics (1996), *Employment, Unemployment and Income Survey*, Jordan: Department of Statistics, Government of Jordan.

Economist Intelligence Unit (2005), 'Quality-of-life index 2005', accessed 9 August 2010 at www.economist.com/media/pdf/quality_of_life.pdf.

Economist Intelligence Unit (2010), 'e-readiness rankings 2009', accessed 9 August at http://graphics.eiu.com/pdf/E-readiness%20rankings.pdf.

Al-Faleh, M. (1987), 'Cultural influences on Arab managerial development', *Journal of Management Development*, **6** (3), 19–33.

Fry, L.W. (2003), 'Toward a theory of spiritual leadership', *The Leadership Quarterly*, **14** (6), 693–727.

Greenleaf, Robert K. (1977), *Servant Leadership*, Mahwah, NJ: Paulist Press.

The Heritage Foundation (2010), 'Ranking the countries', accessed 9 August 2010 at http://www.heritage.org/index/ranking.aspx.

Hofstede, G. (1980), *Culture's Consequences*, Beverly Hills, CA: Sage.

House, R.J. and R.N. Aditya (1997), 'The social scientific study of leadership: Quo vadis?' *Journal of Management*, **23** (3), 409–73.

Hutchings, K. and D.T.H Weir (2006), 'Guanxi and wasta: a comparison', *Thunderbird International Business Review*, **48** (1), 141–56.

International Labour Organization (ILO) (2008), 'Economic development through technical skills project', report, Geneva: ILO.

Jordan Department of Statistics (2009), 'Jordan in figures 2008', accessed 10 August 2010 at http://www.dos.gov.jo/jorfig/2008/jor_f_e.htm.

Kanungo, R. and M. Mendonca (1996), *Ethical Dimensions of Leadership*, Thousand Oaks, CA: Sage.

A.T. Kearney and *Foreign Policy Magazine* (2007), 'Globalization index 2007', accessed 9 August 2010 at www.atkearney.com/index.php/Publications/globalization-index.html?q=globalization+index.

El Kharouf, A. (2000), *Factors Influencing the Employment of Women, from the Point of View of Employed and Non-employed Women in Amman City, Jordan*, UNIFEM and UNESCO, Jordan: The National Library.

Al Khatib R. and F. Abu Farsakh (1996), 'Leadership styles prevailing at Al Yarmouk University and School of Science and Technology as perceived by teaching staff', *Journal of Arab League Universities*, **3**.

Al-Kilani, A. (1988), *Analysis of Leadership Styles and Variables Like Decision Making and Problem Solving: A Sample of Jordanian Managers*, Amman: Jordan University.

Massad, J.A. (2001), *Colonial Effects: The Making of National Identity in Jordan*, New York: Columbia University Press.

Mernissi, F. (1987), *Beyond the Veil: Male-Female Dynamics in Modern Muslim Society*, London: Saqi Books.

Mernissi, F. (1991), *The Veil and the Male Elite: A Feminist Interpretation of Women's Rights in Islam*, translated by M.J. Lakeland, New York: Addison-Wesley Publishing Company.

Mernissi, F. (1992), *Islam and Democracy: Fear of the Modern World*, New York: Addison-Wesley Publishing Company.

Metcalfe, Beverly D. (2007), 'Gender and HRM in the Middle East', *International Journal of Human Resource Management*, **18** (1), 54–74.

Mizel, F. et al. (1994), 'Organizational dimensions and its impact on leadership styles': *Jordan University Studies Journal*, **2**.

Muna, F. (1986), *The Arab Executive*, London: Macmillan.

'National Agenda: The Jordan we strive for' (2006), accessed 10 August 2010 at www.nationalagenda.jo/Portals/0/EnglishBooklet.pdf.

NIC (1997), 'Women in Jordan: a synopsis', accessed 3 June 2010 at www.gov.com.jo/Qnoorjo/main/womenjo.htm.

Al Omari, K. (1994), 'Employees' attitudes towards different aspects at Jordan University', Masters thesis, University of Jordan.

Rania (2008), 'Women empower', accessed 23 July 2010 at http://web.archive.org/web/20080702145801re_/www.queenrania.jo/content/sectionPage.aspx?secID=womn.

Al-Rasheed, A.M. (1996), 'Traditional Arab management: evidence from empirical comparative research', PhD thesis, University of Kent.

Al Rasheed A.M. (2001), 'Features of traditional Arab management and organization in the Jordan business environment', *Journal of Transnational Management Development*, **6** (1,2), 27–53.

Reporters Without Borders (2010), 'Worldwide press freedom index 2009', accessed 9 August at http://en.rsf.org/press-freedom-index-2009,1001.html.

Al-Rimawi, A.Sh., E.K. Karablieh, A.S. Al-Qadi and H.F. Al-Qudah (2006), 'Farmers' attitudes and skills of farm business management in Jordan', *The Journal of Agricultural Education and Extension*, **12** (3), 165–77.

Ryan, Curtis R. (2011), 'Hashimite Kingdom of Jordan', in D.E. Long, B. Reich and M. Gasiorowski (eds), *The Government and Politics of the Middle East and North Africa*, 6th edn, Boulder, CO: Westview Press.

Said, E. (1978), *Orientalism: Western Conceptions of the Orient*, revised edn 1995, London: Penguin.

Saif, I. and D. DeBartolo (2007), 'The Iraq war's impact on growth and inflation in Jordan', report for the Center for Strategic Studies, University of Jordan.

Sarayrah Y.K. (2004), 'Servant leadership in the Bedouin-Arab culture', *Global Virtue Ethics Review*, **5** (3), 58–78.

Salman, H.K. (1996), *Case Studies in Palestinian Enterprise*, Villanova, PA: Villanova University Press.

Sarayrah, Y.K. (2004), 'Servant leadership Bedouin-Arab culture', *Global Virtue Ethics Review*, **5**, 58–79.

Sendjaya, Sen (2007), 'Conceptualizing and measuring spiritual leadership in organizations', *Journal of Business Information*, **2** (1), 104–26.

Al-Shaikh, F.N. (2003), 'The practical reality theory and business ethics in non-Western context: evidence from Jordan', *Journal of Management Development*, **22** (8), 679–93.

Al-Shaikh, F.N. and L.M. Abbas (2006), 'Innovation and organizational culture: the case of IT companies in Jordan', paper presented at the XIV ABAS International Conference, Limassol, Cyprus.

Al-Shalalfeh, S. (1993), *The Relationship Between Managers' Perception of Their Leadership Style and its Impact on Employees' Morale in High Schools in Amman,* Amman: University of Jordan.

Sharabi H. (1988a), *Neo Patriarchy: A Theory of Distorted Change in Arab Society*, Oxford: Oxford University Press.

Sharabi, H. (1988b), 'Introduction', in H. Sharabi (ed.), *The Next Arab Decade: Alternative Futures*, Boulder, CO: Westview Press, pp. 1–10.

Sharabi, H. (1990), *Theory, Politics and the Arab World: Critical Responses*, London and New York: Routledge.

The Heritage Foundation (2010), 'Ranking the countries', accessed 9 August at www.heritage.org/index/ranking.aspx.

Transparency International (2009), 'Corruption Perceptions Index 2009', accessed 9 August at www.transparency.org/policy_research/surveys_indices/cpi/2009.

United Nations Development Programme (UNDP) (2006), 'Support to bridging the gap between higher education and the labour market in Jordan – phase II', accessed 3 June 2010 at www.undp-jordan.org/UNDPinJordan/WhatWeDo/PovertyReduction/HigherEducationproject/tabid/117/Default.aspx.

UNDP (2009a), 'Human development report 2009: overcoming barriers: human mobility and development', accessed 9 August 2010 at http://hdr.undp.org/en/reports/global/hdr2009/.

UNDP (2009b), 'Human development report 2009: Jordan: the Human Development Index – going beyond income', accessed 9 August 2010 at http://hdrstats.undp.org/en/countries/country_fact_sheets/cty_fs_JOR.html.

UNICEF (1994), *Women's Status*, Amman: United Nations Children's Fund.

Weir, D.T.H. (1999), 'Management in the Arab world: a fourth paradigm', in A. Al-Shamali and J. Denton (eds), *Arab Business: The Globalisation Imperative*, Bristol: Bristol Academic Press, pp. 60–76.

Weir, D.T.H. (2000), 'Management in the Arab world', in M. Warner (ed.), *Management in Emerging Countries: Regional Encyclopaedia of Business and Management,* London: Business Press/Thomson Learning, pp. 291–300.

Weir, D.T.H (2003), 'Human resource development in the Middle East: a fourth paradigm', in M. Lee (ed.), *HRD in a Complex World*, London: Routledge, pp. 69–82.

World Bank (2010), 'World development indicators', accessed 10 August at http://data.worldbank.org/data-catalog/world-development-indicators.

World Economic Forum (2009), 'The Global Competitiveness Report 2009-2010', accessed 9 August 2010 at www.weforum.org/en/initiatives/gcp/Global%20Competitiveness%20Report/index.htm.

Yale Center for Environmental Law and Policy and CIESIN, Columbia University (2010), '2010 Environmental performance index (EPI)', accessed 9 August at http://sedac.ciesin.columbia.edu/es/epi/downloads.html#summary.

9. Business leadership development in Iran

Kate Hutchings, Kavoos Mohannak and Sen Sendjaya

INTRODUCTION

Throughout the twentieth century the economies of the Middle East rose and fell many times in response to the external environment, including European de-colonization and the US and former USSR competing to provide military and economic aid after World War II. Throughout these upheavals the Middle East has remained internationally significant politically and economically, not least for the region's large reserves of oil and gas, as discussed in the Introduction to this volume. In recent decades, Western nations have moved to invest into the Middle East in the rapidly developing technology, tourism and education industries that have proliferated. For its part, Iran has been the world's fourth largest provider of petroleum and second largest provider of natural gas and, despite years of political unrest, has made rapid expansion into information technology and telecommunications. Increased involvement in the global economy has meant that Iran has invested heavily in education and training and moved to modernize its management practices. Hitherto there has been little academic research into management in either Western or local organizations in Iran. This chapter seeks to address that gap in knowledge by exploring business leadership in Iran, with particular reference to cultural and institutional impacts.

STRATEGIC AND ECONOMIC SIGNIFICANCE OF IRAN

Iran is a geopolitically strategic country, located between the Russian Federation and the Persian Gulf which connects to the Indian Ocean through the Strait of Hormus. Iran has long been a great crossroads of the

Middle East, South Asia, Central Asia, Russia and the Turkic lands. The international strategic importance of Iran is often taken for granted, but its long history of empire and cultural domination of its peripheries underline the country's powerful position in international trade, in setting the political balance of Western Asia, and in influencing ideological opinion throughout a wide area beyond its boundaries.

With a 1600 mile frontier with the states of the former Soviet Union in the north, and fronting the important Strait of Hormuz to the south, Iran is a nation of especial geo-strategic significance. In addition, Iran has about 10 per cent of the world's proven reserves of petroleum (see Chapter 1, Table 1.6), and for many years has been one of the world's largest oil exporters (Ali and Amirshahi 2002; Javidan and Dastmalchian 2003). It also possesses the world's second largest reserves of natural gas. The population of approximately 75 million people is comparable only to Egypt and Turkey in the region. In these circumstances, Iran is articulating its strength on the regional and world scenes, as an economy of weight and a key supplier of crude oil and natural gas to the world market. Clearly there is a linkage between the current and likely future role of Iran as an exporter of hydrocarbons and the degree of importance attaching to the country's strategic rating.

At the same time, the oil industry provides Iran with very large components of its budget, foreign exchange and national income. A thriving oil sector means a well endowed national treasury and a comparative abundance of disposable foreign exchange with which to play a prominent part in world affairs. The discovery of oil reserves in the Caspian Sea region in the 1990s changed the strategic status of the countries surrounding this area for the USA and European countries (Ehteshami 2004) which remain energy-hungry. The effect of this discovery for Iran was twofold. First, it added to the total oil reserves controlled by Iran. It also potentially increased the importance of Iran as a transportation route for the Caspian oil and the strategic importance of control over the flow of that oil. Initially experts considered Iran the most economically viable route for the pipelines to transport the oil and gas to Europe (Pahlevan 1998). The second consequence was entirely negative. Coupled with war in Chechnaya, the US was prompted to abandon its traditional policy of making energy goals secondary to other foreign policy objectives and to move to a more assertive policy from the late 1990s onward, including supporting the construction of the Baku-Tbilisi- Ceyhan pipeline: '. . . aimed mainly at excluding Iran and at making Turkey a major actor in the region' (Oktavson 2005).

Domestically, the most important and urgent economic and social issue for the Iranian government in recent years has been the achievement of economic growth and development, especially to tackle the high unemployment rate. In order to achieve economic growth, the government has adopted several economic development plans to rehabilitate the country, to attract investment and to strengthen the Iranian economic structure (BMJIR 2006). In past years the economic institutions as well as the infrastructure of the national economy were reconstructed or strengthened through these development plans. In general, undertaking these economic reforms requires good economic management, sound business leadership and good economic relations with Iran's major trading partners and the world's leading economies. To achieve this, government bureaucracies in Iran concerned with the economy place most importance on the enhancement of the techno-economic capacity of the modern society and the important role that private business can play in economic growth. Under such factors, the economic policy of contemporary Iran has been shaped under the complex influence of a number of internal and external factors. Naturally, the changes that have taken place in the aftermath of the Islamic Revolution have affected not only politics and society but also the country's economy and the way that government managed the economy in general and private business in particular (Abrahamian 1992). Iran's status as a strategic hub, partner and interlocutor in oil distribution between East and West, combined with attempts at economic diversification, has been fraught with conflict, ambiguity and political turmoil. The recent commitment to a second term of Ahmadinejad's presidency has reasserted strong commitment to conservative Islam, which promotes the goals of advancement enshrined within goals of Islamic Shari'a. Modernization is thus constructed within different economic and social parameters and creates an unstable climate for international business relations.

SIGNIFICANCE OF THE STUDY OF LEADERSHIP IN IRAN

Iran suffered economically and socially through political unrest following the revolution of 1979, through an eight-year war with neighbouring Iraq, and still has high levels of unemployment and inflation. Some have argued that Iran began its industrialization process too late ever to catch up with Western nations. However in recent years it has expanded rapidly in the fields of information technology and telecommunications (Ebrahimian 2003). Remarkable social changes have coincided with deliberate government policy favouring information diversification. Increased involvement in the global economy means that Iran, like many of its fellow Middle Eastern nations, has invested heavily in education and training and moved to modernize its management and human resource management (HRM) practices (Ramazani 1982).

Iran, like most of the other nations in the Middle East, has witnessed brisk investment in secondary and tertiary education. The government increased the share of the education budget, provided double shift schools, and broadcast educational programmes on television (Kamyab 2004). The government has also been relatively bold in expanding education opportunities for women (Esfandiari 2004).

There has also been an emphasis on English language training and on management development programmes in the public and private sectors (Analoui and Hosseini 2001), there have been moves to increase women's representation in the workforce (Kousha and Mohseni 1997; Schramm-Nielsen and Faradonbeh 2002) and projects to build Iranian universities modelled after American schools – for example, the Shiras University was modelled on The University of Pennsylvania, while Sharif University was modelled on MIT (Lorentz 1995; Clawson and Rubin 2005) as well as the introduction of Harvard style executive training programmes.

Hitherto there has been little academic research into management and HRM in either Western or local organizations in Iran. This chapter seeks to partially address that gap in knowledge by exploring business leadership in Iran with particular reference to the impact of cultural and institutional forces on leadership development.

THE CHARACTERISTICS OF IRANIAN LEADERSHIP

Over the past 20 years, Iran has been pursuing an isolationist approach. This is in part due to the legacy of Ayatollah Khomeini, but it is also now exemplified by the position of Iran in the global political culture (Keddie 1999). The US administration, along with allied NATO members, marginalized Iran following the election of Ahmadinejad in 2005 and 2009. The Government embarked on a massive process of Islamicization of the population, beginning at preschool and pervading every aspect of life in the society. Aside from sporadic media reports on political events in Iran, very little is known about their leadership and managerial practices (Javidan and Carl 2004). The extant literature on Iranian leadership is rather sparse. A search on the topic produced a very small number of publications, with Javidan and Dastmalchian dominating its research (Dastmalchian, Javidan and Alam 2001; Javidan and Carl 2004). Chen and Velsor (1996, cited in Dastmalchian et al. 2001) concluded that there is a limited knowledge bank of non-traditional and non-Western leadership behaviours. Scholarship on leadership is largely associated with political leadership, prevailing discourses of servant leader models, social reform and advance attained via a chosen moral leader (Halliday 2005), and the importance of team leadership (Zaccaro, Rittman and Marks 2005).

On the other hand, as a subject of inquiry, leadership has been considered an omnipresent theme that occurs in almost every form of human study, be it anthropology, social psychology, human relations, sociology, education, political science, theology, or business (Rost 1993). In his review of more than 8000 leadership studies which range from the great man theory in the early 1900s to contingency theory in the 1970s to excellence theory in the 1980s, Bass (1990) concluded that endless leadership research has failed to produce a systematic, coherent, and integrated understanding of leadership. The same sentiment was observed by Barnard (1948, p. 80) nearly 60 years ago: 'Leadership is the subject of an extraordinary amount of dogmatically stated nonsense.'

Nevertheless, decades of meticulous leadership research has resulted in a vast amount of scholarship on the subject (Yukl 2002). A comprehensive review of these divergent views of leadership is simply beyond the scope of this manuscript. We will instead highlight two leadership models, charismatic leadership and transformational leadership, in light of their relevance to the context of Iran.

More generally, however, Analoui and Hosseini (2001) found that there is a general trend of male, rather than female, occupancy of managerial positions in Iran. This remains true in most developing countries. In fact, research suggests that there has been a constant association of leadership with heroic masculinity. Sinclair (1998) offered two possible reasons: first, the association of the stereotypical characteristics of white managerial men to the defining characteristics of managers; and second, the deeply embedded social and cultural experiences that each of us was brought up with within our family, school and social structures which elevate man as the ideal symbol. These attitudinal and organizational biases have contributed to the long-standing problem of the glass ceiling, which always transpires, in overt and covert ways, at lower and middle management levels. In Iran, 'glass ceilings' exist for female managers as most of them have only managed to reach the middle managerial positions.

Charismatic Leadership

The relevance of charisma in Iranian leadership has been highlighted in several important studies in the area. The Greek word 'charisma' was first defined by Weber (1947, p. 48) in his seminal book *The Theory of Social and Economic Organization* as: 'a quality of an individual personality by virtue of which he [or she, the leader] is set apart from ordinary men and treated as endowed with supernatural, superhuman, or at least specifically exceptional qualities.' As a relational and attributional phenomenon (Conger and Kanungo 1998), charisma is based neither on rules, positions, or traditions but rather on followers' perceptions and convictions that leaders possess extraordinary qualities which set them apart from ordinary people.

This elusive attribute of charisma in Iranian leadership was highlighted in Dastmalchian et al.'s study (2001). As part of the GLOBE (Global Leadership and Organizational Behaviour Effectiveness) project, they examined the interrelationships between societal culture, organizational culture, leadership, and societal achievements. On the basis of the data they collected from 300 middle level managers from over 60 organizations in three industries (telecommunications, food processing and banking), they found a number of unique and interesting aspects of Iranian charismatic leadership which, they suggest, need to be understood within the modern day context of Iran as well as the historical-cultural background of the country. The notion of leadership in Iran has historically been closely associated with the deep rooted authoritarian tradition (Mackey 1996; Hillman 1990, cited in Dastmalchian, et al. 2001). Mackey (1996, cited in Dastmalchian et al. 2001) established that, within the Iranian concept of leadership, a leader possesses charisma because he/she is endowed with supernatural powers that set him/her apart from ordinary humans and commands a special grace and otherworldly qualities. Its monarchy is a function of personality where authority is bestowed to the charismatic leader rather than being imposed by the institution of the throne. Thus, this ideal and expectation of charismatic leadership constitutes one of Iranian culture's defining characteristics.

In the organizational context, charisma is typically seen when the leader 'envisions a desirable future, articulates how it can be reached, sets an example to be followed, sets high standard of performance, and shows determination and confidence' (Bass 1999, p. 11). Some exclusive characteristics of charismatic leaders include a tendency to dominate, strong conviction in their own beliefs, need to influence others, and high self-confidence (House 1977). Iranian leaders have been noted to be dominant in their approach. Amirshahi (1997, cited in Ali and Amirshahi 2002) discovered that at the Iranian public institutions, there is a centralization of power and authority at the top, and inefficiency is almost the norm. In the private sector, he identified authoritarian style, lack of motivation, absence of participation, and centralization of management practices. Schramm-Nielsen and Faradonbeh (2002) also found out that paternalism is common, as employees expect their superior to help out in financial cases as well as private matters. Special funds are set aside in the companies for such purposes.

Empirical studies provide substantial evidence that compared to non-charismatic leaders, charismatic leadership behaviours have direct and indirect positive effects on higher performance at individual, business unit, and organizational levels (Avolio, Waldman and Einstein 1988; Barling, Weber and Kelloway 1996; Howell and Hall-Merenda 1999; Kirkpatrick and Locke 1996; Lowe, Kroeck and Sivasubramaniam 1996). Charismatic leaders cause followers to perform beyond expectations by increasing followers' perceived self-efficacy as a mediating factor (Shamir, House, and Arthur 1993). Laboratory studies also suggest that charisma, identified in three core elements, namely vision, vision implementation, and communication style, is positively correlated with follower performance (Kirkpatrick and Locke 1996). Javidan and Dastmalchian (1993, cited in Dastmalchian et al. 2001) carried out a comparative study of Iranian and Canadian managers using a sample of 106 Canadian and 158 Iranian managers. A review of the study by Javidan and Carl (2004) revealed that two elements of charismatic leadership – eloquence and tenacity – are endorsed in both cultures. In addition, the core aspects of three other dimensions, vision, intellectual challenge, and self-sacrifice, were the same, with minor differences at the periphery.

Research suggests that charismatic leadership behaviours produce higher follower performance by increasing followers' perceived self-efficacy as a mediating factor (Shamir et al. 1993). Self-efficacy is defined as 'the belief in one's capabilities to organise and execute the courses of action required to produce given attainments' (Bandura 1997, p. 3 as quoted in Shea and Howell 1999). The means whereby the charismatic leader enhances followers' perceived self-efficacy include communicating high performance satisfaction, expressing confidence in followers' abilities to contribute to the mission, and emphasizing the relationships between effort and important values (Shamir et al. 1993). Interestingly, Shamir et al. (1993) assert that the effects of charismatic leadership on performance are likely to be higher if the following situational variables occur: poorly defined and hard-to-measure performance goals; unclear means to achieve goals; and the leader's inability to link extrinsic rewards to individual performance. Other catalysts of charismatic leadership include an uncertain environment, stressful groups, and the organic structure of the organization (Conger and Kanungo 1998). These catalysts are typically found in developing nations where uncertainties and ambiguities somewhat compel followers to conform to the leaders. Iran is no exception, as demonstrated in Al Ali and Amirshahi's survey (2002) of 768 Iranian managers. Their study reported that toward their superiors, they are generally conformist and sociocentric. This tendency to conform is augmented by their collectivism in their work and life orientations.

A caveat needs to be mentioned in our (in fact, in any) discussion of charismatic leadership. The process that charismatic leaders undertake to bring followers to a high level of performance generally comes at a high price. The strong identification of followers with the leader's extraordinary qualities is likely to result in followers' unhealthy dependence upon the leader (Conger 1989; Graham 1988). This dependence is manifested in followers' typical reactions to charismatic leaders: unquestioning acceptance of the leader; trust in the correctness of the leader's belief; willing obedience to the leader; and similarity of followers' beliefs to those of the leader (House 1977). As followers become more dependent on the leader, their capacity to think critically and act independently in the absence of the leader diminishes over a period of time (Gemmill and Oakley 1992; Kelley 1988; Vanderslice 1988), and their desire to please the leader turns into a sense of duty and obligation (Conger 1989). As a result, followers grow accustomed to thinking and acting only in reaction to external authority, namely leaders, where obtaining the leader's approval is of utmost importance for them in any given context (Conger 1989). These dark and subtle aspects of charismatic leadership have been well documented in the literature (Bass 1985; Conger 1991; Conger and Kanungo 1987, 1998; Gronn 1995; Howell 1988; Kets de Vries 1995; Yukl 1999).

Transformational Leadership

Bass (1985) and his colleagues expanded the idea of charismatic leadership, and building on Burns' model of transforming leadership (Burns 1978) proposed the theory of transformational leadership based on the notion of charisma. Empirical and conceptual studies on transformational leadership have flourished ever since (Bass 1999). Transformational leaders empower and mobilize followers to work for transcendental goals that go beyond their immediate self-interests for the good of the group, organization or country. Transformational leadership consists of four key dimensions: Idealized Influence (Charisma); Inspirational Motivation; Intellectual Stimulation; and Individualised Consideration. Table 9.1 outlines the typical behavioural attributes associated with each dimension (Bass 1997). Proponents of transformational leadership argue that transformational leaders will cause followers to perform beyond expected levels of performance as a consequence of the leader's influence. Followers are willing to go the extra mile because of their commitment to the leader, their intrinsic work motivation, or the sense of purpose and mission that drives them to excel.

Table 9.1   Four dimensions of transformational leadership

Idealized Influence (Charisma)	'Leaders display conviction; emphasise trust; take stands on difficult issues; present their most important values; and emphasise the importance of purpose, commitment, and the ethical consequences of decisions. Such leaders are admired as role models generating pride, loyalty, confidence and alignment around a shared purpose'.
Inspirational Motivation	'Leaders articulate an appealing vision of the future, challenge followers with high standards, talk optimistically with enthusiasm, and provide encouragement and meaning for what needs to be done'.
Intellectual Stimulation	'Leaders question old assumptions, traditions, and beliefs; stimulate in others new perspectives and ways of doing things; and encourage the expression of ideas and reasons'.
Individualized Consideration	'Leaders deal with others as individuals; consider their individual needs, abilities, and aspirations; listen attentively; further their development; advise; teach; and coach'.

Source: Bass 1997, p 133

As transformational leadership is an extension of charismatic leadership, one would expect that some of its aspects are found in Iranian leadership. Javidan (1994 1996, cited in Javidan and Carl 2004) demonstrated that the Iranian view of leadership includes a leader with a mental map, who shares a new paradigm, has a global outlook, is enthusiastic, and is a credible communicator. A successive study by Dastmalchian and Javidan (1998) found the concepts of visionary and high-commitment leadership confirmed within the Iranian sample. The study stated that there was strong support among the 143 Iranian executives surveyed for the concept of empowerment. This points to the conclusion that encouraging employee participation, setting motivational goals, removing bureaucratic barriers and rewarding performance lead towards building a loyal workforce. These findings were also reinforced in a study comparing Iranian and Taiwanese managers (Javidan and Dastmalchian 1995, cited in Dastmalchian et al. 2001).

Javidan and Dastmalchian's follow-up report on the GLOBE project (2003) revealed that Iranian managers expect their leaders to be visionary (having foresight, being prepared and future oriented) and inspirational (being positive, encouraging and dynamic). They also prefer leaders who are performance-oriented and have high integrity and those who are decisive and willing to make personal sacrifices. The strong preference for visionary leaders seems to be rooted in the Iranian culture of high performance orientation and its strong values of uncertainty avoidance and future orientation. Charismatic leaders help reduce uncertainty through their integrity and performance orientation and help increase performance orientation through their inspirational and excellence oriented visions.

In addition, Iranian managers reported strong preferences for leaders who were honest, cooperative and dependable, and who were not hostile, cynical, egoistic or vindictive. The strong desire for team-oriented leadership seems to be rooted in the Iranian managers' collectivistic values (Zaccaro, Rittman and Marks 2001). In addition, rather than having the opportunity to participate, Iranians tend to prefer autocratic leaders who are humane and benevolent and are cognizant of employee emotions and well-being. They prefer a formal relationship with their leaders but at the same time expect them to show concern for employees and their families (Javidan and Dastmalchian 2003).

CULTURAL, LEADERSHIP AND ORGANIZATION DEVELOPMENT

Basin-Asadi (cited in Namazie and Tayeb 2006) argues that Iran's national culture comprises three influences: traditional/ancient, Islamic and Western. When Hofstede undertook his landmark study of cultural dimensions in the early 1970s, he found that Iran, like most other Middle Eastern and indeed Muslim-based societies, had high uncertainty avoidance and power distance – a situation which has only increased since the overthrow of the Shah in 1979 and the re-emergence of Islamic fundamentalism (ITIM International 2003). Importantly, though, the more recent GLOBE study suggests that Iran is now less concerned with avoiding uncertainty (Dastmalchian, Javidan, and Alam 2001). Being mildly risk averse and tolerating a high level of power and income/wealth inequality within the society, Iranians expect leaders to make the decisions on behalf of society and organizations rather than adopt the participative decision-making favoured in many Western societies. Curiously, the origins of an emphasis on uncertainty avoidance mean that, although there are many regulations in society, the inequalities of power mean that rules are often subverted. Hofstede (ITIM International 2003) suggests that leaders have virtually ultimate power and authority and rules reinforce and support those who have power and change tends to be a result of insurrection (as occurred in 1979) rather than through democratic means.

Though slightly higher on individualism than the Muslim countries' average, Iran is still highly collectivist; this is reflected in its focus on family and the importance of extended family and close contacts and replication of familial relationships in the workplace. It is important to note that, although in the GLOBE study Iran was found to be highly in-group collectivist, it is low on social collectivism (Dastmalchian, Javidan, and Alam 2001); so collectivism will be strong within organizations and within departments but not across departments or organizations. Loyalty to society, the group and the organization overrides emphasis on legalities. While there is no doubt that globalization has had its impacts on development and modernity for Iran, there is still an underlying focus on relationship building, an observance of Shari'a law, and a long-term orientation (Hutchings and Weir 2006a; Hutchings and Weir 2006b; Weir and Hutchings 2005). What this means for leadership is that organizational leaders feel a responsibility to protect group members in a paternal manner, albeit within a context in which some may profit more than others from their more favourable *wasta* relationships.

In terms of masculinity, Iran scores similar to the world average and, interestingly, lower than Western industrialized Anglo nations like Australia, Canada, the US and the UK (see Hofstede 2001). This indicates that Iran does have a relatively high degree of gender differentiation of roles, with males having a significant portion of the society and power structure. As discussed later in the section on women as leaders, while Iranian women have increasing educational and employment opportunities, they are still underrepresented in management and leadership roles. Iran is still a very patriarchal society in which women are revered for their feminine qualities and emphasize modesty and dignity and men are positioned as primary income earners (Kandoyti 1996). On the GLOBE study, Iran scored eighth lowest of 61 countries on the dimension of gender egalitarianism and there was no strong desire reflected to change this state (Dastmalchian, Javidan and Alam 2001).

On other measures used in the GLOBE study, Iran scored low on assertiveness, meaning that there is an emphasis on avoiding confrontation and aggressiveness. Humane orientation scored strongly, reflecting a strong cultural norm to be altruistic, and performance orientation was also very high (Dastmalchian, Javidan and Alam 2001), both of which suggest that leaders who are benevolent in their approach to management will be viewed favourably by employees.

Recent Cultural Impacts

Ali and Amirshahi (2002) argue that a struggle continues in Iran between conservative and reformist groups with a tilt towards obedience and compulsion and predestination rather than freedom of choice – so while there are tendencies towards individualism, loyalty and obedience to superiors still remain fundamental. Moreover, Ali and Amirshahi (2002) suggest that the primary values of Iranian managers are conformist and sociocentric, even though this is at odds with public pronouncements of the current regime and global market-orientation. Moreover, the country continues to have tensions between a religious theocracy and democratic values. Both the ancient Persian and Islamic traditions continue to have considerable influence over the shape of management activities and thought. Dastmalchian, Javidan and Alam (2001) suggest that the key characteristics of Iranian leadership are familial, humble and faithful (having historical roots in Iranian and Islamic culture) and being planners and receptive (which they view as a result of societal changes post-revolution in 1979). They also found two charismatic and narcissistic leadership qualities which they define as supportive and dictatorial, but caution these require further investigation (Dastmalchian, Javidan and Alam 2001).

While HRM is not a new concept to Iran, most organizations do not have an actual HRM department and, as a result, practices employed are substantively different from those commonly utilized in the West, with little clear distinction between HRM and HRD as exists in the West. For instance, Namazie and Roshan (2003) note that recruitment is usually from family and friends of current employees (particularly in family businesses); public sector organizations tend to be change averse; performance appraisals are not usual and, where they do exist, tend to be ad hoc and informal; training is regarded as important but evaluation is rare; and career development is not considered a key purpose of the training that is provided. Again, HRM practices, particularly in recruitment and selection, have a strong tradition in cultural values such as the importance of family and assisting those who have close network connections. Leadership in HRM is generally easier to achieve in private rather than public companies, but use of Westernized best practice HRM is slow to be adopted. Indeed, in terms of managerial and leadership knowledge generally, Mosadeghrad and Tahery (2004, cited in Mosadeghrad and Yarmohammadian 2006) found that Iranian managers have insufficient information about leadership theories and Mosadeghrad and Yarmohammadian (2006) argue that, if Iranian managers had greater knowledge of the value of participative management, they may have greater awareness of the impact of their leadership style on employee job satisfaction. Further, an understanding of the fundamental underpinnings of Iranian culture and how it is changing as a result of external forces for global integration is key to appropriating leadership styles which keep pace with these changes.

INSTITUTIONAL IMPACTS ON LEADERSHIP

In Iran, as in many other countries, institutional forces affect organizations' processes and decision making. As global business expands, it becomes more obvious that business organizations do not operate in a vacuum. Within institutional theory literature, perspectives derived to examine institutional forces have both an economic orientation and a socio-cultural orientation. For example, Suhomlinova (1999) found that government institutions and influences had a negative impact on Russian enterprise reform. At the individual level, Lau (1998) suggested that political and market pressures were the institutional constraints faced by chief executives in Chinese enterprises. Thus, it seems that many emerging economy firms such as Iranian business organizations and executives were influenced by the existing institutional arrangements and constraints.

At the macro level, the nature, scope and dynamics of political economy institutions have a significant impact on the performance of business organizations. At the organizational level, executives operating in a global marketplace draw on their cultural backgrounds, experience and values as they chart business strategies and operational tactics for their organizations. The performance of Iranian business organizations, like other business organizations all over the world, is influenced by the political economy in which they operate and the values of the executives who direct them. Iranian business leaderships, like other executives, are the products of their unique socio-culture values and beliefs. In this context, the attitudes, behaviours, and leadership styles of Iranian executives are reflections of the collective dynamic interactions of their unique cultural orientation and marketplace realities. Thus, any attempt to understand the different facets of Iranian executives and the performance of their organizations must address the Iranian culture and its political economic realities and constraints.

As mentioned, the Iranian culture is well rooted in tradition, with a strong emphasis on cultural institutions such as religion and family. The Islamic Revolution of 1979 impacted all facets of the Iranian society and its core values. This revolution created and promoted a social environment characterised by a unique blend of morality that is based on both Islamic values and national pride. In this context, Iranian executives had to realign their values and business practices in order to be consistent with that of the religious, social, and political values and practices of their post-revolution culture.

Yasin et al. (2002) present the results of a survey dealing with the impact of economic and cultural values on Iranian business organizations. According to this study, although Iranian executives perceive the government and religious institutions as the dominant forces, the majority of these executives expressed an optimistic view of the future direction of the Iranian economy (Yasin et al. 2002). Moreover, the majority of the surveyed executives tended to view trading with global business organizations as positive. Their results also clearly show that the Iranian business leaderships' values are in a state of transition. In this context, while religious-based values still dominate, to a certain extent, global business realities and the values associated with them may be forcing Iranian executives to reconsider some of their religious-based values (Yasin et al. 2002). Therefore, it appears that Iranian business leaders demonstrate a higher level of courage and demand for change, which in turn points unmistakably towards a process of change promoting institutionalized and transparent structures.

As mentioned earlier, Iran has experienced two decades of economic and political difficulties after the Islamic Revolution, which have all, socially, politically and economically, greatly impacted the Iranian economy. However, in recent years, there are signs to indicate that the Iranian revolution has begun to mature into well-established social, political, and economic institutions. Despite the economic and political isolation imposed by the West, the trend toward integrating the Iranian economy into the global economy has been positive in recent years. Efforts by the Iranian former president, Mohammad Khatami, to improve the economic condition through attracting foreign investment, increasing non-oil exports, accelerating privatization and reducing red tape within the governmental bureaucracy, although they have not fully achieved their proposed objectives, have nevertheless had great impact on the political economy of institutions. However, government institutions still suffer from considerable bureaucratic procedures, mismanagement and corruption. Khajehpour (2000) presents the results of a survey dealing with obstacles to private sector investment in Iran. The ten most important of these obstacles are listed:

- Unsustainable policy making
- General lack of stability of regulations
- Foreign exchange regulations
- Labour laws and regulations
- Financial problems
- Corruption
- Foreign trade regulations
- Tax laws and regulations
- Inflation
- Price controls.

Despite these constraints, institutions can also facilitate strategy, allowing enterprises to react to and play a more active role in an intuitional environment if firms have an adaptive ability that allows them to move beyond institutional constraints. The drastic events of the past 25 years in Iran significantly affected the performance of Iranian business organizations. Business executives and entrepreneurs found themselves having to do business in a market place which is heavily regulated by the government, often experiencing shortages of critical raw material and out of control inflation. These economic constraints, coupled with the significant political and cultural change due to the revolution, forced many business organizations to emphasize efficiency as opposed to effectiveness. However, in recent years the Iranian government, in its attempts to rebuild the economy, appears to be redefining the scope of the revolution in ways which encourage more openness. To promote the globalization and openness of the business sector, government is encouraging joint business ventures and international investments. Considering Iran's strategic geopolitical position and its vast natural and human resources, the country has great potential to be a formidable international economic player. This is especially true since the Iranian business culture appears to be adopting market-based values as opposed to strictly religion-based values (Yasin et al. 2002). As a consequence of its gradual orientation towards a free market-oriented economy based on private enterprises, especially in non-oil industrial domains, Iran's foreign trade will be less and less planned by governmental bodies. This, in turn, means that a growing portion of foreign exchange will be made by private traders.

In this context, Iranian business executives are experiencing market-leaning institutional change, gradual relaxation of public ownership and control, and the development of the private sector. Institutional reform, in terms of strengthening the role of the private sector, provided proper incentives and changes to corporate culture that enabled firms, even public-owned ones, to make improvements. For example, in recent years private sector banks and NGO credit cooperatives are competing for the deposit and loan businesses of very large state-owned banks. In turn, state-owned banks are upgrading their branches and services with faster response time. It seems that the private sector is gaining strength and competition is increasing. A customer now has a choice of data services and mobile telephone services as the grip of the state monopoly is loosened. The change of generations can also be observed in Iranian business leadership, technocrats, and government officers. Therefore change, at all levels of the vast public and private structure, is notable because the Iranian economy is transforming. Namazie (2004) suggests that there are six key effects on Iranian management of the reforms and restructuring that has occurred since 1997, namely:

- Rapid development of management courses and training
- Iranian managers entering into international negotiations and discussions on the development of business
- The emergence of strategic alliances and joint ventures in import and export
- Difficulties in international management as a result of two decades of isolation
- New young managers who have been trained/educated abroad whom have taken over family businesses
- The influence of foreign company practice on management in Iran.

(Namazie 2004)

WOMEN AS LEADERS IN BUSINESS AND PUBLIC LIFE IN IRAN

After the revolution, the enhanced interest in the study of Iranian women focused mainly on the impact of Islamic ideology on the social, economic, political and legal position of women (Afshar 1985; Higgins 1985; Mahdavi 1983; Momeni 1981, cited in Ghorayshi 1995). There were hardly any studies done on women's experiences with work, the labour market and work organizations (Bagherian 1991; Moghadam 1988, cited in Ghorayshi 1995). In 2003, Shirin Ebadi, an activist, was awarded the Nobel Peace Prize in recognition of her work in Iran for human rights, women's rights and children's rights. Through her, the prize acknowledged the struggles Iranian women (and Middle Eastern women generally) face in their quest for rights and a respectable place in society (Esfandiari 2004; Monshipouri 2004).

However, Iranian women do enjoy a better status than their counterparts in other Islamic countries. It is not Islam as a creed that is repressive, but cultural traditions that developed, sometimes as a result of interpretations of the Holy Scriptures. Iranian women are allowed to vote and are eligible to stand alongside men. The new constitution also gives them the right to work and study, and in urban areas they overwhelmingly assert those rights (Schramm-Nielsen and Faradonbeh 2002). They are now a visible and significant part of the country's elite public college campuses. For over a decade, the number of women attending institutions of higher education has been growing steadily. In most cases, women outperform men at all levels (UNDP 2003, pp. 193–5, cited in Neal, Finlay, and Tansey 2005). For instance, in 2003, women constituted 62 per cent of the student population who passed the national college entrance examination (Shavarini 2006).

Women in Political Leadership Roles

Women are also a common sight in the political arena – they include a female vice-president in the first Khatami government (Andersen and Seeberg 1999, p. 28, cited in Schramm-Nielsen and Faradonbeh 2002), and a female diplomat now representing Iran in the United Nations in New York (L'Express 1999, cited in Schramm-Nielsen and Faradonbeh 2002). The manager of Tehran University is a woman, who is also member of Parliament; however, she is one of only 11 women members (less than 4 per cent of the total) (Berlingske Tidende 2000, cited in Schramm-Nielsen and Faradonbeh 2002).

In 1998, nine women tried to stand for the Assembly of Experts. In 1997, four women registered to run for the presidency, as did two women in the 2001 election, and in both 2005 and 2009 one woman, Rafat Bayat, registered to run. In these elections, all the women were rejected by the Council of Guardians (Wright 2000, p.136, cited in Schramm-Nielsen and Faradonbeh 2002). Nonetheless, women are making their presence felt – almost one-third of government employees were females in 1999 and more than 300 women won in Iran's first local elections in 1999.

Women in the Public Sector

Women are increasingly entering the workforce and rising to leader-ship positions in the public and private sectors (Al-Lamki 1999; ILO 1998; Salloum 2003; UNDP, cited in Neal et al. 2005). Iranian women now hold public offices in national and local administrations and have civil jobs in all professions (Schramm-Nielsen and Faradonbeh 2002). Women employed in the public sector are mostly professional and highly educated. They also tend to be concentrated in the fields of education and health care. A great number of employed women are concentrated in teaching jobs and although they have some authority, they are not involved in any crucial decision-making (Shahidian 1991, cited in Kousha and Mohseni 1997).

Women in Leadership in Business Organizations

In the private sector, Analoui and Hosseini (2001) discovered that there is general trend of male occupancy of managerial positions in Iran. This remains true in most developing countries. On the whole, organizations seemed to show a preference for male employees. It was felt that the male managers were thought of highly and perceived as being more 'reliable' in terms of work effectiveness. In Iran most female managers have only managed to reach middle managerial positions due to the presence of 'glass ceilings', as discussed above. Schramm-Nielsen and Faradonbeh (2002) warned that, since it is taken for granted that a man would be in charge, female business persons and negotiators are recommended not to bring male subordinates, so as to prevent having to stress who is in authority.

However, Al-Lamki (1999, cited in Neal et al. 2005) has challenged the stereotypical and persistent Western view that Arab women are overwhelmingly repressed in the Arab workplace and Arab societies in general. In almost all Arab countries, the number and proportion of women entering the workplace is rising year on year. Historically, most Arab cultures have been relatively comfortable with women wielding power and authority (Guthrie 2001, cited in Neal et al. 2005). In Iran, there are numerous women running their own businesses. In the Islamic world, women even have an advantage compared to their sisters in the West, inasmuch as what they gain, they may keep to themselves. They are not obliged to share their earnings with their husband, who is supposed to be the sole supporter of the family (Schramm-Nielsen and Faradonbeh 2002). Currently, growing numbers of Iranian women have become lawyers, doctors, professors, newspaper and magazine editors, engineers, business executives, economists and television newscasters. In 1998, more than a third of university faculties were female (Wright 2000, p. 137, cited in Schramm-Nielsen and Faradonbeh 2002). The Islamic world has a long tradition of female business women, going back to pre-Islamic times, since the Prophet Muhammad's first wife, Khadidja, was a wealthy merchant (Schramm-Nielsen and Faradonbeh 2002).

However, all these examples need to be set in perspective. They cannot and should not be taken to imply that the fight for equality of women in Iran is all over. Schramm-Nielsen and Faradonbeh (2002) suggest that the general spirit is still phallocratic and misogynist compared to most Western countries and Iranian women still have a long way to go before they break through the 'glass ceiling' and assume a position of equality with their male counterparts.

CONCLUSIONS AND IMPLICATIONS

The increasing convergence and interdependence between nations in many realms (political, cultural, technological, and so on) has created the need to understand how cultural differences affect and shape business leadership (Henry and Springborg 2001). To this end, the GLOBE leadership studies cited in this chapter to shed light on Iranian leadership represent the most recent and ambitious leadership study, involving 62 different countries grouped under ten clusters. Among the important findings in the studies are the desired leadership attributes for the Middle East cluster, in which Iran is placed. Middle Eastern leaders should strive to be self-protective, humane-oriented, autonomous, charismatic, team-oriented, and partici-pative (House et al. 2004). While Iranian leadership demonstrates some similarities to the desirable attributes of the Middle East cluster, it also exhibits some idiosyncratic attributes. What transpires from the studies of Javidan and Dastmalchian (2003) is that the ideal Iranian leader is an autocratic leader who is benevolent and humane. Participative style and team decision making are not as important as the capacity to be the 'father' figure who directs and controls, while simultaneously shepherding the followers and caring for their welfare.

Overall, our chapter provides some important insights into what consti-tutes effective leadership in Iran. In order to address this issue with cred-ibility, however, subsequent studies which test the findings of the studies cited in this chapter are needed. The validation of these findings will be achieved if future studies are conducted in various settings (industries, sectors, etc.) using more rigorous quantitative and qualitative methods than have been used in the past. Future studies need to account for the many contexts that leaders operate in, as is commonly done in country-specific leadership studies. For example, it was found that Iranian manag-ers working in larger firms tended to be somewhat more inner-directed (more egocentric) and individualistic in their values. This could reflect the residual cultural influence of the pre-Islamic Revolution era, coupled with the impact of globalization. Hence, Iranian managers in larger organiza-tions tend to have more in common with their counterparts in Western business environments than their colleagues in smaller enterprises do (Alavi and Yasin 2003). However, to what extent this convergence is true across industries and settings remains unknown.

Given the relevance of the transformational leadership model in the Iranian context, and the dominance of male leadership in the country, it may be of interest to examine the way women lead in Iran. Research suggests that transformational leadership is synonymous with the femi-nine style of leading. Druskat (1994), for example, found that compared to male leaders, female leaders exhibit more frequent transformational leadership behaviours and less frequent management-by-exception behav-iours. This finding corroborated an earlier study by Rosener (1990) who reported that women are more likely than men to display transformational leadership behaviours. In fact, Rosener (1990) argued that women leaders succeed because of, not in spite of, certain leadership characteristics that are commonly considered as feminine. In light of these research findings, the study of gender differences in Iranian leadership will be pertinent for overall leadership development in the country. Notwithstanding the social-political context and cultural prejudices which may inhibit women's leadership in Iran, such studies may advance our understanding of the convergent influences of culture and gender in country-specific leadership and its impacts on global leadership.

It is of relevance to note here that the GLOBE studies generated a list of universally desirable and undesirable leadership attributes (House et al. 2004). According to this list, an ideal portrait of a global leader would be one who exhibits high integrity, charisma and people skills, and is not autocratic or ruthless. A cursory review of this list in light of the perceived attributes of Iranian leaders may point to the perception that there is moderate support for convergence between Iranian and global leadership. For example, the perception that leaders are naturally gifted with certain qualities that non-leaders do not have (often categorized as 'charisma') seems to flourish in both the Iranian and the global context. On the other hand, it is also clear that Iranian autocratic leadership style is not desirable in the global leadership arena. However, these speculations need to be empirically verified by further studies. The outcomes of such studies would be important and relevant for Iranian leaders who endeavour to be more effective in the global arena, as well as for expatriate managers who want to successfully lead others in Iran.

Finally, several notes on research assumptions and methodologies deserve mention. All cross-cultural studies cited in this manuscript, most notably the GLOBE studies, were based on the implicit leadership theory (ILT) that assumes leadership to be a function of the implicit beliefs that individuals have about leaders. Hence, leadership is merely the perception that individuals have of a leader. This conceptualization of leadership is rather limiting and fails to acknowledge other equally valid perspectives, such as those that are behavioural and competency-based. It also fails to consider what is termed post-heroic leadership theorizing, which extends our understanding of the leader as an individual whose role is enacting leadership. Rather, leadership is viewed as a dynamic and evolving set of social relations, resulting in a culturally and socially contingent set of interactions, relationships and processes (Grint 2005). While this chapter has only touched on gender and ethnic configurations, these will undoubtedly have a bearing in Middle East states that have distinct hierarchies and protocols for business communication (Metcalfe 2011; Stead and Elliot 2009; see also Chapter 13).

Future research in culture-specific leadership needs to consider these perspectives. Further, critical investigations will need to have a broad understanding of the political economy in Iran, and international relations with world leaders. Ahmadinejad was elected president on a platform of providing a sustainable livelihood to all Iranian citizens. This is premised on economic development being underscored by Islamic principles. Whatever his intentions, it is difficult to disentangle relations between the governing council and the clerical council and to discern policy planning processes and outcomes, with the influence of former supreme leader Ayatollah Khomeini still highly significant. Put simply, Islamic philosophy will contrive to have a greater impact on initiatives for organization reform and public governance, potentially more than other states.

The second concern has to do with the methodology of cross-cultural comparisons which are based on a single measure of each of the variables examined and, often on a single source. In such studies, the findings may be confounded by biases inherent in the method of data collection, which do not reflect true variations in the variables. The generalizability of the findings may be adversely affected by this sort of common method bias. We recommend future studies in Iranian leadership (or that of other countries) should employ multiple methods of data collection (such as survey questionnaires, interviews and observation) and sources (perhaps leaders, followers and company databases).

RECOMMENDATIONS FOR INTERNATIONAL MANAGERS

Western organizations which have subsidiary operations in Iran cannot expect to lead and manage as they may do at headquarters, at least not in the current state of leadership and business management development in Iran. Accordingly, the following are offered as recommendations for international managers to maximize their adaptation to Iranian organizational practices:

- While the society suggests an emphasis on rules and regulations in accord with uncertainty avoidance, long-standing traditions of relationship building, and an observance of Shari'a law, mean that rules may be subverted for those who have the right connections.
- While the Iranian government has invested heavily in training and management development programmes, there will be substantive differences in education levels (and workforce capability) between urban and rural areas.
- Relationship building is central to business success and use of connections and intermediaries are key.

- Family is central to society and familial relations are reflected in relationships in the organization, so the manager may be thought of as uncle or father.
- Despite increased investment in female education, men still dominate in leadership positions in political life as well as public and private organizations and women may not always be well accepted in a leadership role, particularly in regions that have remained traditional. Women's roles are strongly guided by Shari'a law which reflect a traditional patriarchal order. The debate on women's role is critically examined in Chapter 12.
- Western females may have more leadership opportunities than local women as they will be viewed differently, but they need to remember to be respectful towards local cultural practices and are legally obliged to adopt the *hijab* in public spaces.
- The growth in Islamic revivalism and the politicization of religion will have important implications for how organisations are led and managed and foreign managers need to be cognizant of different approaches reflected by differing religious groupings.
- Managers in large, private organizations are more likely to adopt Westernized leadership practices than those in smaller and public organizations.
- The concept of HRM is relatively new to Iran and leaders are still expected to be paternalistic in their selection and reward practices.
- Authoritarian management styles are favoured over a participative approach. While there is evidence that Iranian employees are seeking empowerment through visionary leaders, they still expect the leader to be benevolent and make the correct decisions on their behalf.
- It is critical that international managers realize that all business activities must be in accordance with Islamic values and the teachings of the Qu'ran.

REFERENCES

Abrahamian, E. (1992), *Iran Between Two Revolution*, Princeton, NJ: Princeton University Press.

Alavi, J. and M.M. Yasin (2003), 'Managerial values and culture: where do Iranian executives stand?', *The Academy of Management Executive*, **17** (4), 147–9.

Ali, A.J. and M. Amirshahi (2002), 'The Iranian manager: work values and orientations', *Journal of Business Ethics*, **40** (2), 133–43.

Analoui, F. and M.H. Hosseini (2001), 'Management education and increased managerial effectiveness: the case of business managers in Iran', *The Journal of Management Development*, **20** (9), 785–94.

Avolio, B.J., D.A. Waldman and W.O. Einstein (1988), 'Transformational leadership in a management game simulation: impacting the bottom line', *Group and Organisation Studies*, **13**, 59–80.

Barling, J., T. Weber and E.K. Kelloway (1996), 'Effects of transformational leadership training on attitudinal and financial outcomes: a field experiment', *Journal of Applied Psychology*, **81**, 827–32.

Barnard, C.I. (1948), *Organisations and Management*, Cambridge, MA: Harvard University Press.

Bass, B.M. (1985), *Leadership and Performance Beyond Expectations*, New York: Free Press.

Bass, B. M. (1990), *Bass & Stogdill's Handbook of Leadership: Theory, Research, and Managerial Applications,* 3rd edn, New York: Free Press.

Bass, B.M. (1997), 'Does the transactional-transformational leadership paradigm transcend organisational and national boundaries?', *American Psychologist*, **52** (2), 130–39.

Bass, B.M. (1999), 'Two decades of research and development in transformational leadership', *European Journal of Work and Organisational Psychology*, **8** (1), 9–32.

Bank Markasi Jomhouri Islami Iran (BMJIR) [Central Bank of Islamic Republic of Iran] (2006), *Economic Profile*, no. 42, third quarter, 1384 (2005/2006), Tehran: BMJIR.

BP (2010), *Statistical Review of World Energy*, June.

Burns, J.M. (1978), *Leadership*, New York: Harper & Row.

Clawson, P. and M. Rubin (2005), *Eternal Iran: Continuity and Chaos*, New York: Palgrave Macmillan.

Conger, J.A. and R.N. Kanungo (1987), 'Toward a behavioural theory of charismatic leadership in organisational settings', *Academy of Management Review*, **12** (4), 637–47.

Conger, J.A. and Kanungo, R.N. (1998), *Charismatic Leadership in Organisations*, Thousand Oaks, CA: Sage Publications.

Conger, J.A. (1989), *The Charismatic Leader: Behind the Mystique of Exceptional Leadership*, San Francisco, CA: Jossey Bass.

Conger, J.A. (1991), 'The dark side of leadership', *Organisational Dynamics*, **19**, 44–55.

Dastmalchian, A. and M. Javidan (1998), 'High-commitment leadership: a study of Iranian executives', *Journal of Comparative International Management*, **1** (1), 23–37.

Dastmalchian, D., M. Javidan and K. Alam (2001), 'Effective leadership and culture in Iran: an empirical study', *Applied Psychology*, **50** (4), 532–58.

Druskat, V.U. (1994), 'Gender and leadership style: transformational and transactional leadership in the Roman Catholic church', *Leadership Quarterly*, **5** (1), 99–119.

Ebrahimian, L.D. (2003), 'Socio-economic development in Iran through information and communications technology', *The Middle East Journal*, **57** (1), 93–111.

Ehteshami, A. (2004), 'Iran's international posture after the fall of Baghdad', *Middle East Journal*, **58** (2), 179–94.

Esfandiari, H. (2004), 'The woman question', *Wilson Quarterly*, 56–63.

Gemmill, G. and J. Oakley (1992), 'Leadership: an alienating social myth?', *Human Relations*, **45** (2), 113–29.

Gorayshi, P. (1995), 'Women, paid work and the family: in the Islamic Republic of Iran', *Journal of Comparative Family Studies*, **27** (3), 453–66.

Graham, J.W. (1988), 'Transformational leadership: fostering follower autonomy, not automatic followership', in J.G. Hunt, B.R. Baliga, H.P. Dachler and C.A. Schriesheim (eds), *Emerging Leadership Vistas*, Lexington, MA: D.C. Heath, pp. 73–79.

Grint, K. (2005), 'Problems, problems, problems: the social construction of leadership', *Human Relations*, **58**, 1467–94.

Gronn, P. (1995), 'Greatness re-visited: the current obsession with transformational leadership', *Leading & Managing*, **1** (1), 14–27.

Halliday, F. (2005), *The Middle East in International Relations: Power, Politics and Ideology*, Cambridge: Cambridge University Press.

Henry, C.M. and R. Springborg (2001), *Globalization and the Politics of Development in the Middle East*, Cambridge: Cambridge University Press.

Hofstede, G. (2001), *Culture's Consequences: Comparing Values, Behaviours, Institutions and Organisations across Nations*, 2nd edn, Thousand Oaks, CA: Sage.

Hooijberg, R. and J. Choi (2000), 'From selling peanuts and beer in Yankee Stadium to creating a theory of transformational leadership: an interview with Bernie Bass', *Leadership Quarterly*, **11** (2), 291–306.

House, R.J. (1977), 'A 1976 theory of charismatic leadership', in J.G. Hunt and L.L. Larson (eds), *Leadership: The Cutting Edge*, Carbondale, IL: Southern Illinois University Press, pp. 189–207.

Howell, J.M. and K.E. Hall-Merenda (1999), 'The ties that bind: the impact of leader-member exchange, transformational and transactional leadership, and distance on predicting follower performance', *Journal of Applied Psychology*, **84** (5), 680–94.

Howell, J.M. (1988), 'Two faces of charisma: socialised and personalised leadership in organisations', in J.A. Conger, R.N. Kanungo and associates (eds), *Charismatic Leadership: The Elusive Factor in Organisational Effectiveness*, San Francisco, CA: Jossey-Bass, pp. 213–36.

Hutchings, K. and D. Weir (2006a), 'Guanxi and Wasta: a comparative examination of the impact of internationalisation and modernisation on traditional ways of networking in China and the Arab world', *Thunderbird International Business Review*, **48** (1), 141–56.

Hutchings, K. and D. Weir (2006b), 'Understanding networking in China and the Arab world: lessons for international managers', *Journal of European Industrial Training*, **30** (4), 272–90.

ITIM International (2003), Geert Hofstede™ cultural dimensions, accessed 5 November 2006 at www.geert-hofstede.com/hofstede-iran.shtml.

Javidan, M. and D.E. Carl (2004), 'East meets West: a cross-cultural comparison of charismatic leadership among Canadian and Iranian executives', *Journal of Management Studies*, **41** (4), 665–91.

Javidan, M. and A. Dastmalchian, (2003), 'Culture and leadership in Iran: the land of individual achievers, strong family ties, and powerful elite', *The Academy of Management Executive*, **17** (4), 127–242.

Kamyab, S. (2004), 'Education in Iran: an overview', *College and University*, **79** (4), 57–60.

Kandoyti, D. (1996), *Gendering the Middle East*, Syracuse, NY: Syracuse University Press.

Keddie, N. (1999), *Roots of Revolution*, New Haven, CT: Yale University Press.

Kelley R.E. (1988), 'In praise of followers', *Harvard Business Review*, **66** (6), 142–8.

Kets De Vries, M.F.R. (1995), *Life and Death in the Executive Fast Lane: Essays on Irrational Organisations and their Leaders*, San Francisco, CA: Jossey-Bass.

Khajehpour, B. (2000), 'Domestic political reforms and private sector activity in Iran', *Social Research*, **67** (2), 577–98.

Kirkpatrick, S.A. and E.A. Locke (1996), 'Direct and indirect effects of three core charismatic leadership components on performance and attitudes', *Journal of Applied Psychology*, **81**, 36–51.

Kousha, M. and N. Mohseni (1997), 'Predictors of life satisfaction among urban Iranian women: An exploratory analysis', *Social Indicators Research*, **40**, 329–57.

Lau, C.M. (1998), 'Strategic orientations of chief executives in state-owned enterprises in transition', in M.A. Hitt, J.E. Ricart, I. Costa and R.D. Nixon (eds), *Managing Strategically in an Interconnected World*, Chichester: Wiley, pp. 101–17.

Lorentz, J.H. (1995), *Historical Dictionary of Iran*, Lanham, MD: Scarecrow Press.

Lowe, K.B., K.G. Kroeck and N. Sivasubramaniam (1996), 'Effectiveness correlates of transformational and transactional leadership: a meta-analysis review of MLQ literature', *Leadership Quarterly*, **7**, 385–425.

Metcalfe, B.D. (2010), 'Diversity, equality and work organization in the Middle East', in M. Ozbilgin and J. Syed (eds), *Diversity Management in Asia: A Research Companion*, Cheltenham, UK and Northampton, MA, USA: Edward Elgar.

Monshipouri, M. (2004), 'The road to globalisation runs through women's struggle', *World Affairs*, **167** (1), 3–14.

Mosadeghrad, A.M. and M.H. Yarmohammadian (2006), 'A study of relationship between managers' leadership style and employees' job satisfaction', *Leadership in Health Services*, **19** (2), 6–28.

Namazie, P. (2004), 'The transferability of HRM practices and policies in IJVs: an examination of the macro and micro environmental factors in IJVs based in Iran', PhD thesis: Middlesex Business School, London.

Namazie, P. and A. Roshan (2003), 'Factors affecting the transferability of HRM practices in joint ventures based in Iran', *Career Development International*, **8** (7), 357–66.

Namazie and M. Tayeb (2006), 'Human resource management in Iran', in P.S. Budhwar and K. Mellahi (eds), *Managing Human Resources in the Middle East*, Abingdon: Routledge, pp. 20–39.

Neal, M., J. Finlay, and R. Tansey (2005), '"My father knows the minister": a comparative study of Arab women's attitudes towards leadership authority', *Women in Management Review*, **20** (7), 478–97.

Oktav, O.Z. (2005), 'American policies towards the Caspian Sea and the Baku-Tbilisi-Ceyhan pipeline', *Perceptions: Journal of International Affairs*, **10** (Spring), 17–34.

Pahlevan, T. (1998), 'Iran and Central Asia', in T. Atakabi and J. O'Kane (eds), *Post-Soviet Central Asia*, New York: Taurus Academic Studies, pp. 73-90.

Ramazani, R.K. (1982), *Revolutionary Iran: Challenges and Response in the Middle East*, Baltimore, MD: John's Hopkins University Press.

Rosener, J.B. (1990), 'Ways women lead', *Harvard Business Review*, **68**, November-December, 119–25.

Rost, J.C. (1993), *Leadership for the Twenty-first Century*, Wesport, CT: Praeger.

Schramm-Nielsen, J. and H.A. Faradonbeh (2002), 'Society and management in Iran', Copenhagen Business School working paper.

Shamir, B., R.J. House, and M.B. Arthur (1993), 'The motivational effects of charismatic leadership: a self-concept based theory', *Organisation Science,* **4** (4), 577–95.

Shavarini, M.K. (2006), 'Wearing the veil to college: the paradox of higher education in the lives of Iranian women', *International Journal of Middle East Studies*, **38**, 189–211.

Shea, C.M. and J.M. Howell (1999), 'Charismatic leadership and task feedback: a laboratory study of their effects on self-efficacy and task performance', *Leadership Quarterly*, **10** (3), 375–96.

Sinclair, A. (1998), *Doing Leadership Differently*, Melbourne, VIC: Melbourne University Press.

Stead, V. and C.J. Elliott (2009), *Women's Leadership*, Basingstoke: Palgrave Macmillan.

Suhomlinova, O. (1999), 'Constructive destruction: transformation of Russian state-owned construction enterprises during market transition', *Organisation Studies*, **20**, 451–84.

Vanderslice, V.J. (1988), 'Separating leadership from leaders: an assessment of the effect of leader and follower roles in organisations', *Human Relations*, **41** (9), 677–96.

Weber, M. (1947), *The Theory of Social and Economic Organization*, New York: Free Press.

Weir, D. and K. Hutchings (2005), 'Cultural embeddedness of knowledge sharing in China and the Arab world', *Knowledge and Process Management,* **12** (2), 89–98.

Yasin, M.M., J. Alavi, and T.W. Zimmerer (2002), 'An examination of the impacts of economics variables and cultural values on Iranian business organisations', *Cross Cultural Management*, **9** (1), 3–18.

Yukl, G. (1999), 'An evaluation of conceptual weaknesses in transformational and charismatic leadership theories', *Leadership Quarterly*, **10** (2), 285–305.

Yukl, G. (2002), *Leadership in Organisations*, 5th edn, Upper Saddle River, NJ: Prentice Hall.

Yukl, G. (2008), 'How leaders influence organizational effectiveness', *Leadership Quarterly*, **19** (6), 708–22.

Zaccaro, S.J., A.L. Rittman and M.A. Marks (2001), 'Team leadership', *Leadership Quarterly*, **12** (4), 451–83.

10. Leadership in Egypt

Gillian Rice

INTRODUCTION

The importance of Egypt in the Middle East and in the world has been much analysed in the aftermath of the unrest and revolutions which spread through the region and led Hosni Mubarak to step down on 11 February 2011. The nature of leadership in Egypt has also been scrutinized as never before. The strong man has been toppled by the unempowered, the old guard by the young, the traditionalist by the technologically aware. In all this the army was almost a spectator, stepping in after Mubarak's departure to take control with a commitment to oversee a transition to free and fair elections: there is something appealingly symbolic about a revolution organized through social networks and taking place in full view not only of the world's media, but also in sight of the Cairo museum, repository of 5000 years of Egyptian history.

Whatever the future of national leadership in Egypt, the repercussions for the future role of the army, of the young, of communications technology and of external powers, remains to be seen – as do the implications for other states now troubled with violence, including Algeria, Bahrain, Iran, Jordan and Libya. Egypt has long held a central position in the Middle East. The fact that it is home to the League of Arab States gives Egypt considerable political influence. Egypt also exerts cultural influence over the region in at least three ways: first, through its historically strong publishing and film industries; second, through its status as an educational centre (Al-Azhar, the world's oldest university, was established in 972 CE); and third, Egypt has the largest population of any nation in the Middle East, with Egyptian expatriates working in key roles in many other Middle Eastern nations, both as professionals and labourers. Egypt is experiencing changes in leadership culture as younger business professionals, more influenced by Western education and ideas, assume more prominent roles.

THE POLITICAL, ECONOMIC, SOCIAL AND CULTURAL CONTEXT OF EGYPT

In order to provide a framework for the discussion of leadership in Egypt, this section reviews the political, economic, social and cultural context of the country. Egypt is a less affluent, predominantly Muslim country. Over the last few years business leaders had become more involved with government, reinvigorating economic liberalization policies in pursuit of development. Egypt's economy experienced relatively rapid economic growth and some areas, such as telecommunications, expanded significantly. However, in a market-oriented economy exposed to global competition, to achieve continued success that reaches all levels of a society with considerable income inequality, leadership capacity, teamwork, and innovative thinking are all essential.

Before the revolution of 2011, Egypt was a republic with very limited democratic features. There were direct presidential elections in 2005 and the next election is due in 2011, but competition was, in effect, not permitted under the regime of President Hosni Mubarak, who ruled Egypt since the assassination of Anwar Sadat in 1981 and was grooming his son Gamal to replace him. According to the Economist Intelligence Unit, constitutional amendments passed in March 2007 did not represent reform, but a tightening of political control and further curbs on civil rights (EIU ViewsWire 2007a). While opposition parties were allowed, and over 70 are in existence, their formation was tightly controlled and they have often boycotted elections. In the most recent elections of November and December 2010, as well as some boycotts, there were allegations of widespread irregularities (Human Rights Watch 2010). The largest opposition party is the Muslim Brotherhood, the members of which circumvented a ban imposed in 1954 by running as independents. There was thought to be little threat to the stability of the regime (EIU ViewWire 2007b) until the popular uprising early 2011, culminating in the removal of Mubarak from power and an interim military government up to a 'free and fair' presidential election planned for 2012 following parliamentary elections in November 2011.

Egypt has maintained strong ties to the US for many years and this relationship is expected to continue, albeit under pressure, as although the US supports democratization, Egyptians disapprove of US policies in the Middle East region. Egypt also has a close partnership with the EU and is strengthening ties with Russia and China. Egypt's population was 83 million in 2009 (World Bank 2010). Although Egypt's economy has expanded steadily in recent years, with a long term average growth rate of approximately 5.5 per cent (Oxford Economic Country Briefings 2007), rising to 7.2 per cent in 2008 before falling back due to global economic conditions to 4.7 per cent in 2009 (World Bank 2010), this growth is insufficient for a rapidly increasing population and unofficial estimates of unemployment range from 15 to 25 per cent (Gundling and Zanchettin 2007). Gross National Income (GNI) per capita for 2009 is $2070 (World Bank 2010).

Gamal Abdel Nasser, who overthrew the monarchy in a coup in 1952, pursued radical nationalist economic policies. During Sadat's presidency, economic policy shifted to an 'open-door' policy, and politically, he signed a peace treaty with Israel in 1979. This led to isolation within the Arab world for a time, which ended under Mubarak's rule. Mubarak continued Sadat's opening up and privatization of the Egyptian economy, but progress has been extremely slow. An economically liberal cabinet, appointed in July 2004, 'restarted' economic reform. Success in implementing politically difficult economic reforms depends, however, on the degree of support for them by the president. The government cut taxes by more than half in 2004 and the personal income tax rate and corporation tax rate are both 20 per cent. Private consumption has risen, but so has inflation, which was 11.8 per cent in 2009 (World Bank 2010). In terms of corruption perceptions, Transparency International rates Egypt as 2.8 on a scale of 0 (highly corrupt) to 10 (highly clean). Egypt ranks joint 111th out of 180 countries; the highest (cleanest score) in 2009 was 9.4 and the lowest was 1.1 (Transparency International 2009).

Egypt's urban population has remained stable for the past 30 years, at about 42 per cent. The structure of GDP by output is as follows: agriculture, 15 per cent; industry, 37 per cent; and services, 48 per cent (Oxford Economic Country Briefings 2007). Egypt's economy is built upon four main sources of revenue: petroleum and related exports, tourism, expatriate workers' remittances, and receipts from the Suez Canal. Before the global economic crisis beginning in 2008, the Suez Canal saw a strong increase in shipping traffic as a result of the surge in economic activity in Asia. Egypt's tourist arrivals reached a record nine million in 2006 as Red Sea and Sinai resorts attracted more winter visitors from Europe. The four primary sources of revenue slightly offset the widening trade deficit: as a proportion of GDP, the current-account surplus was approximately 2 per cent in 2007 (EIU ViewsWire 2007a), with the largest proportion of Egypt's exports, over a third, destined for EU countries.

Flows of foreign direct investment (FDI) rose strongly as Egypt's privatization programme accelerated and as the economy opened up further to foreign investors in areas such as telecommunications and banking. In 2006, Italy's leading banking group, Intesa Sanpaolo, bought one of Egypt's large state-owned banks, the Bank of Alexandria (Oxford

Economic Country Briefings 2007). The net flow of FDI is similar to the amount received by India, and were it not for the political instability of the Middle East, economic progress would proceed at a faster pace (Platt 2007). While some, such as Yasser El Mallawany, chairman and CEO of EFG-Hermes Holding, an investment bank and the leading securities broker on the Cairo and Alexandria Stock Exchange (CASE), are positive about the economic reforms and see Egypt as being in a 'paradigm shift' that is boosting business confidence (Platt 2007), others are more sanguine. Leftist members of parliament charge that privatization policies favour foreign investors and the wealthy at the expense of the poor and the public interest (El-Din 2007). One prominent business leader, Ismail Osman, the former chairman of the state-owned construction company Arab Contractors, argues that enterprises should remain state-owned but be run as private companies, by changing the leadership and improving management. His experience suggests success can be achieved. Arab Contractors was the first state owned company to create a human resources department. When he assumed leadership in 1993, the company's volume of work was worth about LE 1 billion (approximately US$ 175 million) and increased at a rate of LE 1 billion for the next nine years, providing jobs for 60000 people in 26 countries, and returning the company to profit (Nasr 2007).

Galal Amin, a prominent economist, believes that any economic progress in Egypt will be short-lived. The sale of many state assets to foreign investors through the revitalized privatization programme, he argues, will not lead to the reinvestment of profits in Egypt. He is also troubled by the decline of the manufacturing economy in favour of the service economy (Ahmed 2006). Such concerns are not new. Over 20 years ago, the economic liberalization policy also concentrated on trade, the importance of consumer items and the expansion of services such as tourism and hotel management (Tuma 1988). The emphasis on conspicuous consumption and changes in lifestyles which accompanied this policy aggravated inflation and unemployment and resulted in a 'new class'. Despite its small size, this group accumulated much economic and political power during the 1980s (Jabber 1986). This class consists primarily of entrepreneurs, professionals and high salaried employees of the private economy. Furthermore, because Egypt's service sector relies heavily on tourism, the economy is highly vulnerable to security developments and terrorist attacks (EIU ViewsWire 2007b). There are, nevertheless, some encouraging prospects for manufacturing because Egypt's labour costs are among the lowest in the Middle East and, along with state-subsidized energy and abundant water from the Nile, these imply that Egypt can compete with India, China and Turkey as a low-cost supplier to Europe

(Rachid 2006). Egypt has numerous trade agreements that provide it pref-
erential access to Europe, the USA, Turkey and other parts of Africa and
the Middle East. The economic climate means that conditions are suitable
for smaller Egyptian companies to expand. Egypt's biggest challenges are,
however, to improve managerial skills and to raise productivity so that all
Egyptians can benefit from any economic progress. Herein lies the challenge for leaders in organizations.

Closely integrated with the political and economic features of Egyptian
society are the cultural characteristics that play a significant part in
the improvement of managerial leadership and behaviour. Considerable
diversity exists in Egypt, as the Egyptian people are the result of an
intermingling of races over the past six thousand years (Gundling and
Zanchettin 2007). The strongest influences on society are those most
recent: the administrative and Islamic heritage of the Ottomans, the colonial rule of the British, and the pan-Arab nationalism of Gamal Abdel
Nasser. Although outsiders may view them as Arab, the inhabitants of
Egypt see themselves rather as Egyptians and therefore different from
members of other Middle Eastern societies. Egypt is, of course, dynamic,
and today is influenced by people from the Gulf States in two ways. One is
when Egyptian expatriate workers live in those countries for several years
and acculturate to their temporary domiciles before returning home. The
second occurs when people from the Gulf, who formerly came to Egypt
during the summer months, become year-round residents and establish
personal and business relationships with local Egyptians.

Ninety per cent of Egyptians are Muslim and although there is a Coptic
Christian minority, Islam has an overwhelming influence on society. The
teachings of Islam derive from the Qur'an (a book which Muslims believe
was revealed by God to Muhammad in seventh-century Arabia), and
from the *sunnah* (the recorded sayings and behaviour of Muhammad).
The goals of Islam are not primarily materialist. They are based on
Islamic perspectives of human well being which emphasize brotherhood/
sisterhood and socioeconomic justice, and require a balance of both the
material and spiritual needs of all people (Chapra 1992). God is viewed
as the sole creator of the universe and people are equal before God. This
ideal notion implies cooperation, and equality of effort and opportunity.
Muhammad described Islam as the 'middle way' and urged Muslims to be
moderate and balanced in all their endeavours. Islam condemns greed and
disregard for the needs and rights of others. The individual profit motive
is not the chief motivator in Islam; instead, achieving social good should
guide entrepreneurs and leaders. Islam places a greater emphasis on duties
than rights, because if duties are fulfilled by everyone, then self-interest is
held within bounds and the rights of everyone are safeguarded.

In Egypt, the reality of present-day Muslim life is far from the ideal possibilities delineated in Islamic teachings. Nevertheless, the Egyptians are a religious people closely attached to their religious culture and identity. There is a growing perception among them that many Islamic cultural traits are being superseded by Western, especially US, values, institutions, and practices. Egyptians have internalized three behaviours to enable them to deal with the difficulties of life in an autocratic, bureaucratic society with changing economic conditions (Tuma 1988). These behaviours are indecision, procrastination and indifference. People do not answer requests firmly, but say *insha'Allah* (God willing). They do not do today what they can do tomorrow and say frequently that they will do something *bukra* (tomorrow), as if time had no cost. They accept indecision and procrastination and their effects with apparent indifference, and say *ma'alesh* (it doesn't matter), even though the costs may be substantial.

The distinction between values and practices exists in all societies. House et al. (2004) report on these distinctions for several cultural dimensions in the GLOBE study of leadership in 62 societies. A brief explanation of some of the findings for Egypt follows. Egypt has moderate practices ('as is') scores but higher values ('should be') scores for the dimension 'future orientation' (saving for the future, being intrinsically motivated, having flexible and adaptive managers and a longer term strategic orientation). With respect to practices for 'gender egalitarianism,' Egypt falls into the middle of the countries studied. It has a practices score of 2.81 and a higher values score of 3.18 (on a scale of 1 to 7, where increasing numbers mean more of a practice or value). Even this latter score for what 'should be,' however, is towards the bottom of all country values scores on the gender dimension. In terms of 'assertiveness' in social relationships, Egyptians are moderate, and the practices score is only slightly higher than the values score. Egypt's practices score on 'power distance' of 4.92 is quite high, and its values score is lower at 3.24, but still quite high compared to other societies. For 'humane orientation' (being concerned, sensitive to others, tolerant of mistakes and generous), Egypt's practices score is very high (ranking sixth of all societies): 4.73. Its values score on this dimension is a little higher at 5.17. Egypt ranks moderately on 'uncertainty avoidance' (the extent to which people seek order and consistency) with a practices score of 4.06 and a higher values score of 5.36 (where Egypt ranks fifth of all societies).

The GLOBE Project distinguishes between 'societal institutional collectivism' (group loyalty emphasized at the expense of individual goals; the economic system emphasizes collective interests over individual interests) and 'societal in-group collectivism' (pride, loyalty and interdependence in families). Egypt scores quite highly on institutional collectivism and is very high on in-group collectivism. There is virtually no difference between the practices and values scores for Egypt on these variables. Hofstede (1991) also reported that Egyptians are an extremely collectivistic people. Interdependence is seen as a duty and a moral obligation. Egyptians exhibit strong group loyalty and cohesiveness, and a person's self-respect depends primarily on the respect others have for him or her (Patai 2002). In this context, business and family background are closely connected in Egypt. The extended family provides emotional and financial support and is frequently the first source of *wasta* (from the Arabic, *wisata*, meaning 'mediation'). Gundling and Zanchettin (2007) explain wasta as 'personal connections' and even a form of affirmative action, which provides access to government or business connections for individuals who lack other forms of power or status. Status in all forms is vital in a society with fairly high power distance. The correct formal titles are used frequently, even among close friends. In a nation with large income inequality, socioeconomic status is important. In initial meetings, Egyptians mention family achievements, and engage in name dropping in order to establish their status. This helps build networks. Egyptians prefer to do business with people they know and like and who they consider as friends. They are extremely hospitable and generous and exchange gifts often (Rice 1999). Further discussion of wasta is given, in a Jordanian context, in Chapter 8.

There is a pronounced, overt top-down hierarchy in Egyptian organizations. Directions come from the top and quality performance means following directions. While US managers, for example, believe in employee empowerment, Egyptian subordinates, in general, expect orders from their superiors; there are three business subcultures, however (Hatem 2006). The first is the government subculture characterized by rigidity and conservatism. In traditional organizations there tends to be micromanagement (Gundling and Zanchettin 2007). The second subculture comprises Egyptian family owned businesses and merchants. These have been resistant to Western infiltration of their identities and culture. However, according to Hatem (2006), the new generation's exposure to Western education is easing this resistance. A third subculture is the emerging Westernized subculture of Egyptian businesspeople who have been exposed to Western education and who have acquired new characteristics that mix their ethnic roots with new managerial styles. These are often the senior managers of joint venture companies and have proven very successful in managing their companies in the Egyptian market. Smaller companies and multinational organizations are run more informally than public sector or traditional organizations, and with a more collaborative management orientation.

In Islam, distinction between managers, workers and professionals is acceptable. For example, the Qur'an includes the following: '. . . it is We (God) who portion out between them their livelihood in the life of this world: and We raise some of them in ranks so that some may command the work of others. But the Mercy of your Lord is better than the (wealth) which they amass' (Qur'an 43:32). At the same time, a basic Islamic principle, based on Qur'anic teachings, is consultation between the leader and the followers (House et al. 2004). Regardless of hierarchy, trust and respect are crucial for Egyptian employees. They tend to be extremely loyal and if there is mutual trust and respect, will work long hours and even forgo compensation in order to be obliging and respectful (Grundling and Zanchettin 2007). Egyptians stress their affiliations and place more value on the quality of life and relationships than on task accomplishment. Job satisfaction and motivation are based more on quality of organizational life than on the promise of rewards. Spending time with people is an activity in itself and individuals define themselves in terms of their affiliations (Hatem 2006).

DEVELOPMENTS IN LEADERSHIP THEORY: THE EGYPTIAN CONTEXT

Leadership is culturally contingent (House et al. 2004) because it is inevitable that leaders' actions and followers' responses reflect the forms of behaviour viewed as legitimate and appropriate within their societies (Shahin and Wright 2004). That cultural differences might limit the universality of leadership theories is a proposition central to the GLOBE study of leadership (House et al. 2004). The study partially bases its culturally endorsed implicit leadership (CLT) theory on the foundations of implicit leadership theory, value-belief theory and implicit motivation theory. Implicit leadership theory implies that individuals have implicit beliefs and assumptions that differentiate leaders from followers and effective leaders from ineffective leaders (Lord and Maher 1991). The premise of value-belief theory is that the beliefs held by members of cultures influence the degree to which the behaviours of individuals, groups, and institutions within cultures are enacted, and the degree to which they are regarded as legitimate (Triandis 1995; Hofstede 2001). According to implicit motivation theory (McClelland 1985), the essential nature of long-term human motivation can be understood in terms of three nonconscious motives: achievement, affiliation, and power (social influence). The GLOBE study of 62 societies (House et al. 2004) identifies six global CLT leadership behaviours or dimensions. These are depicted in Table 10.1 along with a brief description and Egypt's scores and rank on each dimension. The dimensions are listed according to Egypt's rank compared to other societies. Thus, Egypt ranked very highly on

Table 10.1   Egypt's leadership profile

GLOBE CLT Leadership Dimensions	Definition of Dimension	Range of Scores for 62 Societies (on a scale of 1 to 7)	Egypt's Score	Egypt's Rank (out of 62 societies)
Self-protective leadership	Ensures the safety and security of the group through status enhancement and face-saving.	2.5 – 4.6	4.21	4
Autonomous leadership	Independent and individualistic leadership behaviours.	2.3 – 4.7	4.49	5
Humane-oriented leadership	Supportive and considerate leadership.	3.8 – 5.6	5.15	19
Participative leadership	Leaders include others in decisions and their implementation.	4.5 – 6.1	4.69	43
Team-oriented leadership	Effective team-building and the implementation of a common goal among team members.	4.7 – 6.2	5.55	52
Charismatic/ value-based leadership	Ability of leaders to inspire, motivate and encourage high performance outcomes from followers, based on a foundation of core values.	4.5 – 6.5	5.57	53

Source: Compiled from information provided in House et al. (2004).

self-protective leadership and autonomous leadership and in the top third of societies for humane-oriented leadership.

Another investigation by Shahin and Wright (2004) that focuses specifically on Egypt can offer additional insights into findings from the GLOBE study. Shahin and Wright obtained data from 70 managers and 173 subordinates at ten Egyptian banks, including public sector banks, joint venture banks, and private investment banking companies. The questionnaire included the questions from MLQ Form 5x-Short (Bass and Avolio 1995), translated into Arabic, to measure the eight factors of the leadership model developed by Bass and Avolio (1994) and based primarily on US research. This model includes four kinds of transformational leadership (idealized influence, inspirational motivation, intellectual stimulation, and individualized consideration), three kinds of transactional leadership (contingent reward, active management-by-exception, and passive management-by-exception) as well as non-leadership (laissez-faire). Factor analysis revealed eight somewhat different leadership factors for the Egyptian sample: positive leadership, reluctant decision-making (similar to passive management-by-exception and laissez-faire), enthusiastic leadership (with elements of inspirational motivation and intellectual stimulation), bureaucratic leadership, social integration, authoritarian leadership, and individual consideration (similar to the same factor in the US-based model of leadership). Therefore, Shahin and Wright (2004) identify four factors different from those of earlier studies focusing on US culture.

The factor, 'authoritarian leadership', Shahin and Wright (2004) argue, is consistent with leadership in Egypt and could derive from the high level of power distance in the society. This factor helps to explain the GLOBE finding that Egypt ranked fifth out of 62 societies on 'autonomous leadership,' a dimension reported to range from impeding outstanding leadership to slightly facilitating outstanding leadership (House et al. 2004).

The factor, 'bureaucratic leadership' (Shahin and Wright 2004) is similar to 'passive management-by-exception', and reflects the *ma'alesh* cultural behaviour described by Tuma (1988). It also suggests a blame culture. This means that when things go wrong, blame is attributed to other people for their mistakes or their failure to follow the rules, whilst implicitly absolving oneself from any responsibility. This finding is consistent with Egypt's high ranking (four out of 62) for self-protective leadership, one of the GLOBE study's leadership behaviours, which is formed from five sub-scales: self-centred, status conscious, conflict inducer, face saver, and procedural. An interview study of leaders in state owned manufacturing firms in Egypt by Elbanna and Childs (2007) found that the top managers in many cases could not take strategic decisions without getting approval from their holding companies. In some firms, top managers were taking some strategic decisions merely in response to governmental policies, such as the decision to initiate an early retirement policy, which was a government policy related to its privatization programme (Elbanna and Childs 2007). When making strategic decisions (or perhaps avoiding making them), deference to authority and following procedures, according to Elbanna and Childs (2007), is exacerbated by the general business context, especially political uncertainty. Leadership in Egypt also continues to be hampered by limited experience. For example, Mostafa (2005) describes a 'decrepit bureaucracy' in Egypt. He observes that the Minister of Foreign Trade and Industry, part of the new cabinet appointed in 2004 by Mubarak to revitalize the economy, who has leadership experience with a multinational corporation, stated his intention to encourage business-people to generate their own strategic initiatives, instead of the previous process of the government 'dictating solutions from the top.'

The factor 'social integration' (Shahin and Wright 2004) fits well with the Egyptian need to maintain harmony in the workplace. Relationships or 'ties' among individuals within an organization's social network can be either strong or weak (Bruton et al. 2007). Strong ties involve frequent interaction, a high level of intimacy, and mutual trust; features that can ease the implementation of strategy. Yet at the same time, strong ties can suppress constructive conflict (Leana and Van Buren 1999) and limit the range, diversity and breadth of social resources available to an organiza-tion (Nahapiet and Ghoshal 1998). These tendencies can erode an organi-zational leader's ability to respond quickly to competitive challenges.

'Positive leadership', the first leadership factor revealed in the analy-sis by Shahin and Wright (2004), interestingly includes aspects of both transformational and transactional leadership. The combination of these aspects could be a symptom of the Egyptian centralized form of manage-ment and could also be a function of the high levels of both collectivism and power distance (Shahin and Wright 2004). In a study of employee cre-ativity in Egypt, contrary to expectations, a controlling, hierarchical work environment was positively associated with employee creative behaviour (Rice 2006). She found that in Egyptian organizations, a structured hier-archy with autonomous leadership is not necessarily incompatible with a caring atmosphere, work enjoyment, and a requirement for employees to provide initiative and ideas. The GLOBE study (House et al. 2004) found that Egyptian respondents view humane-oriented leadership positively. Trompenaars and Hampden-Turner (1998) argue that in countries with large power distances (such as Egypt), typically reflected in structured, hierarchical work environments, dependence on powerful people is a basic need that can be a real motivator. This supports the perspective of Howell (1988), discussed by Shahin and Wright (2004), who suggested that a 'per-sonalized' charismatic leader is one whose need for unquestioning trust, obedience and submission creates dependency and conformity, as opposed to the 'socialized' charismatic, who develops and stimulates followers by providing greater empowerment and autonomy. This type of charismatic leader is dissimilar to transformational leadership (Bass and Avolio 1994) and does not motivate people to perform beyond their expectations and fulfil their higher order needs. Rather, the leader uses power to influence followers to perform their normal activities. According to Shahin and

Wright (2004), this type of leader in Egypt also exhibits strong elements of transactional leadership, because people are dependent on those in authority. Obedience to a leader is also a reflection of the Islamic teachings which strongly influence Egyptian culture. The Qur'an clearly states: 'O you who believe! Obey Allah, and obey the Messenger, and those charged with authority among you' (Qur'an 4:59). For example, after a leader is elected, he or she is considered to have received a pledge of allegiance from the community. Both the majority who voted for him or her and the minority who may have voted against him or her now owe them obedience and allegiance (Beekun and Badawi 1999).

The dependence on authority is closely linked to risk avoidance. In Egypt, most people prefer the comfort of proven ideas and shy away from exploring risky options. Egypt ranks fifth out of 62 societies on uncertainty avoidance values (House et al. 2004). The GLOBE analyses indicate that societal uncertainty avoidance values are positively associated with team-oriented, humane-oriented, and self-protective leadership attributes. Mostafa (2005) also found that Egyptians prefer a more structured, team-oriented approach to avoid losing face or to avoid feeling excluded. This result supports Hickson and Pugh (2001) who concluded from a review of relevant studies that Egyptians are sensitive to personal relationships (especially with superiors), and are cautious and slow to take decisions. Egyptian managers are thus relatively respectful of leadership and hierarchical distance, fatalistic, and inclined to act according to the particular relationship involved rather than according to rules or general standards (Elbanna and Childs 2007). Thus, it is relationships that matter in Egypt, not rules. Relationships are much more important than tasks (Hatem 2006).

In addition to cultural explanations of leadership in Egyptian business organizations, it should be noted that the job market is extremely limited in Egypt because economic growth cannot absorb all young people entering it. There are also limits to mobility within the nation as only 6 per cent of Egyptian land is inhabited. The prospects for promotion are also limited and so both younger and older managers behave in ways that will legitimize the status quo (Mostafa 2005).

LEADERSHIP PRACTICE IN EGYPTIAN ORGANIZATIONS: AN ILLUSTRATION

Unheard of by most in Egypt a few years ago, corporate social responsibility (CSR) is increasingly popular among the nation's business community. The Center for Development Service (CDS) is working with the Cairo and Alexandria Stock Exchange (CASE) to produce a sustainability index to rate the CSR performance of Egyptian companies. Multinationals such as Vodafone and Shell brought the concept of CSR to the Egyptian economy and to companies like Americana, Mansour and Oriental Weavers, who are all dedicating part of their profits to give back to society (El-Sayed 2007).

In Egypt, exemplifying business leadership in social and environmental responsibility for 30 years, however, have been Ibrahim Abouleish and his son, Helmy. The success of their family run company, the Sekem Group, a high-profile organic agrifoods business based just outside Cairo, was recognized in 2003 by both the Schwab Foundation and the Right Livelihood Foundation. The Schwab Foundation selected Ibrahim Abouleish as one of the world's 'Outstanding Social Entrepreneurs'. The Right Livelihood Foundation awarded him the prestigious 'Alternative Nobel Prize,' with a statement that: 'Sekem demonstrates how a modern business model combines profitability and success in world markets with a humane and spiritual approach to people while maintaining respect for the environment' (Sekam 2007).

Ibrahim Abouleish innovated when he introduced the concept of organic farming to Egypt in 1979. Today, organic is a worldwide trend in the agricultural industry. To both Ibrahim and Helmy Abouleish, growing organic produce and cotton, and seeking plants for new, natural, plant-derived medicines, is part of a vision about which they have long been passionate. Ibrahim Abouleish worked as a medical pharmacologist in Europe before returning to Egypt because he wanted to contribute something to his homeland. He had concerns about both education and health in Egypt and his dream was 'to build a society, not a company' (Mostafa, 2004). His business philosophy is expressed in the following:

> business people, the leaders of our economy, had very strange ideas about community. They believed that the revenue generated by their companies was theirs alone. What about the workers in their enterprises and the consumers who buy their products? Some of the profits must be returned to the community in which they operate. (Mostafa 2004)

Sekem has numerous organic and quality certifications as well as Fair Trade certification. Egypt's leading organic products exporter, Sekem exports about 90 per cent of its production (fresh produce, pasta, rice, flour, legumes, cereals, oils, honey, herbal teas and cotton). It is also credited with developing a plant-protection system that significantly reduced pesticide use in the entire country (Namatalla 2005).

In the workplace, the Abouleish leadership also operates very differently from other Egyptian organizations. At the beginning of the day, workers gather in circles to chat and share ideas. There is also an end of the week celebration with Qur'anic recitation, a musical performance, and discussion of accomplishments and concerns. The 4000 employees form part of an egalitarian community. The consultation and egalitarianism is unusual in Egypt, but actually reflects Islamic teachings on leadership. Islam stresses consultation in all affairs through the injunction in the Qur'an: 'who conduct their affairs through mutual consultation' (Qur'an 42:38). Also, in Islam, the position of leader is not to be sought as an ambition; rather the leader should arise from the authority of the community. Kriger and Seng (2005) discuss how a spiritually guided leader engages in what Kanungo and Mendonca (1994) call 'socialized power,' and is advised not to seek 'personalized power,' as 'socialized power is the use of power for the service of others'.

Sekem also provides outreach services to the community. There is a school on the farm for local children (free for those who cannot afford to pay), and as they grow older, they choose between a vocation or continuing with studies. Sekem's state-of-the-art hospital also serves the surrounding communities. According to reports on its website, Sekem is planning to open a university in the near future.

One of Sekem's service projects which has received considerable attention both in Egypt and Europe is the innovative Chamomile Children Project. The purpose is to contribute to local economic development and to children's education simultaneously. Among the large poor segment of Egyptian society, although child labour is illegal in Egypt, children often leave school and work to help support their families. Sekem hires about 80 children from age 12 as 'Chamomile Children:' throughout the year they work half-days on the farm doing light agricultural labour. For the rest of the day, they attend school and are supported by specially trained teachers or social workers. Eventually, the children receive their primary education certificate, a prerequisite for entering into vocational training programmes. They receive meals at Sekem and free medical care at the hospital, as well as a salary of about LE 150 – approximately half of what a teacher earns in Egypt (Abouleish 2007).

Quigley et al. (2005) explain that in countries like Egypt with high levels of in-group collectivism, charismatic/value-based, team-oriented, humane-oriented and self-protective leadership behaviours are likely to be perceived as responsible types of leadership. Egyptians also have high future orientation values which are positively associated with self-protective and humane-oriented leader behaviours (House et al. 2004). The combined effect of these two particular leadership types might result in a paternalistic, yet benevolent, leadership style. The very high humane-orientation practices in Egypt mean that Egyptians view humane-oriented leadership as effective and consider responsible leaders to be those who are friendly, compassionate and supportive. Undoubtedly, the Abouleish leadership at Sekem exhibits charismatic/value-based and humane attributes. Therefore, even though some might argue that Sekem is an atypically-led organization in Egypt, the style of its leaders is compatible with predictions based upon Egyptian culture as well as extant leadership theory.

As a sign of his success as one of Egypt's new, younger business leaders, Helmy Abouleish was asked to serve as the Executive Director of the Ministry of Trade and Industry's Industrial Modernization Center (IMC). The IMC is a public sector organization with a private sector approach. It grants assistance to companies based on their ability to export. The organization, partly supported by the European Union to operate from 2001 to 2006, was performing poorly, and in the three years from 2002 to 2005 spent only LE 28 million of its LE 426 million budget (Allam 2005). During Abouleish's tenure the number of companies that were helped increased tenfold (Bossone 2006) and procedures were simplified and quickened (Allam 2005), but Abouleish insists that under no circumstances were funds provided to an applicant without a clear plan for how the support will lead to better competitiveness. He is adamant about working according to the standards of transparency and corporate governance (Oteify 2005).

Earlier, Helmy Abouleish was chair of the Egyptian Junior Business Association, an organization he co-founded, where he realized that the only way to address unemployment was through industrial development. Interviewed by Andrew Bossone (2006), Helmy Abouleish said the following, which clearly reveals his vision, as well as the lack of responsibility that permeates the culture he lives within:

> Starting with Sekem, values and corporate responsibility were the principles I was living with and were being applied very successfully. At Sekem, the philosophy is all about human development; nothing else matters. I never thought about profits. Now, going to the IMC, this is exactly the idea [these companies need]. Invest in your people. The only competitive advantage we have is our people. The biggest challenge is not the capability. There are very successful companies that are competitive with anyone in the world that are owned and run by Egyptians. The perception I'm fighting is that changing the path of development lies with somebody else or with the government. The perception now is that it's big brother's responsibility to feed, educate, find the right girl for you, and find you a flat, and in the end to bury you. When you think this way, you can't take the future of your country in your own hands. (Bossone 2006)

Abouleish believes that the pursuit of business objectives can and must be combined with the delivery of benefits to the local community and that it is vital for both the private sector and civil society to take responsibility for the development of Egypt (Bossone 2006). Abouleish's perceptions of the unwillingness of Egyptians to take responsibility mirrors the high power distance in the society. This high level of power distance is positively related to greater corruption and lower civil liberties, and negatively related to economic prosperity, competitive success, societal health and human development (Quigley et al. 2005).

Risk, renewal, regulation, relationships and reputation: these are five areas that Beardsley et al. (2007) emphasize companies must master in order to manage their complex contracts with society. They write that business leaders must find ways to incorporate sociopolitical issues more explicitly and proactively into their strategic decision-making processes. Such issues are not peripheral tasks for the public relations (PR) department or the corporate social responsibility (CSR) department, they argue, but require the most senior leadership and extensive coordination throughout an entire organization. Mastery of risk refers to predicting and handling new risks that result from changing societal expectations. In the case of Sekem, Ibrahim Abouleish recognized the risks of poor health and a lack of education among Egyptians and acted accordingly in building his social entrepreneurship model. Renewal means to approach changing social expectations as opportunities for growth by creating new products and processes and entering new markets. Over the years the Abouleish leadership has extended Sekem's reach into new product areas and has concentrated on exporting. By carefully managing regulation, companies should shape short-term and long-term policy agendas to reflect both social expectations and the company's commercial interests. Sekem's leadership has lobbied and worked with the government to reduce enormously the use of pesticides in Egypt. Managers must identify which stakeholders are important and how to build relationships with them. Sekem has focused on local stakeholders (local families and communities, for example) but has not neglected global and European stakeholders (non-governmental organizations, business partners, the European Union) from whom it has been able to obtain grants and assistance. Finally, reputation means fostering public trust in the company, not merely with the PR function, but also with action. Sekem's documented achievements have led to it receiving international recognition. In 2007, its profile was raised further at home through an official visit by Suzanne Mubarak, wife of the former president, Hosni Mubarak, to observe the Chamomile Children Project (Sekem 2007).

CHALLENGES FOR LEADERSHIP DEVELOPMENT IN EGYPTIAN ORGANIZATIONS

Egypt is a transitional economy. Business leadership in Egypt is also in transition. The two most prominent challenges for leadership are the lack of control over the external environment and Egyptians' limited experience in private organizational settings.

In their interview study of almost 300 managers in state-owned and private Egyptian enterprises, Elbanna and Child (2007) found evidence consistent with a view that, in countries like Egypt where executives perceive a lack of control over the external environment, they are likely to discount it in strategic decision making. Cultural influences such as indecision, procrastination and indifference discussed by Tuma (1988) undoubtedly contribute to this tendency. Interviewees in the study by Elbanna and Child (2007) highlighted the political instability of the Middle East region, as well as the threats internally to the Egyptian economy that hinder planning. The latter include high interest rates, lack of liquidity and changes in regulations as the shift to privatization progresses.

In an environment where one feels one has little or no control, how can one make decisions and lead? The recent emergence of the private sector means that Egyptian executives have limited experience and knowledge of how to operate and lead in private organizational settings. In some instances this can reduce the competitiveness of Egyptian firms on the world stage, at a time when Egypt is attempting to increase its exports and its integration into the global economy.

Although the external environment has many uncontrollable elements, inside organizations, human development is the key. This refers to human development of all the employees in an organization. Followers affect the leadership process. Leaders may react to the performance of their followers rather than initiate this performance (Greene 1975). It is also important to note that the impact of leader behaviour is amplified over time. Qualitative analysis of a longitudinal research study of more than 200 knowledge workers in 26 project teams in seven diverse US companies revealed that leaders' behaviours can lead to positive or negative spirals in team dynamics and performance, whereby the effects of leader behaviours become augmented over time (Amabile et al. 2004). The analysis of the project teams suggests that the effects of leader behaviours are neither static nor unidirectional. In the Egyptian culture, where relationships are more important than tasks, similar positive or negative spirals in the interaction between leaders and followers will occur. Positive spirals might be expected to be more prevalent under humane-oriented leadership where a caring atmosphere and trust engendered by the leader result in loyalty and extra efforts on the part of subordinates.

What might be the role of Islam in improving leadership behaviour in Egypt? Kriger and Seng (2005) observe that 82 per cent of people in the world espouse and hold spiritual or religious worldviews and so it is highly likely that those who exercise leadership roles in organizations, and who believe in spiritual or religious belief systems, will have their leadership behaviour shaped by the underlying values and attitudes of those world-views. Ibrahim Abouleish, the founder of Sekem, when asked by an interviewer if he was a religious man, replied that he was a Muslim and that his ideas came out of a modern, progressive understanding of Islam (Mostafa 2004). In his opinion, he explained, there are no new ideas without a moral or ethical background. Thus, the Islamic beliefs of the majority of the Egyptian people might contribute to improved leadership behaviors in organizations. Beekun and Badawi (1999) emphasize how the characteristics of effective leaders identified by Kouzes and Posner (1995) in a survey of over 2500 of the most successful leaders in the US are remarkably Islamic. The top four characteristics are: honesty, competence, having a vision and being forward looking, and inspiring. Islam also encourages leaders to have additional attributes: strength of character, patience, humility, kindness, self understanding, the willingness to seek consultation, impartiality, modesty, responsibility and being a good follower (that is, being willing to abide by the same rules that apply to their followers).

Beekun and Badawi (1999) refer to 'dynamic followership', a normative concept in Islamic leadership. Although Islam stresses that followers should obey their leader, it does not condone blind subservience. A well-known report about Umar, one of the leaders who succeeded Muhammad, exemplifies this behaviour. On a particular occasion, Umar suggested that the quantity of dowry paid by the man to the woman should be fixed at the time of the marriage ceremony. A woman immediately stood up and explained that according to Islamic principles and based on the evidence in the Qur'an, he was incorrect. Umar realized his mistake and said, 'the woman is right and the leader of the Muslims is wrong'. This anecdote clearly shows that Muslim followers of both genders should not remain passive bystanders should the leader err. Muhammad is reported to have said, 'The best struggle in the path of God is to speak a word of justice to an oppressive ruler' (Beekun and Badawi 1999).

As discussed earlier in this chapter, the lack of a sense of responsibility on the part of many Egyptians is problematic in a positive dynamic leader-follower process or spiral. Societies like Egypt with high power distance values prefer a more equitable distribution of power with participation of the followers and mutual consultation. Leaders can try to achieve this, but the proper support, guidance and training must be given (Quigley et al. 2005), whether this uses a spiritual or a secular approach. Living in a society with unequal power distance means that Egyptians lack the knowledge and skills to assume their responsibilities successfully: witness the slow start of the Industrial Modernization Centre funded by the European Union.

Traditionally, Egyptians followed orders. They expected direction, but change has now occurred irrevocably. The future of Egypt's business organizations lies with the younger generation who are becoming more comfortable in the private sector: younger, more globally-oriented managers with different points of view, energy, and the enthusiasm to learn and contribute to the development of their society.

REFERENCES

Abouleish, K. (2007), 'Suzame Mubarak visits SEKEM', SEKEM Insight, **61**, 1–2.

Ahmed, H. (2006), 'The dissenter', accessed 15 August 2007 at www.businesstodayegypt.com/article.aspx?ArticleID=7000.

Allam, M. (2005), 'Winds of change at the IMC', accessed 31 August 2007 at www.businesstodayegypt.com/article.aspx?ArticleID=5973.

Amabile, T.M., E.A. Schatzel, G.B Moneta and S.J. Kramer (2004), 'Leader behaviors and the work environment for creativity: perceived leader support', *The Leadership Quarterly*, **15**, 5–32.

Bass, B.M. and B.J. Avolio (1995), *Multifactor Leadership Questionnaire Form 5x-Short*, Redwood City, CA: Mind Garden.

Beardsley, S.C., S. Bonini, L. Mendonca, and J. Oppenheim (2007), 'A new era for business', *Stanford Social Innovation Review*, **5** (3), 56–63.

Beekun, R.I. and J. Badawi (1999), *Leadership An Islamic Perspective*, Beltsville, MD: Amana Publications.

Bossone, A. (2006), 'Helmy Abouleish', accessed 31 August 2007 at www.businesstodayegypt.com/article.aspx?ArticleID=6710.

Bruton, G.D., G.G. Dess and J.J. Janney (2007), 'Knowledge management in technology-focused firms in emerging economies: caveats on capabilities, networks, and real options', *Asia Pacific Journal of Management*, **24**, 115–30.

Chapra, M.U. (1992), *Islam and the Economic Challenge*, Herndon, VA: International Institute of Islamic Thought.

El-Din, G.E. (2007), 'Privatization blows', accessed 31 August 2007 at http://weekly.ahram.org.eg/2007/842/ec1.htm.

EIU ViewsWire (2007a), 'Egypt economy: business climate overview', 12 June, New York.

EIU ViewsWire (2007b), 'Country risk summary', 25 June, New York.

Elbanna, S. and J. Child (2007), 'The influence of decision, environmental and firm characteristics on the rationality of strategic decision-making', *Journal of Management Studies*, **44** (4), 561–91.

Greene, C.N. (1975), 'The reciprocal nature of influence between leader and subordinate', *Journal of Applied Psychology*, **60**, 187–93.

Gundling, E. and A. Zanchettin (2007), *Global Diversity: Winning Customers and Engaging Employees within World Markets*, Clerkenwell and Boston, MA: Nicholas Brealey International.

Hatem, T. (2006), 'Human resource management in Egypt', in P.S. Budhwar and K. Mellahi (eds), *Managing Human Resources in the Middle East*, London and New York: Routledge.

Hofstede G. (1991), *Cultures and Organizations: Software of the Mind*, London and New York: McGraw-Hill.

House, R.J., P.J. Hanges, M. Javidan, P.W. Dorfman and V. Gupta (eds) (2004), *Culture, Leadership, and Organizations: The GLOBE Study of 62 Societies*, London and Thousand Oaks, CA: Sage Publications.

Howell, J.M. (1988), 'Two faces of charisma: socialized and personalized leadership in organizations', in J.A. Conger and R.N. Kanungo (eds), *Charisma Leadership: The Elusive Factor in Organizational Effectiveness*, San Francisco, CA: Jossey-Bass, pp. 213–36.

Human Rights Watch (2010), 'Egypt: elections marred as opposition barred from polls', accessed 24 December 2010 at www.hrw.org/en/news/2010/11/29/egypt-elections-marred-opposition-barred-polls.

Jabber, P. (1986), 'Egypt's crisis, America's dilemma', *Foreign Affairs*, **62**, 961–80.

Kanungo, R.N. and M. Mendonca (1994), 'What leaders cannot do without: the spiritual dimensions of leadership', in J.A. Conger (ed.), *In Spirit at Work: Discovering the Spirituality in Leadership*, San Francisco, CA: Jossey-Bass, pp. 162–98.

Kouzes, J. and B. Posner (1995), *The Leadership Challenge: How to Get Extraordinary Things Done in Organizations*, San Francisco, CA: Jossey-Bass.

Kriger, M. and Y. Seng (2005), 'Leadership with inner meaning: a contingency theory of leadership based on the worldviews of five religions', *The Leadership Quarterly*, **16**, 771–806.

Lord, R. and K.J. Maher (1991), *Leadership and Information Processing*, Boston, MA: Unwin-Everyman.

McClelland, D.C. (1985), *Human Motivation*, Glenview, IL: Pearson Scott Foresman.

Mostafa, H. (2004), 'The Sekem way', *Egypt Business Today,* March.

Mostafa, M. (2005), 'Factors affecting organizational creativity and innovativeness in Egyptian organizations: an empirical investigation', *Journal of Management Development*, **24** (1), 7–33.

Namatalla, A. 'The best investment', accessed 31 August 2007 at www.businesstodayegypt.com/article.aspx?ArticleID=4959.

Napahiet, J. and S. Ghoshal (1998), 'Social capital, intellectual capital and the organizational advantage', *The Academy of Management Review*, **23**, 242–66.

Nasr, S. (2007), 'Privatisation glitches', accessed 31 August 2007 at http://weekly.ahram.org.eg/2007/837/ec1.htm.

Oteify, R. (2005), 'Center stage', accessed 31 August 2007 at www.businesstodayegypt.com/article.aspx?ArticleID=5643.

Oxford Economic Country Briefings (2007), The Egypt Report, Oxford: Oxford Business Group. June 21.

Patai, R. (2002), *The Arab Mind Revised Edition*, Long Island City, NY: Hathersleigh Press.

Platt, G. (2007), 'The new Arab economies', *Global Finance*, **21** (4), 20–24.

Quigley, N.R., M. Sully de Luque and R.J. House (2005), 'Responsible leadership and governance in a global context: insights from the GLOBE study', in J.P. Doh and S.A. Stumpf (eds), *Handbook of Responsible Leadership and Governance*, Cheltenham, UK and Northampton, MA, USA: Edward Elgar, pp. 352–79.

Qur'an (undated), English translation of the meaning, revised version of translation by Abdullah Yusuf Ali, Medina, Saudi Arabia: The Presidency of Islamic Researches, King Fahd Holy Qur'an Printing Complex.

Rachid, M. (2006), 'Factories shoot up as a lot of things start falling into place', *Financial Times*, December 13, p. 2.

Rice, G. (1999), 'Islamic ethics and the implications for business', *Journal of Business Ethics*, **18**, 345–58.

Rice, G. (2006), 'Individual values, organizational context, and self-perceptions of employee creativity: evidence from Egyptian organizations', *Journal of Business Research*, **59**, 233–41.

El-Sayed, N. (2007), 'You've been rated', accessed 31 August at www.businesstodayegypt.com/article.aspx?ArticleID=7163.

Sekem (2007), accessed 1 September 2007 at www.sekem.com/Files/PDFs/si_0607_english.pdf.

Shahin, A.I. and P.L. Wright (2004), 'Leadership in the context of culture: an Egyptian perspective', *Leadership and Organization Development Journal*, **25** (6), 499–511.

Transparency International (2009), 'Corruption Perceptions Index 2009', accessed 29 July 2010 at www.transparency.org/policy_research/surveys_indices/cpi/2009/cpi_2009_table.

Triandis, H.C. (1995), *Individualism and Collectivism*, Boulder, CO: Westview Press.

Trompenaars, F. and C. Hampden-Turner (1998), *Riding the Waves of Culture: Understanding Diversity in Global Business, Second Edition*, London and New York: McGraw-Hill.

Tuma, E.H. (1988), 'Institutionalized obstacles to development: the case of Egypt', *World Development*, **16**, 1185–98.

World Bank (2010), *Data: Egypt, Arab Rep.*, accessed 19 November 2010 at http://data.worldbank.org/country/egypt-arab-republic.

11. Leadership in Turkey: toward an evidence based and contextual approach[1]

Mustafa F. Özbilgin

INTRODUCTION

The field of leadership in non-Western contexts is saturated with studies which draw on constructs developed in Western contexts. This generalization also applies to studies of work values (including Hisrich, Bucar and Oztark 2003) and leadership (including Smith 1997 and Pasa 2000) in Turkey. Except for the GLOBE study (Kabasakal and Bodur 2002), which allows for *emic* and *etic* insights to be gathered, most studies reported in this chapter provide us with etic understandings of leadership in Turkey as they draw on replications of survey instruments which were designed in Western contexts in Turkish settings or using comparative data with common measures of leadership (these include Brodbeck et al. 2000). As leadership theory in Turkey draws heavily on theoretical frames which are developed elsewhere, it is a truism to say that there is dearth of *a posteriori* (inductive) research on leadership in the country. In this chapter, I argue that the unique contextual setting and dynamics of leadership in Turkey requires us to also engage in field studies which provide emic insights, which frame leadership in Turkey using concepts, theories and paradigms that are developed specifically with the Turkish context in mind.

While I do not wish to understate the value of replication or large-scale comparative studies such as the GLOBE project (see Kabasakal and Dastmalchian 2001), in this chapter I outline the reasons why we also need studies which provide situated (cross-sectoral), embedded (ethnographic), contextual (sensitive to history and geography) and rich insights into leadership in Turkey. In order to achieve this, I first explain the economic rationale that renders leadership a significant topic to study in international contexts. With the recognition that leadership behaviours are often path dependent (dependent on history and context) (Smith 1997), I highlight the significance of history in accounting for the current practices of leadership in Turkey. After this, I turn to current studies of leadership at work and in organizations in Turkey and review their key findings. Finally, I provide a set of recommendations for future study and practice of leadership at work in Turkey.

ECONOMIC RATIONALE FOR STUDYING ABOUT LEADERSHIP IN INTERNATIONAL CONTEXTS

There is extensive literature on the business case for good leadership. A large number of studies suggest that there is a complex relationship between practices of leadership and performance at work. Briefly reviewing this literature, which is dominated by studies in industrialized countries, I would like to suggest that studying leadership in developing countries and non-Western contexts, such as in Turkey, is not only important in order to understand how leadership works in the Turkish context, but also to reveal how leadership contributes to organizational survival and success there.

One interesting study which examines the linkages between leadership and performance was conducted and reported by Agle et al. (2006). Based on a survey of 128 major US corporations, the study made use of 770 questionnaire responses from top management team members, objective stock market and accounting data, and measures of environmental uncertainty to reveal that organizational performance correlates with subsequent perceptions of CEO charisma. However, perceptions of CEO charisma were not interrelated with subsequent organizational performance, even after the moderating effect of environmental uncertainty is considered. Their findings have significant implications, suggesting that the charisma of the CEO may be a construct that is contingent upon organizational success. In other words, success may lead to the recognition of charisma, rather than charisma being the cause of success. Therefore, charisma is likely to be recognized in circumstances where organizations are going through trajectories of growth and success. As a result, the study demonstrates the situated and temporal nature of the connection between CEO charisma and organizational success: charisma is situated in success, and it remains temporally specific, as periods of organizational success are bounded by time. For example, in their study of leadership in Turkey and the USA, Ensari and Murphy (2003) note that prototypical leadership behaviour and high performance engender the attribution of charisma to a leader. Therefore, it is important to exercise caution when exploring causation between leadership charisma and organizational performance.

Kula (2005) notes that leadership duality (existence of director and CEO, rather than only one organizational leader) is negatively correlated with firm performance in Turkey, unless controlled for firm size. Therefore, there is a link between leadership structure and performance. In their study of a North American sample, Mehra et al. (2006a) demonstrate that social network ties of leaders are correlated with group performance. Bartram et al. (2007) examined the linkages between HRM and performance in healthcare in their study of 132 Australian public healthcare providers. Their study reveals that strategic plans are often misinterpreted or reappraised between layers of management and this leads to a diverging gap between performance aims and outcomes. The findings of this study points to the significant role that an 'engaging manager' or leader (Costanzo and Tzoumpa 2008) can play in achieving transfer and implementation of performance objectives by involving all essential parties. Chen et al. (2007) report that leadership, empowerment and performance are intricately interlinked at multiple levels, and that leadership has an impact on performance outcomes at the individual, group and organization levels. Effective and strategic deployment of resources, however, requires that the macro-business context, stakeholder relations and other contextual and relational variables are captured in strategy formulation. Shea-Van Fossen, Rothstein and Korn (2006) reveal a positive link between strategic planning, which takes account of internal and external considerations and performance. Therefore, it is not sufficient to examine leadership and performance linkages without an attention to the broader contexts, in which leadership is constructed, exercised and enacted.

Although skilled leadership is positively correlated with high performance and positive individual and organizational outcomes in the extant literature (see Eker et al. 2004 for impact of leadership on job satisfaction in Turkey), the nature, antecedents, correlates and consequences of leadership could not be fully appreciated outside the situated contexts in which leadership is practiced. I argue, therefore, that there is need for further research to examine the linkages between leadership and performance in the context of Turkey, using instruments and constructs that are indigenous. Achieving this goal requires research to focus on idiosyncrasies of leadership, paying due regard to history and geography of Turkey. Having outlined the complex relationship between leadership and performance, I now turn my attention to the historical context, which underpins the current practice of leadership in Turkey.

HISTORICAL CONTEXT OF LEADERSHIP IN TURKEY

Leadership presents an important organizing logic in political, social and economic life in Turkey. Turkish history, not unlike other national histories around the world, is crowded with stories of charismatic leadership, centred on national episodes of heroism, change and transformation which are strongly attributed to the charisma of these leaders (Kabasakal and Bodur 2004). The single most influential charismatic leader in Turkey is Mustafa Kemal Ataturk (1881-1939), the founder of the modern Turkish Republic, whose leadership and far sighted reforms have distanced the modern Turkish Republic from its theocratic, autocratic and imperial past (the Ottoman Empire). As a military commander and civil leader, Ataturk epitomizes the model of charismatic leadership, which stretches to all aspects of his public and private life and presents a strong archetype of leadership in Turkey, displaying such characteristics as charisma, benevolence, paternalism, statesmanship, intellectualism, strategic thinking and determined service to democratic, secular and modernist ideals.

Long Service in Leadership

In line with examples that were set by Ataturk and previous Ottoman imperial leaders, political leadership presents the dominant model of leadership in Turkey. Political leadership in the Ottoman Empire was characterized by long service in leadership roles, only disturbed by dramatic episodes of radical change. The pattern of valuing long service to leadership has outlived the Ottoman Empire and it manifests itself in contemporary Turkish political scene. Today, a strong culture of long service remains among political leaders in Turkey persists. This is supported by a social culture which values seniority and age over youthfulness and older people receive more respect and recognition than younger people in Turkey. This is in clear contrast to Western appreciation of youthfulness over seniority, and also to the fact that Turkey has one of the youngest populations in Europe. The culture of respect for age and seniority is often associated with countries in the Arabic (Kabasakal and Bodur 2002), Middle Eastern (Kabasakal and Dastmalchian 2001) or European (Koopman et al. 1999; Smith 1997) clusters in cross-cultural studies. It is important to note, though, that positioning Turkey in an Arabic or Middle Eastern cluster would be a contested choice both in Turkey and abroad.

Legacy of Nepotism

In Turkey, there is a strong tradition of nepotism in public sector employment, which is reminiscent of the Ottoman era, in which it was typical to see transfer of public posts from father to son. Today there are considerable inefficiencies across the public sector employment practices in Turkey as large number of employment opportunities are created for supporters of ruling parties in the public services sector, with absolute disregard for principles of meritocracy and equal opportunities. Therefore, public sector leadership in Turkey continues to have a flair for nepotism based on political, ideological and other arbitrary and extracurricular ties. The same does not fully apply to the private sector, which operates with more dynamism in the increasingly liberalized business context of Turkey. Nevertheless, nepotism manifests in different forms and ties in the private sector work, including ties based on family membership, graduate networks, religious sects, birthplace and other arbitrary social ties (Özbilgin and Woodward 2003). Nepotism or lineage based networks are not unique to formal sector organization in Turkey. In their ethnographic study of Southeastern Turkey, Johansen and White (2002) demonstrate that a number of relations and networks of lineage provide bases of support for leadership in society. Hence, it is possible to find different approaches to leadership in public and private sectors of work, and the underlying structures of inequality and nepotism legitimate only particular forms of leadership, which may distract attention from interests of economy and productivity.

Legacy of Leadership in Context

While leadership is often associated with private sector work employment or political settings in Turkey, Bilgin Aksu (2003) demonstrates that leadership is an important factor in organizational readiness for management of quality and performance in public sector settings. Therefore, if counterproductive logics of work organization (discrimination and nepotism) can be eliminated, it may be possible to leverage leadership as a means to improve performance at work. However, this is a remote ideal, as Turkish models of leadership do not exist outside the dominant logics of work, employment and organization in the country. Turkish models of leadership are neither subdued nor subtle. In their study on leadership in Turkey, Pasa, Kabasakal and Bodur (2001, p. 584) conclude that: 'An ideal leader is described as a decisive, ambitious, assertive person who is somewhat aggressive but controlled at the same time, and has a hands-on approach to problems. This image of an ideal leader is in line with the high power distance and highly assertive characteristics of Turkish society'.

In their paper, which draws on GLOBE data from Turkey, Pasa Kabasakal and Bodur (2001) explain that leadership in Turkey is underpinned by collectivism, which is supported by paternalistic approach to work, at the organizational level. The authors also explain that hierarchical-autocratic leadership is the dominant style of leadership in the organizations studied. In comparison to other countries in Europe, there is a stronger leader-follower relationship, which allows for a level of leader worship in Turkey. This is demonstrated through strong and overt attachment to leaders in public and private life. One aspect of this leader worship ritual is that the emotional attachment of the followers is often polarized across the spectrum of love and hate. While the leaders, who are currently worshipped are loved and elevated to a super-human status, leaders who fall from grace also receive strong emotional reactions as they are often metaphorically cannibalized, their past achievements and failures were tarred with the same broad brush. Therefore, the dominant leadership archetype in Turkey resembles a zero-sum game in which the winner takes all, and there is limited scope for leadership with normal ebbs and flows of success and failure, and sharing of power and authority.

Legacy of Tempered Leadership

In order to understand the reasons why there is such a strong pattern of leader-follower relationship, we need to turn to history. There are some historical explanations for this passionate form of leader-follower relationship. Historical models of leadership in Turkey tend to transcend the leadership achievements from a core activity to all aspects of the leader's life. This is evident in the way the lives of Ottoman Sultans or more recent leaders in the republican era are portrayed in historical texts, even today. One important example of this phenomenon is the way Ataturk's life is portrayed in the battleground, as a statesman, as a father to his adopted daughters, and as a mentor to the Turkish public in his many encounters with citizens of the country. Ataturk is depicted as a leader with exceptional integrity and charisma across all aspects of his life. Historical models of leadership in Turkey are imbued with halo effects of charisma across all aspects of leaders' lives. The permeable nature of private and public sphere in terms of the way leaders are assessed in Turkey renders halo or spill over effects from one aspect of their lives to other domains. This means that negative or positive assessment of a leader's attributes in one domain of private and public life would spill over to the other domains. There are two implications of the dominance of this model of charismatic leadership. First, leadership transcends work and life divide in Turkey. Leaders are expected to demonstrate leadership across all aspects of their work and personal lives. Therefore, Turkish politics and business are crowded with leaders whose personal lives draw as much attention as, if not more than, their leadership in their professions.

Second, and consequently, leadership in Turkey requires attention to a broader set of constituent groups and contexts in order for us to understand the power and influence of the leader. Blurring of the boundaries between private and public life of leaders means that leaders in Turkey need to negotiate their leadership with a broader range of constituent groups and subject their leadership to broader public gaze than leaders in other countries in which leadership is limited to the work domain. Although charismatic leadership normally enjoys a strong hold on power and influence, in Turkey this power is tempered by diverse demands and expectations of the groups to whose gaze and demands the leader is subjected. Therefore, leaders in political, social and economic life in Turkey receive considerable media coverage and they are scrutinized in the press across a wide range of issues including their leadership performance at their roles, and their leadership as private individuals: their interaction and conduct with the general public, their friends, families as well as their overall demeanours and appearance. Therefore, a singular focus on leadership at work, which underpins much of the Western constructs of leadership, may not fully account for the tempered nature of the leader's power and influence in Turkey.

Legacy of Family Ideology

Another important historical and cultural construct for understanding leadership in Turkey is the dominance of family ideology in the country. Turkish society is wedded to a family ideology with very strong ties. Family ideology is reified in many aspects of social life. There are frequent references to a 'Turkish family structure' in daily press and public speeches as a way to judge the private and public actions of individuals. Turkish family ideology is often used as a lens through which individual actions are scrutinized across all aspects of social life. Resultantly, Turkish leaders are often obliged to act according to the moral and social requirements of this family ideology, which sets a range of expectations of respect and protocols of exchange among its members. Individuals are often held accountable for actions of their family members. Family honour is a concept which cuts across class and context in Turkey.

Another way that family ideology manifests itself in organizational formations is through the dominance of family logics in management across the spectrum of small, medium and large firms in Turkey. It is a truism to say that small firms are more likely to draw on family labour in Turkey. When small firms in Turkey grow, they tend to retain some aspects of their family legacies. Özkaya and Özbilgin (2007) identified that there is a queuing system by which large firms first employ family members for prized posts and failing that they would recruit from outside the family and turn to professional managers, selected on the basis of merit. Therefore, even the large firms continue to drawn on family labour. Leadership structures of the largest Turkish firms in the stock exchange retain a large number of family members.

Legacy of Gender Equity, Inequity and Diversity

Leadership in Turkey is also highly gendered. Historically, there are very few examples of women in leadership positions in the pre-republican Ottoman era. Women were allowed to take up posts in public and private sector employment only as the new Turkish republic dissolved the religious stricture of the Ottoman sex-segregation in employment. Owing much to the legacy of the republican reforms that Ataturk championed in Turkey, there are some strong examples of female leadership in public and private sectors of work in modern Turkish history.

Nevertheless, the archetypal leader in Turkey remains a family man, who enjoys the stable support of a loving family. While Ergeneli and Arikan (2002) demonstrate in their study on a Turkish sample that there is no difference between ethical perceptions of men and women in Turkey, leadership is a gendered construct. For example, Celikten's research (2005) on women leaders in the education sector in Turkey suggests that organization of work and expectations from leaders are structured along gendered lines in ways which disadvantage women in leadership. Clearly, there may be exceptions that do not conform to this archetype, including female and single male leaders. Turkish society and its concomitant culture are subject to rapid pace of transformations. Most obvious of these transformations is the emergence of diversity in the leadership class. In recent years, the homogeneity of the leadership elite in Turkey has been challenged with entry of large numbers of people with rural backgrounds in political and commercial life in Turkey (Yamak 2006). Facilitated by rampant migration from rural to urban areas, introduction of neoliberal logics in governance of society and economy, and consequent loss of political philosophies (Cizre-Sakallioglu and Yeldan 2000), it is possible to talk of peasantification of the leadership elite in Turkey. This was partly the outcome of Ataturk's western facing campaign to achieve social mobility based on merit (education, skills and experience) rather than class, or blood line in Turkey. What took place in Turkey was a sea change in the leadership diversity, with entry of large numbers of people with diverse backgrounds to Turkish politics. A new breed of female business leaders has also attracted some media attention in recent years in Turkey. In a similar way, the Anatolian Tigers, firms from rural Asia Minor which achieved national and international business success, and the commercial leaders who are behind this success are given popular coverage in the Turkish press. Coupled with these, there was also the emergence of leaders who subscribed to a political Islamic agenda of economic and social organization in Turkey (Mellon 2006). Furthermore, Simsek (2004) notes that new and emergent social movements have had transformational effects on Turkish social and political life and institutions with unprecedented impact. These changes present a challenge to leadership homogeneity. Despite the apparent diversification of the leadership elite, it is too early to judge whether such diversity will lead to more inclusive leadership models in Turkey.

Legacy of Geopolitical Connectedness

Turkey is a country with high levels of connectedness to the international scene. It is located between Europe and Asia and has a large number of neighbours, including Armenia, Azerbaijan, Bulgaria, Georgia, Greece, Iran, Iraq and Syria. It is a member of the European Council and an accession country of the European Union. It has strong international trade links with a large number of countries and large numbers of students from Turkey are educated across Europe and the US on full government bursaries. Despite such strong connectedness to Europe and the Western World, the rise of right-wing nationalism in Europe and their anti-Turkish sentiments during talks around Turkish membership to the EU hardens Euro-scepticism in Turkish people (Gunes-Ayata 2003). Recent political victories of AKP, an Islamic party, elevated it to the status of ruling party in Turkey and added to the domestic and international concerns that Turkey may be turning its face East to the Muslim world if its long standing project of Europeanization fails. There are reports of popular backlash in Turkey against Europe, secularism, and the national modernization projects. Adding to these is the poor welcome that Turkish migrants receive in some European countries and these migrants' recently increased interest in organizing around Muslim clerics (Kroissenbrunner 2003). There is need for studies to explore these patterns and the effects of the dissonance that juxtapositions of oriental versus occidental values and, secularism versus religious beliefs as well as discrimination and exclusion of Turkey across Europe will engender.

Long service in leadership, legacies of nepotism, context, constraints and ideologies of family and gender equity, as well as geopolitical connectedness, are examined in relation to the role of history in explaining current forms of leadership in Turkey. Having reviewed the significance of history in accounting for current forms of leadership, I now go on to scope the contemporary literature on leadership in Turkey.

LEADERSHIP AT WORK IN TURKEY – SCOPING THE LITERATURE

In this section, I review the literature on leadership at work in Turkey. First, I identify a number of weaknesses in the current literature. Then, I examine the life cycle of leadership in Turkey. The metaphor of cross-roads is often attributed to Turkey's geography, status in the world economy, politics, as well as social and cultural life. This metaphor suggests, on the one hand, a tension between two polarized choices, and on the other, a confused and fragmented identity. From a purist orthodox perspective, the metaphor renders the situation of Turkey less desirable than more homogeneous models or conceptions of national, social, cultural and political identity in industrialized countries. It is also possible to consider, from a pluralist heterodox perspective, the position of Turkey as a strength which allows the country to experience and have access to multiple structures, beliefs and cultures. In this review, I adopt the perspective that there is indeed strength in such pluralism, heterodoxy and diversity in terms of the way leadership can be framed in Turkey.

What is Wrong with Theorization of Leadership in Turkey?

As outlined in the introductory section, there are several shortcomings of academic studies of leadership in Turkey. First, the research area suffers from the replication of studies which use research instruments, such as survey scales, developed predominantly in Western Europe and North America. For example, Brodbeck et al. (2000) report a major European comparative study which set out to demonstrate that culture presents the key reason for variations in terms of leadership constructs across Europe. Turkey is included in this study and its suggested difference was attributed to a cultural difference from other clusters of countries in Europe. Second, there is lack of critical attention to issues of power in leadership. Leaders in Turkey often assume and enjoy an unchallenged hold on power (Pasa 2000). However, Turkey is now subject to stronger international pressures (including membership talks with the EU) to democratize its employment relations and its concomitant processes of employment relationship. Although research from the USA fails to identify a causal link between sharing of leadership at the team level and improved organizational performance (Mehra et al. 2006b), there is need for critical studies to examine how power may be (or should be) shared, negotiated and delegated in leadership at the organizational level in Turkey. This does not simply require analyses of the interplay between leadership and power, but also a courageous engagement with culturally sensitive issues of equity across all social fault lines in Turkey.

Life Cycle of Leadership Learning in Turkey

There is a life cycle of leadership learning. Leadership is learned through a series of interactions, experiences and reflections in an individual's life-time. Therefore, leadership learning starts at birth in the context of family. Family care and education provide important bases of learning about leadership. Parents, carers, and other significant players in the family are instrumental in teaching notions of leadership to young children. Family members impart folk stories and historical archetypes of leadership, which leave the children with varied examples. The professional class, level of education, rural-urban background, and size of a family and other factors affect the choice of leadership archetypes that children learn.

Turkish folk stories have archetypes of both power-seeking leaders (Ottoman Sultans in their pursuit of expanding their territories of land and power, or pre-Islamic folk heroes as they are portrayed to possess much power and influence to gather large groups of followers) and anti-establishment visionary leaders (Ataturk as he established a democratic country out of a theocratic empire, Nasreddin Hodja who took a stance against religious bigotry and social hypocrisies, Bektashi and Mevlana whose religious leadership was one which welcomed inclusion rather than exclusion). The latter counterbalance the power-seeking leadership models with more democratic models of leadership which relegate the power back to people in the country. Therefore, the choice of stories in each family will inform the early learning of an individual and colour their understanding and appreciation of leadership.

After family, the main source of leadership learning is the formal education in Turkey. The education system is highly competitive in Turkey, which has a compulsory primary education system, followed by second-ary and tertiary (higher) education, which receive a competitively selected small proportion of the available population of students. Schools in Turkey, similar to their counterparts in Europe and the USA, do not have explicit items in the curriculum on leadership. Nevertheless, leadership ideology and stories are abundant in texts of literature, culture, history and social life in the curriculum in the Turkish education system.

Only about 20 per cent of over one million students who enter university exams are admitted to study in Turkish universities. Therefore, university education remains a relatively elite pursuit. There are over 100 universities which have public or private status. University courses which deal with issues of leadership at work are also few and far between. As a result, universities fail to educate students to understand the wider possibilities of leadership, which goes beyond what is available in the folk culture. Aycan and Fikret-Pasa (2003) surveyed Turkish students regarding what motivates them to select their future jobs and their preferred leadership style. The study revealed that the students are motivated by having power, authority, a positive work environment and possibilities of career advancement as well as financial outcomes. Congruent with Turkish cultural history, students have also opted for a charismatic leadership model as their preferred model of leadership. Although student experience offers a poor proxy for their career and leadership experiences after graduation, the study nevertheless provides an assessment of beliefs, opinions and expectations of university students in Turkey and reveals the significance of cultural context in choices of careers and leadership styles of Turkish students.

Besides deficiencies in terms of leadership training in the higher education sector, Turkish university education mainly caters for European and North American markets as higher education does not prepare students for management and leadership in Turkey. One manifestation of this is the education in European languages. Most prestigious universities in Turkey offer education in English, German and French languages. In these universities, texts and papers used for instruction are mainly in these foreign languages and refer to studies conducted in these international contexts. Although the individual lecturers may attempt to introduce papers based on studies in Turkey, this is often lacking. Therefore, students who are educated in business management acquire knowledge that prepares them to work and do research in Western European and North American settings. Indeed, most students would require extensive training upon graduation if they are to take up jobs in Turkey. The exception to this is the proliferation of MBA programmes which admit students with experience in industry. Even then the teaching materials are often based on studies in other countries.

The situation is also the same with teaching of leadership in Turkey. Leadership theory draws heavily on theory developed elsewhere and migrated to Turkish settings like a straitjacket in a way which ignores contextual requirements of Turkey.

A consequence of the ongoing problems that plague Turkey's economic development – and an education system which prepares students better for employment abroad is that Turkey loses a considerable number of talented people, who leave the country for education abroad and fail to return after graduation (Tansel and Gungor 2003). While some authors interpret this as brain drain or talent loss, this also has some unexpected outcomes as migration adds to the connectedness of Turkey to the rest of the world. Many talented migrants retain active links in Turkey and the Turkish higher education sector. Turks who are educated abroad and live there can serve as conduits for exchange, introduction and transfer of new models of leadership to Turkey.

Leadership learning after graduation does not only take place in formal settings. There are also civil society organizations, mosque schools, sermons by religious sects and esoteric communities which serve as sources of leadership learning. These groups and organizations present their own takes on leadership. In a country which has a tradition of secularism, the emergence of esoteric sects and religious groups with strong ideologies is a new phenomenon, dating back to the 1980s military coup, which strengthened religious groups in order to suppress left-wing movement in Turkey. The heritage of the 1980s is that today, Turkey has a religiously inspired government and many of its secular institutions are tacitly or explicitly contested. An outcome of these changes is that religion serves as an inspiration for models of leadership in Turkey.

In the Turkish context, military experience cannot be discounted in understanding the conception of leadership and how autocratic models of leadership are so deeply rooted. While the Turkish military has served as a significant force for the Westernization and modernization project of Turkey (Tank 2006), military service and its organization have a different impact on the country's routines of work and organization. A period of military service is compulsory for men of military age in Turkey. The duration of the service varies extensively based on education and job status (living and working abroad). Military service experience is characterized by a period of indoctrination in which the military style of leadership is instilled in the soldiers. This autocratic style of leadership is reproduced across the Turkish organizations, as old military generals also hold significant posts in the boards of some very large Turkish companies. Further, Turkey has a tradition of military involvement in civil politics. In his analysis of Turkish political elites, Arslan (2004) demonstrates that two-thirds of the country's presidents have indicated military education as the primary source of their education. The compound effect of these on the way leadership is shaped in Turkey is that autocratic and bureaucratic leadership models spill over from military organization to organizations in other sectors of employment. Nichols, Sugur and Demir (2002) provide a counter-argument to conception of Turkish managers' and leaders' styles as autocratic. In their study of the white goods sector, they find that, in terms of care for workers, Turkish workers rate their managers more favourably than do British workers who rated their managers in a similar study. Furthermore, in their study among public, private and multinational firms, Olmez. Sumer and Soysal (2004) found that Turkish managers are less concerned about standardization and assessment when compared to their foreign counterparts. Therefore, there is a degree of puzzlement in terms of leadership behaviours and their context-specific origins. It seems that military service operates as one of the strong influences on leadership learning, but it is not the sole basis for such learning.

Leadership is also learned through experience of work. In the world of work, however, there is very little emphasis on evidence-based policy and practice. There are some structural problems such as relevance of education (vocational, school or higher education) to employment experience (Simsek and Yildirim 2000). The linkages with academic research and business practice remain unsupported not only in the field of leadership but also in other cognate fields, such as human resource management. For example, Aycan (2001) noted that human resource management in Turkish organizations is a developing field, which operates with concepts from foreign language literatures, based on research abroad. The dearth of academic education in the field, coupled with the reluctance of business professionals to rely on evidence-based practice, deem the field susceptible to loss of credibility. Collaboration between academy and industry is important not only because the industry would benefit from it, but also because research in action (in the process of collaboration) can help researchers generate emic insights which are sorely lacking in the Turkish context.

Economic and Social Context and Leadership in Turkey

The economic system in Turkey can also account for the leadership models that can exist in its business context. Under the leadership of Turgut Ozal (a contemporary of Margaret Thatcher who admired Thatcher's policies of liberalization and privatization), Turkey has started a process of economic liberalization, moving away from its state-controlled economic system (Karatas 2001). With this change in its economic system, certain commercial logics have also migrated to public and private sectors. These included opportunism associated with entrepreneurial activity, and winner-takes-all culture, which underpinned the overall logic of liberalization. In a comparative study between British, Irish and Turkish managers, Arslan (2001) identified that Turkish managers displayed higher achievement (congruent with achievement orientation in high growth economies) and lower power orientation (associated with paternalistic attitudes) than their British counterparts, arguing that recent economic growth and cultural context respectively may explain these differences. Despite an apparently vibrant economy, consequences of the winner-takes-all culture and opportunism have been felt most in terms of widening of the income gap between rich and poor in Turkey, as it is the case in other countries which have gone through such liberalization processes, such as the US and the UK.

In line with changes elsewhere, trade unionism was also badly effected in the process of liberalization in Turkey. While previously unionization was polarized along political lines, the present unionization is further segregated along religious lines. Therefore, liberalization of economy and emergence of religiously inspired unionization has segregated union movement, effectively reducing its power. Despite these changes, in line with national ambitions to join the EU, Turkish government has started attributing greater value to social dialogue as an important mechanism through which good governance can be supported (Sural 2007). However, the agenda of social dialogue and change requires political will and leadership to champion these new forms of workplace representation.

Tempering the Agency of Leaders in Turkey – Democratization, Equality, Social Culture and Group Dynamics

Despite evidence of some strong forms of leadership and leader-follower relationship in Turkey, agency of leaders is tempered by the process of democratization, requirements of equality, and dynamics of social culture and group. Democratization is a long journey for Turkey. Onis (2002) refers to the linkages between business and government leadership to deliver this type of tempering of the state and corporate power. Embedding democracy and equality is one of the key historical challenges in Turkish workplaces and a significant agenda item in Turkey's EU membership bid. Democratization and equality demand similar attention to the tempering of the otherwise absolute power that leaders may hold. Gender equality, as it affects the whole population in any country, is an important marker of the way leadership power is framed.

Turkey is a paradoxical country in terms of gender equality at work. Turkish women with higher education achieve better career status than their European counterparts (Özbilgin and Woodward 2003). However, women who are less educated are more likely to experience poverty, 'honour' killings, and local and religious pressures to conform to strict gender norms. This polarized picture, therefore, requires particular attention to issues of leadership. Leaders by definition come from better educated and more influential segments of social life in Turkey. Therefore, it is reasonable to expect a healthy proportion of female leaders, as women with education have better chances of holding positions of power and influence in Turkey than their Western counterparts. As indicated earlier in the chapter, there are exceptional female leaders in business, social life and politics in Turkey. However, some commentators argue as far as to suggest that the dominant cultural norms of paternalism and autocracy deem Turkish workplaces unsuitable outlets for women to join. They go on to explain that multinational firms may provide better employment opportunities to Turkish women outside these cultural norms (Taylor and Napier 2001). However, this approach assumes that Turkish women are (and wish to remain) outside the autocratic and paternalistic cultural norms in Turkey. I would argue that the dominant leadership ideology in Turkey would be shared and similar among female and male leaders. Connectedness of leadership styles with dominant ideologies in the country renders gender representation in leadership positions a rather simplistic measure for gender equality in business.

Women have always been used as part of the leadership discourses. Most political parties engage with debates on gender and work as part of their agendas. There is, for example, polarization of opinion around the issue of headscarves. While the current ruling party is sympathetic towards headscarves, the other parties advocate a secular line in which they argue that religious symbols should be kept out of state institutions. Alptekin Oguzertem (2003) argues that the headscarf[2] debate divides Turkish women. There is a fault line in Turkish society across interpretation of secularism and Islam in terms of women's head covers, when there are more significant issues such as feminization of poverty, illiteracy and unemployment, as well as problems with 'honour' killings, prenatal care and women's health. The superficial nature of the ongoing debates in Turkey suggests that women are still used as means rather than ends of social policy.

The current ruling party, AKP, sends mixed messages in terms of its approach to gender equality. On the one had, the party declares its commitment to join the European Union and commits itself to undertake the structural reforms which well prepare Turkey and on the other hand, the revised constitution which they prepared brought in protective legislation which places women to the level of children, workers with disabilities and old age citizens, in need of protection. The party also purged the gender equality clause in the constitution, the only piece of legislation which provided equal opportunity under previous administrations. These legal changes do not comply with the spirit of the AKP's espoused commitment to join the EU.

Besides equality of opportunity, another important challenge to absolute power of a leader is sharing of power by the leadership group (Ataman 2002). A leadership group is often a tightly connected group of individuals who collectively lead the country under one leader. Ataman notes that even charismatic leaders in Turkey had very effective leadership groups with which they share leadership authority and power. In the context of organizations, Celikten's (2001) study of assistant school principals suggests that the leadership group in school administration does not enjoy a democratic sharing of duties. Despite the significance of the role that a leadership group may play in delivering good governance, a leadership group itself may suffer from inequitable sharing of power and authority.

While democratization, equality and leadership groups may challenge the leaders' absolute hold on power, in the context of Turkey, the limited nature of equality legislation, the slow pace of the democratization process as well as the complex dynamics of power sharing in groups renders leadership power relatively uncontested.

DISCUSSION: TOWARDS AN EVIDENCE-BASED THEORY OF LEADERSHIP IN TURKEY

Leadership is important to study in organizational contexts. While successful leadership can make a contribution towards survival of the firm, poor leadership may lead to organizational failure. Bozbura (2004) finds that there is a strong positive correlation between the intellectual and relational capital that organizations hold and the shareholder value within Turkish firms. Leadership as a relational construct and as part of the relational capital of the organization therefore is linked with the shareholder value of the organization.

Reflecting on the relation between leaders and their context, Day (2001) provides a critique of leadership development theory, distinguishing it from leader development. This critique is pertinent for the Turkish case, as almost all studies of leadership in Turkey are underpinned by the philosophy of leader development, rather than leadership development, and therefore, the main emphasis is placed on the leader as the individual, rather than leadership as a negotiated and relational process.

Leader development is based on a traditional, individualistic conceptualization of leadership. The underlying assumption is that more effective leadership occurs through the development of individual leaders. It also assumes that leadership is something that can be added to organizations to improve social and operational effectiveness. On the other hand, leadership development has its origins in a more contemporary, relational model of leadership. This model assumes that leadership is a function of the social resources that are embedded in relationships. In this manner,

> leadership . . . emerges with the process of creating shared meaning, both in terms of sensemaking and in terms of value-added. From this approach everyone is considered to be a leader. Rather than asking the question 'How can I be

an effective leader' the more pertinent question from the relational approach is 'How can I participate productively in the leadership process'. (Day 2001, p. 605)

Construction of leadership as a relational construct, rather than an individual trait or as a simple exchange relationship, has wider implications to our understanding of individual and group constructs at work. For example, in their study of bank managers, Ergeneli, Ari and Metin (2007) also provide support for the idea that empowerment, which is often correlated with leadership, is a relational construct and that trust is essential for empowerment of work groups.

One of the reasons why leadership research has remained stunted and largely EU- and US-centric is the absence of a link between academic research and organizational policy making in Turkey. Evidence-based policy making is in its inception in Turkey. Practitioners do not turn to academic evidence, particularly from Turkey, in order to improve their leadership skills. Despite allocation of research funds for social themes through national agencies such as TUBITAK as well as from international sources, social science research remains under-funded in Turkey. Lack of adequate funding for research on leadership theory has rendered leadership theory thin on the ground. Academic research therefore becomes an end in itself (loosely regulated merely in terms of career advancement of the individual researcher) rather than a means for social and organizational development. Leadership research, which is conducted in pursuit of career advancement, rather than broader social or economic ends, does not engage at a deep level with the contextual requirements of the subject, neither would it be linked with leadership development initiatives or policy in Turkey. The absence of a link between academic research and social policy has been partly responsible for the acontextual nature of much of the leadership research and styles of leadership, which draw on emotive discourses rather than empiricism, characterize the Turkish context. Indeed, the public speeches of leaders often revert to some collective values, rather than evidence. In the context of Westernization and Europeanization in Turkey, there is need for evidence-based leadership, if leadership is to gain accountability and credibility in Turkey.

NOTES

1.   I would like to thank Eda Ulus for reading and commenting on this chapter. Her suggestions were very useful.

2. 'Headscarf' in English may give the impression that all types of head covering are a point of contention in Turkey. This is not the case. I refer to the turban, the folding and fastening style of which is associated with the specific sect to which the person belongs. Therefore, headscarf mentioned here is a symbol of a politicized form of Islam.

REFERENCES

Agle, Bradley R., N.J. Nagarajan, J.A. Sonnenfeld and D. Srinivasan (2006), 'Does CEO charisma matter? An empirical analysis of the relationships among organizational performance, environmental uncertainty, and top management team perceptions of CEO charisma', *Academy of Management Journal*, **49** (1), 161–74.

Alptekin-Oguzertem, Y. (2003), 'Covered or uncovered? Female leadership to lift barriers keeping girls out of schools in Turkey', paper presented at the 5th European Feminist Research Conference, 20–24 August, Lund University, Sweden.

Ardichvili, A. (2001), 'Leadership styles and work-related values of managers and employees of manufacturing enterprises in post-communist countries', *Human Resource Development Quarterly*, **12** (4), 363–83.

Arslan, A. (2004), 'Social anatomy of Turkish top political elites in contemporary Turkey', *International Journal of Human Sciences*, **65**, 1–28.

Arslan, M. (2001), 'A cross-cultural comparison of achievement and power orientation as leadership dimensions in three European countries: Britain, Ireland and Turkey', *Business Ethics: A European Review*, **10** (4), 340–45.

Ataman, Muhittin (2002), 'Leadership change: Özal leadership and restructuring in Turkish foreign policy', *Alternatives Turkish Journal of International Relations*, **1** (1), 120–53.

Aycan, Z. (2001), 'Whatever happened to individual-level studies of work motivation?' *Cross-Cultural Bulletin*, **35** (2), 6–13.

Aycan, Z. and M. Eskin (2005), 'Relative contributions of childcare, spousal support, and organizational support in reducing work–family conflict for men and women: the case of Turkey', *Sex Roles*, **53** (7/8), 453–71.

Aycan, Z. and S. Fikret-Pasa (2003), 'Career choices, job selection criteria, and leadership preferences in a transitional nation: the case of Turkey', *Journal of Career Development*, **30** (2), 129–44.

Bartram, T., P. Stanton, S.Leggat, G. Casimir and B. Fraser (2007), 'Lost in translation: exploring the link between HRM and performance in healthcare', *Human Resource Management Journal*, **17** (1), 21–41.

Bilgin Aksu, M. (2003), 'TQM readiness level perceived by the administrators working for the central organization of the Ministry of National Education in Turkey', *Total Quality Management*, **14** (5), 591–604.

Bozbura, F.T. (2004), 'Measurement and application of intellectual capital in Turkey', *The Learning Organization*, **11** (4/5), 357–67.

Brodbeck, F.C. et al. (2000), 'Cultural variation of leadership prototypes across 22 European countries', *Journal of Occupational and Organizational Psychology*, **73** (1), 1–29.

Celikten, M. (2001), 'The instructional leadership tasks of high school assistant principals', *Journal of Educational Administration*, **39** (1), 67–76.

Celikten, M. (2005), 'A perspective on women principals in Turkey', *International Journal of Leadership in Education*, **8** (3), 207–21.

Chen, Gilad, B.L. Kirkmanb, R. Kanferc, D. Allend and B. Rosen (2007), 'A multilevel study of leadership, empowerment, and performance in teams', *Journal of Applied Psychology*, **92** (2), 331–46.

Cizre-Sakallioglu, U. and E. Yeldan (2000), 'Politics, society and financial liberalization: Turkey in the 1990s', *Development and Change*, **31**, 481–503.

Costanzo, L.A. and V. Tzoumpa (2008), 'Enhancing organisational learning in teams: has the middle-manager got a role?', *Team Performance Management*, **14** (3), 146–64.

Dastmalchian, A., M. Javidan, and K. Alam (2001), 'Effective leadership and culture in Iran: an empirical study', *Applied Psychology: An international review*, **50** (4), 532–58.

Day, D.V. (2001), 'Leadership development: a review in context', *Leadership Quarterly*, **11** (4), 581–613.

Eker, L., E.H. Tuzun, A. Daskapan and O. Surenkok (2004), 'Predictors of job satisfaction among physiotherapists in Turkey', *Journal of Occupational Health*, **46**, 500–505.

Ensari, N. and S.E. Murphy (2003), 'Cross-cultural variations in leadership perceptions and attribution of charisma to the leader', *Organizational Behavior and Human Decision Processes*, **92**, 52–66.

Ergeneli, A. and S. Arikan (2002), 'Gender differences in ethical perceptions of salespeople: an empirical examination in Turkey', *Journal of Business Ethics*, **40**, 247–60.

Ergeneli, A., G. Sag, I. Ari and S. Metin (2007), 'Psychological empowerment and its relationship to trust in immediate managers', *Journal of Business Research*, **60** (1), 41–56.

Gunes-Ayata, A. (2003), 'From Euro-scepticism to Turkey-scepticism: changing political attitudes on the European Union in Turkey', *Journal of Southern Europe and the Balkans*, **5** (2), 205–22.

Hisrich, R.D., B.Bucar and S. Oztark (2003), 'A cross-cultural comparison of business ethics: cases of Russia, Slovenia, Turkey, and United States', *Cross Cultural Management*, **10** (1), 3–28.

Johansen, U.C. and D.C. White (2002), 'Collaborative long-term ethnography and longitudinal social analysis of a nomadic clan in Southeastern Turkey', in R. Kemper, and A.P. Royce (eds), *Chronicling Cultures: Long-term Field Research in Anthropology*, Walnut Creek, CA: AltaMira, pp. 81–101.

Kabasakal, H. and M. Bodur (2002), 'Arabic cluster: a bridge between East and West', *Journal of World Business*, **37**, 40–54.

Kabasakal, H. and M. Bodur (2004), 'Humane orientation in societies, organizations, and leader attributes', in R. House, P. Hanges, M. Javidan, P. Dorfman and V. Gupta (eds), *Culture, Leadership, and Organizations: The GLOBE Study of 62 Societies*, Thousand Oaks, CA: Sage, pp. 564–601.

Kabasakal, H. and A. Dastmalchian (2001), 'Introduction to the special issue on leadership and culture in the Middle East', *Applied Psychology: An International Review*, **50** (4), 479–88.

Karatas, C. (2001), 'Privatization in Turkey: implementation, politics of privatization and performance results', *Journal of International Development*, 13, 93–121.

Koopman, P.L. et al. (1999), 'National culture and leadership profiles in

Europe: some results from the GLOBE study', *European Journal of Work and Organizational Psychology*, **8** (4), 503–20.

Kroissenbrunner, S. (2003), 'Islam and Muslim immigrants in Austria: socio-political networks and Muslim leadership of Turkish immigrants', *Immigrants and Minorities*, **22** (2/3), 188–207.

Kula, V. (2005), 'The impact of the roles, structure and process of boards on firm performance: evidence from Turkey', *Corporate Governance*, **13** (2), 265–76.

Mehra, A., A.L. Dixon, D.J. Brass and B. Robertson (2006a), 'The social network ties of group leaders: implications for group performance and leader reputation', *Organization Science*, **17** (1), 64–79.

Mehra, A., A.L. Dixon, D.J. Brass and B. Robertson (2006b), 'Distributed leadership in teams: the network of leadership perceptions and team performance', *The Leadership Quarterly*, **17** (3), 232–45.

Mellon, J.G. (2006), 'Islamism, Kemalism and the future of Turkey', *Totalitarian Movements and Political Religions*, **7** (1), 67–81.

Nichols, T., N. Sugur and E. Demir (2002), 'Globalised management and local labour: the case of the white-goods industry in Turkey', *Industrial Relations Journal*, **33** (1), 68–85.

Olmez, A.E., H.C. Sumer and M. Soysal (2004), 'Organizational rationality in public, private and multinational firms in Turkey', *Information Knowledge Systems Management*, **4**, 107–18.

Onis, Z. (2002), 'Entrepreneurs, citizenship and the European Union: the changing nature of state-business relations in Turkey', prepared for E. Fuat Keyman and Ahmet İçduygu (eds), *Challenges to Citizenship in a Globalizing World: European Questions and Turkish Experiences*, revised version of the paper presented July 2001 at the ISA Hong Kong Convention.

Özbilgin, M.F. and D. Woodward (2003), *Banking and Gender*, London and New York: Palgrave–I.B. Tauris Publishers.

Özkaya, M.O. and M.F. Özbilgin (2007), 'Boundaryless careers in Turkey: the case of top-ranking firms in the Istanbul Stock Exchange', paper presented at the Academy of Management Meeting, 1-6 August, Philadelphia, PA.

Pasa, S.F. (2000), 'Leadership influence in a high power distance and collectivist culture', *Leadership & Organization Development Journal*, **21** (8), 414–26.

Pasa, S.L., H. Kabasakal and M. Bodur (2001), 'Society, organisations and leadership in Turkey', *Applied Psychology: An International Review*, **50** (4), 559–89.

Shea-Van Fossen, R.J., H.R. Rothstein and H.J Korn (2006), 'Thirty-five years of strategic planning and firm performance research: a meta-analysis', *Academy of Management Proceedings*, pp. 1–6.

Simsek, S. (2004), 'New social movements in Turkey since 1980', *Turkish Studies*, **5** (2), 111–39.

Simsek, H. and A. Yildirim (2000), 'Vocational schools in Turkey: an administrative and organizational analysis', *International Review of Education*, **46** (3/4), 327–42.

Smith, P. (1997), 'Leadership in Europe: Euro-management or the footprint of history?' *European Journal of Work and Organizational Psychology*, **6** (4), 375–86.

Sural, A.N. (2007), 'A pragmatic analysis of social dialogue in Turkey', *Middle Eastern Studies*, **43** (1), 143–52.

Tank, P. (2006), 'Dressing for the occasion: reconstructing Turkey's identity', *Southeast European and Black Sea Studies*, **6** (4), 463–78.

Tansel, A. and N.D. Gungor (2003), ' "Brain drain" from Turkey: survey evidence of student non-return', *Career Development International*, **8** (2), 52–69.

Taylor, S. and N.K. Napier (2001), 'An American woman in Turkey: adventures unexpected and knowledge unplanned', *Human Resource Management*, **40** (4), 347–64.

Yamak, S. (2006), 'Changing institutional environment and business elites in Turkey', *Society and Business Review*, **1** (3), 206–19.

12. Making a difference in a troubled country: the case of entrepreneurial and female leadership in Yemen

Nabil Sultan

INTRODUCTION

The modern history of Yemen is a complex and troubled one. The twentieth century witnessed the withdrawal of colonial powers, foreign-backed war and financial dependency; Yemen was a Cold War battleground and went through reunification and civil war. At the end of the first decade of the twenty-first century, Yemen has been described as a 'failing state' (Barron 2008; Colton 2010) with a severely damaged economy, resentment of the ruling Northern powers and sections of the country in open armed revolt. Yemen has both the largest and poorest population on the Arabian peninsula, with over 20 million people in an area similar to that of Ireland (MEDEA 2008), among whom the unemployment rate is estimated to be as high as 40 per cent (Colton 2010).

Yet this is the region of Arabia known to Ptolemy as *Eudaimon Arabia* – Fortunate Arabia, a term adopted by the Romans as *Arabia Felix*; Herodotus described the region as '. . .scented with [the spices of Arabia], and exhales an odor marvellously sweet' (in Ovendale 1998; see also Halliday 2007). This fanciful description reflects the importance of Yemen at that time in the trade in incense and spices. The Incense Route along the Western part of the Arab peninsula was the predecessor of the Indian Spice Route (Artzy 1994), and the origin of much of the frankincense, one of the most important and valuable items of trade, was Wadi Hadramaut in what is now the eastern part of Yemen (Shackley 2002). This ancient wealth is remembered in tales of the queen known to Arab scholars as Bilqis and in the Qur'an as the Queen of Sheba (Saba). The people of Yemen were also very successful in their exploitation of rain water by developing an advanced irrigation system, including the famous Marib dam, whose purpose, according to one account, was not to retain water but to deflect the runoff from the infrequent rains into irrigation canals

which helped agriculture and made that region the only area of the peninsula to be self-sufficient in agriculture (Baynard et al 1980, pp. 7–9; Cohen
and Lewis 1979; UNDP 2009).

The interior of Yemen would go into a long decline as trade shifted
from the overland routes to maritime routes along the Red Sea, although
the port of Aden remains important. Yemen was early to accept Islam,
and this would shape the development of the region over the next
centuries.

In the early nineteenth century, after further political upheavals, Yemen
was divided between occupation of the North by the Ottoman Empire and
the seizure of Aden by Britain in 1839. British occupation did little for the
non-strategic rural areas of the South Yemen interior, where traditional
tribal leadership was maintained (Milton-Edwards 2009).

For the remainder of this chapter I will discuss how this historic background has led to the current, troubled political and economic context of
Yemen. I will then look at theories of leadership and strategy in modern
Yemen, at the tradition of entrepreneurial leadership, at new challenges,
especially those arising from the crisis of the Gulf War and Yemeni civil
war of 1994, and at the special case of women in modern Yemen. This
will be investigated in more depth through case studies, and I will close by
looking at the severe economic, social development and leadership challenges facing Yemen in the future.

THE ECONOMIC AND SOCIAL DEVELOPMENT OF MODERN YEMEN

As discussed above, the colonial legacy of the Arabian peninsula led to
Yemen entering the twentieth century as two states, the borders of which
had been drawn by the occupying powers, the Ottomans and Great Britain.
I therefore begin by discussing the two states and their development prior
to unification.

North Yemen

The Ottoman Empire ceased to exist after the peace which ended World
War I. Therefore, after 1918, North Yemen was ruled by Imam Yahya
Hamid al-Din, an autocrat who declared the country a monarchy. He
isolated his country from the rest of the world and as a result the population remained backward and poor. Assassinated in 1948, he was succeeded
by his son Imam Ahmad who ordered the execution of the conspirators.
Imam Ahmad continued his father's policies of enforced isolation: it

was reported that in the 1950s, after the new nationalist military regime of Egypt began broadcasting revolutionary propaganda, he ordered the confiscation of all radio sets. Despite attempts on his life, he survived and publicly executed those who conspired against him. Imam Ahmad died of natural causes in 1962 and was succeeded by his son Muhammad al-Badr, a more open minded individual. However, his rule only lasted for a few days before he was ousted by a military coup supported by Egypt's military regime under Nasser (Burrowes 2011, p. 208).

The new regime began the difficult task of building a new nation state almost from scratch. The Imamate was abolished and North Yemen became, for the first time in its history, a republic, the Yemen Arab Republic (YAR), headed by a military president, Abdulla al-Sallal. He was supported by an Egyptian military presence and opponents regarded him as an Egyptian stooge. Also, the coup had failed to capture Imam Muhammad who began to rally troops, plunging the country into a civil war in which Saudi Arabia supported the royalists (Burrowes 2011) and nearly 70 000 Egyptian troops supported the Republic (Cleveland and Bunton 2009). In 1967, with the departure of the Egyptians following defeat in the war with Israel, al-Sallal was removed in a bloodless coup and replaced by Abdul Rahman al-Iryani, a *qadi* (religious scholar) who was widely respected. Al-Iryani had been implicated in the 1948 coup but pardoned by Imam Ahmad only minutes before he was due to be beheaded. In the ten years that followed, there was reconciliation between the factions, a new constitution in 1970, elections and, following al-Iryani's resignation in 1974, the popular but short-lived presidency of Ibrahim al-Hamdi (Burrowes 2011). However, in 1977 al-Hamdi was assassinated by one of his generals, Ahmad Hussein al-Ghashmi, who installed himself as president. Less than a year later, al-Ghashmi himself was killed by a bomb delivered to him in a suitcase by a messenger, alleged to have been sent by South Yemen's president, Salem Rubaya Ali.

There followed a 12-year period in which President Ali Abdullah Saleh presided over an era of initially increased stability and, with the discovery of oil, increasing prosperity (Burrowes 2011), a period that ended with Saleh the president of a newly unified nation.

South Yemen

South Yemen became a British Protectorate after the occupation of 1839. The British administration ensured the rural areas of the country remained, as they have always been, under the control of their tribal leaders, whom they supported with financial and other forms of assistance: but the British policy was essentially one of neglect. As a consequence, many of those areas remained largely deprived and had very basic public services in terms of education, health and infrastructure. Local infighting and banditry was common in most of the tribal areas. This was particularly evident in Hadhramaut (a large region to the east of the country) which caused many of its people to migrate to places such as Indonesia, Singapore and East Africa (a new phase of the historical phenomenon known as the Hadhrami diaspora). By 1934, about a quarter of the Hadhramis lived outside Hadhramaut, with the Dutch East Indies (modern day Indonesia) being their largest colony (Jonge 1993, p. 75).

By contrast, after the Second World War, Aden underwent rapid economic development under British rule. In the late 1950s its port ranked fourth after London, Liverpool and New York in number of ships handled and its social services were more advanced than those of many European countries of the time (Bidwell 1983, pp. 81–2). As a consequence, trade prospered and the city attracted many people from within South and North Yemen and many other parts of the world (Cohen and Lewis 1979).

However, when independence came rapidly in 1967 following Britain's announcement of its intention to withdraw from all of its positions East of Suez, Aden's economic progress, trade and industry were dealt a double blow with, in the same year, closure of the Suez canal (as a result of the Arab-Israeli war) and the rise to power of a Marxist regime, the leaders of which came mainly from the deprived regions of South Yemen's rural areas. South Yemen became known as the People's Democratic Republic of Yemen (PDRY), ruled by one party, the Yemeni Socialist Party (YSP), which maintained strong links with the Soviet Union and sought to spread its 'revolution' to other parts of the region.

South Yemen was governed by the coleadership of Salim Ruba'i Ali and Abd al-Fatah Isma'il from 1969 to 1978 until ongoing violence saw the execution of Salim Ruba'i Ali and the exile of Abd al-Fatah (Burrowes 2011). The regime was disrupted by violence again in 1986 when the newly appointed President, Ali Nasir Muhammad, ordered his bodyguard to machine gun most of the members of the party's *politburo* during a meeting, precipitating violence in which the returned Abd al-Fatah Isma'il was killed along with over 5000 others and Ali Nasir was ousted, to be succeeded until unification by Haidar Abu Bakr al-Attas.

With a long desired reunification coming about in 1990, to the surprise of many, Ali Abdullah Saleh became president of the single nation, the Republic of Yemen. Until the 2011 Arab Spring events, his premiership has survived a war of secession in 1994, ongoing economic crisis triggered by mass repatriation of workers during the 1990 Gulf Crisis (Colton 2010) and growing protest in the South against Northern dominance (Day 2008).

As discussed elsewhere in this volume, the characteristic style of leadership in the nations of the Middle East is highly influenced by the tone set by national leaders. The constant instability of Yemen has meant that decision making in political relations and in organization systems is characterized by a pragmatic 'rules of the game' approach (Gentile 2006; Alley 2010). Business development and entrepreneurship are compromised by informal systems of patronage (Utting 2006). Indeed, Alley (2010) observes that, since 1978, Saleh's rule has been based on a politics of informal patronage that extends to national level agenda setters and includes tribal elites, religious leaders, traditional merchants and technocrats, commonly known as 'merchant, shaykh, officer and modernist' (Alley 2010, p. 390–91). Disruption to this system, especially its strong component of tribal Zaidi elites, can be a risky endeavour as evidenced by the June 2011 events, when Saleh's presidential mosque was bombed (allegedly by tribal strongmen supporting youths revolting in Yemen's Arab Spring), almost costing him his life. This system is discussed further in the section below on emerging Yemeni leadership.

It is important to note that, while informal associations and networks are embedded in political and economic history, the requirement for modernization and redevelopment has meant that the patronage system is changing and extending more broadly to include new investors and entrepreneurs (Alley 2010, pp. 391–3).

DEVELOPMENTS IN LEADERSHIP IN YEMEN

Yemenis, even by Western accounts, are generally regarded as hard-working and entrepreneurial people (Cohen and Lewis 1979, p. 525; Le Guennnec-Coppens 1997, p. 168). However, most of the current economic and social literature on Yemenis as people tends to focus more on the 'deprived', 'struggling', 'uneducated' and 'unskilled' aspect of their lives, whether as rural or urban dwellers in their own country or as migrants living in the oil-rich neighbouring Gulf countries (Clarence-Smith 1997). Little has been written on the entrepreneurial and leadership aspects of successful Yemenis with any serious analysis. The following pages will attempt to shed some light on this issue within the context of modern leadership theories, while highlighting some of the cultural, economic and historical factors particular to Yemeni society and considering critically the dominance of Western theories on authority and leadership.

This neglect of entrepreneurial leadership could be due to a number of factors. Most Yemeni entrepreneurs found success outside their own country, in places as distant as Southeast Asia or as near as Saudi Arabia and parts of Africa. Additionally, many of the successful large enterprises that currently exist in Yemen (especially in the north) are relatively new. Only after the 1962 revolution did enterprises start to grow and prosper in private ownership. Privately owned enterprises in South Yemen, particularly those of large and medium size that emerged and thrived during British rule, were nationalized without compensation in 1969 by the country's Marxist regime and the establishment of any significant private enterprise was prohibited. This state of affairs was to last until 1990, the year unity between South Yemen and North Yemen was declared (Al-Aswami 2005).

However, I contend that there is enough material evidence to form the basis for an exploration of Yemeni entrepreneurial leadership. It must however be noted that the definition of what leadership is has often been problematic for both practitioners and academics (Ford 2006, p. 237). Persuasive answers have proved elusive, and findings have been inconclusive and inconsistent (Collinson 2005, p. 1423). Nevertheless, some generalizations seem to have emerged from this body of literature. For example, Rost collected 221 definitions of leadership ranging from the 1920s to the 1990s which, according to Ciulla (2005, p. 160), seem to say the same thing: that 'leadership is about a person or persons somehow moving other people to do something'. As such, some authors criticized the main theories of leadership for being conceptualized primarily at the 'dyadic' or 'dualistic' (leader-follower) level where the overriding concern is with managerial effectiveness (Collinson 2005, p. 1420; Yukl 1999, pp. 290, 295, 301; Zoller and Fairhurst 2007, p. 1333). An alternative approach is possible. According to Ciulla (2005, pp. 160–61), scholars who worry about constructing the ultimate definition of leadership are asking the wrong question. The whole point about studying leadership, according to her, is to answer this question: what is good leadership?

Good Leadership and Responsible Leadership

The word 'good' here has two senses; morally good leadership (guided by ethical principles) and technically good leadership (effective at getting the job done). Ciulla (2005) asserts that a good leader is an ethical and an effective leader who brings about good change. However, she also accepts that there could be situations where the level of ethics and effectiveness in a leader is different. For example, some leaders could be highly ethical but not effective and vice versa (see Grint 2000, 2005).

Authors such as Alexander and Wilson (2005, pp. 137–56) argue that integrity and altruism are essential qualities of a 'responsible' style of leadership (see also Asongo 2007). In their experience of examining thousands of managers, Alexander and Wilson recognize that the presence of integrity (at the core of which is honesty and trustworthiness) and altruism (concern for the welfare of others) in an individual can be a source of strength for addressing situations created by negative human behaviour, whether self-serving, negligent or deliberately malevolent. In such situations, people often turn to those who possess a different kind of strength which shows up as integrity, altruism and ethical fitness and watch what they do and say to guide their own behaviour (Bass 1997; Bass and Steidlmeier 1999).

Socially Responsible Leadership: A Western View

While Alexander and Wilson (2005) focus on the question of leadership within the context of the workplace, an increasing number of authors now recognize the importance of looking beyond the confines of the organization as an entity in order to identify responsible leaders. Proponents of this approach see leaders as socially responsible accountable not only to their shareholders but also to stakeholders, represented by employees, local communities and the environment (Karp 2003, p. 16; Waldman and Siegel 2005, p. 208; Roper and Cheney 2005, pp. 99–100). Such leaders are morally conscious, open towards the diversity of stakeholders inside and outside the corporations, and are aware of and understand the responsibilities of business in society (Ples 2007, p. 438). Key to their success, according to Maak (2007, p. 331), is their ability to enable and broker sustainable and mutually beneficial relationships with stakeholders to create stakeholder goodwill and trust. The result is ultimately a trusted business participating in society to the benefit of a multitude of stakeholders.

Karp (2003, p. 19) argues that, in the coming decade, commercial organizations will increasingly need to earn the right to operate profitably due to increased pressure from various groups such as owners, customers, employees, NGOs and international organizations responsible for monitoring global labour standards and a code of ethics (see also UNDP 2003). Many corporations have recently incorporated policies designed to align private gain with public purpose in order to be seen as socially responsible. According to Waldman and Siegel (Waldman and Siegel 2005, p. 208) there is growing realization that a company does not exist in isolation from its community and the society surrounding it. Collins and Porras (2000, pp. 8, 68, 69) found that many of the world's then most successful and 'visionary' companies, including Ford, Hewlett-Packard and Merck, while valuing profits, also pursued a cluster of other objectives (many intended for the welfare of employees, customers and society) and that such companies, paradoxically, make more money than the more 'purely' profit-driven companies.

However, the concept of Corporate Social Responsibility (CSR) remains problematic for some people who argue that there is no sufficiently explicit or detailed evidence of what CSR entails and no developed or convincing body of literature that can clearly articulate the value to organizations of engaging in such behaviours, while others are concerned that it might be no more than the latest management fad (Hazlett, McAdam and Murray 2007, pp. 670–71). Some scholars, such as Milton Friedman, argued that corporations should pursue their economic self-interest and that attempts to promote corporate social responsibility amount to moral wrong (Friedman 1970). Friedman, to whom the statement 'the business of business is business' is attributed, argued that, in a democratic society, the government was the only legitimate vehicle for addressing social concerns (Asongu 2007, p. 13). Other entrepreneurial leaders, however, disagree. For example Anita Roddick, founder of The Body Shop, argued that the business of business should not just be about money and private greed; it should be about responsibility and public good (2000, p. 24).

The concept of CSR is thought to have emerged in 1953 with the publication of a book by Howard Bowen entitled *Social Responsibilities of the Businessman* (1953). However, forms of CSR emerged during the nineteenth century in Europe and North America, encapsulated in the works of foundations and trusts endowed by leading industrialists of the day in an attempt to shape community around particular (often quasi-religious) virtues (Sadler 2004, p. 858). Nevertheless, it was only during the late 1990s that the idea of CSR was widely disseminated and was promoted by all constituents in society, from governments and corporations to non-governmental organizations and individual consumers (Lee 2008, p. 1).

During that period, many large Western transnational corporations began to attract criticism for their global environmental management and labour practices (Utting 2005, 2006; UNDP 2003). The development of global communications facilitated the international transmission of some of the bad practices of those corporations, thus leading to increased public awareness and campaigning activities. In the face of such negative publicity, those corporations, while contending that poverty globally was principally a government responsibility, nevertheless responded by espousing CSR (Jenkins 2005, p. 527). Moreover, support for CSR by such companies was also a reaction to initiatives, both national and international, aimed at establishing codes of corporate conduct (Sadler 2004, pp. 853, 860–62). However, there is now growing acknowledgement that both management and stakeholders (defined as those whose relations to the enterprise cannot be completely contracted for, but upon whose cooperation and creativity it depends for its survival) can influence the profitability of companies (van Tulder and van der Zwart 2006, p. 142). A meta-analysis integrating 30 years of research concluded that there was a positive association between CSR and CFP (Corporate Financial Performance) across industries and across study contexts (Orlitzky, Schmidt and Rynes 2003, p. 423).

Lee (2008, p. 2) cites the story of Henry Ford and his great grandson, William Clay Ford Jr., as evidence of the dramatic change in people's perception of CSR. In 1917 Henry Ford stood in a Michigan courtroom defending his decision to reinvest Ford Motor Company's accumulated profits on plant expansion while slashing the price of Model T vehicles. Henry Ford stated that the purpose of his company was to do as much as possible for everybody concerned, to make money and use it, give employment, and send out the car where the people could use it and that 'business is a service not a bonanza'. Ford's idea of business as a service to society was derided by shareholders and resulted in the court granting the Dodge brothers (the largest shareholders of the company after Ford) their request for maximum dividends in 1919.

Eighty years later Henry Ford's great grandson William Clay Ford Jr. took control of the company and again tried to convince his company's stakeholders of the importance of business as a service to society, saying: 'We want to find ingenious new ways to delight consumers, provide superior returns to shareholders and make the world a better place for us all' (Lee 2008). This time, however, the younger Ford did not have to worry about lawsuits. Rather, he received considerable support from various stakeholders in the company, including shareholders.

Responsible and Transformational Leadership

The discussion above illustrates how social perceptions of leadership and organization evolve over time and how this is reflected in more development oriented approaches to people management. The concept of the transformational and transactional leader was first proposed by political scientist James McGregor Burns in his book *Leadership* to describe political leaders. To Burns (1978, pp. 19, 20) a transformational leader is someone who engages with others in a relationship in such a way that leader and follower raise one another to higher levels of motivation and morality, as opposed to a transactional leader who engages with others in a contractual self-serving relationship. The concept was later built upon by Bass (and later his colleague Avolio) who extended its applicability to organizational leaders (Conger 1999, p. 151). Bass and Avolio (1994, p. 3) argue that transformational leaders motivate others to do more than they originally intended and often more than they thought possible. In response to critics, Bass and Steidlmeier (1999, p. 184) further differentiate between authentic transformational leaders (whose conduct rests on a moral foundation of legitimate values) and pseudo-transformational leaders who consciously or unconsciously act in bad faith.

Bass and Steidlmeier (1999, p. 186) highlight the sense of responsibility that authentic transformational leaders hold towards others. They argue that authentic transformational leadership provides a more reasonable and realistic concept of self: a self that is connected to friends, family and community, the welfare of whom may be more important to oneself than one's own welfare. According to Bass (1997), transformational leaders go beyond their self-interest for the good of their group, organization or society and, as such, they are unlikely to engage in unethical practices as they are guided by terminal values such integrity and fairness. The morality of transformational leadership, according to Bass and Riggio (2006, p. 16), is therefore critical.

Research on 95 pairs of managers and subordinates belonging to a large US non-profit, national human services organization revealed that transformational leaders ranked 'responsible' higher than other attributes such as cheerful, intellectual and ambitious. Moreover, there was a preference given by transformational leaders to moral values (which Burns links to transformational leaders) over competence values (Krishnan 2001, pp. 128, 130). Another study which examined the statistical relationship between transformational leadership and the perceived integrity of New Zealand managers (using a sample of 1354 managers), as rated by their subordinates, peers and superiors, showed that transformational leaders were rated as having more integrity than non-transformational leaders (Parry and Proctor-Thompson 2002, p. 75).

Ethics and Leadership: A Yemen Lens

It follows from the discussion above that ethics and morality underpin the behaviour of responsible transformational leaders who can make a positive impact on people's lives, both inside and outside the confines of the organization. According to Mohammed however, much of the contemporary discussion of CSR seems largely based on a Western orientation informed by Western religious values (Mohammed 2007, p. 8). Similarly, CSR has evolved in response to issues or problems that are specific to management and organizations in a Western development context. This view is also echoed by Shahin and Wright (2004, p. 499) who argue that most leadership theories are North American in origin and may not be appropriate for application on a worldwide basis.

An investigation of CSR from a different cultural perspective will help enrich our understanding of leadership in a Yemeni cultural context and reveal important insights into the forces that influence the presence of CSR and the leaders who engage in such practice. As was noted in Chapter 1,

Islam has played an important role in shaping the knowledge and behaviour of leaders. Further, Islam has nurtured community cooperation in the context of the historical neglect of social duties on the part of the state. This community orientation and concern reflects the principles of CSR. Social responsibility is an obligation that is called for in the Qur'an and is in keeping with the conduct of the Prophet Muhammad (originally a trader widely known for his honesty) and the few disciples who ruled after him. According to Benthall (1999, p. 11) it is doubtful whether any other world religion has an equivalent to the Islamic principle that a hungry person has the right to share in the meal of one who is well fed. Moreover, Islam also places great importance on trust and honesty in dealing with one another and in trade. The Qur'an, in more than one place, warns against unfair trading.

Beekun and Badawi (1999, pp. 28–9, 39) argue that, from an Islamic perspective, Muslim leaders should be honest, not only because being so makes them better leaders but also because they are accountable for their deeds to a very high authority, Allah. They also argue that the Qur'an explicitly links the concept of *amanah* (honesty) to leadership and quote the story of the Prophet Yusuf (Joseph) in the Qur'an as evidence. The Qur'an reveals how Yusuf was placed in a responsible and leadership role (in charge of the granaries and storehouses of the kingdom) by the king of Egypt after the king indicated that he had great trust in him:

> So the king said: 'Bring him to me; I will take him specially to serve about my own person.' Therefore when he had spoken to him he said: 'Be assured this day you are before our own Presence with rank firmly established and fidelity fully proved!' (Yusuf) said: 'Set me over the storehouses of the land: I will indeed guard them as one that knows (their importance). (Yusuf, 12: 54-5)

Self- transformational Leadership

In this section I demonstrate how the concept outlined above of an ethical, Islamic leadership model in a specifically Yemeni context can be applied to the idea of self-transformational leadership. The concept of 'self-transformational leadership' is an extension of what Manz (1986) and Neck (2006) term 'self-leadership'. Self-leadership is a self-influencing process through which people achieve the self-direction and self-motivation necessary to perform. It consists of specific behavioural and cognitive strategies designed to positively influence personal effectiveness. Such strategies are largely grouped into three primary categories: behaviour-focused, natural reward and constructive thought pattern strategies.

Behaviour-focused self-leadership strategies are designed to encourage positive, desirable behaviours that lead to successful outcomes. Natural reward strategies are designed to help create feelings of competence and self-determination, which in turn energise performance-enhancing task-related behaviours. Constructive thought pattern strategies are designed to identify and replace dysfunctional beliefs and assumptions with more constructive thought processes (Neck 2006, p. 272).

However, Manz and Neck describe self-leadership within the 'organizational' context, claiming that the concept is mostly concerned with explaining ways to enhance organizational performance through individual-dependent thinking and acting (Alves et al. 2006, p. 342). The concept of self-leadership is a US-originated model and is grounded in US cultural values (Alves et al. 2006, p. 348; Neck 2006, p. 286). The concept does not, for example, extend to include the possibility of some individuals having the capacity to self-lead themselves outside the organizational context in order to achieve the self-direction and self-motivation necessary not merely to improve organizational performance, but to succeed as individuals. On that basis, I argue, the concept of self-leadership can also be extended to apply to situations where the individual (rather than the organization) and Yemeni culture are of central importance. Moreover, the term 'self-transformational leadership' seems to be more fitting in this extended context than self-leadership, since the ultimate beneficiary of this process is the individual.

It is beyond the scope of this chapter to examine the many constituents of each of the three self-leadership strategies proposed by Manz and Neck from the perspective of the self-transformational leadership concept. It is suggested that self-transformational leadership can be defined as a self-empowering process which can enable people to achieve the self-direction and self-motivation necessary in order to counter and overcome the dysfunctional beliefs and assumptions (often fostered by factors such as tradition or stereotype) that other individuals or society hold toward them and to escape the economic and social consequences of those beliefs. This process, I argue, can assist in the social and psychological transformation of Yemen's troubled economic development and reverse the perception of a 'failed state'. This transformation is embodied in the persons of the two self-transformational female Yemeni leaders presented in the case studies later in this chapter.

YEMENI LEADERSHIP: AN ISLAMIC AND CULTURAL PERSPECTIVE

The Entrepreneurial Leaders of Hadramaut

For many Yemenis, their wealth and prosperity in the ancient past is proof of their industriousness and wisdom (Carapico 1998). No more evidence is required than that provided by the Prophet Muhammad when he described them as 'the most gentle, pious and wise of people', a statement which many Yemenis often repeat (particularly in times of crisis) in order to remind themselves of the 'high' values that their ancestors maintained (Freitag 1997).

The socially responsible Yemeni entrepreneurial leaders discussed in the introduction to this chapter are products of the conservative Islamic regime that characterized the rural areas where many of them originated. The devotion of these areas was particularly evident before the rise of Arab nationalism and socialism in the 1950s and 1960s, when completion of reading the full text of the Qur'an by a family child was an event that often called for family celebration (Baynard 1980).

The leaders originating in these areas saw it as a duty to provide vital public services denied to local communities by either colonial regimes (the case in most of South Yemen and areas of Southeast Asia and Africa where many Yemenis settled) or an autocratic and backward Imamic regime (as in North Yemen).

Private sector Yemeni enterprises tend to be family owned. According to Roper and Cheney (2005, p. 99) the relative autonomy of privately owned companies allows the consistent pursuit of social values, sometimes against the prevailing wisdom of financial analysts and in marked contrast to some competitors. A close examination of some of the success stories of Yemeni entrepreneurs indicates that religion and the desire to address the inequalities of resource allocation and neglect by the state played an important role in their achievements both as successful entrepreneurs and as leaders (Burrowes 2011).

Yemenis, particularly those originating from the Hadramaut region, known as *Hadhrami*, developed a reputation in the eighteenth, nineteenth and twentieth centuries for being successful entrepreneurs, particularly in Southeast Asia, Africa, Saudi Arabia and Aden. Sir Richard Burton, the nineteenth century British orientalist, remarked, 'it is generally said that the sun does not rise upon a land that does not contain a man from Hadramaut' (Burton 1966, p. 58). Hadhramis were also famously known for their integrity and altruistic credentials which may be ascribed to their conservative Islamic upbringing. This is not surprising given that the region of Hadhramaut was historically known as an Islamic teaching centre (Le Guennec-Coppens 1997).

The Hadhrami diaspora began in the early eighteenth century and lasted up to the Second World War, by which time about 110 000 Hadhramis are thought to have lived in southeast Asia, some 90 000 of them in present day Indonesia (Lukas 2002, p. 5). The diaspora also extended to Africa, where they settled in areas such as Zanzibar, Kenya and the Comoros Islands.

In Singapore during the nineteenth century they formed an influential economic elite with substantial land holdings and trading widely in clothing, spices and tobacco. They also built mosques and schools and assisted in the upkeep of poor families (Bafana 1996 p. 5). This pattern of entrepreneurial success combined with social responsibility was repeated throughout the diaspora.

Hadhramis also became involved in politics. For example, in Malaysia, Sayyid Jamal al-Layl and his descendents have ruled the border state of Perlis since 1843 when they assisted the Sultan of Kedah in expelling the Thai occupiers. In East Africa, Sharif Abu Baker bin Sayyid Sharif Husayn became the king of Moheli in the Comoro Islands during the seventeenth century and Sayyid Abu Baker bin Sheikh al Masila Ba-Alawi was enthroned in Vanga and Wasini in southern Kenya in the early eighteenth century (Le Guennec-Coppens 1989, p. 185–91).

In Batavia (Jakarta) a group of wealthy Hadhrami entrepreneurs and property owners established Jamiyyat al-Khayr (Benevolent Society) in 1901, the main aim of which was to lay the foundation for a more modern type education, styled on a Western curriculum but incorporating more traditional Islamic subjects. The drive for education received a major boost in 1914 when Hadhrami merchants established the Arab Society for Reform and Guidance (Jamiyyat al-Islah wa al-Irshad al-Arabiyya), which exists to this date. It comprises over one hundred branches throughout Indonesia and has around 50 000 members, with activities including running kindergartens, primary and secondary schools and hospitals. The Irshadis saw education in languages and modern science as key to overcome the backwardness of the Islamic community and to bringing progress (Mobini-Kesheh 1997, pp. 231–40). In East Africa Hadhramis controlled the Islamic schools and played a significant role in the development of Swahili literature, especially poetry.

Hadhrami migrants in Southeast Asia and Africa also brought Islam with them, were largely responsible for the Islamization of those regions and were good ambassadors of their faith. However, it would be a mistake to assume that all Hadhrami entrepreneurs were of the high standard described so far. There is historical evidence of some Hadhrami engagement in money lending or usury (prohibited by Islam) (Clarence-Smith 1997, p. 301) and slave trading (Islam encourages the freeing of slaves) during the nineteenth century (Ewald and Clarence-Smith 1997, p. 290).

Saudi Arabia was another destination for the Hadhrami diaspora. In 1969 Hadhramis living in Saudi Arabia were estimated to number between 150 000 to 180 000 (Freitag 1997, p. 320). Many of them rose to become powerful entrepreneurs such as Salim Ahmed Ben Mahfouz, Abdullah Ahmed Baqshan, Bamawada, Bakhashab and Bin Laden. The businesses established by these people employ thousands of people and continue the socially responsible Hadhrami tradition. Many of them have charities such as the Awon Foundation and Taybah Welfare Association (IRIN 2007).

It is apparent from the foregoing that Yemen has an established indigenous tradition of entrepreneurship combined with a tradition of social responsibility, with entrepreneurial leaders making religious, educational and social provisions where the state has failed to do so. In the sections that follow I outline the political realities and challenges that exert constant pressure on such socially responsible entrepreneurs: and then present case studies of three diverse individuals who have provided inspirational leadership examples in spite of those challenges.

The Social, Economic and Political Realities of Yemen: Murder and Political Rivalry

Hardship and bloody struggle have been characteristic of the Yemeni experience in the post-colonial era. During the 1970s, wars between South Yemen and its dominant neighbour Saudi Arabia raged across their borders and a proxy war was conducted with Yemen's other neighbour, Oman, through support for the Popular Front for the Liberation of Oman and the Arabian Gulf (Barron 2008).

Some of the political violence of Yemen's recent history is discussed in the section above on economic and social development. More recently, after unification, a campaign of assassination killed or injured approximately a hundred southern officials. That this violence was associated with returned Arab-Afghan *mujahedeen* responding to the fall of the Soviet Union is indicative of Yemen's political complexity. The same 'Afghan' fighters would be involved in supporting President Saleh when civil war broke out in 1994 and North Yemen came out victorious. In this war, President Saleh was also helped by North Yemen's Zaydi tribal leaders. This event further strengthened the power of North Yemen's tribal leaders and encouraged the emergence of a powerful and influential Islamist elite which espoused the strict Wahhabi sect doctrine.

Before unification, border wars between South and North Yemen took place on a number of occasions. President Ali Abdulla Saleh, who comes from a tribal background, found it necessary to rely on the support of his country's powerful northern tribal leaders and a coterie of close friends and relatives to ensure his survival in this volatile region. Yemen's northern tribes were well armed and remained for a long time beyond government control; indeed, since 2004 there has been renewed armed confrontation in the north western province of Sana'a (Day

2008). President Saleh's attempts to protect his power base have had far-reaching effects on the political environment and have led to a *realpolitik* approach, the consequences of which are discussed below (Abdulhafez and al-Udeini 2006).

Economic Boom and Inflation

During the 1970s and the 1980s many Yemenis travelled to Saudi Arabia and other parts of the Gulf to work as low-paid manual labourers. The remittances sent by those labourers to their relatives in Yemen reached an annual record high of $1.4 billion (Carapico and Myntti 1991, p. 25) and were a vital source of hard currency for the country. The influx of this money into the country boosted trade, but at the same time created inflationary pressure in the economy. In 1990, with the Iraqi occupation of Kuwait, President Saleh failed to condemn Iraq's aggression. On that basis, he was deemed by many Gulf and world leaders to be sympathetic with the invaders rather than the victims, who had for a long time provided economic assistance to Yemen. The result was the repatriation of hundreds of thousands of Yemeni workers from Saudi Arabia and other countries. The effect of this action on the Yemeni economy was considerable. Many of those who were forced to return to Yemen suddenly found themselves out of work (Colton 2010).

President Saleh's awareness of the precarious nature of Yemen's politics, as discussed above, forced him to place great reliance on the support of North Yemen's powerful Zaidi tribal leaders, and on a large circle of his family members and tribesmen drawn from his own Zaidi tribe of Sanhan. The result was a new era of favouritism, nepotism, self-enrichment and corruption. Few state resources were available to spend on development projects or public utilities such water – in 2004 only 31 per cent of the population had access to safe drinking water (WHO 2006, p. 57) – or electricity, the supply of which is often cut off for several hours each day in many of the country's major cities. Yemen continues to be ranked at the bottom of the low income countries with a Gross National Income (GNI) of US $ 875 or less in 2005 (UNDP 2007, p. 375).

Another area that government money was withdrawn from was the salaries paid to government employees. With already low remuneration eroded by inflation, corruption among low-level government bureaucrats increased (Sultan 1993, p. 383). A field study of corruption in Yemen conducted by the Yemen Polling Centre and funded by the Centre for International Projects Enterprise (affiliated with the American Trade Chamber in Washington) revealed that low salaries and the absence of religious motives were the primary causes of the spread of bribery in Yemen

(Abdulhafez and al-Udeini 2006, p. 13). Transparency International, the organization engaged in measuring the level of worldwide, lists Yemen as number 141 of 179 countries with a Corruption Perceptions Index (CPI) in 2008 of 2.3: the worst is Somalia with a CPI of 1.0 and the best is Denmark, CPI 9.3 (Transparency International 2009).

EMERGING YEMENI LEADERSHIP: A NEW BREED OF PRAGMATIC ENTREPRENEURIAL LEADERS

The economic situation described above has allowed new elite groups to prosper, if at the expense of the population as a whole. A USAID report (Robinson et al. 2006, p. v) identifies five elite groups as the main beneficiaries from the structure of corruption in Yemen. These are consistent with the concept of 'merchant, shaykh, officer and modernist' described by Alley (2010). The two most important are also the two with the most overlap: tribes and the military-security establishment. Leaders of key tribes contribute the lion's share of senior military and security officers.

The third powerful elite group is the business community. There is some overlap with the military-security elite as Yemen's military controls an extensive array of commercial activities, some legal and some extra-legal. However, the traditional business elite are non-tribal, and they have remained important players in this new political economy, although their relative decline and generally pessimistic view of Yemen's future have prompted some businesses to leave the country. In addition, a parasitic bourgeoisie of tribal businesses has grown in recent years and derives virtually all of its income from state contracts, often awarded under corrupt circumstances (Alley 2010). The distinctiveness of the business community has been further superseded in the person of President Saleh himself. In 1997 this 'army and tribal man par excellence' became a partner in the prominent business and industrial enterprise Hayel Saeed Anam (HSA) (Alley 2010). The HSA group is generally considered an example of the socially responsible leadership that still exists in Yemen. The group is still run by members of the family of Hayel Saeed Anaam, discussed further in a case study in this chapter, who are still running and expanding his commercial empire, which has a strong presence in Yemen and a growing global expansion programme.

A further type of elite group is the 'dispensable' elite which consists of the technocratic class that remains essential to run the state in a relatively modern way, and regional elites that enjoy high status within important local constituencies. The state has far more ability to promote and demote individuals within these elite groups than it does with tribal, military and business elites.

In this new phase of Yemen's political and socio-economic development a new breed of leaders has emerged who show entrepreneurial advancement and a broad commitment to transformational leadership in business practices (Sadler 2004). They fit Weber's (1924/1947) description of 'pragmatic' leaders who often tend to have an in-depth understanding of the social system and the causal operating variables and who exhibit Machiavellian tendencies epitomized by a lack of moral system and willingness to manipulate others in order to achieve their objectives (Bedell, Hunter, Angie and Vert 2006, p. 65; see also Collinson 2005). In the case of Yemen, this is exemplified by a culture of corruption and bribery (Strategic Media 2005): however, evidence for future hope for more ethical business and social relations is given in the case studies of entrepreneurial and inspirational leaders that follow.

The Particular Case of Women: Inequality and Discrimination

Evidence from Yemen's history suggests that women were able to assume important leadership roles (Ahmed 2003). The case of the pre-Islamic Bilqis or Queen of Sheba (mentioned in this chapter's introduction) is one major example. The Qur'an portrays this queen in a very positive way, describing her as a prudent leader who was prepared to listen to advice when faced with a major dilemma – a demand from King Solomon that she and her people give up worship of the sun and instead worship his God. Her advisers informed her that they would accept whatever decision she took (out of pure belief in her leadership qualities); she visited King Solomon in person to appease him with gifts and when Solomon refused these she declared her faith in his religion, thus sparing her people destruction.

Yemen also produced two great Islamic female leaders during the eleventh and twelfth centuries who shared power with their husbands but ruled in their own names: Queen Asma al-Sulayhiyya (1066–1074 CE) and her daughter-in-law Queen Arwa (1074–1138 CE). They were the only two queens in Muslim Arab history to have had the Friday *khutbahs* (sermons) pronounced in their names (Colburn 2002, p. 25).

Many Yemeni women played an important role during the struggle against Turkish occupation and Imamic rule in North Yemen (al-Siyaghi 2005) and British occupation in South Yemen (Ahmed 2003). Despite this tradition of female leadership and political activism, many Yemeni women, as is the case in many Arab countries, continue to suffer from various forms of inequality (Molyneux 1979). Women, particularly in rural areas, are sometimes denied their full inheritance by male members of their family without their knowledge and without any legal justification, and engagement in commercial activity by Yemeni women is often discouraged by local custom and tradition.

In rural areas, only 30 per cent of girls, as opposed to 73 per cent of boys, are enrolled in primary education. Nearly 86 per cent of working women are in the agricultural sector, largely as non-waged workers. No laws exist to protect women from sexual harassment and women who end up in prison or detained (especially for cases involving moral issues) are often abused by their male prison or police officials (Metcalfe 2008). Yemeni women are also hugely under-represented in the judiciary and government bodies. There are other social, cultural and health factors that impact on Yemeni women negatively, such as lack of reproductive health-care (especially in rural areas) and lack of legal provisions to safeguard their freedom to make decisions about their health or reproductive rights. Moreover, some harmful traditional practices, such as female genital mutilation, still exist in some Yemeni regions (Basha 2005).

Representation of women in parliament has declined from 11 (all originating in former socialist South Yemen) in 1993 to only one in the 1997 election, even though the number of women registered to vote increased from 18 per cent in 1993 to 27 per cent in 1997 and 42 per cent in 2003. As discussed in Chapter 13 of this volume, this lack of women's representation is common to many ME states.

The socialist regime of South Yemen which ruled from 1968 to 1994 tore down many of the traditional barriers which relegated women to second class citizen status. Women were encouraged to go out unveiled and to join the police, army and other public professions. In 1974, the South Yemeni regime passed a new Family Code which abolished divorce by repudiation, limited polygamy to exceptional circumstances, gave divorced women child custody rights and outlawed early marriages and marriages arranged without the consent of both parties (Molyneux 1979, p. 7). Some women were even promoted to high positions in the political apparatus of the ruling party.

In the more conservative and largely tribal and rural North, Yemeni women's rights continued to be ignored. The government of the new unified Yemen even implemented a new Personal Status Law in 1992 which opted to integrate the more conservative and discriminatory laws that previously applied under North Yemen's family codes. This has resulted in the annulment of the equal status of women that was enshrined in South Yemen's family code of 1974 (Basha 2005).

Furthermore, the support President Saleh received from radical Islamists in the 1994 civil war forced him to tolerate the growth of a Wahhabi-style (i.e. strict) form of Islam. They have built religious schools based on Wahhabi teaching and fostered a Wahhabi culture which has impacted negatively on women. Many urban women, who in the past were able to walk or work without covering their faces, found themselves obliged to cover themselves in black from head to toe. Non-compliance with this new code of public 'decency' was often met with verbal abuse (Metcalfe 2008).

The Yemeni civil service and public sector are the main providers of employment for the Yemeni workforce. However, women only represent 9.3 per cent of that workforce (Basha 2005). Many of them fail to advance to leadership positions despite their high qualifications. Some Yemeni women activists attribute this issue to traditional factors such as male perceptions of women as weak and to badly formed Islamic views held by religious clerics (al-Ajel 2007). Moreover, in a largely corrupt and male dominated public workforce, where corruption thrives and relies on personal relations and connections, it is difficult to see how women can advance their careers. Research has shown that women are less likely to engage in corrupt practices than men (Amos-Wilson 1999, p. 130; Hashmi 2005; Honour, Barry and Palnitkar 1998, pp. 195–196; Macharia 2007; Olubi 2006). Corruption, according to an African female leader, can bring disgrace, and women hate to tarnish the image of their husbands and families (Olubi 2006).

CASE STUDIES

Entrepreneurial Leadership During and After British Rule in South Yemen: The Case of Hayel Saeed Anaam

In this section I present a case study of an individual who embodies the distinctive attributes of Yemeni leadership described earlier in this chapter. Hayel Saeed Amaan had a traditional grounding in knowledge of the Qur'an and in living according to its tenets. He was a successful entrepreneur who looked, and travelled, beyond his native North Yemen to begin his entrepreneurial venture; he was a self-transformational leader who advanced from a poor weaver to control one of Yemen's most significant corporations; and he was throughout his career a socially responsible business leader. He has become an icon of Yemeni success in business and a role model for his high standards of integrity and philanthropic qualities.

This case study is based on interviews held with members of his family and some of his surviving staff and friends by Egyptian journalist al-Ashmawi (2004) and al-Saqqaf, a journalist from Yemen (2003). Additional information was obtained from one of his relatives, Dirhim

Abdo Saeed, Head of Longulf, a subsidiary of the Hayel Saeed Anaam (HSA) Group.

Hayel was born in 1902 in the Ta'izz province of North Yemen, then still part of the Ottoman empire. As well as studying the Qur'an he learned weaving skills from his father and then had an early introduction to entrepreneurial activity when he would accompany his father to market with the cloth they produced. However, economic circumstances forced him to look for employment outside Yemen, perhaps inspired in part by the Qur'anic verse 'And whoever fears Allah – He will make for him a way out', which his son Abdul Wasa Hayel remembered him repeating often and believing very strongly.

Working passage on a French merchant ship out of Aden, Hayel progressed to a job in an oil factory in Marseille and then became supervisor in another French factory. He was able to employ a number of fellow Yemenis and became more religious and close to Arabic friends from North Africa with *sufi* Islamic leanings. The outbreak of World War II found him in Somalia working as an agent in animal hides for a French businessman based in Aden. After setbacks including the sinking of the ship carrying his first consignment, Hayel began to succeed and found himself importing cloth and food products from Aden and selling them in Somalia. He became known as a responsible and honest trader and because of this he was able to take a significant step in developing his business when French company Besse & Co. agreed to supply him with large quantities of goods on credit.

Following the departure of the British from South Yemen in 1967 Hayel, along with other businessmen, had assets nationalized and property seized. However, Hayel had already established some presence in North Yemen, encouraged by the overthrow of the Imamic regime in 1962. Despite the loss of his assets in Aden, Hayel continued to honour his debt obligations to the foreign companies that provided him with goods on credit. He owed $1.5 million, a great deal of money at that time, and while others claimed *force majeur* and wrote off debts, he asked for a grace period of six months. In fact, Hayel was able to pay back his entire debt within three months. This further enhanced his reputation for honest and responsible trading and was an important factor in his success after he left Aden. His son, Abdul Wasa Hayel, maintains that integrity and honesty have been the mainstay of their success: 'Because we have established ourselves over the years as good reliable partners, the companies we deal with often give us favourable payment conditions without us even asking' (Strategic Media 2005, p. 14).

Hayel expanded his business empire further when he moved into manufacturing, building Yemen's first food factory, reputedly inspired by a crowd of Yemeni school children demonstrating against the small portions of jam and cheese in their food. The entire business grew to become a global conglomerate with an estimated turnover of close to $2 billion and employing some 22000 people worldwide, of whom 19000 people are in Yemen alone. During his life, Hayel's responsibility as an entrepreneur was widely acknowledged. He helped build schools, mosques and roads. As well as supporting stakeholders in the wider community, his social responsibility extended to his workforce. He was known to be very close to his subordinates, listened to their concerns, helped resolve their problems and visited them when they fell sick. His behaviour with his employees was described as being more akin to the behaviour of a trade union official than that of an owner of a business.

Hayel died in 1990 but his legacy continues through one of Yemen's major companies, the HSA Group, managed by his sons, grandsons and other members of his family and maintaining a reputation for corporate social responsibility. The HSA Group is pouring substantial resources into the al-Saeed Foundation, the Group's main charitable organization which supports initiatives in poverty relief; support of orphans, disabled and elderly people and widows; building and renovating schools and mosques; and proving assistance to many civil society organizations who work in the humanitarian, educational and developmental fields.

SELF-TRANSFORMATIONAL FEMALE YEMENI LEADERS: TWO CASE STUDIES

As described earlier, the environment for Yemeni women is socially and culturally challenging. Despite this, a few female figures rose to lead highly successful careers with leadership responsibilities and to become leadership role models for many Yemeni women. Case studies of two women are presented here, each coming from a totally different social and educational background: they are Amat al-Alim al-Sowsowa and the woman known in Yemen as the Queen of Oranges, Amena al-Imrani.

Both women have gone through a long process of struggle in a male-dominated culture and succeeded in overcoming the traditional, cultural and stereotypical barriers that contributed to Yemeni women's marginalization, poverty and backwardness, eventually becoming leaders. They typify the model of self-transformational leadership described earlier.

Amat al-Alim al-Sowsowa

Born in 1958 to a relatively liberal family in the city of Taiz, Amat al-Alim started working on her family's farm when she was nine but soon left when she began to stand out at school through hard work and enthusiasm. One of the people who stood by her and supported her was her mother who did not want her, according to Amat al-Alim, to end up like her. Her mother struggled financially after the death of her father (a poor local judge), a situation which led the young Amat al-Alim to aspire to a more equitable society where women would be less dependent on their men.

Amat al-Alim's first involvement with the media came at age eight when she participated in the chorus of a children's show on a local radio station. Then at the age of 12 she became a news announcer, sitting on her mother's lap in order to reach the microphone. While studying in Egypt, she would go home in the summers to work. During one visit she walked into a local television station, where the chief suggested she read the news. She was 17. 'My hair was pulled back in braids. I had no makeup or great features, and I was scared to face the camera. I tried out and was ordered to anchor the news that night. Next morning, I was the news of the town,' she was later to recall (Boustany 2003).

She also worked as a journalist on the local newspaper where she found fame writing a widely read column which focused on women's rights. She later moved to television to work on a children's programme. She encountered a great deal of male hostility when she appeared unveiled on television, was attacked in the local newspapers and mosques and was accused of single handedly leading Yemen's women astray. Despite the pressure she persisted in this role. In addition she obtained a BA in Mass Communications from Cairo University and later gained a USAID scholarship to study for a Master's degree in International Communications at the American University in Washington DC. In 1984 she became Deputy TV Programmes Director at Sanaa TV, the most senior position in Yemen to be held by a woman at that time. She was also Chief Editor of Mutabaat Elamiah, a monthly magazine specializing in communications and media affairs.

Describing her problems with the people who saw her setting a bad example to other women she says: 'The men looked at me as a representative of all women. If I failed they would say that all women were no good. But at the same time that gave me the strength to continue, to struggle more, to fight more' (Arabia Felix 2005).

Amat al-Alim joined the General People's Congress (GPC), Yemen's ruling party. She became Undersecretary at Yemen's Ministry of Information from 1997 to 1999 and Chairperson of the National Women's Committee. A vocal proponent of women's rights, she led the Yemeni Women's Union from 1989 to 1991.

She was later appointed Yemen's ambassador to Sweden, Denmark and the Netherlands, where she was Yemen's Permanent Representative to the Organization for the Prohibition of Chemical Weapons, based in

The Hague. After her ambassadorial assignment she became Minister of Human Rights in Yemen in 2003. After that appointment, she became the first woman human rights minister in Yemen's history. During her tenure in this office she initiated the country's first national human rights report, and established a public human rights resource centre.

In March 2006 Amat al-Alim was appointed Assistant Secretary-General, Assistant Administrator of UNDP and Director of its Regional Bureau for Arab States in New York. This was a major career achievement for Amat al-Alim who began her international career as a consultant to UNDP and its sister agencies.

Amat al-Alim should be considered an inspirational leader and role model for her achievement in a male-dominated profession, for her persistence in the face of very public criticism and for her profile on both the national and the international political stage. She has published and lectured extensively and received numerous awards and distinctions, including Officier dans l'Ordre National de la Légion d'Honneur (France) and the Medal of the Egyptian Committee for Afro-Asian Solidarity (Egypt).

Amena al-Imrani (the Queen of Oranges)

Like Amat al-Alim, Amena al-Imrani was of a poor family background. Unlike the cultured and USA-educated Amat al-Alim, Amena is an illiterate in her late fifties who built a small empire selling fruit and became known as the 'Queen of Oranges'. She started business selling coral necklaces: when a woman who owed money promised Amena that when her peaches ripen she would sell them and pay her, Amena instead accepted the peaches and sold them herself. The profit she made on this transaction started her story in fruit.

She started selling fruit to retail buyers, helping to support her husband and her daughters (now numbering seven). Just as Amat al-Alim's mother supported her daughter, Amena's husband supported his wife, unlike her mother and brothers who thought she was shaming the family and refused to talk to her for many years. This is understandable, given the conservative culture of Yemeni society and the fact that she was dealing with men deemed to be at the bottom of the social hierarchy.

Interestingly, Amena now supports many of the family members who once ostracized her. Interviews with some Arab female leaders indicate that parents play an important role in shaping the character and self-confidence of those leaders, which lends support to the widely accepted view that early socialization is an important factor in shaping people's personal traits and other leadership qualities (Al-Lamky 2006, p. 56). This was clearly evident in the case of Amat al-Alim. In the case of Amena, however, her husband was the source of much of the support and encouragement she needed.

Amena works every day from sunrise to late in the evening and never takes weekend breaks. Her only day of rest is the first day of *Eid*. Her hard work, perseverance and honesty paid off in a near monopoly of the orange market in Yemen through buying directly from a large list of farmers (about 400) across the whole country and selling to retailers in Sanaa's central fruit market. She also exports fruit to several Arab countries including Saudi Arabia, Egypt and Sudan. She sells almost 200 tons of fruit daily, employs 40 staff and operates a fleet of lorries. She thinks her title 'Queen of Oranges' does not do her justice and prefers to be called the 'Fruit Madam' as a testimony to her ability to beat men in all types of fruit, not just oranges. She named her company *Nasr* (victory) in order to reflect this fact (Al-Hammadi 2007).

Despite her inability to read or write, Amena has a strong (and numerate) memory with an intimate understanding of how the fruit market works which enables her to work out every aspect of her daily income, thus preventing any possibility of being cheated by her employees.

Like Amat al-Alim, Amena is a self-confident woman who refused to cover her face and who stood in the face of many cultural and traditional challenges and succeeded. However, what makes Amena a unique case is her ability to make it in the face of overwhelming odds; poverty, lack of education, age, a male-dominated society hostile to women, a highly competitive market whose clients are men of largely low social status and family opposition.

Amena does value education. She sent all her daughters to private schools and hopes to see them graduate from university and eventually help her in her business. However, she sees hard work as central to any success. Many educated people, according to her, are unable to benefit from their educational certificates.

Amena's entrepreneurial success was recognized by many local (including the president of Yemen) and international observers as unique. Her advice to other women is summed up in these words: 'tell them you can take the initiative even if you have nothing. Just have the motivation, just have in mind that you can do it, and you will do it' (Elwazer 2007).

FUTURE CHALLENGES FOR LEADERSHIP DEVELOPMENT

Yemen has a complex modern history of post-colonial transition, state formation and conflict. Many of the challenges it faces in terms of natural resources and their allocation, corruption and political instability are common to the rest of the region. However, Yemen can also draw on a rich tradition of leadership, both in entrepreneurial commerce based on the Hadhrami entrepreneurs discussed in this chapter and modern women leaders who can be considered in a tradition going back to Bilqis.

Yemen's modern history was largely shaped by political forces (both foreign and indigenous) that did little to improve the welfare or wellbeing of its people, particularly those who came from poor rural backgrounds. Ironically, many Yemeni individuals (largely of rural backgrounds) rose to become amongst the wealthiest people of their generation, commanding the respect and admiration of large sectors of society. This is shown in the case studies above. Many of those successful entrepreneurs built a reputation for themselves based on a strong adherence to high moral values such as integrity and altruism which reflected their conservative Islamic upbringing. Moreover, they were also hardworking and industrious people who valued work and their workers. They became socially responsible (and transformational) leaders who took upon themselves the task of making a difference to the lives of many people by providing work opportunities and, in many situations, vital social services denied to them by the state.

Yemen's volatile and sometimes violent political history has had an impact on the country's development and economic future. Many Yemenis (such as those who originated from Hadhramaut) migrated from their own country to different regions of the world and built successful, socially responsible enterprises that continue to exit to this day, while some held public leadership roles in their new societies.

Despite a government-driven programme of democratization and pluralism, political (and consequently economic) power is still largely vested in a small number of people. In this atmosphere, a new type of 'pragmatic' entrepreneurial leadership emerged. This issue was not discussed in any great details in this article, but could provide an interesting topic for future research. As Alley (2010) has asserted, the politics of patronage is complex and continually shifting.

Despite inheriting a tradition of female leadership, Yemen, like many other Arab countries, continues to exercise numerous forms of discrimination against women which impact negatively on their social and economic wellbeing. However, a growing number of Yemeni women are taking a more proactive lead of their lives despite hostility from many sectors of Yemen's traditional society and in some instances from their own relatives. Some managed to self-transform themselves and became successful leaders both of men and women. This chapter presented two examples of such women.

REFERENCES

Abdulhafez, A. and K. Al-Udeini (2006), *Bribery in Yemen*, Sana'a: Yemen Polling Centre.

Ahmed, S.M. (2003), 'Yemeni revolution festivals: the feminist role in confronting the occupation: the woman took part in the battle fronts . . . and led demonstrations against the British occupation' accessed 4 November 2010 at www.26sep. net/newsweekprint.php?lng=arabic&sid=6657.

Al-Ajel, F. (2007), 'Female leadership ignored in Muslim countries', *Yemen Times*, accessed 4 November 2010 at www.yementimes.com/defaultdet. aspx?SUB_ID=25396.

Albahar, A. (1996), 'A page from the past', *Al-Mahjar*, **1** (1).

Alexander, J. and M. Wilson (2005), 'Foundations of responsible leadership: from self-insight to integrity and altruism', in J. Doh, and S. Stumpf (eds), *Handbook on Responsible Leadership and Governance in Global Business*, Cheltenham, UK and Northampton, MA, USA: Edward Elgar.

Alley, A.L. (2010), 'The rules of the game: unpacking patronage and politics in Yemen', *Middle East Journal*, **64** (3), 387–409.

Alves, J.C. *et al.* (2006), 'A cross-cultural perspective of self-leadership', *The Journal of Managerial Psychology*, **21** (4), 338–59.

Amos-Wilson, P. (1999), 'The women in blue shalwar-kameez', *Women in Management Review*, **14** (4), 128–35.

Arabia Felix (2005), 'Amat al-Alim al-Soswa: Minister of Human Rights', *Arabia Felix*, accessed at 30 March 2010 www.arabia-felix.com/arabia-felix-3.html.

Artzy, M. (1994), 'Incense, camels and collared rim jars: desert trade routes and maritime outlets in the second millennium', *Oxford Journal of Archaeology*, **13** (2), 121–47.

Al-Ashmawi, A. (2004), 'Hayel Saeed: A legend of charitable practice', *Al-Ahram Al-Arabia*, accessed 4 November 2010 at arabi.ahram.org.eg/arabi/ Ahram/2004/7/3/HYAH5.htm.

Asongu, J.J. (2007), 'The history of corporate social responsibility', *The Journal of Business and Public Policy*, **1** (2), 1–18.

Bafana, H. (1996), 'The Arab identity: Dilemma or non issue?', *Al-Mahjar*, **1** (1)

Barron, O. (2008), 'Things fall apart: Violence and poverty in Yemen', *Harvard International Review*, Summer, 12–13, accessed 4 November 2010 at www.entrepreneur.com/tradejournals/article/184710760.html.

Basha, A. (2005), 'Women's rights in the Middle East and North Africa: Yemen (a special country report)', *Freedom House*, accessed 4 November 2010 at www. freedomhouse.org/template.cfm?page=384&key=26&parent=2&report=56.

Bass, B.M. (1997), 'The ethics of transformational leadership', in *Kellogg Leadership Studies Project*, transformational leadership working papers, The James MacGregor Burns Academy of Leadership.

Bass, B.M. and B.J. Avolio (1994), 'Introduction', in B.M. Bass and B.J. Avolio (eds), *Improving Organizational Effectiveness Through Transformational Leadership*, Thousand Oaks, CA: Sage.

Bass, B.M. and R.E Riggio (2006), *Transformational Leadership*, 2nd edn, Mahwah, NJ: Lawrence Erlbaum Associates.

Bass, B.M. and P. Steidlmeier (1999), 'Ethics, character, and authentic transformational leadership behavior', *The Leadership Quarterly*, **10** (2), 181–217.

Baynard, S. *et al.* (1980), 'Historical setting', in R. Nyrob (ed), *The Yemens: Country Studies*, The American University Foreign Area Studies, Washington, DC: Foreign Area Studies.

Bedell, K., S. Hunter, A. Angie and A. Vert (2006), 'A historiometric examination of Machiavellianism and a new taxonomy of leadership', *Journal of Leadership and Organizational Studies*, **12** (4), 50–72.

Beekun, R.I. and J. Badawi (1999), *Leadership: An Islamic Perspective*, Beltsville, MA: Amana Publications.

Bidwell, R. (1983), *The Two Yemens*, Harlow and Colorado, USA: Longman-Westview.

Boustany, N. (2003), 'Our enemy in Yemen is ignorance', *Gulf News (Online Edition)*, 14 September, accessed 4 November 2010 at www.mafhoum.com/press6/160S30.htm.

Bowen, Howard (1953), *Social Responsibilities of the Businessman,* New York: Harper & Brothers.

Burns, J.M. (1978), *Leadership*, New York: Harper & Row.

Burrowes, Robert D. (2011), 'Republic of Yemen', in David E. Long, Bernard Reich and Mark Gasiorowski (eds), *The Government and Politics of the Middle East and North Africa*, 6th edn, Philadelphia, PA: Westview Press, pp. 205–32.

Burton, R.F. (1966), *First Footsteps in East Africa*, 3rd edn, London: Routledge and Kegan Paul.

Carapico, S. (1998), *Civil Society in Yemen: The Political Economy of Activism in Modern Arabia*, Cambridge: Cambridge University Press.

Carapico, S. and C. Myntti (1991), 'Change in North Yemen 1977–1989: A tale of two families', *Middle East Report*, 170, pp. 24–47.

Ciulla, J.B. (2005), 'Integrating leadership with ethics: is good leadership contrary to human nature?', in J. Doh, and S. Stumpf (eds), *Handbook on Responsible Leadership and Governance in Global Business*, Cheltenham, UK and Northampton, MA, USA: Edward Elgar.

Clarence-Smith, W.G. (1997), 'Hadhrami entrepreneurs in the Malay world, c. 1740 to c. 1940', in U. Freitag and W. Clarence-Smith (eds), *Hadrami Traders, Scholars, and Statesmen in the Indian Ocean, 1750s – 1960s*, Leiden, Netherlands: Brill.

Cohen, J.M. and D.B. Lewis (1979), 'Capital-surplus, labor-short economies: Yemen as a challenge to rural development strategies', *American Journal of Agricultural Economics*, **61** (3), 523–28.

Colburn, M. (2002), *The Republic of Yemen: Development Challenges in the 21st Century*, London: Stacey International.

Collins, J.C. and J.I. Porras (2000), *Built to Last: Successful Habits of Visionary Companies*, 3rd edn, London: Random House Business Books.

Collinson, D. (2005), 'Dialectics of leadership', *Human Relations*, **58** (11), 1419–42.

Colton, N.A. (2010), 'Yemen: a collapsed economy', *Middle East Journal*, **64** (3), 410–26.

Conger, J.A. (1999), 'Charismatic and transformational leadership in organizations: an insider's perspective on these developing streams of research', *The Leadership Quarterly*, **10** (2) 145–79.

Elwazer, S. (2007), 'Yemen's "Queen of Oranges"', CNN, 28 December, accessed 4 November 2010 at http://edition.cnn.com/2007/BUSINESS/12/28/queen.oranges/index.html#cnnSTCVideo.

Ewald, J. and W.G. Clarence-Smith (1997), 'The economic role of the Hadhrami

Diaspora in the Red Sea and the Gulf of Aden', in U. Freitag, and W.G Clarence-Smith (eds), *Hadrami Traders, Scholars, and Statesmen in the Indian Ocean, 1750s – 1960s*, Leiden, Netherlands: Brill.

Ford, J. (2006), 'Examining leadership through critical feminist readings', *Journal of Health Organisation and Management*, **19** (3), p. 236–51.

Freitag, U. (1997), 'Conclusion: the diaspora since the age of independence', in U. Freitag, and W.G. Clarence-Smith (eds), *Hadrhami Traders, Scholars, and Statesmen in the Indian Ocean, 1750s–1960s*, Leiden, Netherlands: Brill.

Friedman, Milton (1970), 'The social responsibility of business is to increase its profits', *The New York Times Magazine*, 13 September, pp. 32–3.

Gentile, M.G. (2006), 'Is there free will in business? Leadership and social impact management', in J.P. Doh and S.A. Stumpf, *Handbook on Responsible Leadership and Governance in Global Business*, Cheltenham, UK and Northampton, MA, USA: Edward Elgar.

Grint, Keith (2000), *Work and Society*, Cambridge: Polity Press.

Grint, Keith (2005), 'Problems, problems, problems: the social construction of leadership', *Human Relations*, **58**, 1467–94.

Le Guennnec-Coppens, F. (1989), 'Social and cultural integration: a case study of the East African Hadramis', *Journal of the International African Institute*, **59** (2), 185–95.

Le Guennnec-Coppens, F. (1997), 'Changing patterns of Hadhrami migration and social integration in East Africa', in U. Freitag, and W.G. Clarence-Smith (eds), *Hadrhami Traders, Scholars, and Statesmen in the Indian Ocean, 1750s–1960s*, Leiden, Netherlands: Brill.

Halliday, F. (2007), 'Yemen: murder in Arabia Felix', *Open Democracy*, accessed 4 November 2010 at www.opendemocracy.net/gloablisation/global_politics/yemen_murder_arabia_felix.

Al-Hammadi, K. (2007), 'The Queen of Yemen's oranges', *Mareb Press*, 1 September, accessed 4 November 2010 at http://marebpress.net/articles.php?print=2448.

Handy, C. (2002), 'What's a business for?', *Harvard Business Review*, **80** (11), 96–102.

Hashmi, H. (2005), 'Psychology: are women less corrupt?', *Daily Times*, 29 September, accessed 4 November 2010 at www.dailytimes.com.pk/default.asp?page=story_29-9-2005_pg3_5.

Hazlett, S., R. McAdam and L. Murray (2007), 'From quality management to socially responsible organisations: the case for CSR', *International Journal of Quality & Reliability Management*, **24** (7), 669–82.

Honour, T., J. Barry and S. Palnitkar (1998), 'Gender and public service: a case study of Mumbai', *The International Journal of Public Service Management*, **11** (2/3), 188–200.

IRIN (2007), 'Yemen: Saudi charities boost health, education projects', *IRIN*, accessed 4 November 2010 at www.alertnet.org/thenews/newsdesk/IRIN/688f51bc1cb5cddec8cafff9d592985f.htm.

Jenkins, R. (2005), 'Globalization, corporate social responsibility and poverty', *International Affairs*, **81** (3), 525–40.

Jonge, H. (1993), 'Discord and solidarity among the Arabs in the Netherlands East Indies, 1900–1942', *Indonesia, The East Indies and the Dutch*, Vol 55, pp. 73–90.

Karp, T. (2003), 'Socially responsible leadership', *Foresight*, **5** (2), 15–23.

Krishnan, V.R. (2001), 'Value systems of transformational leaders', *Leadership and Organization Development Journal*, **22** (3), 126–31.

Al-Lamky, A. (2007), 'Feminizing leadership in Arab societies: the perspectives of Omani female leaders', *Women in Management Review*, **22** (1), 49–67.

Lee, Min-Dong Paul (2008), 'A review of the theories of corporate social responsibility: its evolutionary path and the road ahead', *International Journal of Management Reviews*, **10** (1), 53–73.

Lukas, H. (2002), 'The perception of Indonesia's history and culture by Western historians and social scientists', a paper based on a one-day seminar organised by the Indonesian Embassy, 16 December, Brussels.

Maak, T. (2007), 'Responsible leadership, stakeholder engagement, and the emergence of social capital', *Journal of Business Ethics*, **74** (4), 329–43.

Macharia, L. (2007), 'Why there are such few women business leaders in Kenya and what to do about it', *Business Daily*, 26 October, accessed at www.bdafrica.com/index.php?option=com_content&task=view&id=3917.

Manz, C.C. (1986), 'Self-leadership: toward an expanded theory of self-influence processes in organizations', *The Academy of Management Review*, **11** (3), 585–600.

MEDEA (2008), 'Yemen', accessed 28 October 2010 at www.medea.be/index.html?page=2&lang=en&doc=208.

Milton-Edwards, B. (2009), *Contemporary Politics in the Middle East*, 2nd edn, Cambridge, and Malden, MA: Polity Press.

Mobini-Kesheh, N. (1997), 'Islamic modernism in Colonial Java: the al-Irshad movement', in U. Freitag, and W.G. Clarence-Smith (eds), *Hadhrami Traders, Scholars, and Statesmen in the Indian Ocean, 1750s–1960s*, Leiden, Netherlands: Brill.

Mohammed, J.A. (2007), 'Corporate social responsibility in Islam', unpublished PhD thesis submitted to the Faculty of Business at the Auckland University of Technology, New Zealand.

Molyneux, M. (1979), 'Women and revolution in the People's Democratic Republic of Yemen', *Feminist Review*, **1**, 4–20.

Neck, C.P. (2006), 'Two decades of self-leadership theory and research: past developments, present trends, and future possibilities', *Journal of Management Psychology*, **21** (4), 270–95.

Olubi, Dotun (2006), 'Women are less corrupt than men, says award winning teacher', accessed 29 October 2010 at www.sunnewsonline.com/webpages/features/womanofthesun/2006/june/13/womanofthesun-13-06-2006-004.htm.

Orlitzky, M., F.L. Schmidt and S.R. Rynes (2003), 'Corporate social and financial performance: a meta-analysis', *Organization Studies*, **24** (3), 403–41.

Othman, M.R. (1997), 'Hadramis in the politics and administration of the Malay States in the late eighteenth and nineteenth centuries', in U. Freitag and W.G. Clarence-Smith (eds), *Hadrhami Traders, Scholars, and Statesmen in the Indian Ocean, 1750s–1960s*, Leiden, Netherlands: Brill.

Ovendale, R. (1998), *The Middle East Since 1914*, 2nd edn, London: Addison Wesley Longman.

Parry, K.W. and Proctor-Thomson S.B. (2002), 'Perceived integrity of transformational leaders in organisational settings', *Journal of Business Ethics*, **35** (2), 75–96.

Ples, N.M. (2007), 'Understanding responsible leadership: role identity and motivational drivers: the case of Dame Anita Roddick, founder of The Body Shop', *Journal of Business Ethics*, **74** (4), 437–56.

Roddick, A. (2000), *Business As Unusual,* London: Thorsons.

Roper, J. and G. Cheney (2005), 'Leadership, learning and human resource management: the meanings of social entrepreneurship today', *Corporate Governance,* **5** (3), 95–9.

Sadler, D. (2004), 'Anti-corporate campaigning and corporate "social" responsibility: towards alternative spaces of citizenship', *Antipode,* **36** (5), 851–70.

Al-Saqqaf, I. (2003), 'A story of a blessed Yemeni man', *Yemen Times,* accessed at http://yementimes.com/print_article.shtml?i=789&p=report&a=1.

Al-Siyaghi, N. (2005), 'Special edition for the 43rd anniversary of the revolution: women who helped the revolutionaries with support and participation', accessed at www.26sep.net/newsweekprint.php?lng=arabic&sid=22552.

Shackley, Myra (2002), 'The frankincense route: a proposed cultural itinerary for the Middle East', *Historic Environment,* **16** (2), 12–17.

Shahin, A.I. and P.L. Wright (2004), 'Leadership in the context of culture: an Egyptian perspective', *The Leadership and Organisation Development Journal,* **25** (6), 499–511.

Strategic Media (2005), 'Yemen: poised to prosper', *Foreign Affairs,* November/December 2005 accessed 4 November 2010 at www.smlstrategicmedia.com/yemen1.html.

Sultan, N. (1993), 'Bureaucratic corruption as a consequence of the Gulf migration: the case of North Yemen', *Crime, Law and Social Change,* **19** (4), 379–93.

Transparency International (2009), 'Corruption Perception Index 2008', *Transparency International,* accessed 4 November 2010 at http://transparency.org/content/download/46187/739801/.

van Tulder, R. and A. van der Zwart (2006), *International Business-Society Management,* London and New York: Routledge.

United Nations Development Programme (UNDP) (2003), *Ownership, Leadership and Transformation: Can We Do Better for Capacity Development,* New York: UNDP.

UNDP (2007), *Human Development Report 2007/2008,* New York: UNDP.

UNDP (2009), *Arab Human Development Report 2009: Challenges to Human Security in the Arab Countries,* New York: UNDP.

Utting, P. (2005), 'Corporate responsibility and the movement of business', *Development in Practice,* **15** (3/4), 375–88.

Utting, P. (2006), 'Challenging the knowledge business', in P. Utting (ed.), *Reclaiming Development Agendas,* UNRISD, Basingstoke: Palgrave Macmillan.

Waldman, D.A and D. Siegel (2005), 'The influence of CEO transformational leadership on firm-level commitment to corporate social responsibility', in J. Doh and S. Stumpf (eds), *Handbook on Responsible Leadership and Governance in Global Business,* Cheltenham, UK and Northampton, MA, USA: Edward Elgar.

Weber, M. (1924[1947]), *The Theory of Social and Economic Organization,* translated by A. M. Henderson and T. Parsons, New York: The Free Press.

World Health Organization (WHO) (2006), *Health System Profile: Yemen,* Cerio: WHO Regional Health Systems Observatory.

Yukl, G. (1999), 'An evaluation of conceptual weaknesses in transformational and charismatic leadership theories', *The Leadership Quarterly,* **10** (2), 285–305.

Zoller, H.M and G.T. Fairhurst (2007), 'Resistance leadership: the overlooked potential in critical organization and leadership studies', *Human Relations,* **60** (9), 1331–60.

13. Women, leadership and development: reappraising the value of the feminine in leadership theorizing in the Middle East

Beverly Dawn Metcalfe and Lulwa Mutlaq

I believe strongly in the rights of women. My mother is a woman. My sister is a woman. My daughter is a woman. My wife is a woman.
King Abdullah of Saudi Arabia, interview with Barbara Walters 2005

I mean, what is a woman? I assure you I do not believe that anybody can know until she has expressed herself in all the arts and professions open to human skill.
Virginia Woolf, Professions for Women 1932

INTRODUCTION

In this chapter we advance the theorizing of women's leadership development in the Middle East. We explore the growth of women leaders in the region and show how current leadership knowledge presents only a partial picture of the complexity of women's leadership roles and practice. Our intention is to enhance the value of the feminine in theorizing as a corrective to Western constructions which have largely privileged masculinist accounts. Further, our intention is not to recreate hierarchical gender positioning, but to show that a re-reading through a feminist Islamic lens can reveal a feminine logic which has often remained silenced and marginalized.

The past two decades have seen the appearance of Muslim scholars whose writings bear a keen resemblance to those of Muslim modernists of the nineteenth and early twentieth centuries (Ramadan 2009). Their writings include feminist re-interpretations of Qur'anic verses and analyses of the authenticity of reports of the Prophet's traditions as well as clarifications of Islamic history. These works are often ripostes to traditionalist and fundamentalist views of women's rights and roles.

The past three decades have also seen three practising Muslim women come to power: Benazir Bhutto in Pakistan and, in Bangladesh, Khaleda Zia and Sheikha Hasina. While they are certainly not the first women to rule over Muslims, they have brought renewed relevance to debates concerning whether Muslim women may assume positions of leadership over men. This question is inextricable from debates surrounding globalization processes, the status of women in Islam and gendered interpretations of traditional duties of Muslim rulers and women. As this chapter will show, Islamic feminists have re-read the Qur'anic verses and hadiths in a contemporary light, emphasizing examples of female leadership. These include scholars such as Amina Wadud (2006), Fatima Mernissi (1991), Leila Ahmed (2002), Kecia Ali (2006) and Tariq Ramadan (2009) who highlight that Islam does not ascribe leadership to men alone and who cast doubt over the claims conservatives have made since shortly after Prophet Muhammad's death.

The chapter firstly explores the nature of Islamic resurgence and its implications for women. The chapter then reviews critiques of the Qur'an and hadith pertaining to women's leadership which are being revisioned to incorporate a feminine logic. The chapter considers the current status of women in the Middle East and provides selective data on their progress in leadership and political roles. We outline the current cultural value systems that shape women's work experience and outline the institutional structures and nature of governance regimes to show how women's issues are largely sidelined in government planning. The second half of the chapter examines current gender and leadership theory, highlighting how it has little relevance for understanding gender and leadership in Middle East states. New developments that challenge models of post-heroic leadership suggest a feminist Islamic lens can open up new understandings of the dynamics of leader-follower behaviour in the twenty-first century which focus on a relational ethics of social care and mutual engagement. We then detail current global initiatives sponsored by international organizations which have assisted women's leadership development.

A leadership development framework is proposed which outlines how development agendas can be nurtured in partnership with four key stakeholders, including national government machineries, private institutions, international development agencies and women's active participation in lifelong learning via NGOs and women's organizations. It is intended that this critique can assist administrative planners in the development of women's empowerment policy frameworks in the Middle East. We aim to reassert the value of feminine traits as the global skills now required for effective leadership (Ramadan 2009). These traits includes those relational and nurturing capacities often associated with female leadership styles and inherent in the model of Islamic leadership theorizing discussed in Chapter

1. We argue that in their active participation in women's organizations and in promoting Islamic feminisms, women are challenging the prevailing social ethics which requires that they eschew a career and define their self-identity in the home sphere. Women have advanced in leadership roles in the Middle East and championed commitment to social and cultural change. Islamic leadership, we argue, can be conceptualized as intrinsically feminine.

HISTORICAL OVERVIEW OF WOMEN'S DEVELOPMENT AND GROWTH OF ISLAMIC RESURGENCE

Before we undertake an explanation of ideologies and practices of leadership in politics and institutions, it is necessary to give a brief background to the recent socio-historical reforms and changing political and economic agendas, especially in Islamic states, that have impacted women's social status and identity. These dynamics are especially relevant to the understanding of women's rights, the dialectical and religious justifications for such practices, as well as the framework within which ideas are emerging out of fundamentalist views of society. Our focus will be on Sayyid Qutb (Akbar Ahmed 1992; Esposito 2002; Haddad 1993). This is in part due to his 'privileged' place in modern Islamic thought, but more importantly in order to reveal some of the dichotomies of his views, which appear progressive and liberal in the political and religious fields, but very conservative regarding the status of women, underscoring a paradox within the general framework of his thought (Haddad 1993; Shehadah 2000). In contextualizing the debates on women's advances in leadership, we outline views on Islamic resurgence (more commonly referred to in the 1970s as fundamentalism) as introduced in Chapter 1, and how they are creating a complex nexus for women's development progress, whilst maintaining what are viewed as 'literal' or 'traditional' interpretations of Islam.

The term 'fundamentalism' began to be used in the 1970s in reference to a growth in political Islam (Ahmed and Donnan 1994; Esposito 2005; Ramadan 2009), but was soon replaced by the terms revivalism and resurgence (Esposito 2005). That said, since 9/11 and subsequent associated terrorist and military activity worldwide, fundamentalist discourse has been promoted and, within that discourse, the role of women has been much analysed. Significantly, the commodification of women's social status in international relations discourse has led to it being used as a legitimizing factor for a range of political and military interventions (including Iraq and Afghanistan). Fundamentalism refers to the induction of radical changes in recently accepted modalities and traditions with the express purpose of unifying Islam as a dynamic and transformatory force (Chapra 1993; Lunn 2009; Shehedah 2000).

The modern revitalization of Islam was developed by two Muslim organizations in the 1930s and 1940s: the *Muslim Brotherhood*, founded in Egypt by Hassan al-Bann in 1928, and the *Islamic Society* organized in Pakistan by Mawlana abu-A'la al Mawdudi in 1941. Their impact extended to all Arab and Islamic countries, advocating a revolutionary ideology to convert society and liberate people through to the 1970s. This ideology tends to adopt a literal interpretation of Islamic scriptures (in all jurisprudence) as it concerns social reform and reconstruction of Islamic society. In so doing, it challenges Western versions of governance and development (Chapra 1982; Lunn 2009; Utting 1996).

The most significant proponent of these ideologies, advocating Islam as revolutionary, is Sayyid Qutb (Esposito 2002, 2005; Haddad 1993). Part of the Islamic resurgence concentrated on the centrality of the family in social and economic relations, and consequently women in Muslim societies began to experience, from the late 1970s, constraints in their daily lives, including curbs on female mobility. The era of first-, second- and third-wave feminist movements in the West from the 1960s to 1990s was, in Muslim societies, interpreted as Western decadence, undermining tenets of Islamic belief (Leila Ahmed 1992). Accordingly, all revivalists incorporated the status of women as a major part of their corpus: the most radical of them stipulating complete segregation of women to the domestic environment (Oman), and segregation generally in the economic sphere (Saudi Arabia) (see Handoussa 2006; Wikin 1991). The process of segregation has been shaped by cultural changes in Middle East states and has become heightened with symbolic expressions of religiosity expressed in wearing the veil. In sum, Islamic resurgence proposed a natural bio-logical order. This positioned men as leaders, protectors and caretakers of women and the family, while women nurtured and propagated the family, the nucleus of society. As we will show however, this biological difference does not infer deference, but rather confers social relations that engender complementary and equal roles for men and women in society.

Qutb was aghast at American bias against the Arabs and support for Israel, at the materialism of American culture and Western societies generally, and also at the growth of sexual freedom. He thus began to question secular economic and social systems, which he regarded as a failure of both Marxism and capitalism to provide for human wellbeing. His discontent with American values and ways of life led him to advocate Islamic ideals as a way of protecting and enhancing Arabic and Middle Eastern values and history (Ahmed 2002, see also Sahli 2008) and he began to argue that political and economic regeneration could only be achieved through following Islam (Shehadah 2000). He returned to Egypt, joined the Muslim Brotherhood and developed his ideas concerning *al-hakimiyyah* (the sovereignty of God) and *al-jahiliyyah* (the decadence of society) and came to view forms of governance that did not adhere to Shari'a as morally deficient. A reformist position was thus transformed into a radicalist one purporting that the welfare of human citizens would come through adherence to the precepts of Divine Law (Haddad 1993, pp. 77–78; see also Roald 2001). Qutb's message argued for a monotheistic path that would deliver social justice to humankind, with Islam conceived as a 'divine regulator' in all aspects of human life. We summarize Qutb's revolutionary aims for an Islamic state and women's position in Table 13.1. The overall aim of the mission of Islam is to: Propel life to renewal, development and progress and to press human potentialities to build, go forth and to elevate (Qutb Fi al-Tarikh, *Fikra wa minhaj* (History, idea and methodology), in Shehadah 2000, p. 48).

CAN A WOMAN BE A LEADER IN AN ISLAMIC STATE? A REFLECTIVE VIEW OF ISLAMIC SCHOLARSHIP

Can a woman be leader in an Islamic-governed state? There is a hadith that states: 'those who trust your affairs to a woman, will never know prosperity' (al-Bukhari's Salah). This hadith has been used as a 'sledgehammer' (Mernissi 1991, p. 4) throughout the centuries as a means of excluding women from participation in public life. However, during the whole period of his Prophetic missions in Mecca (610–622 CE) and in Medina (622–632 CE), Muhammad gave a major place to women in his public life. Khadija, his first wife, was the first woman to profess her commitment to the new faith, after revelations to Muhammad. Khadija was also a successful career woman in her own right before she married Muhammad, and was known as formidable and trustworthy in negotiating contracts and business settlements. Another wife of the Prophet, Aisha, was leader of an army at the age of 42 in the 'Battle of the Camel' (650 CE) which challenged the legitimacy of the fourth caliph, Ali (Mernissi 1991).

Feminist scholars have noted that Muhammad consulted women and included women's opinions in his deliberations and judgements (Leila Ahmed 2002; Ali 2006; Badran 2005; Al Faisal 2006; Al-Hassan Golley 2004; Wadud 2006). Mernissi, a Moroccan scholar, revealed, through her deconstruction of Islamic sacred texts, ambiguities in the founda-tional authority of the hadith relating to women's ability to hold leader-

Table 13.1   Sayyid Qutb perspectives on women and Islam

Organizing Concept of Women's Role	Values and Belief in Qutb
Overarching aim of family	The cornerstone of society responsible for building moral citizens.
Male-female relations	Balance and equilibrium are to be aimed for in private realm as its benefits peaceful happiness for mankind.
Woman's status	Islam orders no woman marries against her will. Marriage to be permanent to ensure stability. Man rules the home and protects wife. Furthermore, to nurture peace women are to avoid adornment and mixing with men to avoid temptation and seduction.
Divorce	Is the safety valve of marriage.
Polygamy	Safety valve of marriage, and desirable when surfeit of women during war. All wives are to be treated equally (Surah IV:3).
Equality of men and women	All humans decreed equal except in aspects relating to experience and responsibility. They are equal in spiritual and religious fields as well as in economic and property matters. Inheritance rights for men are to allow proper provision for wives and family.
Women and work	Qutb maintains women in the West are obliged to work as men stopped supporting them. This resulted in them being demeaned and exploited. Islam does not deny women work, but rather to have positive careers that enhance humanity. Qutb believes the West has commoditized women's sexuality and ignored the elevation of women's education, mind and character (Qutb 1952).
Women's role in the family	Capitalist and communist systems in principle grant men and women equal opportunity in work, and place a burden on women's caretaking responsibilities. This exonerates men from their responsibility to support and protect women.
Women's rights	Afforded to women in Islam centuries ago. Biological difference between men and women and complementary roles. Motherhood is important for women's and society's development and continue with them.

Source: Adapted from Haddad 1993; Shehedah 2000.

ship positions. Examining a number of the accounts of *fuqaha* (religious scholars) during the first few centuries she highlights that hadith could only be transmitted and accepted by those who were 'learned' in the Islamic sciences. Further, those who, in their everyday relations with people, did not 'act justly' or who gave 'false testimonies' could not be relied upon (attributed to Imam Malik ibn Anas). Abu Bakr was a companion of the Prophet Muhammad, and when the Prophet learned of the death of King Kirsa of Persia, he inquired who would be their new leader. He was advised that power would reside with Kirsa's daughter. It was on learning this information that Abu Bakr claimed to hear Muhammad speak the hadith subsequently documented by al-Bukhari and cited above.

However, Abu Bakr was punished for *qadhf* (slander) by giving false testimony in court concerning a woman's infidelities. He was sentenced to flogging. This in itself could be a reason for discounting the hadith. Mernissi (1991) highlights that al Tabari, who was a religious authority in the same era, also contested the validity of the hadith (Mernissi 1991, p. 6).

The hadith is commonly referred to even today to exclude women from leadership roles and positions of authority. Mernissi's insights reveal to us the complexities of interpreting and verifying hadith and the social and historical context in which they were constituted, as well as how one can attempt to assess them in light of contemporary knowledges. She states: '. . . the relationship to time, the relationship to power, and the relationship to femaleness become connected to a discourse of identity' (Mernissi 1991, p. 21).

Mernissi provides authentic and authoritative reasoning concerning attitudes towards women's leadership role in early Islam. Similar to other Muslim scholars (Ahmed 1992, Ahmed and Donnan 2004; Handoussa 2006; Roald 2001), she argues that the problematic position of women in Muslim societies is the result of male-dominated (mis)interpretation of the holy texts of Islam, not of Islam itself. In addition, scholars such as Leila Ahmed (2002), Shehedah (2000) and Haddad (1993) claim that Qutb was selective in his choice of quotations from the Qur'an and hadith, reaffirming the ways in which scripture is openly subject to interpretation in accordance with social and historical contexts.

The foregoing discussion is significant in laying the foundations for understanding women's continually changing role and how it is constituted by the intersecting dimensions of cultural history and the dynamics of Islamic jurisprudence. In the following section, we examine characteristics of work culture and social practices that exist in the present day that shape a woman's social identity and her engagement in the public sphere. We then move on to describe current developments in gender and leadership theorizing. We show how Islamic female leadership identity

Table 13.2   WEF rankings for selected countries, 2010

	Gender Gap Score	Economic	Education	Health	Political Empowerment
Bahrain	110	115	60	110	120
Egypt	125	121	110	52	125
Iran	123	125	96	83	129
Jordan	120	126	81	87	117
Kuwait	105	107	83	110	114
Oman	122	129	90	61	128
Saudi Arabia	129	132	92	53	131
UAE	103	120	37	110	60
Yemen	134	134	132	81	130

Source: Hausmann et al. 2010.

and behaviours are constituted and stress the relational, social and collaborative. In particular, there is a focus on consultation, on principles of equality and fairness, and on building trusting relations with followers. To position Islamic knowledges of leadership, we review gender and leadership writings in a contemporary light and elucidate similarities in the feminization of leadership discourse. We show that an Islamic feminist lens can unveil the value of the feminine in leadership theorizing and that this should be celebrated among Middle East women.

Women and Work in the Middle East

The previous analysis shows how women's social identity is historically positioned within intersecting social pressures (Al-Dajani 2010). On the one hand, there is a cultural legacy that is intertwined with progressive agendas: on the other, there is the prevalence of traditional (or masculinist) discourses. This may perhaps help explain why the Middle East region has made less progress on development indicators, especially with regard to women's economic and political empowerment, than any other region of the world. Middle East scores for gender empowerment gaps, compiled by the World Economic Forum (Hausmann et al. 2010) in a survey of 134 countries, reveal the advances which Middle East states have made in some fields, especially in education: but also how limited has been progress against other empowerment indices. The scores in Table 13.2 show countries' overall world ranking and the empowerment ranking in respect of: (a) economic participation, which includes participation in the labour force, wage equality and ratio of women to men among legislators, senior officials and managers; (b) education empowerment, which includes ratios between men and women and access to, and involvement in primary, tertiary and university education; (c) health empowerment, which incorporates life expectancy; and (d) political empowerment, which measures the gap between men and women in politics and in senior decision making roles in private and public organizations. The Middle East states are primarily grouped in the lower quartile on account of limited advances made in the economic and political spheres (Hausmann et al. 2010).

Empowerment indicators are measures of economic, social and political inequalities, and reveal the gendered processes present in work and organization systems (Syed 2010). Scholars have argued that gendered occupational structures have caused inequalities in society (Acker 2005, 2006; Bierema 2005) and the inequalities in career choices are particularly prevalent for women in the Middle East, since the rate of women's labour market participation is the lowest in the world (Hausmann et al. 2010; UNDP 2010; UNIFEM 2004). Table 13.3 provides selected data for Middle East countries and the USA and UK and expands on the indicators discussed above.

The Middle East countries can be divided into three categories, depending on their labour and natural resource endowments: labour-abundant and natural resource-rich countries, labour-abundant and natural resource poor countries, and labour-importing and natural resource-rich countries (UNDP 2005; UNIFEM 2004). The rate of women's participation in the work force tends to be higher in countries with abundant labour and relatively limited resources such as Egypt, Lebanon, Morocco and Tunisia (UNDP 2005, 2009; UNIFEM 2004). GCC countries, endowed with substantial natural resources and which import labour, show atypically high rates of women's participation. Kuwait, Bahrain and Qatar are the three countries with the highest levels of women's employment, although the situation is more typical in Saudi Arabia.

The Middle East, as explained in Chapter 1, is diverse economically, socially, historically and politically, yet its people are linked in a variety of ways. The great majority are linked by a common language (Arabic), religion (Islam) and cultural identity and heritage (Ahmed and Donnan 1994; Akbar Ahmed 2002; Ali 1999; UNIFEM 2004). Globalization has created new employment opportunities, especially in oil and gas-rich economies such as Bahrain, Qatar, UAE and Saudi Arabia, and labour market policies such as Emiritization, Omanization, Bahrainization and Saudization (or Gulfization) have led to the 'feminization' of public employment (Al Dabbagh 2009; JCCI 2009; Kingdom of Bahrain and ILO 2002; Kingdom of Bahrain and UNDP 2003; Moghadam 2000, 2005).

Table 13.3   Gender statistics in selected Middle East countries

Country		Female percentage of:								
	Seats in parliament		Minister Positions*		Economic Activity Rate		Legislator Managers		Professional/ Technical Workers	
	2007	2010	2007	2010	2007	2010	2007	2010	2007	2010
Bahrain	7.5	13.8	(2000) 9	11	31	34	10	22	19	18
Egypt	4.3	2	(1962) 6	9	22	24	9	11	30	34
Jordan	6	6	(1982) 11	7	29	25	n.d.	n.d.	29	29
Kuwait	3	8	(1996) 0	7	50	47	n.d.	14	n.d.	34
Oman	2	0	(1995) 10	9	24	27	9	9	33	33
Qatar	0	0	(1996) 8	0	37	51	8	7	24	20
Saudi Arabia	0	0	(2010) 0	0	22	19	31	8	6	27
UAE	23	23	(2006) 6	17	39	43	8	10	25	22
UK	20	22	(1924) 20	23	69	69	33	35	46	47
USA	16	17	(1952) 14	33	70	68	42	43	55	57
Yemen	0	0	3	6	31	21	4	2	15	15

Compiled from Hausmann et al. 2010.

Notes:
* The date in brackets indicates the first year a woman was appointed minister. It should also be noted that in a number of states there are women ministerial positions attributable to royal birth.

It should be highlighted that there is considerable academic debate concerning the validity of gender statistics and their accuracy, including within and between UN agencies themselves. The above data is based on UN and ILO data sets and may disagree substantially with official statistics from some of the countries concerned. For example, female labour participation stated above is in many cases significantly higher than that officially recognized.
    This can be ascribed in part to the fact that the collection and collation of gender-based statistics is a relatively recent activity in many of the countries. In addition, the calculation of gender inequality indices has been changed considerably in the UN 2010 reports.

As in Western societies, Middle East occupational structures are strongly gendered, with the majority of women employed in health, education and social care. There is also evidence of vertical segregation, with women concentrated in lower level roles (Handoussa 2006; Tzanntos and Kaur 2003; UNDP 2009; UNDP 2010; UNIFEM 2004). However, unlike Western societies, in some countries women are also barred from certain professions – for example, architecture, some fields in medicine and engineering occupations (Bahry and Marr 2005; JCCI 2009; Kingdom of

Saudi Arabia 2003). There are additional limitations that hinder women's progress in organizations, including: the persistence of gender stereotypes, limited training budgets for women (Metcalfe 2007), biases in recruitment and selection practices, and few female role-models in public leadership (Adler 2004; El-Azhary Sonbol 2003; Eagly et al. 2007; Meyerson 2007).

However, several high-profile leaders have challenged gender stereo-types and promoted women's capabilities. These include Queen Rania of Jordan and Sheikha Lubna al-Qasimi of the UAE, now minister of Foreign Affairs and a businesswoman in her own right. Sheikha Mozah Bint Nasser al Missned, the second wife of Sheikh Hamad bin Khalifa Al Thani, Emir of the State of Qatar (Moza 2010), has three key respon-sibilities: education development; families and health; and heritage and culture. As Chairperson of the Qatar Foundation for Education, Science and Community Development and President of the Supreme Council for Family Affairs, Sheikha Mozah has spearheaded activities and projects in basic and higher education, establishing several high quality, non-profit private schools and learning institutions for children and young people in Qatar. As a UNESCO Special Envoy, Her Highness's main mission is to promote education for all children and the improvement of the quality of education throughout the world. Like Queen Rania she is liberal minded, and only adopts the veil in the Gulf. She has supported the expansion of the world-renowned Al Jazeera televison newstation in Doha, especially into children's broadcasting (Moza 2010).

Princess Haya Bint Al Hussein, daughter of the King of Hussain of Jordan and youngest of the five wives of His Highness Sheikh Mohammed Bin Rashid Al Maktoum, Prime Minister of the UAE and Ruler of Dubai, is also a woman who has pioneered humanitarian and community and health reform in the Arab world. Princess Haya has engaged in a range of humanitarian activities and founded *Tikyet Um Ali*, the first Arab NGO dedicated to overcoming local hunger, in her native Jordan. She now chairs Dubai's *International Humanitarian City*. She was an ambassador for the World Food Programme 2005–2007, and then appointed a UN Messenger of Peace in July 2007 by secretary-general Ban-Ky Moon. She is a founding member of former secretary-general Kofi Annan's Global Humanitarian Forum based in Geneva. As with the other women dis-cussed here, she has progressive views, does not adopt the veil and is a regular commentator (like Queen Rania and Sheikha Moza) on women's development issues at UN conferences. In addition, Princess Haya is an accomplished equestrian and has been twice voted President of the *International Equestrian Society* (Al Hussein 2010). Ultimately, however, it is clear that the majority of female leaders play a community role, rather than support women's development in commerce.

WOMEN AND CULTURE IN THE MIDDLE EAST

There are many vernacular proverbs that generally describe women as inferior, including aspects of deficiencies in moral character and ability (UNDP 2005). Traditionalists reject the notion of equality (at least in respect of Western constructions) between the sexes. They argue that men and women have been created biologically different in order to fulfil different roles in society, and that God has given men responsibility for providing for the family. Equality ideology is premised on difference (Liff 1996; Metcalfe 2007):

> Husbands should take full care of their wives, with the (bounties) God has given to some more than others and with that they spend out of their own money. (Surah 4 Women, 34)

Social and economic structures are thus premised on tribalism and patriarchy, governed through male alliances and networks (World Bank 2004, 2005). Relations in the family are governed by the father's authority over his children and the husband's over his wife. While there have been some changes to challenge this view (for example, Egyptian women obtaining the right to divorce), advances have been primarily seen in Middle East countries other than those of the Persian Gulf. Male control of the economic, social, cultural and legal and political levels of society remains the abiding legacy of patriarchy. The existence of 'family law' permits men's control, specifically the personal status law that is the classic embodiment of this problem (Badran 2005). As we will show, however, women have created space for development opportunities and for engagement in women's organizations, and have contributed to economic, political and cultural activities.

In addition to legal structures, social and cultural practices in Middle East countries discriminate against women (Seikaly 1994). Constitutional provisions for the protection of women's rights exist in the majority of states (for example, Kuwait Constitution 1996, Bahrain National Charter 2001, and of course Turkey's secular constitution), but are often ignored, contradicted or not enforced (UNDP 2005). Some contain provisions for the equality of men and women in, for example, public offices in Saudi Arabia, and political rights and duties (UAE). Some contain principles of equal opportunity, affirming the state's responsibility to maintain the family, to protect motherhood and to guarantee a proper balance between women's duties towards their families and their work in society (for example, Jordan), and in prohibiting the employment of women in certain industries or at specified times (Morocco, Qatar and Bahrain). However, interpretation of these constitutions reaffirms a commitment to difference, thereby potentially codifying gender discrimination in the household and economy. Importantly, the constitutions underline the family as the most important foundation of an Islamic state.

The implication of these interpretations is the prevalence of discriminatory practices in work and social relations. If one examines the field of employment law one will note that it is guided by *urf* (custom) and Shari'a, which reflect the need to protect women and create a moral work environment. As such, employment legislation is limited and does not cover sexual discrimination, since discrimination is perceived as being embedded within Shari'a. In Saudi Arabia, Bahrain, Oman and Qatar, oil companies support gender segregation by subsidizing sex-separate offices and educational facilities. This work organization structure limits development choices for women (Moghadam 2005; Al Mughni 2001; Wikan 1991). Metcalfe (2006) found that in sex-segregated organizations in Bahrain and Oman there were limited funds for skills development for women since training budgets were largely allocated to men. It was also found that private sector organizations preferred to recruit men for organization roles, as women are seen as more costly. A further study examining gender, diversity and human resource development found that equal opportunities or diversity issues did not constitute part of general strategic management procedures since equality was considered as being constituted within the guidelines of Islamic Shari'a (Metcalfe 2007).

There are also a number of social practices that govern men's and women's roles in work organizations. As already highlighted, gender, work and social relations are governed by a traditional patriarchal structure. Women's most important role, according to society, is as a homemaker and mother, while the man's responsibility is to support and protect the wife and the family. Hence, women enjoy limited, if any, recognition for their contribution to the family, and are often seen as legally, financially and socially dependent on men. Men's responsibility for women is illustrated by a cultural practice relating to the maintenance of women's modesty. This involves protecting women from male contact other than within her immediate family. This cultural practice of *qiwama* (protection) requires that a man must 'protect' a woman's honour and sexuality. Job and career opportunities are thus likely to be realized through male networks and connections. There are also restrictions imposed on women which limit their mobility within their country (for example Oman, Bahrain, KSA, Kuwait), as well as women having to obtain permission to travel overseas from their husband or guardian (for example Bahrain, Oman, KSA). These cultural practices create gendered work relations and organization structures and sustain sex-segregated work spaces and, similarly, sex-segregated occupations.

Fiona Farrell's work in the UAE (2008) found that none of the women in her study of the private banking sector were aware of government initiatives and women's organizations that assist women's development. This illustrates the way in which support is often through specific class and social networks (Hutchings et al. 2010 Metcalfe 2007, 2008). Figure 13.1 summarizes the gendered social practices that limit women's full participation in the public sphere.

The foregoing discussion has highlighted the significance of interpretations of Islamic jurisprudence and cultural practices in shaping gender relations, which determine the spheres of public action where men and women can operate. The importance of Islam as a social and organizing influence is shown in research which examines how the Qur'an and hadith provide a moral framework which guides the behaviour of all men and women. The achievement of the 'well being' (*falah*) of all men and women (Ali 1999) is an underlying philosophy in all human activity and communications. The concepts of unity (*itihad*) and justice, balance and equilibrium ('*adl*) have a significant bearing on ethical behaviours in management and organization relations. Middle East scholars also note that the Qur'an is explicit in identifying the different but complementary roles of men and women (Liff 1996; Roald 2001). A recurring theme is the equal but different identities of men and women: 'And the male is not like the female' (Surah, The Family of Imran 3:36).

The commitment to difference in shaping gender and work relations is perhaps best encapsulated by reviewing the status of Arab countries signed up to the United Nations CEDAW convention (see Table 13.4). Of the 22 Arab League states, 16 have ratified or acceded to CEDAW, although most have stated reservations with respect to women's social status and rights. Arab states argue that they are not opposed to the principles of CEDAW but wish to maintain their commitment to Islamic Shari'a. This stresses that men and women be treated differently, not unequally. The eminent Iranian philosopher Mutahhari (died 1979) eloquently argued the importance of the *difference* theorizing prevalent in early Islamic philosophy as well as current literatures:

> According to Islam, a woman and a man are . . . appropriated equal rights. [However,] women and men, on the basis of the very fact that one is a woman and the other is a man, are not identical with each other in many respects. The world is not exactly alike for [the two] of them and their natures and dispositions were not intended to be the same. Eventually this requires that in very many rights, duties and punishments, they should not have an identical placing. In the western world they are now attempting to create uniformity and sameness in laws, regulations, rights and functions between women and men, while ignoring the innate and natural differences. It is here that the difference between the outlook of Islam and that of western systems is to be found. (Muttahari 1998, in Mahallati 2010, p. 1)

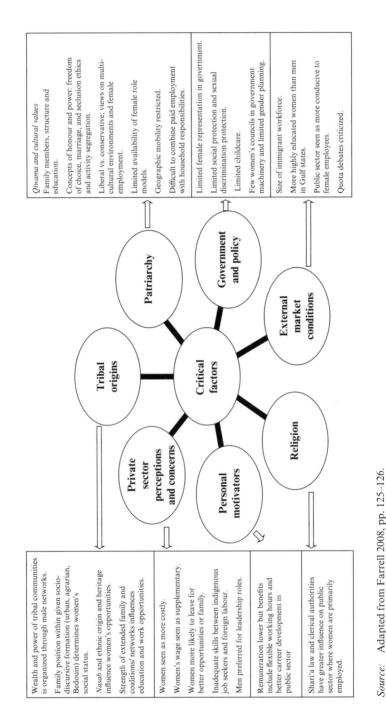

Qiwama and cultural values
Family members, structure and education.

Concepts of honour and power: freedom of choice, marriage, and seclusion ethics and activity segregation.

Liberal vs. conservative: views on multi-cultural environments and female employment.

Limited availability of female role models.

Geographic mobility restricted.

Difficult to combine paid employment with household responsibilities.

Limited female representation in government.

Limited social protection and sexual discrimination protection.

Limited childcare.

Few women's councils in government machinery and limited gender planning.

Size of immigrant workforce.

More highly educated women than men in Gulf states.

Public sector seen as more conducive to female employees.

Quota debates criticized.

Wealth and power of tribal communities is organized through male networks.

Family position within given socio-discursive formation (urban, agrarian, Bedouin) determines women's social status.

Nasab and ethnic origin and heritage influence women's opportunities.

Strength of extended family and coalitions/ networks influences education and work opportunities.

Women seen as more costly.

Women's wage seen as supplementary.

Women more likely to leave for better opportunities or family.

Inadequate skills between indigenous job seekers and foreign labour.

Men preferred for leadership roles.

Remuneration lower but benefits include flexible working hours and better career development in public sector

Shari'a law and clerical authorities have greater influence on public sector where women are primarily employed.

Critical factors: Patriarchy, Government and policy, External market conditions, Religion, Personal motivators, Private sector perceptions and concerns, Tribal origins

Source: Adapted from Farrell 2008, pp. 125–126.

Figure 13.1   Gendered social processes impacting women's leadership participation

Table 13.4   Selected Arab states and CEDAW accession and reservations

State	Date of Signature	Date of Ratification	Reservation by article number:						Total Reservations
			2	7	9	15	16	29	
Jordan	03/02/1980	01/07/1992 Ratify			9/2	15/4	16/1 (c) (d) (g)		3
Algeria		22/5/96 Accession	2		9/2	15/4	16	29/1	5
Iraq		03/08/1986 Accession	2		9/1 9/2		18	29/1	4
Kuwait		02/09/1994 Accession		7(a)	9/2		16/1 (f)		4
Lebanon		21/04/1997 Accession			9/2		16/1 (c)(d) (f) (g)		3
Egypt	16/07/1980	18/09/1998 Ratify	2		9/2		6	29/1	4
Saudi Arabia	07/09/2000	07/09/2000			9/2			29/1	2
Bahrain	18/06/2002	18/07/2002 Accession	2		9/2	15/4	16	29/1	5
UAE		18/06/2006 accession			9/2	15/4	16/1		3

Note:
Article 2: Condemns discrimination against women in all forms and agree to pursue all appropriate means to eliminate it (particularly incorporating principle of equality in laws and actions)
Article 7: Political and public life (voting and participation in public office and NGO)
Article 9: Nationality of mothers to be passed to children
Article 15: Women's equality with men before the law
Article 16: Equality of rights in marriage and family relations
Article 29: Settling of disputes by arbitration or International Court of Justice
* Saudi Arabia has made a general reservation against the CEDAW convention as follows: 'In case of contradiction between any term of the Convention and the norms of Islamic law, the Kingdom is not under obligation to observe the contradictory terms of the Convention' (see UNIFEM, 2004).

Source: Compiled from United Nations Datasets 2004, 2010.

The range of structural and cultural barriers that limit women's opportunities are entwined with differing notions of human development (World Bank 2004, 2005). Revivalists interpret texts through a traditionalist lens and in seeking to maintain balance and equilibrium, sustain and create what Metcalfe has termed an 'Islamic gender regime' (Metcalfe 2007, 2008). This Islamic gender regime refers to the cultural practices that govern patriarchal gender relations as well as the institutional frameworks in nation states that are engineered to sustain commitment to an Islamic constitution. Yet, as already outlined, the dilemma for women's development is how to expand opportunities for women whilst maintaining commitment to Islamic values and Arabic or Persian heritage.

An alternative approach is to envision women's development through a new reading of Islamic jurisprudence, one that engenders a new form of gender relations (Ramadan 2009; Roald 2001). Islamic feminist critiques and their relevance for understanding female leadership in the Middle East will be expanded upon following a review of current gender and leadership writings.

GENDER AND LEADERSHIP DEVELOPMENT: NEW THEORETICAL DIRECTIONS

Leadership scholarship which, as discussed in Chapter 1, emerged in the USA in the 1950s, has largely concentrated on Western societies, and this is true whether the focus is on men or women. Studies also focus on minority populations, and extensively utilize military and political figures (Collinson 2005; Grint 2005, 2009). Over the last 30 years, critiques of women and leadership broadly focus on three key questions, still underpinned by Western theorizing:

1. Can women be leaders?
2. Do male and female leaders differ in their behaviour and effectiveness in organizations?
3. Why do so few women reach top leadership positions?

The overwhelming majority of leadership studies ascribe stereotypically masculine characteristics as congruent with leadership qualities (for example, Eagly and Carli 2003; Vecchio 2003). Leadership success is associated with demonstrating tough, aggressive and competitive behaviours. Women's leadership capabilities are thus often questioned on account of their caring and nurturing disposition. The description of the differences in male and female leadership styles has created a gender hierarchy which positions women leaders as 'lesser than' (Eagly and Carli 2007). This, however, not only assumes Western constructs of gender difference, but also a Western oriented perspective of what constitutes successful leadership.

Texts have drawn heavily on masculinist assumptions when discussing leadership qualities such as decision making, risk taking and visionary power, generally concluding that when critiquing managing and leading we are defining male characteristics and attitudes (Billing and Alvesson 2000; Collinson 2005; Stead and Elliot 2009). As noted by organization and management scholars: 'the leaders we read about, the leadership activity we read about, and the theory we read about, are forms and relations of, "idealised masculinity even when the pronoun is she" ' (Oseen 1997, p. 170). This is not to suggest that we cannot think about feminine leadership styles. We would follow Fondas (1997) here when she argues that feminization has been surfaced within prevailing masculine norms and values rather than articulated in its own right. As Billing and Alvesson state (2000, p. 144), we should be wary of using feminine leadership as a slogan for change and transformation in organizations. These ideas have to some extent been challenged in reviews concerning feminine leadership, and claims for women possessing specifically feminine and 'different' advantages (for example Eagly and Carly 2007; Vecchio 2003).

Yet critical organization scholars have stressed, as would we, that the feminization of leadership writings have been largely marginalized and the gendered power relations and fluid gender identities not explicitly named. Scholars suggest that descriptions of leadership use characteristics that are culturally associated with females, and that these texts function as 'carriers of a feminine ethos' and tend to become embedded within masculinist accounts (Fondas 1997, p. 359). The recognition by scholars of the gendering of theory formulation is important because it evidences forms of subordination and domination and of dualistic sex/gender hierarchies, and of subsequent hierarchies in knowledge construction (Luce Irigaray 1985a, 1985b). As commentators note, within Western philosophical traditions we have inherited approaches to knowledge formation that recognize sexual difference as male sameness, with male mastery of knowledge embedded within, and outside of, social reality (Grosz 1994; Irigaray 1985a, 1985b).

New developments in leadership theorizing emerging since 2005 illustrate the complexity of leadership relationships and attest to the importance of structural, social, political, historical and institutional dynamics (Grint 2009, 2005). The 'feminization' of leadership, through what have been termed 'post-heroic' leadership studies, draws on collaborative and relationship building behaviours as important for effective community, social and organization development. Leadership is thus characterized not as a 'style', but as an emergent process and as something that is fluid and formed through networks of influence (Stead and Elliot 2009). David Collinson states that leadership skills are formed and reformed through 'multi-directional social interactions and networks of influence' (2005, p. 422; see also Binns 2008). Chapter 1 of this volume highlighted that

Islamic models of leadership rest on a relational and social ethic that requires leaders and followers to work together for mutual gain, and to demonstrate commitment to performing good deeds, and completing tasks efficiently, as well as working towards broader social development goals. We would argue that these behaviours constitute qualities traditionally stereotyped as feminine but that are now seen as universalizing qualities, whether employed by men or women.

VALUING THE FEMININE IN ISLAMIC LEADERSHIP THEORIZING

We would argue that the tenets of Islamic leadership are intrinsically feminine as they stress those nurturing qualities that aim to build human capabilities, develop trusting and meaningful relationships, engineer systems and policies to tackle social injustices and help build the solid foundations of Islamic communities. Unlike in the West, these are values and qualities respected and valued in both men and women in the Middle East, and draw unashamedly on the nurturing qualities of 'mother earth' in holistically building the capacities of all individual stakeholders.

The skills and approaches needed to enact power within leadership are: the willingness to show and guide, to acknowledge interdependence between partners; building trusting relationships; practising humility; and an ethics of care for all within the social and organization network. This is a departure from individualistic leadership development concerns to one that is more holistic and fosters broader social capital goals. In a Middle East context therefore, the process of doing leadership would be viewed as a collective social practice (see Binns 2008), emerging out of the requirement to nurture knowledge in organizations and society, secure stability, justice and balance (*'adl*), and build and maintain trust behaviours, arrived at through *shura* (consultative) efforts. Global research has shown that women have excellent nurturing and relationship building qualities. Doing leadership 'differently' (Sinclair 2005) is about valuing the feminine in leadership theorizing.

Building on this we would like to refer to the discussion on leadership in Chapter 1. In order to be an effective leader in Islamic communities, one must show *Ihsan*, a love of Allah. This requires attaining personal qualities associated with *sabr* (patience), *ubudiyyah* (servitude), *jihad* (struggle in the intellectual sense) and *ijz* (humility). In addition, a key skill in acknowledging one's humility is the process of critical self-reflection. This is entitled *musahabah* and requires the leader to look inwardly at his or herself to see what was amiss in their service to Allah and fellow citizens (see also Cunliffe 2009). These themes will be discussed further in Chapter 14.

Leadership in Islam is a relational ethical practice, a process of interaction between leaders and followers, which should be based on mutual engagement and trust. In this way, business leaders can be seen as corporate *khalifah*, who are not only responsible for their business growth but are also accountable to God for their actions as leaders. The principle of *maslahah* governs the actions and behaviour of leaders/followers. Therefore, instead of typical aggressive, ego-centric, personal-interest oriented leaders, more humane and ethical conduct is expected from leaders in Islam who are tasked with serving the public good. This is a holistic view of leadership which is concerned with the moral growth and development of individuals, organizations and societies.

Feminine Knowledge and Becoming

From an Islamic perspective, leading has a strong connotation of leading toward knowledge and righteousness through words and acts, identifying the leader as a knowledge figurehead, as well as perceiving him or her as a role model in a holistic sense. The role of leadership by virtue of being involved in knowledge building, and of guiding individuals to raise themselves to higher levels (Surah *Ripped Apart*, 84: 19), concerns 'embodied reflective practice' (Cunliffe 2009; Kempster and Stewart 2010; Metcalfe 2008) and the 'process of becoming' (Choudhury 1993, p. 6; Beekun and Badawi 1999). Indeed, reflection has been embedded in feminist epistemologies and underpins all forms of social inquiry (Braidotti 2003) as well as women's learning of the embodied materialities of their everyday lives. Carving an ethical organization and social identity is a learning journey, developing social sensitivities and ethical awareness, achieved through *jihad*, *mujahadah* and an acknowledgement of the sacred (Grint 2009). The process of leadership as an exchange relation requires benevolence, humility, and contemplation. Unlike Western models which focus on organization effectiveness, Islamic perspectives attempt to engender harmony and balance (*'adl*) and work towards sustaining a natural order that encompasses organization and social considerations.

The significance of this task is important in Islamic communities as seeking knowledge has a collective dimension: each individual is responsible for sharing and dissemination. This process incorporates building the *ummah* (community) and, ultimately, global Muslim societies and communities. Thus, institutional leadership (whether religious or organizational) continues to involve more than organizational management, it also includes a moral obligation for the holistic development of the leaders and followers of the community.

We argue that women's leadership in Islamic communities can be described as relational leading. This approach acknowledges the cultural process of exchange in leader-follower relations, one that is premised on overall commitment to humanistic development and a shared social ethics. Rethinking leadership as a feminized ethical interaction requires a review of Western notions of morality and power relations. Within both Western and Islamic discourse, women's sensitivities and identity are silenced, unnoticed, entombed within masculinist constructions of knowing. Consequently, effective leadership activity within Western traditions represents, as already described, toughness, resilience and competitiveness, all characteristics of hegemonic masculinity. Our perspective of feminized relational ethics does away with gender dualisms as the characteristic behaviours are valued by both men and women. However, for the purposes of 'undoing gender' in leadership theorizing, we utilize the label feminine as a corrective, a 'signifier' device, to show how femaleness and feminine subjectivity can be reread, be made visible, noticed. As Irigaray argues, to use the 'feminine word deliberately' dislodges traditional forms of knowledge and knowing premised on Western notions of cultural masculinism (1985a, 1985b).

To make our point clear, Islamic leadership is intrinsically feminine. The practical ethics of leadership and relational power is governed by feminized principles of equity, complimentarity, reciprocity and an ethics of social care. The feminine leadership ethic requires enacting power with, not over. However, while in the West this may be interpreted as powerlessness, and feminization also as a sign of 'lesser than' leadership abilities, in an Islamic community this approach is understood as doing leadership with humility, benevolence and collaboration. This observation reaffirms the social and historical ways in which the feminine/masculine are constituted and have different signifying labels in diverse geo-political contexts.

GLOBAL STRATEGIES, TRANSNATIONAL FEMINISMS AND LEADERSHIP DEVELOPMENT

Middle East governments, women's organizations and transnational organizations have been arguing that the continued and sustainable road forward for economic development is the deployment and utilization of the region's female resources. Various international development reports and successive World Bank reports have argued that the empowerment of

Middle East women, recognizing their right to participation and leadership in public administration roles and development processes, is a significant aspect of the region's economic and social development (see Farrell 2008; UNDP 2006, 2009). We have shown that Middle East women are under-represented in middle and senior leadership positions. Yet there are exemplars of women's leadership role models in the Middle East, including al Quasim (Farrell 2008). How then can we redress this? In the following we detail the advances of women in entrepreneurship, politics and business, and development networks. This incorporates global initiatives to enhance women's status and capacities. We look at global partnerships, women's organizations and networks, women's role in TNCs and women's entrepreneurial development. Following this review we provide a women's development framework that unites government, organization, international agency and individual strategies to advance women's empowerment and development.

WOMEN'S GLOBAL DEVELOPMENT PARTNERSHIP INITIATIVES

A key area for fostering women's development has been through government involvement with private research agencies and TNCs in global networks that support women's leadership development. We detail three such initiatives here.

Aspen Middle East Initiative

This is supported by Booz and Company and the Saudi Telecom Company, the mission of this venture is to foster values-based leadership, encouraging individuals to reflect on their ideals and development roles in society.

World Economic Forum

The World Economic Forum has launched an initiative entitled *Women Leaders and Gender Parity Programme*. The initiative is committed to promoting women's leadership in public communities and in contributing to global dialogue about women's development. Its focus is to research global issues impacting the talent pool for women's leadership development and assist countries in closing the gender gap. It produces an annual Gender Gap Report by nation and in the future will prepare a Corporate Best Practice report through assessment of the 1000 largest companies in the OECD and BRIC countries.

Without the Borders: Change the World

Without Borders is a collaborative venture between primarily Arab governments and industry which aims to overcome the gender divide in the Arab region and promote women's leadership. Based in Austria, it provides information about empowerment through internet based support and online training in all aspects of women's employment, political participation and in expanding women's role in building societies. They argue that, 'when women get involved from education to economics, from faith to family, from credit to creditability and from governance to good will – everything gets better' (Women without Borders 2005).

Women's Organizations and Networks

A key factor in assisting women's leadership development is the growth of women's organizations and networks (Moghadam 2005; Naples 2002; Roald 2001). While it has been found that women's networks have limited impact on career progression in the Middle East (Bierema 2005), they have been pivotal in creating learning and training support, especially in the area of employment rights, personal status law and leadership skills. Women's organizations have grown markedly, especially in the Gulf region. Women are bound together by a global feminist consciousness that nurtures coalition and network building (Acker 2006; Walby 2005).

Meyerson (2007) found that women's networks in organizations in the USA were beneficial for women's learning and development. She found that they:

- Provided useful contacts
- Allowed them to access senior leaders
- Provided an environment to discuss openly career development issues
- Helped them gain confidence
- Helped them learn about how organizations' systems worked.

In the Middle East region, women's organizations have been pivotal in supporting community development and family planning as well as providing vocational education (Metcalfe 2009). While some women's organizations concentrate on promoting traditional female roles such as child care, health education and religious education (for example, the UAE Women's Federation, now the General Women's Union, founded by Queen Fatima), there are an increasing number that are dedicated to advancing women in leadership and public administration roles.

Specifically, these organizations contribute to women's development in progressive ways through provision of literacy programmes, raising legal awareness about employment and personal status rights and provision of training programmes for work related skills (motivation, teamwork, communication, ICT) as well as participation in politics and public administration. Other women's organizations unite professional women and offer a development forum for enhancing women's skills and political knowledge about global feminism and movements. In Saudi Arabia, following the national dialogue on women's rights and duties in 2003, women's organizations began to unite to discuss women's role in society. Al-Dabbagh's (2008) research is based on women leaders of women's organizations who demonstrated intergroup leadership in Saudi Arabia. This involves coalition building and bringing networks together to tackle social and human injustices. Al-Dabbagh (2008) found that women's organizations energized commitment to political planning and promoted women's active role in the economy.

The Jordan Forum for Women and Business aims to: 'empower women's participation in all social, cultural, legal, business and economic development in Jordan, through education, advocacy, networking, training and professional support' (UNDP 2005). In addition, the Bahrain Businesswoman's Society (BBS) was recently successful in acquiring funding from UNIFEM to support entrepreneurial and leadership development skills training and has trained hundreds of women in the last few years (Metcalfe 2007).

It is important to note, however, the complexity of the support systems for women's development. Many women's organizations cannot be managed independently and are often subject to government checks, or are tied to a religious party (Badran 2005). In addition, most women's organizations are united by their predominantly middle class background and their commitment to retain and expand their civic rights (Bahry and Marr 2005).

Women and Transnational Corporations

There is some evidence that transnational corporations located in the Middle East region are supporting women's advancement in the public sphere. Shell and General Electric, for example, are promoting women in business through leader and entrepreneur of the year awards (Metcalfe 2006, 2008). These awards provide women leaders with recognition and status and help challenge cultural and gender stereotypes about women's role in business (Adler 2004). Shell and General Electric have also established a women's Middle East Network to help foster and support knowledge transfer and learning for senior leader figures in the region. Their current HR strategies also provide for building diversity objectives into long term succession planning. It should be noted, however, that the majority of TNCs tend to employ international female staff, rather than local female staff, at middle and senior levels.

Contrary to this, evidence from various studies of gender and work in the global economy revealed that TNCs' commitment to an equality philosophy in regional subsidiaries is uneven, and that TNCs are more likely to perpetuate inequalities between men and women (see Hearn et al. 2011).

A good example is that current government policy in Saudi Arabia advocates part-time work for women as this 'suits the special circumstances of many women' (Kingdom of Saudi Arabia 2003, p. 112). TNCs and the private sector are, however, reluctant to reform employment systems since part-time arrangements are not a common feature of work practices in Middle East states. This highlights the ways in which transnational processes and local specificities intertwine (Walby 2005).

Women's Leadership and Entrepreneurial Development

Reluctance by TNCs to tackle sensitive local organization and managerial cultural practices that are at odds with their global corporate philosophy has meant that women's advancement in business has been increasingly supported by international agencies such as the ILO and UN (Hearn et al. 2011; Metcalfe 2007). This is significant since it is international organizations that are taking the lead in social and equality transformations. An example is the micro-start initiative in Bahrain that has been able to help more than 2000 low-income entrepreneurs in the Arab region since 1998. The programme was funded with US$ 1 million from the government of Bahrain and US$ 500 000 from UNDP. The Alexandria Business Association (ABA) is playing a key role in Bahrain's Micro-start Project as an international micro-finance service provider (UNIFEM 2004). Women's entrepreneurial advance has grown markedly over the last five years (Hausmann et al. 2010). This is attributable to reluctance by private organizations to recruit women. There has also been an expansion of e-business opportunities that women can manage from their family home. Data is scarce on e-business as statistics focus on women in paid employment in the private or public sectors. A number of important achievements have been made by women in the sphere of leadership and entrepreneurial development. In just five years, the Bahrain Chamber of Commerce grew from having no female members to 1785. Dr Lulwa Mutlaq, Vice-President of the Arab Banking Co-operation, was voted President of the Bahrain Management Society, a predominantly male organization in the

Gulf (Metcalfe 2007). In Saudi Arabia, the Chambers of Commerce and Industry are setting up female provisions to assist entrepreneurial development including information and advice with business start-ups and finance and legal counselling. In addition, Chambers of Commerce are expanding provision for specialist women's training including, inter alia: banking, finance, public relations, managing small enterprises, and the management of social services (Kingdom of Saudi Arabia 2003). The Princess Basma Resource Centre in Amman Jordan provides similar services (Metcalfe 2006).

At the regional level, the OECD's Centre for Entrepreneurship has been assisting women's entrepreneurship training in Morocco and Turkey. The World Bank has established a development project, Investment Climates and Women's Entrepreneurship, which is part of a larger gender project in the Middle East and North Africa (MENA) (World Bank 2006), which is assessing the opportunities for women entrepreneurs in MENA client countries to promote women's entrepreneurship.

WOMEN, LEADERSHIP DEVELOPMENT AND SOCIAL CHANGE IN THE MIDDLE EAST

Current government machineries provide little support to women's empowerment. Indeed, large numbers of Middle East (primarily Gulf) states have no specialist women's ministry or government institution responsible for developing national plans. Table 13.5 details a governance and institutional framework for women's development. Significantly, it demonstrates that leadership development initiatives have been instigated by NGOs and international agencies. More importantly, women are sidelined from democratic processes as there are few dedicated ministries to manage women's affairs.

Governance and National HRD Frameworks for Women's Empowerment and Leadership Development

Table 13.5 represents the responsibility of a number of stakeholders and partners in governing women's development. Scholars have highlighted the importance of leadership skill strategies as part of nation and capacity building (Metcalfe and Rees 2007; Metcalfe 2011). We draw on the definitions of Metcalfe (2011) of female capacity building which focus on multi-stakeholder partnerships systems for human development. Thus, a 'national' policy of skills formation is normally devised by governmental education and industry administration departments: not organization

Table 13.5   Women, governance and institutional frameworks for development

Country	Women's National Action Development Plan	Government Department	Leadership and Management Development Initiatives	Women's Professional and Networking Organizations
Bahrain	Bahrain National Charter (2002).	Supreme Council for Women (2002).	Royal Women's University. Crown Prince leadership Programme.	Bahrain Businesswomen's Society (BBS). Bahrain Management Society.
Egypt	National Strategy for Women (1996).	National Council for Women (2002).	Women at Work IBM Regional Development Programme.	Egyptian Business Society.
Jordan	National Strategy for Women (1993).	Jordanian National Council for Women (1993).	Princess Basma Women's Development Centre.	Jordan Forum for Women in Business.
KSA	Women's development Plan to be implemented by CCI No women's council.	No women's council.	Chambers of commerce.	Women's NGOs.
Kuwait	No women's development plan.	No women's council.	Chambers of Commerce and Industry. Springboard Women's Programme (SWP)	Kuwaiti Culture. Arab Women Development organization.
Qatar	Women's Development Plan 1996 in line with MDG Goals after 1995 Nariobi	Women's Affairs Department (1996). Family Affairs Committee- (1998).	Qatari Business Women's Award Since 2007. SWP.	Qatari Business Women's Forum.

Table 13.5   (continued)

Country	Women's National Action Development Plan	Government Department	Leadership and Management Development Initiatives	Women's professional and Networking Organizations
Oman	No women's development plan.	General Directorate for Women's and Children affairs.		Omani Women's Association. (Free organizing generally outlawed).
UAE	UAE Women's Federation (1975, now General Women's Union).	General Women's Union (Family Affairs under each Emirate).	2008 Dubai Women's Establishment (DWE) Leadership Programmes. Emirati Business Woman's Award. SWP.	Dubai Business-women's Council (2003). Abu Dhabi Business Women's Committee (2002).

Source: Compiled from multiple source.

agencies, although they can play a part. Capacity and HRD initiatives can be regionally oriented within a nation state, or incorporate partnerships with other governments (as with Women's Arab League). Significant to national HRD strategy is that they promote partnership relationships for learning between government, industry, NGOs and professional and labour institutions. Women's national HRD planning in the Middle East should incorporate four components:

1. The development of a national women's development strategy that incorporates all elements of MDG priority areas including women's role in politics and the economy as well as better provision for health and education opportunities.
2. The establishment of a specialized women's unit in government institutions in order to ensure that women's concerns are considered in public policy and development.
3. The development of specific national women's leadership training initiatives. Priority is to be given to initiatives that incorporate collaboration with multinational agencies.

4. Consultation and involvement of women's organizations in policy
    planning and development, and the encouragement of networks of
    women's organizations, helps to assist their advancement. (adapted
    from Metcalfe 2011)

While a detailed critique of the democratic structure and governance
systems is beyond the scope of this chapter (see Esposito 2005 for an
excellent summary; Gulf Centre for Strategic Studies 2004; UNIFEM
2004; World Bank 2005), the Beijing conference called for countries
to develop National Action Plans (NAPs) for women. Metcalfe (2011)
revealed that the progress of Middle East states is highly variable, with
Gulf states having less detailed women's development plans and being
less likely to have official women's bodies in government institutions.
Indeed, women's development planning has been outsourced to 'quasi'
women's organizations such as the GWU in UAE, the JCCI in Saudi
Arabia, or the Family Affairs Committees in Oman and Qatar, which do
not tend to focus on economic and political empowerment. Policy initiatives to support women have been via international agencies such as the
UN-, or UK-sponsored DFID programmes like Springboard Leadership,
detailed in Table 13.5. As already highlighted, development efforts for
leadership capacity building have been primarily driven by grassroots
women's organizations, working informally and outside official state
structures.

Despite limited institutional and political governance frameworks in
many Middle East states, it should be emphasized that the leadership
initiatives outlined in Table 13.5 are having a profound impact on social
and economic values and are being continuously resisted and challenged.
The Jordanian national strategy focuses on the empowerment of women
in six fields: legislation, political activity, economic activity, social activity,
educational activity, and health activity. Their commitment stipulates any
women's strategy should:

> . . . be consistent with the Jordanian constitution, Jordanian national charter,
> Islamic Jurisprudence, values of Arab and Muslim society, principles of human
> rights, aspiration to progress and development, regional and international
> agreements. (Jordanian National Strategy for Women 1993; see also El-Azhary
> Sonbol 2003)

Women's leadership advance is thus supported, but in accordance with
strong family values that underpin the maintenance of an Islamic gender
regime.

DEVELOPING WOMEN LEADERS' CAPABILITIES: A MODEL

The evidence in this chapter has highlighted that globalization processes in the Middle East make salient Islamic values in shaping gender and work systems. Islam is a unifying cultural resource that forms a community of practice and assists in the formation of organization practices and individual subjectivities at institutional, organization and individual identity levels (Acker 2006; Leila Ahmed 1992).

An important consequence of this observation is that leadership development initiatives in Islamic states should embrace the advancement of women's rights as well as recognize the importance of family in society. A key development area then is to help women to be able to combine work and family responsibilities, and this has been the primary characteristic of the development of equal opportunity policies in Western nations (Dickens 1998; Hakim 1996).

Debates on the conceptualization of gender equality are informed by ongoing analysis of the processes of change in gender relations. In particular, there is a question of the extent to which progress for women is associated with economic development as contrasted to democratically-inspired social and civil society development (Acker 2006). However, the mobilization and collective action of women to challenge inequalities is also necessary. Significantly, women should consider themselves as not only able to define self-interest and choice, but also as entitled to make choices (see UNIFEM 2004). As Syed (2010) and Metcalfe (2011) stress, without women's individual or collective ability to recognize and utilize resources in their own interests, resources cannot bring about empowerment. Thus individual agency is an essential aspect of women's empowerment.

Table 13.6 represents a development model that focuses on the intersecting relationships between four stakeholders: government, international organizations, private sector organizations and women's individual activism. These are discussed further below.

1. Government Strategies

To ensure women's economic security, there is a need for an enabling institutional, legal and regulatory framework to facilitate women's access to economic resources and to strengthen existing national HRD structures. At the government level a key objective for women's organizations has been legislative measures that prohibit gender-based discrimination in the workplace since this is largely inadequate in most Middle East states

Table 13.6 Partnership development for women's leadership and empowerment

Women, Development and HR Systems in Organizations	Government	Individual	International Agencies
a) HR systems premised on gender mainstreaming benchmarking tool which encompasses women's development as core value in organizations mission. b) Women only management and leadership programmes and provision of access to mentor and coaches. c) Collaborations and enterprise development with local Chambers of Commerce. d) Facilitation of women's networks for professional skills. g) Collaboration with global partners (for example Booz and company and Saudi Telecom Aspen Institute Leadership. h) Recruitment monitoring statistics to track women's development with option of quota systems. i) Provision of women's support network to assist career. j) Family friendly benefits including PT working, flexitime.	a) Legislative framework and constitution to eliminate discrimination and premised on framework of gender mainstreaming. b) Gender mainstreaming benchmarking tool to evaluate HR. b) Ensure creation and the active role of women's ministries in economic planning. c) Ensure all ministries have national HRD plan for women and provide training and support for vocational provision in key skill areas such as technology, ICT and finance and other professional sectors. d) Provide enabling mechanisms for entrepreneurship support, financial start ups and credit counselling. e) Ongoing strategy for political empowerment of women including quota systems. f) Collaboration with civil society organizations and development.	a) Women participate in professional societies both local and international to demonstrate commitment to skills development. b) Embrace lifelong learning. c) Lead and participate in voluntary and community organizations to assist individual and societal development.	Agencies such as the UN and ILO who have a human development focus can work in partnership with: a) Government b) Transnational organizations c) Civil society organizations – to help empower women especially in economic, political fields primarily through advocating discourse of women's rights and empowerment.

(Moghadam 1997; Metcalfe 2008). There also needs to be reform in educational policy in order to include provision for women in vocational, professional and entrepreneurial activities. This requires some of the women's administrative bodies in Middle East states to give equal emphasis to the work sphere as well as to the domestic sphere. The implementation of these institutional changes would require a greater number of women in public administration roles through gender integration and empowerment planning (Al-Dabbagh and Nusseibeh 2009). This is one area where Middle East states are actively promoting women's leadership and there is current debate about whether quotas are a viable way forward (Al Dabbagh 2009; Badran 2005; UNDP 2005; World Bank 2006). In addition, there needs to a mechanism to reach out broadly to all women regardless of class or ethnicity so that all may benefit from government-sponsored initiatives (see Hutchings et al. 2010; Farrell, 2008).

2. Organization Strategies

To ensure women's economic advance in management and the professions, there is a need for organizations to support general empowerment initiatives in the Middle East through the integration of gender and diversity principles in HRD planning and generally through promoting discourses of equality. This should ensure that women feel they are protected from any form of sexual discrimination. The expansion of women's networks and social and professional organizations, supported by business institutions referred to earlier in this chapter, would provide opportunities for women to share knowledge and assist women's training and skills development. This should potentially include:

   a) Monitoring of recruitment, selection and training statistics
       The measurement of women's advances could be achieved through the establishment of recruitment monitoring and training statistics and further promote the importance of management education and development for women.
   b) Women-only leadership training
       One area that would complement existing business culture is the development of sector-led women-only leadership education and development programmes for women. There is also a need for women to learn how to manage mixed working environments. Training programmes that target women have been introduced in a number of countries, reflecting the growing recognition of the importance of self-employment and entrepreneurship for women's employment. These programmes stress business planning,

credit counselling, marketing and management development (see Springboard).

c) Cultural training
    Cultural orientation programmes should introduce the philosophy of Islam and highlight women's and men's roles and the importance of the connections between work-related values and religion. This training should also introduce the complex nature of men and women's different roles and highlight cultural variation in the societal construction of gender.

d) Mentor programmes
    Develop mentor programmes that include and promote positive leadership role models for women.

3. Individual Strategies

There is a need to build leadership competencies in women, and for women to believe in themselves. There is a need therefore to involve individual women in social and community networks, political alliances and forums to help engender knowledge and collectivism and about political systems and the potentialities for social change (Badran 2005). The globalization of concepts and discourses of human rights and the activities of women's organizations, NGOs and INGOs have supported the development of transnational feminist networks and, as argued in this chapter, stirred feelings for acquiring new knowledges, new rights and new opportunities. Reaffirming the commitment to women's agency, we stress that women must be involved in women's organizations as agents of change rather than as recipients of concessions. Acquiring knowledge and understanding of gender relations and the ways in which these relations may be changed is important for women to move forward (Moghadam 2005). Developing a sense of self-worth and a belief in one's ability to secure desired changes and the right to control one's life are skills that need to be fostered. We would again stress the need for women's organizations and governments alike to expand their opportunities more broadly to enable the participation of all women.

International Organizations

International organizations have played a key role in supporting women's empowerment and leadership development in the Middle East. They have been actively involved since the early 1990s and have facilitated the formation of women's collectives and organizations. The Beijing Platform for Women in 1995 ignited the movement for reform as the vast majority of women attendees from women's organizations from the Gulf were sponsored by UNIFEM or UNICEF. This paved the way for transnational feminist organization development and networking. The key agency Arab Gulf Fund for UN Development Organizations (AGFUND) has pioneered leading education support for women including the Arab Open University, the Centre of Arab Women for Training and Research (located in Morocco) and the Arab Council for Childhood and Development.

The UN has also encouraged country and regional governments to sponsor women and international development. Bridging the Gulf, an NGO, is the most recent venture in Kuwait, sponsored by the EU Commission and the Kuwaiti Ministry of Foreign Affairs, which plays a key role in supporting leadership, political and employment development for women in the Gulf. Bridging the Gulf comprises a council of 41 elected leaders of NGOs and civil society personnel, most of them women, thus providing women with opportunities for acquiring leadership knowledge and skills. The UN also specifically supports women's leadership appointments in its regional offices in Egypt, Qatar, Bahrain, Jordan and Kuwait, again permitting women access to development opportunities. As Hutchings et al. (2010) argue, the development of Middle East women's leadership skills has been nurtured and grown through the region's International Development agencies.

CONCLUSION: FEMINIZING LEADERSHIP, GLOBAL FEMINISM AND SOCIAL CHANGE

This chapter has advanced feminist knowledge of gender and leadership. Positioning our argument in the geopolitical context of heightened religiosity in the Middle East, we used Islamic feminism as a framing device to debate the qualities and behaviours of leaders. We argued that leadership is intrinsically feminine, since it rests on the nurturing of a social and relational ethic, developing trust behaviours, and in engaging in ongoing critical self-reflection so as to acquire deeper understanding of the leader's and followers' needs.

This was not an essentialist position, but rather a mimetic strategy (Irigaray 1985a, 1985b) or what Butler (1994) calls catechrisis. This literary technique invokes a feminine logic to dislodge or disrupt accepted masculinist interpretations. Interestingly, however, the signifiers of feminine/masculine in much leadership theorizing are premised on Western knowledge. The 'feminine' aspect we would identify in Western leadership theorizing is a concept which, in the Islamic world, would apply to both women and men.

While feminization is inherent in descriptors of leadership work in the Middle East, there are still discriminatory practices. A range of global initiatives and case examples were outlined to demonstrate women's leadership advance. To progress women further a development model with multiple stakeholders was presented which provided a range of intersecting strategies to help empower women. This model proposed that a difference equality strategy, acknowledging the importance of the family, was the most appropriate way forward to develop women's leadership capabilities targeting institutional mechanisms, as well as women's individual agency.

Relational Leading: An Ethics of Care and Feminized Development

This chapter suggests that, in an Islamic context, leadership is a collective social practice, governed by a relational social ethic. This brings into play reconfigurations of power, as responsibility for task accomplishment is a collective endeavour. Significantly, the process of redrawing the boundaries of subject/object, power holder/organization actor re-balances relational dynamics so that all are positioned as moral subjects and moral agents (Braidotti 2003).

This is significant, as in reimagining Islamic ethical leadership as intrinsically feminine, it counters those views that encode corporate masculinity as the signifier of efficiency and effectiveness. Power relations are thus framed in the social dynamic of interaction, held in check by one's awareness of Islamic principles of *'adl* (balance) and *musawat* (equality). Underpinning Islamic ethical philosophy is a concern for all leader/follower exchanges. Leaders *are* shepherds of the flock.

Braidotti (2003) argues that relations are enacted through feminist knowledges that acknowledge men and women with particular histories, identities and positions. Sexual difference theory requires an affirmation of a critical expression of women's ontological desire, with women positing themselves 'as female subjects' (Braidotti 2003, p. 43). This resonates with Islamic philosophy requiring that leader/follower engagement is constituted as one that elevates feminized principles of equality, reciprocity and an ethics of care.

However, it is important to note that notions of instrumental masculinity and leadership power and control are not configurations that are characteristic of Middle East leadership behaviours. Relationship morality above all transcends mere 'exchange', since leadership dynamics are a trust. Desires to lead differently, and to be just, are qualities far more highly valued by all (Sinclair 2005).

Significantly, this challenges the idea of masculinized identities as embodying effective leader behaviours. Islamic feminist leadership emphasizes sociability, relationality and an interactive social ethic with followers. It provides an alternative to Western heroic leadership which is often signified by self-mastery and control – and is about doing power; doing leadership; doing hegemonic masculinity (Grint 2005).

As ethical and critical scholars have noted, leadership development is inextricably linked with notions of rights, status and broader community development (Stewart et al. 2007). Western descriptions of leadership have tended not to focus on community and social development issues. In this respect, it should be highlighted that, viewed through an Islamic cultural lens, and thus advocating difference between the sexes, this difference should not be linked to ideas of subordination and deference. Islam is an all embracing concept depicting humanity's relationship to God and represents a programme of life (Ahmed 1992). The analysis presented suggests therefore that we cannot understand the complexity of women and globalization processes in the Middle East without connecting to broader social and economic changes relating to the rights of women in Islamic nations.

Alison Jagger has argued that the wholesale adoption of Western concepts for women in the Muslim world could have negative repercussions, as it could seriously undermine the social and ethical values and practices that threaten social cohesion and the potential for social regeneration. Instead, she suggests that non-Western societies need their own space: 'to look after their own affairs, according to their own values, and priorities' (in Barlow and Akbarzadah 2006, p. 1490).

This approach to Islamic feminism is about reforming current masculinist interpretations of the Qur'an and hadith, and injecting a feminine ethics into leadership and organization logic (see also Meyerson et al. 2007; Ramadan 2009). This requires thinking anew, afresh, women's leadership qualities and their value and worth through a feminist Islamic lens. Feminist re-reading of the sacred texts is a legitimate and historically necessary strategy to improve the status of women and modernize religious thought. It is a strategy that has been used by feminist theologians in their interpretation of Christian scripture, and has assisted in advancing women in religious organization systems (Metcalfe 2009). Thus, Islamic feminism is not primarily about denying Western ideas and values: this would reinforce the dichotomies between Western equality rights and Islamic human rights. As was suggested in the introduction to this volume, the intersecting and organizing processes of Islamization and Westernization (Ahmed and Donnan 1994; Castells 2009; Ahmed 1992; Al-Hassan Golley 2004) led to a continual ebb and flow of social and cultural ideas across and within geographic borders and territories, informing ethics, values and social practices.

However, as Barlow and Akbarzadah (2006) claim: 'A model of Muslim women's rights that does not move beyond the Islamic framework is hostage to the discriminatory aspects of the Islamic legal framework' (2006, p. 1491). This echoes the concerns of some Islamic feminists, who argue that working within the Islamic system reproduces and sustains that system and limits the potential for reform. Yet as Moghadam (2005) argues, US and European feminists work within frameworks of liberal capitalism to improve women's rights, yet they have not challenged that system or called for political reform. It seems that, within a capitalist system, sexual rights and equal opportunities and advancements in education and employment are compatible. Current brands of Islamic feminism, those promoted by Ramadan (2009), Mernissi (2001), Wadud (2006) and Ali (2006), have an important place in the current struggle for a democratic and egalitarian Middle East. Efforts to re-read the sacred texts, to locate and label Islam's egalitarian precepts, are important to reformism. As Barlow and Akbarzadeh (2006) argue, Islamic reformism has a greater resonance with authenticity since it is speaking to the embodied and material lives of men and women, thereby promoting opportunities for grassroots reform. We reassert the message in Chapter 1 of this volume that Islam and economic development can provide alternative models to Western views of industrial change and growth (Lunn 2009).

Islamic feminism is important in the Middle East because it is mobilizing women's organizations, raising political consciousness and reaffirming the rights of women to legitimately hold positions as community leaders, business leaders and political leaders. As Moghadam (2005) has argued, Islamic feminism should embrace theological, socio-economic and political questions that reference religious texts, as well as other relevant cultural sources of knowledge (See also Lunn 2009; Wadud 2006).

In this endeavour, Islamic feminists should ensure commitment to their contribution to, and involvement in, issues such as governance, democracy, poverty and civil society. However, as this chapter has highlighted, not all women's organizations are political in nature, and many have firmly attached themselves to issues such as women's health and family organization. This should not necessarily be seen as a negative or disconnected feminist strategy to assist/position women in narrowly defined roles in society. Rather, it is an example of the dynamic fluidity of feminisms and feminist action as they evolve and develop over time. It also reveals that feminist politics is multi-faceted and shaped by a myriad of social, cultural and economic forces.

As Rupp and Taylor argued in 1999, feminists are social movement actors, are positioned historically and geographically, and work out ethics and equality strategies in different ways. Islamic feminism is then part of the global feminist movement and concerned with challenging inequalities between men and women and all manner of injustices. Moghadam (2000) suggests it is not useful to create divisions and boundaries between Islamic feminism, Western feminism, African feminism and so on, since there has been cross-fertilization of ideologies and strategies. The Beijing Platform for Women adopted in 1995 is a global manifesto for a global women's movement. As this chapter has shown, women's organizations in the Middle East, especially those in the Gulf and Egypt, have played a pivotal role in transforming and building women's leadership knowledges. We would argue, therefore, that while building female leadership capacities as defined by our development model, there is still a requirement for partnership arrangements with the private sector, civil society and international organizations and public agencies. However, without the intervention of women's organizations in assisting women's leadership development and empowerment, and ultimately contributing to social rejuvenation and female capacity building, women's advance is not likely to be realized (Al-Riza 2005).

We began this chapter by asking whether women could lead Muslim communities. Women have shaped economics, culture, politics and education. Moreover, unlike Western industrialized notions of self-transformation, there is increasing recognition that women have ethical and moral qualities to lead, not by exerting power over, but by working with power to facilitate and support mutual collaboration and exchange (Ahmed 2002, p. 247). Re-readings by Wadud and Ali reaffirm the feminine voice as a social actor that has legitimacy. In the contemporary structure of global power, we need a feminism that is vigilantly self-critical and aware. We also need leaders who can inspire the future development of the Middle East and rise to the challenges of state building, as discussed in Chapters 1 and 14. We reaffirm that women not only can, but must, be among those leaders. As al Riza (2006) has argued, women are pursuing this challenge by reflecting on women's past heritage and knowledge, and are preparing to lead future societies towards prosperity.

REFERENCES

Acker, Joan (2005), 'Gender, capitalism and globalization', *Critical Sociology*, **30** (1), 17–41.

Acker, Joan (2006), 'Inequality regimes: gender, class and race in organizations', *Gender and Society*, **20** (4), 441–64.

Adler, Nancy (2004), 'Shaping history: global leadership in the 21st century', in H. Scullion, and Margaret Lineham (eds), *International Human Resource Management: A Critical Text*, Basingstoke: Palgrave.

Ahmed, Akbhar.S. (1992), *Postmodernism and Islam*, London and New York: Routledge.

Ahmed, Akbhar S. and H. Donnan (eds) (1994), *Islam, Globalization and Postmodernity*, London and New York: Routledge.

Ahmed, Leila (2002), *Women and Gender in Islam*, New Haven, CT: Yale University Press.

Ali, Abbas (1999), 'Middle East competitiveness in the 21st century's global market', *Academy of Management Executive*, **13** (1), 102–8.

Ali, Kecia (2006), *Sexual Ethics and Islam: Feminist Reflections on Qu'ran, Hadith and Jurisprudence*, Oxford: Oneworld Publications.

El-Azhary Sonbol, Amira (2003), *Women of Jordan, Islam, Labour and the Law*, New York: Syracuse University Press.

Badran, Margot (2005), 'Between secular and Islamic feminisms: reflections on the Middle East and beyond', *Journal of Middle East Women's Studies*, **1** (1), 6–29.

Bahry, Louay and Phoebe Marr (2005), 'Qatari women: a new generation of leaders', *Middle East Policy*, **12** (2), 104–30.

Barlow, Rebecca and Shahram Akbarazadeh (2006), 'Women's rights in the Muslim world: reform or reconstruction', *Third World Quarterly*, **27** (8), 1481–94.

Beekun, Jamal and Rafik I. Badawi (1999), *Leadership: An Islamic Perspective*, Beltsville, MD: Amana Press.

Bierema, Laura L. (2005), 'Women's networks: a career development intervention or impediment', *Human Resource Development International*, **8** (2), 207–24.

Billing, Yvonne and Alvesson Matts (2000), 'Questioning the notion of feminine leadership: a critical perspective on the gender labelling of leadership', *Gender Work and Organization*, **7** (4), 144–57.

Binns, Jennifer (2008), 'The ethics of relational leading: gender matters', *Gender Work and Organization*, **15** (6), 600–620.

Braidotti, Rosi (2003), 'Becoming woman or sexual difference revisited', *Theory, Culture and Society*, **20** (3), 43–64.

Butler, Judith (1994), 'Bodies that matter', in C. Burke, N. Schor and M. Whitford (eds), *Engaging With Irigaray*, New York: Columbia University Press.

Castells, Manuel (2009), *The Rise of the Network Society: The Information Age: Economy, Society, and Culture*, vol I, 2nd edn, Chichester: John Wiley.

Chapra, Muhammed Umer (1993), *Islam and Economic Development*, Pakistan and Malaysia: Institute of Islamic Thought and Islam Research Institute, Islamabad, Pakistan.

Choudhary (1990), 'The concept of Islamic socio-economic development in contemporary perspective', *The Journal of Development Studies*, 1–10.

Collinson, David (2005), 'Dialectics of leadership', *Human Relations*, **58** (100), 1419–42.

Cunliffe, Anne L. (2009), 'The philosopher leader: on relationalism, ethics and reflexivity – a critical perspective to teaching leadership', *Management Learning*, **40** (1), 87–101.

Al Dabbagh May (2008), *The Context for Intergroup Leadership Among Women's Groups in Saudi Arabia*, May, Dubai: Dubai School of Government.

Al Dabbagh, May and L. Nusseibeh (2009), *Women in Parliament and Politics in the UAE*, Dubai: Dubai School of Government Report for Ministry of State for Federal National Council Affairs.

Al-Dajani, Haya (2010), 'Diversity and inequality among women in employment in the Arab Middle East region: a new research agenda', in Mustafa F. Ozbilgin and Jawad Syed (eds), *Managing Gender Diversity in Asia: A Research Companion*, Cheltenham, UK and Northampton, MA, USA: Edward Elgar, pp. 140–60.

Desai, Manisha and Nancy A. Naples (2002), *Women's Activism and Globalization: Linking Local Struggles and Transnational Politics*, New York: Routledge.

Dickens, Linda (1998), 'What HRM means for gender equality', *Human Resource Management Journal*, **8** (1), 23–40.

Eagly, Alice H. and Linda L. Carli (2003), 'The female advantage: an evaluation of the evidence', *The Leadership Quarterly*, **14** (6), 807–34.

Eagly, Alice H. and Linda L. Carli (2007), 'Overcoming resistance to women leaders: the importance of style', in Barbra Kellerman, and Deborah R. Rhode (eds), *Women and Leadership: The State of Play and Strategies for Change*, San Francisco, CA: Jossey Bass, pp 127–48.

Egypt Council for Women (2006), *National Council for Women's Leadership Strategy*, accessed at 7 January 2011 www.ncwegypt.com/english/index.jsp.

Esposito, John, L. (2002), *The Islamic Threat*, New York and Oxford: Oxford University Press.

Esposito, John L. (2005), *Islam: The Straight Path*, revised 3rd edn, Oxford: Oxford University Press.

Al Faisal, HRH Princess Loulwah (2006), 'The role of Saudi women in King Abdullah's reign: Future vision', presented in the second annual Saudi/British Conference 'Two Kingdoms Dialogue' 16 April, organized by Ministry of Foreign Affairs in association with Committee of International Trade.

Farrell, F. (2008), 'Voices on Emiratization: the impact of Emirati culture on the workforce participation of national women in the UAE private banking sector', *Journal of Islamic Law and Culture*, **10** (2), 107–65.

Grint, Keith (2005), 'Problems, problems, problems: the social construction of leadership', *Human Relations*, 58, 1467–94.

Grint, Keith (2009), 'The sacred in leadership: separation, sacrifice and silence', *Organization Studies*, **31** (1), 89–107.

Grosz, Elizabeth (1994), *Volatile Bodies: Towards a Corporeal Feminism*, Bloomington, IN: Indiana University Press.

Gulf Centre for Strategic Studies (2004), 'The national strategy for women's development', *Bahrain Brief*, **5** (11), 1–4.

Fondas, Nannette (1997), 'Feminization unveiled: management qualities in contemporary writings', *Academy of Management Review*, **22** (1), 257–82.

Haddad, Yvonne (1993), 'Sayyid Qutb: ideologue of Islamic revivalism', in Y. Haddad and John Esposito, *Voices of Resurgent Islam*, Oxford: Oxford University Press.

Handoussa, Heba (2006), *Arab Women and Economic Development*, Cairo: American University in Cairo Press.

Hakim, Catherine (1996), *Key Issues in Women's Work: Female Heterogeneity and the Polarisation of Women's Employment*, London: Athlone Press.

Al-Hassan Golley, Nasar (2006), 'Is feminism relevant to Arab women?', *Third World Quarterly*, **25** (3), 521–36.

Hausmann, Ricardo, Laura D. Tyson and Saadia Zahidi (2010), *Global Gender Gap Report 2010*, Geneva: World Economic Forum.

Hearn, J., B.D. Metcalfe and R. Piekkari (forthcoming), 'Gender, intersectionality and international human resource management' in I. Bjorkman and G. Stahl (eds), *Handbook of International Human Resource Management*, 2nd edn, Cheltenham, UK and Northampton, MA, USA: Edward Elgar.

Al Hussein (2010), Princess Haya Bint Al Hussein, personal website, accessed 7 January 2011 at www.princesshaya.net.

Hutchings, Kate, Beverly Dawn Metcalfe and Brian Cooper (2010), 'Exploring Middle Eastern women's perceptions of barriers to, and facilitators of, international management opportunities', *International Journal of Human Resource Management*, **21** (1), 61–83.

Irigaray, Luce (1985a), *This Sex Which is Not One*, translated by Catherine Porter, Ithaca, NY: Cornell University Press.

Irigaray, Luce (1985b), *Speculum of the Other Woman*, translated by Gillian C. Gill, Ithaca, NY: Cornell University Press.

Jeddah Chamber of Commerce and Industry (2009), Khadija Bint Khuwalid Centre, accessed 7 January 2011 at www.JCCI.org.sa.

Kempster, Stuart and Jim Stewart (2010), 'Becoming a leader: a co-produced auto ethnographic exploration of situated learning of leadership practice', *Management Learning*, **41** (2), 205–19.

Kingdom of Bahrain and ILO (2002), *Employment, Social Protection and Social Dialogue: An Integrated Policy Framework for Promoting Decent Work in Bahrain*, Geneva: ILO.

Kingdom of Bahrain and United Nations (2003), *Millennium Development Goals: First Report*, Manama: Ministry of Foreign Affairs.

Kingdom of Saudi Arabia (2003), *Human Development Report*, Washington, DC: United Nations.

Liff, Sonia (1996), 'Sameness and difference revisited,' *Journal of Management Studies*, **33** (1), 79–95.

Lunn, Jenny (2009), 'The role of religion, spirituality, and faith in development: a critical theory approach', *Third World Quarterly*, **30** (5), 937–51.

Mahallati, Amineh (2010) 'Women in traditional Sharī'a: a list of differences between men and women in Islamic tradition', *Journal of Islamic Law and Culture*, **12** (1), 1–9.

Mernissi, Fatima (1991), *The Veil and the Male Elite: A Feminist Interpretation of Women's Rights in Islam*, Cambridge MA: Perseus.

Metcalfe, Beverly Dawn and Chris J. Rees (2007), 'Feminism, gender and HRD', in J. Stewart, C. Rigg and K. Trehan, *Critical Human Resource Development: Beyond Orthodoxy*, London: FT Prentice Hall.

Metcalfe, Beverly, Dawn (2006), 'Exploring cultural dimensions of gender and management in the Middle East', *Thunderbird International Business Review*, **48** (1), 93–107.

Metcalfe, Beverly Dawn (2007), 'Gender and HRM in the Middle East', *International Journal of Human Resource Management*, **18** (1), 54–74.

Metcalfe, Beverly, Dawn (2008), 'Women, management and globalization in the Middle East', *Journal of Business Ethics*, **42**, 85–100.

Metcalfe, Beverly, Dawn (2009), 'Developing women's leadership capability in the public sector in the Middle East', keynote lecture to the International Conference on Administrative Development: Towards Excellence in Public Sector Performance, 9 November, Riyadh.

Metcalfe, Beverly Dawn (2010), 'Reflections on difference: women, Islamic feminism and development in the Middle East', in Mustafa Ozgilbin and Jawad Syed (eds), *Managing Gender Diversity in Asia*, Cheltenham, UK and Northampton, MA, USA: Edward Elgar, pp. 140–60.

Metcalfe, Beverly Dawn (2011), 'Women, empowerment and development: a critical appraisal of culture, ethics and national HRD frameworks in Arab Gulf States', *Human Resource Development International*, **14** (2), 1–22.

Meyerson, Diane, Robin Ely and Laura Wernick (2007), 'Disrupting gender, revising leadership' in Barbra Kellerman, and Deborah R. Rhode (eds), *Women and Leadership: The State of Play and Strategies for Change*, San Francisco, CA: Jossey Bass, pp. 453–74.

Moghadam, Valentine (1997), 'Globalization and feminism: the rise of women's organization in the Middle East and North Africa', *Canadian Women Studies*, **17** (2), 64–77.

Moghadam, Valentine (2000), 'Islamic feminism and its discontents: notes on a debate', in special issue of *Islamic Feminism and the Politics of Naming, Iran Bulletin*, accessed 5 November 2010 at www.iran-bulletin.org/women/ Islamic_feminism_IB.html.

Moghadam, Valentine (2005), 'Women's economic participation in the Middle East', *Journal of Middle East Women's Studies*, **1** (1), 110–46.

Moza (2010), 'Her Highness Sheikha Moza', personal website accessed 7 January 2011 at www.mozabintnasser.qa.

Al-Mughni, Haya (2001), *Women in Kuwait: The Politics of Gender*, London: Saqi Publishing.

Naples, Nancy (2002), 'Changing the terms: community activism, globalization, and the dilemmas of transnational feminist praxis', in Nancy A. Naples and Manisha Desai, *Women's Activism and Globalization: Linking Local Struggles and Transnational Politics*, New York: Routledge.

Nussbaum, Martha (2000), *Women and Human Development: The Capabilities Approach*, Cambridge: Cambridge University Press.

Oseen, Collette (1997), 'Luce Irigaray, sexual difference and theorizing leaders and leadership', *Gender Work and Organization*, **4** (3), 170–84.

Pfeifer, K. and Martha P. Posusney (2003), 'Arab economies and globalization', in Eleanor Abdella. Doumato and Martha P. Posusney, *Women and Globalization in the Arab Middle East*, Boulder, CO: Lynne Reiner Publishers, pp. 15–35.

Platteau, Jean-Philippe (2010), 'Political instrumentalization of Islam and the risk of obscurantist deadlock', *World Development*, **39** (2), 243–60.

Qur'an (2004), translated by M.A.S. Abdel Haleem New York: Oxford University Press.

Ramadan, Tariq (2009), *Radical Reform: Islamic Ethics and Liberation*, Oxford: Oxford University Press.

Al- Riza, Sarah (2005), 'Women in the Arab region: learning from the past: preparing for the future', paper for the *The Arab World Competitiveness Report*, World Economic Forum, Geneva.

Roald, Anne-Sofie (2001), *Women in Islam: The Western Experience*, London: Routledge.

Rupp, Leila, J. and Verta Taylor (1999), 'Forging feminist identity in an international movement: a collective identity approach to 20th century feminism', in Kare Ask and Marit Tjomsland (eds), *Women and Islamlization: Contemporary Dimensions of Discourse on Gender Relations*, Oxford and New York: Berg.

Sahli, Z.S. (2008), 'Gender and diversity in the Middle East and North Africa', *British Journal of Middle Eastern Studies*, **35** (3), 295–304.

Seikaly, May (1994), 'Women and social change in Bahrain', *International Journal . of Middle Eastern Studies*, **26**, 415–26.

Shehedah, Rustum L. (2000), 'Women in the discourse of Sayyid Qutb', *Arab Studies Quarterly*, **22** (3), 45–55.

Sinclair, Amanda (2005), *Doing Leadership Differently: Gender, Power and Sexuality in a Changing Business Culture*, revised edn, Carlton, VIC: Melbourne University Press.

Stead, Valerie and Carol Elliot (2009), 'Learning from women leaders' experiences', *Leadership*, **4** (2), 159–80.

Stewart, Jim, Clare Rigg and Kiran Trehan (2007), *Critical Human Resource Development: Beyond Orthodoxy*, London: FT Prentice Hall.

Syed, Jawad (2010) 'Reconstructing gender empowerment', *Women's Studies International Forum*, **33**, 283–94.

Truss, Catherine (1999), 'Human resource management: Gendered terrain?', *International Human Resource Management*, **10** (2), 180–200.

Tzanntos, Z and I. Kaur (2003), 'Women in the MENA labour market', in Eleanor Abdella Doumato and Marsha Prosptein Posusney, *Women and Globalization in the Arab Middle East*, Boulder, CO: Lynne Reiner Publishers, pp. 79–99.

United Nations Development Programme (UNDP) (2005), *Arab Human Development Report: Towards the Rise of Women in the Arab World*, New York: United Nations.

UNDP (2009), *World Survey on the Role of Women in Development*, Division for the Advancement of Women, New York: United Nations.

UNDP (2010), *Human Development Report 2010: The Real Wealth of Nations*, New York: UNDP.

UNIFEM (2004), *The Progress of Arab Women*, Division for the Advancement of Women, New York: United Nations.

Utting, Peter (ed.) (2006), *Reclaiming Development Agendas: Knowledge, Power and International Policy Making*, Basingstoke: Palgrave Macmillan.

Vecchio, Robert P. (2003), 'In search of gender advantage', *The Leadership Quarterly*, **14** (6), 835–50.

Wadud, Amina (2006), *Inside the Gender Jihad: Women's Reform in Islam*, Oxford: Oneworld.

Walby, Sylvia (2005), *Measuring Women's Progress in a Global Era*, report for UNESCO, Oxford: Blackwell.

Wikan, Unni (1991), *Behind the Veil in Arabia: Women in Oman*, Chicago, IL and London: Chicago University Press.

Women without Borders (2005), *Women Winning the Future*, Vienna: Women without Borders, p. 3.

World Bank (2004), *Gender and Development in the Middle East and North Africa: Women in the Public Sphere*, Washington, DC: World Bank.

World Bank (2005), *Doing Business in the Middle East and North Africa 2006*, Washington, DC: World Bank.

14. Turning neither to East nor West: social reform and a liberating ethics for leadership development

Beverly Dawn Metcalfe, Fouad Mimouni and Tony Murfin

David, We have given you mastery over the land. Judge fairly between people. Do not follow your desires, lest they divert you from God's path . . .

Qur'an, sura Sad, 38:26

Goodness does not consist in turning your face towards East or West. The truly good are those who believe in God and the Last Day, in the angels, the Scripture, and the prophets; who give away some of their wealth, however much they cherish it, to their relatives, to orphans, the needy, travellers and beggars, and to liberate those in bondage . . .

Qur'an, sura Al Baqara, 2:177

INTRODUCTION

In introducing the topic of leadership development in the Middle East in Chapter 1, we gave an overview of current Western models of leadership and their history. We also outlined the need, as we contend, for a culturally appropriate, Middle Eastern and/or Islamic model of leadership. In the other chapters presented here, the contributors put forward contrasting views on leadership in the nations under consideration, on the influence of individuals, both in government and in wider society, and on the specific characteristics of those leaders presented in the case studies. Inevitably, in a region of study so diverse, there are many knowledges and shades of meaning and understanding of Islamic interpretation. Nonetheless, mainstream leadership assumptions and discourses are inadequate for explaining the cultural diversity of leadership behaviours and practices described in this book (Ali 2005). There is a seductive and, we contend, erroneous tendency to utilize universalist, typically Western models without question (Osland and Bird 2006).

In this chapter, we will argue for a leadership discourse that is culturally apposite to the Middle East. Following a review of the leadership themes which are currently relevant in the region, we introduce a model of leadership based within a framework of faith in which culturally relevant, region specific factors are interwoven to produce an appropriate leadership construct. We then look at the challenges to future economic and social development in the region, constructing our argument around the regional scenarios developed by the WEF (2007). Finally, we evaluate additional social and political challenges to economic stability, and review our findings in light of the uprisings of 2010 and 2011, which have become known as the Arab Spring.

Contemporary workplaces are increasingly important sites of social activity and community, but Western leadership epistemologies assume organization structures premised on neoliberalism and state capitalism (Castells 2009). As shown by our contributors, leadership is a dynamic relational practice and contributes to social and economic relations in a broad range of community ventures. Importantly, contributors argued that that there is no leadership without followership, and the mutual engagement and support of all parties in such a relationship. We highlighted that leadership is considered a trust and is constituted through the formation of a social and relational ethic.

Central to understanding the social context of leader and follower activity within the accounts provided is reflective agency. This process of *musawah* is a collective endeavour to ensure economic and social goals are achieved, but also requires individuals, through a liberating ethics (Ramadan 2009), to draw on personal, organization and ethical knowledges as a means of enhancing self-awareness and performance (Alvesson and Wilmott 1992; Cunliffe 2009). This acts as a check and balance on power abuse and corruption. As Ramadan asserts, reflexivity is grounded in existential seriousness as we question our ways of being and acting, and whether we live our lives responsibly and ethically.

Ramadan's treatise proposes a new approach to Islamic resurgence, injecting Islamic ethical principles in leadership and governance frameworks in relationship to contemporary social and economic developments in the twenty-first century. His approach is rooted in community and political organizational leadership and encourages inter-faith dialogue, cooperation and understanding. Further, the recognition of the diversity of nations, their interconnectedness and interdependence, he argues, are conditions for a positive future for humankind and its social development. These principles were evident in many of the early teachings of Islam, embracing science, ecology, humanities and the social sciences, and are constituents of the liberating ethics he envisions will revive this humanistic goal.

We will return to issues of appropriate leadership culture later. In the section that follows, we first investigate the key themes arising from this investigation into leadership development in the Middle East.

BEYOND BORDERS AND TERRITORIES: KEY LEADERSHIP THEMES

The key common theme that emerged in the chapters presented in this volume is that imposed or bought-in solutions based on Western leadership models are inadequate or insufficient to describe the realities and requirements for leadership in the Middle East. In addition, the reality of Islam as a fundamental basis of thought, behaviour and leadership has been widely described in these chapters. In the case studies, authors presented leaders who were often charismatic, entrepreneurial, self-transformational and deeply rooted in faith and Islamic tradition.

It is perhaps notable that as well as the Western-educated leaders described, for example King Abdullah II of Jordan or Sheikha Lubna al-Qasimi, there are also inspiring successes amongst those who are either un- or self-educated, such as Amat al-Alim al-Sowsowa or Hayel Saeed Anaam.

In the immediate future, emergent leaders will either be Western-educated; locally educated in business or technical schools either associated with or modelled on those of the USA or UK (for example the strategic partnerships in Saudi Arabia discussed by Mimouni and Metcalf in Chapter 7 and the development of Iranian universities based on the University of Pennsylvania and MIT described by Hutchings in Chapter 9); or educated elsewhere in the world but still in systems based on the same established, Western business model. This will, we argue, create turbulent social relations. While calls for curriculum and education reform are recognized and valued by education ministers and professionals, there are at the same time education initiatives which aim to preserve ancient knowledge and history (Castells 2009). The 2005 Arab Human Development Report detailed the requirement for Arab states to invest in education ventures, as an overall process of cultural development, in order to raise the capabilities of its citizens and foster innovation and enterprise development. The Arab Booker Prize, the Guggenheim Centre in Abu Dhabi, and KAUST are examples of outward-looking developments that address this perceived need. Another case is that of Dubai International Knowledge City, successor to Dubai Knowledge Village, a so-called educational free trade zone in which over 400 foreign-owned educational and training institutions are located. Although there is significant external,

especially Western, cultural input, such projects are nevertheless not introducing Western ideology wholesale, as there is also the recognition of an
Islamic cultural tradition and Arab knowledges which are still in use and
still being freshly translated into English and other languages. The aim
is to reintroduce ancient Islamic science and knowledge and interrogate
them in development planning and education curricula (Morgan 2005;
UNDP 2006). It is also noted that, given current enrolment in tertiary education in the region, the pool of potential leaders will become increasingly
rich in women graduates (Chapter 1, Table 1.4).

It is therefore no longer meaningful or relevant to position a global
hegemony of leadership theorizing in Western ideologies and practices.
The fascination with globalization and leadership principles that are universal and timeless, as advocated by several academics, primarily in the
USA (see Campbell 2006), assumes a cultural homogeneity in thinking
and practice, and understates the ongoing shifts in international relations
and political economy that will have trickle-down influence on all nation
states. Western (2008) is clear on this challenge when he seeks to revision
new paradigms that embrace diverse knowledges that are evolved from the
Global South as well as the Global North.

This makes it all the more important that future leadership models
embrace, beyond the role of Islam and the influence of the West, the participation of women managers and leaders in building futures. It is also
necessary to be open to change (Ramadan 2009). In 2010, China's economic growth led to it passing Japan to become the world's second largest
economy (Barboza 2010). This will bring in new influences, new ways of
constructing Middle East territories, and will help redefine cultural flows
and knowledge exchange, within and across borders.

Leadership Territories: Beyond Borders

In Chapter 1, part of our definition of the Middle East was as existing
'between East and West': yet this is a very partial definition only possible
from a viewpoint of Europe or the Coast the East of the USA. From
Shanghai, California or the rest of the Americas, the perception must
be different. Nor should the Middle East define itself based solely on its
geographic position: as the title of this chapter suggests, the Middle East
must find an identity which derives from its own culture and history,
aware of, and informed by the knowledges of East and West, Global
North and Global South, but turning neither to East nor West. This is
likely to be true for the way in which we define and evaluate all leader
follower relationships in organizations and communities in the global
economy. The fluidity of space and place, transnational communication

and the flow of knowledges across and within borders render cultural descriptions of organizational practices partial, in process and emergent (Castells 2009).

The future of leadership development in the Middle East lies in being open to new models – and to new technologies, cultures and changing geopolitical alignments which go beyond the current precedence of a Western business culture fuelled by Middle Eastern oil. Future leaders will be guided by more than free market capitalism and a belief in abundant cheap energy. They will also derive inspiration from environmental movements, ethical philosophies and a global human concern for social justice (Maak 2007; Storey 2004; Thomas and Maak 2009; Western 2008). Indeed, the success of the Emirates, especially Dubai, provides a development model in the form of centralization, strong state control and a rentier contract with citizens that challenges Western neoliberal conceptions of market efficiency (Davidson 2009; Hvidt 2009). Emerging from this, there are concerns about the nature of identities, how they are formed, evolve and are constituted in relation to international economic exchanges.

This engagement of what could be termed transnational perspectives poses challenges for how Middle East states identify and relate to each other. Our concern in this volume has been to open up debate about dominant leadership knowledges, and it is clear that in the current international climate Middle East leadership identities are in a state of flux (Hvidt 2009). How, for example, are other powers interpreting events in Bahrain, Egypt, Libya, Syria and Tunisia and Yemen, or responding to the fact that popular movements powerful enough to topple strong leaders are able to organize, communicate and spread without consideration of national boundaries? And, given ongoing tensions between Iran and the US, what are the prospects for Iranian re-engagement with the West? Further, the Gulf states responded rather late in the day to cross-border challenges such as global climate and energy debates, as discussed in Chapter 1. We feel it relevant to ask how the Middle East states are thinking about, and positioning themselves on, the local, regional and global aspects of the climate change debate.

Throughout this volume, authors have advanced the necessity for Islamic theories of leadership by stressing the relational and social ethics governing leader/follower relations, and the mutual interconnectedness which unites Muslim believers to support and fulfil obligations of a higher spiritual order. In the section that follows we craft a model that embraces the complexity of leadership. As part of this framework we chart leadership development challenges. We then go on to discuss economic and social development scenarios developed by the WEF, before summarizing our findings.

FRAMING A NEW LEADERSHIP MODEL

As Sultan discussed in Chapter 12, Hayel Saeed Anaam, founder of HSA Group, began life as a poor weaver. In Chapter 1 we made use of an extended metaphor of the artisan weaving together disparate concepts to produce a new model: not only the researcher selecting knowledge threads to define their model, but also the leader weaving together influences of culture, development, spirituality and environment to create a distinctive and culturally specific style of leadership which can be further developed by future researchers and practitioners. This insight went behind contingency and transformation models that shape behaviour based on environmental and contextual conditions. Rather, this model questions epistemological assumptions about the nature of life, work, allegiance and values. Specifically, Maak defines the responsible leader as a 'weaver' who weaves together different stakeholders in a coalition and a broker of social capital (Maak 2007). The theme of weaving and all that it implies recurs in several of the chapters.

This may be expected, as the weaving metaphor arises from notions of creation from the complex and multi-threaded approach outlined in Chapter 1 and necessary to understand the requirements for leadership development. This is far from unique, with Storey (2004) describing the leadership constellation, the 'interlocking factors of context, perceived need, behavioural requirements and development methods' (2004, p. 341). We believe that it is useful to extend this metaphor in order to emphasize that we are not merely restating Western theories of leadership and attempting to apply them in a Middle East context: rather we are taking existing 'threads' of epistemologies: theology, history, management, economics, sociology or international relations, as set out in Chapter 1, and configuring them in new ways that may be appropriate to describe leadership in the Middle East. We are not claiming a definitive description of such leadership, but want to emphasize the need to develop new models against which the future leaders of the region can be developed. In developing this model we acknowledge the analogy of Plato who, in *The Statesman*, defined the leader who: 'completes the political web by marrying together dissimilar natures, the courageous and the temperate, the bold and the gentle, who are the warp and weft of society' (Plato tr. Jowett, First World Library 2007). However, the very prevalence of the metaphor of weaving suggests a common cultural construct, searching for explanation of leadership in abstract terms in a convergent process of 'intellectual "bricolage" ' (Lévi-Strauss 1966, p. 17).

Lévi-Strauss, who incidentally considered weaving 'one of the great arts of civilization' (ibid, p. 13), looked to 'mythical reflection' to produce unexpected insights. The bricoleur is unlike the engineer: he does not subordinate tasks to the, 'tools conceived and procured for the purpose of the project' (ibid.). We argue that the Middle East leader must be, to some extent, a bricoleur: he must work with what is at hand because the tools which may be procured from the West for the development of leadership contain embedded assumptions which are not necessarily relevant. The leader-bricoleur will, 'turn back to an already existent set made up of tools and materials, to consider or reconsider what it contains and. . . engage in a sort of dialogue with it [and] index the possible answers which the whole set can offer to his problem' (ibid, p. 18). We contend that Middle East leaders should indeed look to the set of materials and tools available to them, rather than buy-in those from the West that have been designed for a different set of circumstances, a different task.

In a Western, post-industrial society it is perhaps necessary to provide further explanation for the metaphor of the loom and weaver, both in terms of its pre-industrial history and with respect to industrial and historical development, an explanation which cultures closer to the artisanal production of fibre and cloth may find unnecessary. Yet the loom is symbolic in the West not only of the artisan weaver producing finished cloth from spun yarn, but also of industrialization and resistance to it: it is no coincidence that the crime of the Luddites was 'frame breaking' (Hobsbawm 1999).

For our purposes, we consider three elements of the loom: the frame, fixed and unchangeable and within which the work of the weaver is constructed; the warp of fixed threads stretched vertically between the base and head of the frame and held in tension by it; and the weft, woven between the warp by the weaver's skill in such a pattern of intersection and motion as to produce the finished cloth.

It would be possible to conceptualize a frame that is in nature Christian, secular, Marxist or in accordance with almost any ideology and, through the process of bricolage referred to above, to construct a valid model for the associated society or culture. However, as many of the authors in this volume have pointed out, Islam is, in the Middle East, 'an all-encompassing ideology which provides the organizing structure of meaning for political, social and cultural life' (Chapter 1) and constitutes the very frame within which our knowledge tapestry must be constituted and executed. As asserted previously, there is no secular lens and we must build our conception within a frame based on Islam, which we represent as the loom frame, the immutable framework of faith surrounding the concepts depicted within Figure 14.1.

Dimensions of the Leadership Model

Within the frame discussed above is a warp of threads that are fixed solidly and generally outside the control of the individual or society. As shown in

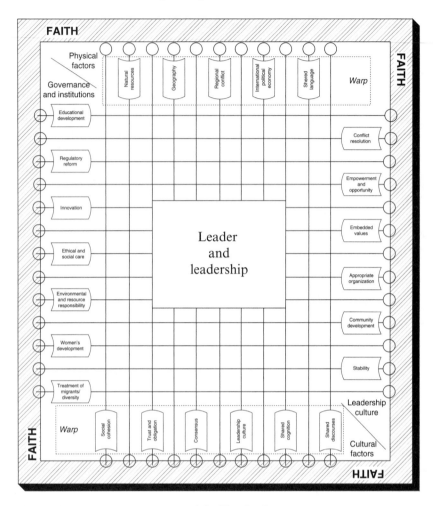

Figure 14.1   Weaving a new model of leadership

Figure 14.1, elements of the warp are identified in two sets anchored at the top and bottom rails:

1. **Physical factors:** There is a fixed physical environment of geographic position, resources both natural and human, of coasts, canals and fertile and desert zones. The factors of international political economy and conflict are so closely related to these factors that we have included them here, and language, whether Arabic or Persian, is, as has been discussed elsewhere, so closely attached to the geography and identity of the area that we consider this also along with the physical factors.

2. **Cultural factors:** There is a distinctive and persistent culture of individual leadership which, as discussed, influences national and regional culture (but which provides a consistent question mark over the stability of succession to long established leaders): however, there is no concept of divine right in Islam, and the concepts and cultures of consensus (ijma) and the community of Islam (umma) are fundamental. We also consider as fundamental to the culture of the region the factors of social cohesion, trust and obligation, including but not limited to wasta, and shared cognition and discourse including not only Islam, but also the heritage of Islamic science and literature.

The weft is more variable and necessarily entails more choices, more decision points, although in no case is there a simple causal relationship between today's decision points and future responses. In our model it is the weft that defines leadership responses and leadership challenges. In Figure 14.1 these are set out horizontally and labelled on the left and right rails and include:

3. **Governance and institutions:** this element of the weft provides the political background which can support ethical and relationship behaviours. These embrace policy initiatives for societal and sustainable development congruent with the growth of an economy, and included in this aspect are migrant labour, including nationalization programmes; the use of resources and environmental responsibility; innovation; public administration; and education policy.

   Also important, as discussed in Chapter 13, is the position of women, and women's development – women have already become a hugely significant but under-used resource of skills and education, and important decisions remain to be made as to their position in some societies (UNDP 2006, 2010).

4. **Leadership culture:** significantly, leadership culture has a responsibility to build cohesive social systems, eradicate conflict, to empower and provide opportunity, to interact with and develop the community, to provide a stable working environment and to embed appropriate values within the organization and societal culture through mutual and supportive social interaction.

This model, in its depiction of the interweaving of multiple factors and interlocking of the social, economic and human system, provides an holistic approach and encompasses development for the individual, the organization and for society and community. In the remainder of this concluding chapter we will discuss in more detail each of these dimensions – frame, warp and weft – in turn, in light of the discussion presented in the foregoing chapters, both as they impact current leadership practice in the Middle East and in response to identified future leadership development challenges.

Faith: A Framework

Our model is underpinned by the Islamic worldview (Platteau 2010). Interestingly, Western, in his broad ranging critical review of leadership theory (2008), outlines how observations in a monastery offered an ideal-type leadership role model, as the Father in his leadership role encompassed supportive and directive behaviours. This environment clearly mirrors Islamic culture (indeed, many Islamic cultures). The ethical dimensions, behaviours and characteristics expected of spiritually committed personnel are fundamental to that individual's existence, on a path, a learning journey, a becoming space or place.

Western, employing the insights of Merton, argues that his ideas can give guidance to develop leadership competences embedded in the spiritual:

> Spiritual direction does not consist merely in giving advice. The man who has only an advisor does not have a director in the fullest sense. Since the spiritual life does not consist in having and thinking, but in being and doing, a director who only gives idea has not begun to form the one he directs. (Merton 1966, in Western 2008, p. 204)

Injecting the spiritual into discourses of leadership development is made more complex by an examination of the social construction of religious orders and beliefs. A case in point is the work of Clifford Geertz, who has substantially influenced organizational sociologists and cultural theorists. In 1966 he proposed that religion can be defined as a cultural system, since religion was a subjective experience. Islamic scholars would view this as an inadequate expression of faith: Talal Asad, in his Genealogies of Religion (1993), argued that Geertz's view of religion was itself a product of his own history and experience, essentially a post-Enlightenment view that saw religion as a discrete phenomenon capable of being isolated from culture in general. Asad argued that religion did not fit into post-Enlightenment critiques of reason and existence. Lincoln, however, argued (cited in Yapp 2004) that an approach to religious organization incorporates: a discourse about transcendence; a set of practices designed to promote an ordered world; a community based on religious discourse; and institutional systems to regulate the above three (see Maak and Plass 2009). Therefore, acknowledging that it would be possible to follow Geertz and construct a post-Enlightenment frame to our model, as we present it in the Middle East context, the frame is Faith.

A Warp of the Fabric of Society

In our discussion of the weaving metaphor we acknowledge links between the artisan and his or her loom and the theorist describing networks, for example Portes (1998): 'the aggregate of actual or potential resources which are linked to possession of a durable network of more or less institutionalized relationships of mutual acquaintance or recognition source'. Such networks of social capital are multi-dimensional and rely on the relationship between a multiplicity of factors which include fixed or semi-fixed issues such as physical environment and society, which form the warp of our model, and the weft of factors more amenable to individual intervention as described below (see Bebbington 2008; Woolcock 1998).

Following the model of Maak (2007), we identify on the warp of our model 'cognitive' and 'relational' dimensions such as: shared cognition; shared language; shared narratives; norms and values; trust and obligation; social cohesion; and level of recognition, in addition to location– and society – specific dimensions such as geography, resources, consensus (*ijma*), community (*umma*) and conflict. It is no coincidence that discussion of these factors forms the core of our introduction to leadership in the Middle East in Chapter 1.

The Weft: Leadership Challenges and Developing the Future

In this section we investigate those variable factors that are to some degree within the control of leadership regimes in organizations and societies and which constitute the weft of this model. Decisions concerning these will shape the development futures of the countries of the Middle East.

Socially Responsible Leadership

The concern to reinvigorate the social ethics of care in organization and leadership theorising underscores the sentiments of Islamic writings on leadership (Ciulla 1995, 2005; Held 2005). They question whether global business leaders are agents of world benefit and a force for good given the dynamics of stakeholder society and the interconnections of stakeholder social capital (Maak 2007; Maak and Plass 2009). As responsible leadership is driven by a commonly shared purpose (Rost 1991) to nurture 'motivation and "morality"' (Burns 1978, p. 20; Maak and Plass 2009, p. 540), their task is to tackle broader social, community and environmental challenges.

Ultimately, development economists and development sociologists have shown how global leaders in transnational corporations (TNCs) have avoided social and environmental responsibilities in less developed nations (Hearn, Metcalfe and Piekarri 2011). Pearson (2007) has shown that the conditions of urban livelihoods in Maguiladoras in Brazil, characterized by poor sanitation and lack of clean water, and where women are regularly subjected to violence and sexual abuse, are marginalized in TNC discourses in which growth and competition dominate. Further, Pearson argues that TNCs in South America openly claim in the media that their involvement with social and community agendas are not their direct responsibility. This illustrates two key issues related to *social responsibility and ethics* in leadership theorizing. Beck who is concerned that global labour social injustices remain an issue for TNCs and state governments, proposed that:

a) CSR and responsible management agents are socially and discursively created, and are not priorities for TNCs in the Global South where there is little regulation or resistance.
b) This reaffirms the need for state governments to intervene to counter exploitation and abuse by empowering institutions and strengthening regulation.

(Beck, 1992)

Managing Migrants and the Working Poor

This model has strong resonances with ethical organizational leadership promoted by a few development management scholars as a requirement for sustainable growth in a global economy. A key omission of international business, HR specialists and leadership scholars is the management of both the working poor and migrant labour. A thorough discussion of this theme is beyond the scope of this chapter, but is relevant due to the large migrant populations detailed in several of the chapters in this volume including Chapter 1.

Although not officially communicated, Gulf states prefer to recruit Muslim migrants from Indonesia, India and Malaysia. These tend to be employed in occupations considered more menial: the 'dormitory' towns positioned outside Dubai, Abu Dhabi and Jeddah, in particular, are reminiscent of the Chinese dormitory towns alongside TNC manufacturing complexes – or, indeed, of the shanty towns associated with nineteenth-century Western industrialization.

How they are treated will affect both development and stability. There is considerable overlap with dimensions of motivation and morality. The development of a similarly motivated technocracy will also depend on the motivational, empowerment and governance environment that is created, and it is essential to generate a diverse economy, reduce reliance on oil and ultimately generate a sustainable (both economically and environmentally) post-oil future.

Current demonstrations in Bahrain seem to reflect injustices between Sunni and Shi'a and also reflect broader ethnic and national discriminatory practices. Public service jobs are traditionally reserved for Sunni nationals, and there is an ethnic hierarchy which prevents advancement. There are, of course, no official statistics and limited research due to access problems. For example, *Khaleej Times* reported that an entire female workforce from the Philippines tested positive for HIV and was deported.

Education Development

Underpinning all of this is of course education – and we highlighted previously the region must develop not only its own educational institutions but its own models, progressively reducing its reliance on or attempt to recreate Western educational models, especially business schools. Education reform needs to concentrate on vocational qualifications relevant to local business needs, and particularly on programmes that nurture innovation, entrepreneurship and development enterprise. We reasserted that the Arabic traditions and legacies, including arts sciences and philosophy, are integral to this knowledge economy building. Several chapters cite the tremendous strides in educational partnerships with global institutions, but, while FDI will be crucial to develop economic growth, there is a need for entrepreneurial development and small scale enterprise development.

Women, Education and Development

As arguably the most under-developed resource in the region, it is necessary to pay particular attention to the requirement to develop and position women in the sustainable future we envision (see Maak and Plass 2009). As the 2005 Arab Human Development Report (UNDP 2006) stated, the region is committed to educating its female resources, but not to their utilization. Issues of women's leadership development are explored fully in Chapter 13.

Gulfization

Gulfization policies have had, overall, only partial success. This reflects, on the one hand, high numbers of professional expatriates, as well as large numbers of migrant workers in low-wage, low-skill service occupations. Farrell (2008) argues that part of the problem is that in rich Gulf states, quotas for nationalization have been 'engineered' to satisfy Ministers of Education. That is, jobs have been created for nationals in both the public and private sector which have no clearly defined role or responsibility. Accurate statistics are therefore difficult to quantify (Rutledge et al. 2011). There will still be a requirement for low-wage, low-skill migrant labour as nationals are reluctant to take on these roles (Davidson 2008, 2009).

ECONOMIC AND SOCIAL DEVELOPMENT: SCENARIOS FOR THE FUTURE

It is normal in a volume such as this to conclude by looking at challenges for the future and possible leadership responses to them. We are fortunate in this in that, as mentioned by Suliman and Hayat in Chapter 4, a number of future scenarios have been mapped out as far as 2025 for GCC countries under the auspices of the World Economic Forum. The trajectories help understand the changes projected for the Middle East as a whole. The scenarios are set out in Figure 14.2 and make use of the environmental images Oasis, Sandstorm and Fertile Gulf as metaphors for possible development futures. In developing the scenarios the WEF worked with thought leaders and leaders in global commercial organizations and in public administration. They were guided by overarching concerns regarding the attainment, or not, of economic growth, governance and democratic reforms to address sustainable competitiveness and, in particular, policy measures to target governance reform, private sector development, entrepreneurship and innovation, security stability and education.

This exercise was specific to the GCC countries, but the implications transcend national boundaries and other Middle East countries face similar challenges in terms of the pursuit of economic growth. GCC states have a particular need to further diversify from their over-reliance on natural resources in the form of fossil fuels, however all Middle East states require the reform of governance systems and democratic reform and to place less reliance on the public sector for job creation. In Egypt, Iran, Jordan and Yemen private sector job growth is seen as vital for the region, not least to ensure ongoing stability, and will require ongoing privatization programmes. All states require upskilling in public administration and governance systems.

While various contributors stressed growth in education participation rates, especially among women, the existing skill base still needs upgrading. This is due to the fact that women's education focuses on the humanities and liberal arts subjects: for example, 40 per cent of all female degree candidates in Saudi Arabia major in Islam. There is a requirement for reform of education provision, especially in the fields of HRD, Strategic

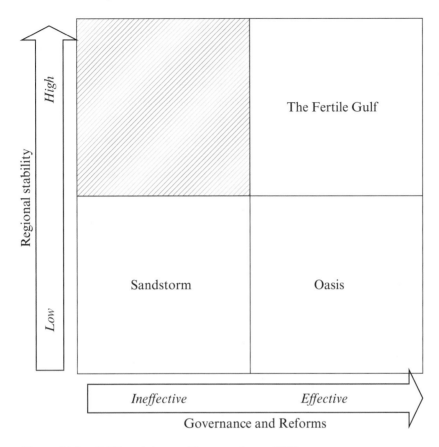

Figure 14.2   GCC and the world: scenarios to 2025

Management and Economics, as well as the need for the establishment of post-doctoral capabilities in the region's universities. A summary of trajectories follows and is detailed in Table 14.1.

Although we will not discuss the bases of the scenarios in detail, the defining event of the Sandstorm scenario is a military encounter between the US and Iran over the latter's nuclear installations, triggering a global economic recession. This scenario was not fanciful – Israel directly threatened an attack on Iranian nuclear installations in July 2008 – and the global economic crisis happened on a similar timescale, even if for very different, and ultimately very Western, reasons.

No country in the region can be ignored in such developments. Similarly, in the more positive 'Fertile Gulf' scenario, the development of

Table 14.1 Development scenarios: leadership development in the GCC to 2025

Economic and Social Indicators	Oasis	Sandstorm	Fertile Gulf
Governance and Public Administration Institutions	Public sector reform leads to rule by technocrats. Reform of private law strengthens private sector development/innovation.	Corruption worsens. Unaddressed tensions. GCC remains vulnerable to terrorism.	Government reform, reduction of red tape and improved communication between ministries. National HRD plan coordinated across public sector/private and entrepreneurial growth.
Higher Education and Training	Education standards are established as part of NHRD strategy and skills coordinated with industry requirements. Governments fund 'on-the-job' training for nationals. Further reduction in reliance on expatriates. Curriculum reform, but with prescribed limits.	Restrictions on curriculum reform and lack of incentives to raise standards. Limited liaison and collaboration with university and vocational sector. Limited opportunities for partnerships with world class research institutions.	Private sector funding for education increases, and alliances formed with international partners to facilitate education reform and curriculum planning. Curriculum reform done in consultation with professional associations and public and private sector organizations. Vocational training and scholarships increased. Universities encouraged to develop world leading research sponsored by government and industry. Growth of management and leadership networks.
Technological Readiness	GCC countries support large scale investment in ICT as part of national skills strategies.	GCC lag behind on ICT adoption as well as private sector limited investments.	Privatization of ICT improves quality. Access to internet and broader control of private agencies of internet management.
Business Sophistication and Innovation	Governments support regional development via regions and economic strength – such as oil and gas added activities. Extended to other diversified industries: some lag.	Sophistication tempered by lack of skills and declining competitiveness of local firms.	The formation of new industry clubs, venture capital to support entrepreneurship, diversification beyond natural resources, and inter and intra knowledge industry transfer. Entrepreneurship and innovation culturally embedded in business philosophy.

Source: Adapted from WEF 2007.

'Silicon Valley'-style centres of technological excellence will have positive effects that cross and transcend national boundaries, including current developments such as Dubai International Academic City and Qatar's Education City.

The scenarios considered looked at, in a creative and speculative framework, essentially a best case, worst case and no change scenario. As will be seen, these scenarios depend largely on the response not only to unpredictable external events but perhaps more importantly to a few key challenges. These challenges are consistent with those identified throughout this book, and included in the model summarized in Figure 14.1: education; governance and regulation; and the treatment of migrant labour.

It is apparent that the time scale chosen by the authors of the scenarios is one over which production of fossil fuels in the region can be expected to remain significant (see Chapter 1) – and that this is therefore the period in which significant economic decisions need to be made in order to ensure a sustainable, developed future in the region.

The scenarios identified are:

> *Oasis* is a story where a focus on technocratic governance and top-down institutional reforms pays off in the form of a well-organized, cohesive and prosperous regional grouping. The region's economic growth, however, remains partially constrained by over-regulation and less-inclusive globalization. Will GCC governments allow regional tensions to spill over and affect their internal security, resulting in a focus on short-term solutions at the expense of tough reforms?
>
> *Sandstorm* is a scenario in which dramatic regional events and domestic unrest contribute to the GCC countries failing to maintain their momentum of reforms, with negative consequences for the region's economic and social development. Will GCC governments succeed in taking advantage of globalization in a more stable regional environment through bold reforms at the institutional and political levels?
>
> The *Fertile Gulf* is a future where GCC governments invest heavily in education and innovation in order to create a healthy private sector while encouraging reforms through a bottom-up process. This results in a more socially integrated and economically diversified region that occupies an increasingly relevant position in the international scene.
>
> (WEF 2007)

Figures 14.3 and 14.4 show two quantitative indicators that can be compared with the scenario predictions: GDP per capita and oil prices, both measures that were discussed in Chapter 1. This progress is significant as we approach the latter part of the first phase of the futures envisioned.

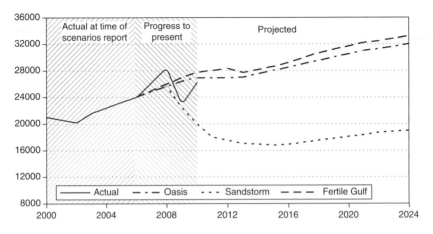

Sources: WEF 2007, updated with data from AIGC

Figure 14.3   Real GDP per capita ($US): scenarios and progress

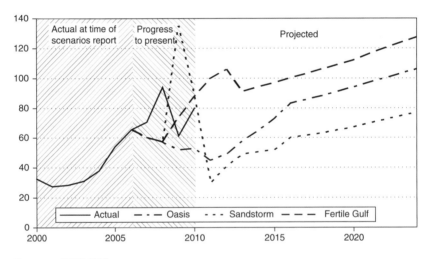

Sources: WEF 2007.

Figure 14.4   Oil price ($US per barrel): scenarios and actual

Development Planning in the Middle East: Discussion

It is clear that those involved in proposing and developing these scenarios
identified relatively few factors amenable to the influence of state leaders
as absolutely key, the envisioned regional conflict aside. In particular,

the difference between the scenarios is engendered by action, or lack of action, on governance and regulatory affairs (most importantly 'creating a good and supportive environment for business) and IT (internet and communication technologies being either embraced and encouraged by governments, or seen as 'subversive' and controlled as suppressed) (WEF 2007, p. 41; see also Davidson 2008, 2009). In the Sandstorm scenario, Mohammad Aziz, fictional caller to a television debate looking back at the scenario events, states: 'the labour situation didn't improve. There was a general shortage of skills . . . we were urged to hire costly nationals who seemed to have less incentive to work hard . . .. It was tough to find competent executives to lead the divisions', and: '. . . the reforms to government bureaucracies were not enough . . . still huge delays and costs in obtaining permits and concessions. Government contracts were awarded arbitrarily' (WEF 2007, p. 37).

In the Oasis scenario, the progress of GCC countries is generally recognizable to observers in 2011, with similar growth in GDP per capita and a moderate degree of economic diversification. In this scenario a GCC Economic Coordination and Development Board has been formed, there is a common currency based on the Euro zone model and progress rests on the 'Three Pillars Policy' of building the private sector, economic diversification and Governance, noting that the Governance pillar includes increased commitment to tertiary education and nurturing innovation and entrepreneurship, especially in the ICT sector.

In the Fertile Gulf scenario, many of the factors are common with Oasis: there has been financial integration and education systems are improved, with specific emphasis on education as a means to economic diversification. Governance and public administration reforms are facilitated through partnership development through multiple stakeholders, including grassroots organizations. However, absolutely key to this scenario is the improved global understanding engendered by G20 and Islamic conferences held in the region in 2009, with the result of:

> real consequences . . . not just in how Islam was perceived internationally, but also on how Islamic groups and leaders related to one another. It was also an acknowledgement from such leaders of the pressure for recognition and inclusion coming from different religious groups, and of the need for consensus as a defence from civil strife. It was therefore an important step in improving the political and social stability within and surrounding the GCC countries. (ibid., p. 48)

Although in this scenario the most important improvements in the business climate, according to a postulated survey, are in workforce education, work ethic and infrastructure (p. 52), how much the future economy has opened up is perhaps summarized in a statement by entrepreneur Najeeb Essa: 'we were able to put together a team that was 80% local, and of which almost half were women' (ibid., p. 51).

Summary of the WEF Scenarios

What conclusions, ultimately, can be drawn from the WEF scenarios? It must be remembered that the main concern of the report is the economic development of the GCC states. The importance of the development of migrant populations, of individuals or of women are not considered as ends in themselves. It should be reiterated that this report concerns the GCC only and does not include many of the countries considered in this volume. This is especially important as it is the natural resources of GCC countries that give them the privilege of having this choice to develop alternative futures. These choices will affect the course of history in other nations in the region, and the scenarios discuss the importance of Egypt as an emergent, even nuclear (ibid., p. 27) power, of Turkey as an important link between the region and EU economies (ibid., p. 47), and of Iran, throughout, as an ongoing point of conflict and instability, including in its support of Shi'i populations and as an ongoing challenge to a US defined world order. The US itself remains the global superpower and influence on, or driver of, security in the region (ibid., p. 10). There is some acknowledgement of the growing importance of Asia, especially in the Oasis scenario. What cannot be predicted is how the external relations of the regions will be reconfigured as a result of the unrest and regime change in the region in 2010 and 2011.

Ultimately, the WEF perspective is one of business, rather than human, development – a perspective in a very much Western, unregulated, free-market paradigm. The more positive scenarios could be seen as a 'development along Western lines', or even as scenarios for which the initiating concept was to ask, 'which Western development model should we choose?' It would be valuable for researchers to revisit this in light of the Western-created economic crisis, entirely a product of the failure of Western business models, a failure anticipated by Dunning (2007) as discussed in Chapter 1 – the failure of markets, failure of institutions and failure of moral virtues: a crisis nonetheless comparable in short-term effect to the global military confrontation and its consequences envisioned in the Sandstorm scenario. We contend that these failures, and the relatively robust response of the Middle East economies to them, provide added impetus to our call for a culturally appropriate leadership model arising from the region and not imposed, either externally or by a Western-educated internal elite. As we maintain, and as development economists such as Hvidt (2009) and Platteau (2010) have shown, stateist, centralized planned economy models, as exemplified by the regimes of the Gulf states, provide alternatives to Western, capitalist economics. However, the events of 2010 and 2011 have shown that the position of even strong, established rulers who try to govern without the consent of the community is uncertain.

Social and Political Challenges to Economic Stability

In the discussion on the leadership model presented above, we outlined specific tasks that focused on building the knowledge and skill capabilities of Middle East citizens. As was shown, this is inextricably tied to myriad political and cultural intersections: the regime structures and tensions that uphold traditional Arabic values, whilst also embracing innovative and market-oriented strategies, characteristic of economic growth models in Western democracies. Tied to this is the fragility of current regimes and leadership succession and it is currently unclear what the outcomes will be, especially given the spreading unrest at the time of writing in early 2011. Whatever happens in the Al Sa'ud dynasty in Saudi Arabia, there is no doubt that the influence of al-Wahhab and Hanbali jurisprudence will persist. While we have seen the decline of Muttawah's influence in some social areas under Abdullah's rule, for example women and education, Muttawah advocates are quite clearly embedded in the Shurah constitutional organization.

In Egypt political discord initially surrounded the 2010 parliamentary elections, with calls of 'irregularities' as well as widespread unrest and electoral dissatisfaction. This appeared suppressed until the much more vigorous, widespread and better-organized protests early in 2011 that led to Hosni Mubarak being deposed after almost 30 years in office. The long-term consequences of these events cannot be predicted, with the army in temporary control but free elections promised, the Muslim Brotherhood no longer banned but stating that it will not run a candidate for the presidency or seek a parliamentary majority, and a general feeling that people power and democracy has prevailed. Nevertheless, religiosity and support for the Muslim Brotherhood and Salafi movement are high, and elsewhere across the Arab world there are calls for an Islamic constitution where none exists and ongoing unrest that may lead to social reform and democratic opportunities for many populations. It is possible to view these events as a triumph of a move to Western-style democracy, enabled by modern communication technologies which ossified regimes failed to understand and control: it is also possible to view the events as examples of an Islamic world view, in which the leader can only govern with the consent (*ijma*) of the community. What the result of these events will be, and whether we will see democratic reform within the framework of Islam, remains unknowable.

Such tensions and conflicts are prevalent, arguably disproportionately prevalent, in general discourses in the West and in international relations and political economy, some of which have been discussed in these chapters, especially as they relate to Islam and culture, the relations between religion and the state, and the utilitarian values of religion. Indeed, Geertz's later work on 'Islam observed' noted how Indonesia and Morocco were so distinct that, despite superficial similarities, the religious differences were so profound that he was led to ask if they were one religion with different aspects, or two religions sharing common features (Geertz 1968). Cultures are the main components that help determine ethics, aesthetics, language, class and gender relations, and are often formulated in conjunction with the geopolitical context. As was shown in Chapter 1 and in subsequent individual chapters, religion and state are often in conflict, and religion may serve to foster obedience or submission to the state, or resistance or rebellion. That said, Shari'a constitutions are premised on a belief that organized state religions and public administrative systems are entwined. Islam and democracy are not just strange bedfellows (Yapp 2004).

LEADERSHIP DEVELOPMENT, LEARNING AND SOCIAL CHANGE

Given the social and economic uncertainties discussed above, the question remains, how can the issue of skills development for leaders in Middle East states be addressed? Our leadership model proposes that learning about leadership roles, behaviours, practices and knowledges is not necessarily about the application of tool kits to develop transformational perspectives, but it is about a life journey, experimentation and discovery. Significantly, this journey is not an individual one, but a collective, shared experience, where the *umma* discover and nurture leadership in themselves and in each other, and as part of aims to develop oneself, an organization and a community. To address this we seek to elucidate: 'the range of ways in which leaders and potential leaders may be trained and developed' (Antonacopoulou and Bento 1994).

Antanocopoulou and Bento's argument (1994) resonates very strongly with ideas about Islamic leadership and development. They stress the significance of what they call 'learning leadership', an approach to leadership that rests on transformational concepts, and where leadership is a process of 'becoming', and learning is a way of being (2004, pp. 81–2).

This strongly supports the value of humility and critical self-reflection in our model, as post-heroic models view leaders as all knowing, visionary and masterful. Islamic leadership is concerned with assessing their and others' capabilities, and being realistic as to what is amiss in their qualities, or in their services to others in the community. Antonocopoulou and Bento phrase this 'vulnerability' (2004, p. 82), since viceregents on earth are only human and will work at overcoming all vulnerabilities (Beekun and Badawi 1991).

The capabilities of leaders in charismatic and post-heroic models covered strategic insight, the ability to deliver change, as well as to perform the ambassadorial function which includes the inter-organizational representation of what the organization stands for (see Storey 2004). Yet our view counters this isolated figure, since leaders who keep learning may ultimately be the source of competitive advantage (Yukl 2008; Storey 2010). Most of the training and development interventions which are available can be classified in terms of four main types:

1. Learning about leadership and organizations which incorporates the theories of motivation and key leadership writers.
2. Self-analysis, team analysis and exploration of different leadership styles. These are based on psychological questionnaires such as Belbin's team questionnaire.
3. Experiential learning and simulation. This mode of provision dates back to John Adair's residential course framework which includes outdoor tasks and challenges. Trainers act as facilitators, though it has been increasingly criticized as it promotes athletic figures.
4. Top level strategic or master classes which are short executive courses which primarily focus on case analysis. Promoted and favoured by Harvard, Wharton and INSEAD.

(Adapted from Storey 2004)

In addition to the above, a range of leadership and development activities exists, including 360-degree feedback, action learning and secondments. Because leadership is perceived as 'doing' rather than 'knowing', there is an inherent bias towards activity based education. This really does not capture the ways in which leadership capabilities are primarily enhanced within the Islamic cultural framework discussed in this volume. The heroic, charismatic and transformational leadership styles, as discussed throughout, were not so evident in the Middle East case examples. Embraced in Islamic ideals, however, is the necessity of transforming capabilities, with the focus on humanistic development (Bass 1985).

The implication is that, with respect to Islamic leadership, management training and development activities can provide the space for leadership learning to become emergent and be discovered. It articulates the view that leadership development is a dynamic capability that can assist in social transformation of traditional leadership mindsets, and refocus Middle East leaders in public agencies and private organizations, not only to the task in hand, but to broader social and ethical agendas.

Dynamic capabilities are central to understanding how creative working conditions can be formed which will allow managers the flexibility to respond to issues in ways that support sustainable innovation. This is because learning changes one's adaptation to new circumstances.

The foregoing suggests that learning leadership shares similarities with Islamic ideologies of doing and reflecting on leadership. In the introduction, we made the case that Islamic leadership challenges post-heroic and traditionally masculinist models. In our previous discussion in this chapter we weaved the interconnections of leadership roles, relationships and aspirations as being governed by social interaction, and of course the overriding dynamic of faith.

We would argue, as do Antonacopoulou and Bento (1994), that learning leadership can be developed. This requires that we move away from economic models or toolkits to models that understand the socially contingent nature of leadership roles and behaviours, as exemplified by our model. This involves acknowledging that the leader is naturally a learner, and that leaders can not only impart knowledge to, but also seek and learn knowledge from their followers.

Reinforcing our position on Islamic leadership, Antonacopoulou and Bento argue that learning leadership offers, 'a window to inner learning,' and thus is premised on leadership as a 'relational process' (Antonacopoulou and Bento 2004, p. 94). Antonacopoulou and Bento propose that this can be nurtured by what they term learning structures. Characteristics of learning structures are set out below.

Leading and Learning Structures

1. Awareness, alertness and attentiveness to one's own and others' learning and development needs.
2. Shared learning and leadership responsibility.
3. Recognition of discontinuity in organization and social life, so as to cope with uncertainties and unforeseen challenges.
4. Mutual cooperation and agreement with leaders/followers to tackle organization and social projects, collectively and for mutual gain.
5. Learning from others' intellectual reasoning as a way of sharing learning processes in collective tasks.

(Adapted from Antanacopoulou and Bento 2004, p. 95)

These learning structures are the window to inner learning and help to transform decision making and practice. We would argue that learning how to become, enact oneself in humility, show learning, engender community learning, promotes the potentialities for social harmony through change:

> Learning leadership therefore presents a fluid image beyond attributes and tasks, beyond behaviours and situations. Learning leadership is the coming together of these features in a complex blend of colour that stimulates our senses to learn to feel the impact of leadership rather than simply insisting on seeing it if we are to testify to its existence. (Antonacopoulou and Bento 2004, p. 95)

This volume began with a stated aim to challenge exclusive Western conceptualizations of leadership. As Storey (2004) has noted, the concerns and agendas of leadership behaviours and practices reflect the way in which a subject is studied, interpreted, communicated and written about. We declared unashamedly that our intention was to move across and between knowledge territories wider than those labelled *organization* and *leadership*, in order to paint a richer picture of the practical diversity of geopolitical, cultural, economic and social dynamics factors which shape leadership processes and how leadership is constituted in a Middle East context. This endeavour, we hope, has shown the many intersecting dynamics that shape conceptualizations of leadership roles and behaviours, and has begun to address the underlying questions which will continue to shape intellectual inquiry into leadership, answering the fundamental questions:

1. What are the attributes or competences, if any, that demarcate the best leaders from the rest?
2. If such attributes and competences can be identified, how can they be accrued or learned?

Eminent leadership commentators such as Pfeiffer in 1977 argued that even CEOs are constrained by market conditions, organization political constraints and other factors, and in consequence their true influence on organization effectiveness is limited. Yukl (2008) concurs, but is more circumspect, arguing that CEOs have only moderate influence.

The implication of this analysis, and what we have attempted to show in this volume, is that we need to closely assess the political, economic and cultural context of leadership actions and behaviours. 'Organization-bound' analyses, often accompanied by limited insight into the economic contexts of business markets, do not capture the prevailing cultural and social norms influencing organizational development and growth. As we have clearly shown, the injection of development sociologists and development economists offers crucial insights into the readiness of 'states', and whether the enabling characteristics (present or not) of governance and political economy will yield beneficial results. While much leadership theorizing has attempted to focus on measuring styles through well-developed questionnaires such as the MLQ, they provide little understanding of the complexities of doing leadership.

Behavioural requirements and competences will nevertheless always be part of any theory of leadership. They express what capabilities and behaviours are expected or required of persons held to be leaders or in leadership positions.

RE-IMAGINING LIBERAL ETHICS IN LEADERSHIP THEORIZING

Throughout this text we have attempted to provide alternative perspectives on leadership theorizing by focusing on the social, geopolitical and cultural dimensions that shape leadership thinking, action and reflective practice in the Middle East. This has involved weaving together relevant literatures from management and organization, Middle East development studies, development, geography and international relations, as well as making direct linkages to Islamic thought and writings which have underpinned the critical orientation of the majority of the chapters presented here.

An important common theme, introduced in the early stages of our analysis and which differentiates this study from typical Western perspectives, is that leadership dynamics in a Middle East context are largely concerned with emancipatory goals and aims. By this, we mean that underpinning leadership ontology is a concern to redress imbalances, acknowledge injustices and foster negotiation and consultation through networks that represent community interests. This is a marked change from leadership activity in Western economies which assumes strategic planning and corporate vested interests for an individual organization or group of companies. Islamic leadership has ultimately a social development orientation, aiming to enhance human wellbeing, livelihoods and productive ventures that benefit the entire community.

We assert that important insights may be gained by contrasting the current goals and insights of the Islamic world with the goals of the Western enlightenment and its explicit rejection of religion, a concept that still underpins the Western-oriented, constructed version of knowledge. Burrell (1997) argues for a 'retro organization' in which organizational development requires rejuvenation and examines not only modern organizational forms but those with histories stretching back to pre-Enlightenment concepts.

In the context of the Middle East, we argue for a culturally-appropriate, faith-based epistemology. In recognizing the centrality of the enlightenment to the modern Western world construct, we argue that leadership theorizing in particular and Western theorizing in general has stagnated, is enclosed within a mindset of neoliberal capitalist hegemony and is in need of rejuvenation. One way to advance this is to reinvestigate concepts from the dawn of the modern period in European thought and to seek in the pre-scientific era ideas and themes of relevance for today (Burrell 1997, pp. 5–6; Western 2008, p. 201). This is exactly what thought leaders are doing across the MENA region, and also what development planners are currently doing with their state-building programmes in Middle East nations. By learning from the past, they seek to look to the future (Morgan 2007; Ramadan 2009).

This perspective has strong resonances with the multitude of literature that examines Islamic organization with Islamic development, traceable to long before the enlightenment and back to the era of the first caliph leaders. There is also resonance, beyond the scope of this chapter to discuss, with key social theory writers such as Nussbaum, Sen and Held, fundamental to the fields of development theorizing, discussed specifically in Chapter 13 and throughout this volume. Essential to their deliberations are responsibilities and rights enshrined in human interactions and not in endeavour towards profit maximization, as are the vast majority of organization systems.

Western's conception of leadership formation (2008) has touched on a value inherent in Islamic organization and social relations. Leadership formation relates to a collective holistic process. It incorporates shared responsibility of stakeholders in the organization (Maak and Pless 2009). Western uses the religious phrase, *charism*, a form of exchange of individual gifts. As well as holistic vision, a radical inclusivity is also required.

Western's insights share parallels with Islamic culture and ideology since embedded in the recognition of how leadership is conceptualized as part of the social and political system is a requirement to connect to wider environmental concerns, broader social development agendas, ethics in organization and everyday social and human interaction. Western calls this 'macro development'. Thus a fundamental flaw common to leadership approaches in the context of the West is their 'micro focus' (Western 2008, p. 201).

The formation and current condition of the modern Middle East are expressed particularly strongly in the interaction of political and economic factors. Whether or not the Muslim Middle East is *dar-al Islam* (the House of Islam), it is certainly the geographic territory where geopolitics, economics and religiopolitics interlock. In the West, political economy asserts an undisputed intersection of political factors, states, conflict and ideology with finance and technology, the mechanisms of economic production. It is only since the nineteenth century that the separation of politics and economics has been emphasized (Hobsbawm 1999). More recently in the West, there has been a move to impose not only a separation between church and state, but also between economy and state, a separation which has had disastrous consequences for the world economy.

We believe that in accepting the need for a faith-based transformational leadership in the Middle East, the West will also be able to integrate pre-Enlightenment concepts and, in those dawn-picked concepts, find its own straight path.

REFERENCES

Ali, A.J. (2005), *Islamic Perspecives on Management and Organizations*, Cheltenham, UK and Northampton, MA, USA: Edward Elgar.

Alvesson, M. and H. Willmott (eds) (1992), *Critical Management Studies*, London: Sage.

Antonacopoulou, Elena and Regina Bento (1994), ' "Learning leadership" in practice', in J. Storey (ed.) (2004), *Leadership in Organizations: Current Issues and Trends*, London: Routledge, pp. 81–102.

Asad, Talal (1993), *Genealogies of Religion: Discipline and Reasons of Power in Christianity and Islam*, Baltimore, MA and London: Johns Hopkins University Press.

Barboza, David (2010), 'China passes Japan as second-largest economy', *New York Times* 15 August, accessed 7 January 2011 at www.nytimes.com/2010/08/16/business/global/16yuan.html.

Bebbington, Anthony J. (2008), 'Social capital and development studies II: can Bourdieu travel to policy', *Progress in Development Studies*, **7** (2), 155–62.

Beck, Ulrich (1992), *Risk Society: Towards a New Modernity*, Thousand Oaks, CA: Sage Publications.

Beekun, Jamal and Rafik I. Badawi (1999), *Leadership: An Islamic Perspective*, Beltsville, MD: Amana Press.

Burns, J.M. (1978), *Leadership*, New York: Harper and Row.

Burrell, Gibson (1997), *Pandemonium: Towards a Retro-Organization Theory*, London: Sage.

Campbell, David P. (2006), 'Globalization: The basic principles of leadership are universal and timeless', in William H. Mobley and Elizabeth Weldon (eds), *Advances in Global Leadership*, vol 4, Oxford and Amsterdam: Elsevier.

Castells, Manuel (2009), *The Rise of the Network Society: The Information Age: Economy, Society, and Culture*, vol I, 2nd edn, Chichester: John Wiley.

Ciulla, Joanne B. (1995), 'Leadership ethics: mapping the territory', *Business Ethics Quarterly*, **5** (11), 5–28.

Ciulla, Joanne B. (2005), 'Integrating leadership with ethics: is good leadership contrary to human nature?', in J.P. Doh and S.A. Stumpf, S.A. (eds), *Handbook on Responsible Leadership and Governance in Global Business*, Cheltenham, UK Northampton, MA, USA: Edward Elgar.

Cunliffe, Ann L. (2009), 'The philosopher leader: on relationalism, ethics and reflexivity – a critical perspective to teaching leadership', *Management Learning*, **40** (1), 87–101.

Davidson, Christopher M. (2008), *Dubai: The Vulnerability of Success*, New York: Columbia University Press.

Davidson, Christopher M. (2009), *Abu Dhabi: Oil and Beyond*, New York: Columbia University Press.

Dunning, John H. (2007), 'A new zeitgeist for international business activity and scholarship', *European J. International Management*, **1** (4), 278–301.

Farrell, Fiona (2008), 'Voices on emiratization: the impact of Emirati culture on the workforce participation of national women in the UAE private banking sector', *Journal of Islamic Law and Culture*, **10** (2), 107–65.

Geertz, Clifford (1966), 'Religion as a cultural system', in Michael Banton (ed.), *Anthropological Approaches to the Study of Religion*, ASA Monographs 3, London: Tavistock Publications, pp. 1–46.

Geertz, Clifford (1968), *Islam Observed: Religious Development in Morocco and Indonesia*, Chicago, IL and London: University of Chicago Press.

Hearn, Jeff, Beverly D. Metcalfe and Rebecca Piekarri (2011), 'Gender, intersectionality and IHRM', in Günter K. Stahl and Ingmar Björkman (eds), *Handbook of Research in International Human Resource Management*, Cheltenham, UK and Northampton, MA, USA: Edward Elgar.

Held, Virginia (2005), *The Ethics of Care: Personal, Political, and Global*, Oxford: Oxford University Press.

Hobsbawm, Eric (1999), *Industry and Empire: From 1750 to the Present Day*, revised edn, London: Penguin Books.

Hvidt, M. (2009), 'The Dubai model: an outline of key development process elements in Dubai', *International Journal of Middle East Studies*, **41**, 397–418.

Lévi-Strauss, Claude (1966), *The Savage Mind*, Chicago, IL: University of Chicago Press.

Maak, Thomas (2007) 'Responsible leadership, stakeholder engagement, and the emergence of social capital', *Journal of Business Ethics*, **74**, 329–43.

Maak, Thomas and Nicola M. Pless (2009), 'Business leaders as citizens of the world. advancing humanism on a global scale', *Journal of Business Ethics*, **88** (3), 537–50.

Nussbaum, Martha (2000), *Women and Human Development: The Capabilities Approach*, Cambridge: Cambridge University Press.

Osland, Joyce and Allen Bird (2006), 'Global leaders as experts', in William H. Mobley and Elizabeth Weldon (eds), *Advances in Global Leadership*, vol 4, Oxford and Amsterdam: Elsevier.

Pearson, Ruth (2007), 'Beyond women workers: gendering corporate social responsibility', *Third World Quarterly*, **28** (4), 731–49.

Pfeiffer, J. (1977), 'The ambiguity of leadership', *Academy of Management Review*, **2**, 104–12.

Plato (2007), *Statesman*, translated by Jowett, Fairfield, IA: 1st World Publishing.

Platteau, Jean-Philippe (2010), 'Political instrumentalization of Islam and the risk of obscurantist deadlock', *World Development,* **39** (2) 243–60.

Portes, A. (1998), 'Social capital: its origins and applications in modern sociology', *Annual Review of Sociology*, **24**, 1024–47.

Qur'an (2004), translated by M.A.S. Abdel Haleem, New York: Oxford University Press.

Ramadan, Tariq (2009), *Radical Reform: Islamic Ethics and Liberation*, New York: Oxford University Press.

Rost, J.C. (1991), *Leadership for the 21st Century*, London and Westport, CT: Quorum.

Rutledge, Emilie, Fatima Al-Shamsi, Yahia Bassioni and Hen Al-Sheik (2011), 'Women, labour market nationalisation policies and human resource development in the Arab Gulf States', *Human Resource Development International*, **14** (2), 183–98.

Storey, John (2004), 'Changing theories of leadership and leadership development', in J. Storey (ed.), *Leadership in Organizations: Current Issues and Key Trends*, London: Routledge.

United Nations Developed Programme (UNDP) (2006), *The Arab Human Development Report 2005: Towards the Rise of Women in the Arab World*, New York: United Nations Publications.

UNDP (2010), *Human Development Report 2010: The Real Wealth of Nations*, New York: UNDP.

World Economic Forum (WEF) (2007), *The Gulf Cooperation Council (GCC) Countries and the World: Scenarios to 2025*, Cologny/Geneva Switzerland: WEF.

Western, Simon (2008), *Leadership: A Critical Text*, Thousand Oaks, CA: Sage Publications.

Woolcock, Michael (1998), 'Social capital and economic development: toward a theoretical synthesis and policy framework', *Theory, Culture and Society,* **27** (2), 151–208.

Yapp, M.E. (2004), 'Islam and Islamism', *Middle Eastern Studies*, **40** (2), 161–82.

Yukl, Garry (2008), 'How leaders influence organizational effectiveness', *Leadership Quarterly*, **19**, 708–22.

Index